Critical Essays on

OSCAR WILDE

CRITICAL ESSAYS
ON
BRITISH LITERATURE

Zack Bowen, General Editor
University of Miami

Critical Essays on
OSCAR WILDE

edited by

REGENIA GAGNIER

G. K. Hall & Co./New York
Maxwell Macmillan Canada/Toronto
Maxwell Macmillan International/New York Oxford Singapore Sydney

PR
5824
C75
1991

G. K. Hall & Co.   Maxwell Macmillan Canada, Inc.
Macmillan Publishing Company   1200 Eglinton Avenue East
866 Third Avenue   Suite 200
New York, New York 10022   Don Mills, Ontario M3C 3N1

Macmillan Publishing Company is part of the Maxwell Communication
Group of Companies.

Library of Congress Cataloging-in-Publication Data

Critical essays on Oscar Wilde / edited by Regenia Gagnier.
        p.   cm.—(Critical essays on British literature)
    Includes bibliographical references (p. 265) and index.
    ISBN 0-8161-8860-2
    1. Wilde, Oscar, 1854–1900—Criticism and interpretation.
  I. Gagnier, Regenia. II. Series.
  PR5824.C75   1991
  828'.809—dc20   91-21925
                                                         CIP

The paper used in this publication meets the minimum requirements of
American National Standard for Information Sciences—Permanence of Paper
for Printed Library Materials, ANSI Z39.48–1984.∞®

10 9 8 7 6 5 4 3 2 1

Printed in the United States of America

Contents

◆

General Editor's Note

◆

The Critical Essays on British Literature series provides a variety of approaches to both classical and contemporary writers of Britain and Ireland. The formats of the volumes in the series vary with the thematic designs of individual editors and with the amount and nature of existing reviews, criticism, and scholarship. In general, the series represents the best in published criticism, augmented, where appropriate, by original essays by recognized authorities. It is hoped that each volume will be unique in developing a new overall perspective on its particular subject.

Regenia Gagnier's introduction and selection of essays on Oscar Wilde mainly concern contemporary American criticism, including three original essays written for this volume. Together they constitute an assessment of what Wilde's work and history mean for the United States at this juncture of world history and social theory. Her introduction follows her general outline of the volume in being divided into four sections: Wilde's living and literary protest against prevailing social values; linguistic studies dealing with Wildean wit in *The Importance of Being Earnest;* Wilde's aesthetic pronouncements in the context of contemporary critical theory; and the sacrificial aspects of Wilde's life and work.

University of Miami   Zack Bowen

Publisher's Note

◆

Producing a volume that contains both newly commissioned and reprinted material presents the publisher with the challenge of balancing the desire to achieve stylistic consistency with the need to preserve the integrity of works first published elsewhere. In the Critical Essays series, essays commissioned especially for a particular volume are edited to be consistent with G. K. Hall's house style; reprinted essays appear in the style in which they were first published, with only typographical errors corrected. Consequently, shifts in style from one essay to another are the result of our efforts to be faithful to each text as it was originally published.

Critical Essays on

OSCAR WILDE

Introduction

◆

REGENIA GAGNIER

Two decades ago a reader could barely have discerned the first glimmerings of the renaissance of Wilde scholarship, criticism, and theory that this volume represents. By then, classic essays in criticism from Wilde's time to the postwar period had been collected in volumes edited by Wilde's early bibliographer Stuart Mason, Karl Beckson, and Richard Ellmann. The roots of sustained *literary*—as opposed to the previously biographical, psychological, ethical, or evaluative—analysis of Wilde's works had been cultivated by Edouard Roditi and Epifanio San Juan, Jr. At the end of the 1970s, a sequence of books confirmed the value of serious literary study of Wilde's works: Alan Bird's treatment of the plays, J. E. Chamberlin's and Rodney Shewan's work in intellectual history, Philip Cohen's sustained ethical approach, and Christopher Nassaar's literary psychology. Representative samples from these works have recently been reprinted in Harold Bloom's Chelsea editions of Wilde criticism.

Since 1900, when Wilde died because, as he said, it would be too much for the English that he should live into the twentieth century, many biographies have appeared, the most thorough and authoritative being, in chronological order, Hesketh Pearson's (1946), H. Montgomery Hyde's (1976), and Richard Ellmann's (1987)—although my own personal favorite remains the one that loved its data not wisely but too well, Rupert Croft-Cooke's *Unrecorded Life* of 1972. The majority of these biographies, including Ellmann's currently definitive work, are typical of the tragic genre of the life of the Great Man, who in this case slouches inevitably toward his doom, which is accomplished through a fatal flaw, in this instance either indiscretion or sexuality: Croft-Cooke's is the comic exception. By the 1970s, the standard editions for scholarship were the Sunflower or Collins editions, neither of which was annotated. Since the early 1980s, the plays have come out in authoritative New Mermaids edited by Russell Jackson and Ian Small, and Oxford has begun to publish a complete scholarly edition, whose most notable recent appearance is the *Oxford Notebooks*.

The purpose of the present volume is not to reprint the classic essays and reviews but, rather, to represent state-of-the-art Wilde criticism as it appears,

1

with two exceptions, in the United States. Limiting the volume to recent material primarily from the United States reflects my desire not to reprint material easily available elsewhere and not to include the same authors as an original collection whose authors are primarily British planned by Ian Small to announce the Oxford edition. Since Wilde's time, Germany and Italy have produced a substantial scholarship on Wilde and the 1890s, some of which will be discussed in this introduction, but most of that work has been and remains textual scholarship, eminently valuable but not of theoretical interest in a volume like this. Wilde is no doubt written of outside Europe and the United States, as his works have been translated into many languages, but my access to that literature has perforce been limited.

To say, however, that this volume represents state-of-the-art Wilde criticism is not to say that it includes only the fashionable (although that is here). This collection is meant to be a testimony to what Wilde represents for our time and place—late twentieth-century life in the United States. As the various contributions show, Wilde means many things for our time. Most important among them, he means—whether in gay activism, social theory, or interpretive margin or latitude—freedom and toleration.

The volume consequently includes a wide variety of contributors. Some have political projects and aspire to intervene in broader cultural life. Some want platforms for personal style, brilliancy, or ingenuity, representing the outré individuality they admire in Wilde. Some are scholars, poets, or journalists. After some arguments with myself, I have included essays far from my own perspective or profession: for example, one of the essays sees *The Importance of Being Earnest* as a deeply reactionary play, and one is intended to provide material for the monastic exercise of *lectio* that leads to meditation, prayer, and contemplation. All schools of criticism represented here, however, have their passionate advocates, and the total of impassioned perspectives makes up our collective critical moment and contribution. In his epilogue to *Oscar Wilde* Richard Ellmann wrote, "We inherit [Wilde's] struggle to achieve supreme fictions in art, to associate art with social change, to bring together individual and social impulse, to save what is eccentric and singular from being sanitized and standardized, to replace a morality of severity by one of sympathy."[1] In the hope of freedom and necessity of toleration, this fin de siècle pays tribute to the last, and to one of Ireland's great verbal artists.

WILDE AND SOCIETY

His chief war was against the Philistines. That is the war every child of light has to wage. Philistinism was the note of the age and community in which he lived[:] in their heavy inaccessibility to ideas, their dull respectability, their tedious orthodoxy, their worship of vulgar success, their entire preoccupation with the gross materialistic side of life, and their ridiculous estimate of themselves and their importance.

—*De Profundis* (Wilde on Jesus Christ)

The history of dandyism is inseparable from that of aestheticism. Aestheticism was a protest against Victorian utility, rationality, and realism, or the reduction of human relations to utility and the market and the representation of this in bourgeois literature. Asserting the diplomatic value of literary criticism in "The Critic as Artist," Wilde criticized the Manchester school that "tried to make men realize the brotherhood of humanity, by pointing out the commercial advantages of peace. It sought to degrade the wonderful world into a common marketplace for the buyer and the seller. It addressed itself to the lowest instinct, and it failed." Aestheticism represented a detachment from praxis indicating a break with imperialist society (Beardsley) and a preoccupation with formal or technical qualities of artistic media (Dowson and Johnson). Its function was to negate the means-end rationality of everyday middle-class life by theorizing art as an autonomous "useless" realm (Wilde). Its consequence was that art lacked overt political content, repeated archaic forms, and courted unproductiveness on the part of artists.

The dandy was the human equivalent of art under aestheticism. He was removed from life, like the Duke in *Zuleika Dobson,* a living protest against vulgarity—the creation of mass needs and desires—and means-end living. Like the dandies in Wilde's comedies, he provided a commentary on a society he despised in the form of wit at its expense. This wit, technically the inversion of the language of popular sentiment, was the major form of the dandy's participation in society. In the early period of Brummell and D'Orsay, he had patrons, but by the 1890s dandies used their wit to be both critical and commercially competitive, ironically commodifying themselves as products in a utilitarian economy. Socially central yet politically marginal and financially vulnerable, their position was often compared with that of women, who were limited in their ability to be dandies by the social constraints on their ability to be commercial. Proclaiming the superiority of his individual style, articulating a credo of idleness, irresponsibility, and artificiality, the dandy affronted the masculine and bourgeois ideology of equality, enterprise, duty, and sincerity.

Historically, dandies appealed to reactionaries through their refinement (taste and tact) and to revolutionaries through their independence. The early dandies embodied the bourgeois gentleman's superiority over a declining aristocracy. George Bryan Brummell, for example, the son of a valet, came to dominate Regency Society. Byron thought that Brummell heralded democracy, yet Brummell's first biographer began the romanticization of the Beau as part of a "natural aristocracy" that would give him reactionary status in an increasingly vulgarized bourgeois economy. In *Of Dandyism and of George Brummell* (1844) the Anglophile Barbey d'Aurevilly argued that dandyism arose within a wealthy society's contradictions between the luxury and power of the establishment and its ensuing boredom, or ennui. The conventions, constraints, and tedium of high society are counterparts to the scarcity and monotony of working-class life. The dandy accepts for his own benefit and others' amusement the materialism of affluent society, while he mocks its superficiality, its (as Wilde would later say) knowing the price of everything and the value of nothing. Applying to Brummell a *mot* from *Pelham,* "he displeased too generally not to be sought after," Barbey likened society's worship of the dandy to "the wish to be beaten of powerful and licentious women."[2] Wilde called one of his dramatic dandies "the first well-dressed philosopher in the history of thought." The dandy was the first to make style the basis of philosophy, of the only philosophy consistent with modern materialist life.

In *The Painter of Modern Life* (1863) Baudelaire also interpreted dandyism in sociopolitical terms as a "cult of the self" arising from "the burning need to create for oneself a personal originality" before "the rising tide of democracy levels everything."[3] Appearing in periods of transition, when the aristocracy is impotent and before the people have become the masses, men of natural abilities arise, whose gifts are those that work or money is unable to bestow. Declining with mass society, "dandyism is a sunset; like the declining daystar, it is glorious, without heat and full of melancholy" (Baudelaire, 28–29). Baudelaire's image of the dandy as "the last representative of human pride" had its most sublime (or Byronic) form in Charles Robert Maturin's Melmoth in *Melmoth the Wanderer* (1820). Melmoth's last intelligible words inspired the dandies of future generations. Torn between a God he was too materialist to believe in and a humankind too materialist for him to respect, he glitters alone in the splendor of material celestiality: "When a meteor blazes in your atmosphere—when a comet pursues its burning path towards the sun—look up, and perhaps you may think of the spirit condemned to guide the blazing and erratic orb."[4] Thus, a century later, in the crass world dominated by the superstar Zuleika, Beerbohm's perfect Duke leaps from a height "on the peak of dandyism . . . on the brink of eternity."[5] Thus also Wilde assumed the name Melmoth during his exile in Paris. These were dandyisms in the tragicomic and high tragic modes.

Dandyism declined with aestheticism after 1895. Dandies, like the dream of autonomous art, were pure. They entertained without belonging. When the trials made out that Wilde was *not* a dandy—dandies, wrote Baudelaire approvingly, did not have erections—the public he had amused for a season deserted him, as it had deserted Brummell and others whose vulnerability was traced to the social and financial insecurity Baudelaire had theorized. Given that Wilde's private life was all too engagé, contradicting his public aesthetic code of critical distance, the aestheticism he had helped to promote fell in the public mind from its height of dandiacal purity to a shameful bohemianism that was to be associated with the art world for decades to come. But in his heyday, the dandy was the ironic conscience of mass society. Ostentatiously brilliant, he still could distinguish between value and price. Aloof and critical, he still retained a desire for community, for the approval of others. He showed the gentleman what he had sacrificed in the age of privacy and massification: individuality, community, beauty.

When I began my *Idylls of the Marketplace: Oscar Wilde and the Victorian Public* in the late 1970s, my goal was to move the study of Wilde in particular and the 1890s in general out of the biographical, psychological, and evaluative modes of previous criticism into a more social, or political, historical context. Thus I saw the dandy in relation to the development of European democracy; aestheticism in relation to the mass-market and mass-media society it opposed; wit as the linguistic subversion of the status quo; the plays in relation to commodity fetishism; Wilde's sexuality as constructed rather than given; art-for-art's-sake in relation to what we might call sex-for-sex's-sake—a movement that opposed itself to "natural" sexuality and purposive reproduction; and *The Ballad of Reading Gaol* and *De Profundis* in relation to the reformation of law and prison. This admittedly sociological approach to the fin de siècle has continued in the work of cultural studies, most recently and fruitfully in John Stokes's *In the Nineties* (1989) and Elaine Showalter's *Sexual Anarchy* (1990).

In Wilde studies per se the critics in the first section of this volume have a primarily sociological interest in Wilde's relation to his larger society. The excerpt from my chapter on *Salome* and *The Ballad of Reading Gaol* from the *Idylls* explores the class and gender ideologies and social events leading to Wilde's trials in 1895. The prosecutors attacked Wilde because his life, to them a low private life, was incommensurate with his putative and public aesthetic code. The press reporting the trials found in Wilde's life the same absence it had discerned in *The Picture of Dorian Gray:* the absence of middle-class life; he presumed to associate with aristocrats, artists, or grooms. As the prosecutors pushed the connections between the art world and domestic and sexual deviation, aestheticism came to represent a secret, private realm of art and sexuality impervious to middle-class conformity. In other words, aestheticism came to mean the irrational in both productive (art) and reproductive (sexuality) realms: a clear affront to bourgeois utility and rationality in these realms and an apparent indication of the art world's divorce from middle-class life.

In "Different Desires: Subjectivity and Transgression in Wilde and Gide" (*Textual Practice*, 1987), Jonathan Dollimore contrasts Wilde's anti-essentialist concept of human nature—best articulated in "The Soul of Man under Socialism"'s depiction of individualism as a dynamic *social* potential—and critique of subjective depth, or "transgressive aesthetic," with Gide's essentialist concept of an authentic self, which nonetheless, according to Dollimore, provides an equally "transgressive" ethic. Seeing Wilde's transgressive aesthetic as anticipating three aspects of contemporary theoretical debate—the critical possibilities of deconstruction, the politics of decentering the subject, and the postmodern critique of subjective depth—Dollimore concludes that an antiessentialist theory of subjectivity can in no way guarantee, a priori, any effect, radical or otherwise. Through such a pragmatic approach to theory, Dollimore is exploring the possibilities of transgression and resistance from within the dominant social forms, what he calls the paradox of marginalities that are interior to, or at least intimate with, the center. In citing Wilde's antiessentialist critique of human nature in "The Soul of Man"—"The only thing that one really knows about human nature is that it changes. . . . Progress is the realisation of Utopias"—Dollimore aligns Wilde, as many of us have, with the Marx of *The Poverty of Philosophy,* who said that all history was nothing but a continuous transformation of human nature.

Two themes explored by Dollimore, the possibilities of resistance from within the dominant social forms and Wilde's synthesis of socialism and individualism, are central to the two essays that complete this section. In "Writing Gone Wilde: Homoerotic Desire in the Closet of Representation" (*PMLA,* 1987) Ed Cohen specifies the continuum of homosocial desire that Eve Kosofsky Sedgwick outlined in *Between Men: English Literature and Male Homosocial Desire,* a text that has become influential in gay studies.[6] Using the homoerotic novel *Teleny,* with which Wilde was associated, and the manifestly "straight" *Picture of Dorian Gray,* Cohen suggests how textual depictions of male same-sex experience both reproduce and resist dominant heterosexuality. He explores the complex representations of a subcultural gender experience within a dominant culture that not only marginalized but criminalized it. Both Dollimore's and Cohen's essays broadly testify to the influence of Michel Foucault's *History of Sexuality.*

In his rousing "Style and Socialism" (*Nation,* 1988), a review of an aspect of Wilde that Ellmann's biography made too little of, Christopher Hitchens too revives "The Soul of Man under Socialism," reminding us that, far from bourgeois essentialism and isolation, Wilde's individualism implied a social program, a solidarity that recognized mutual interest. From a journalist who is also a media analyst and social critic—as Wilde was in his day—Hitchens's reminder is especially poignant at a time when the U.S. media invariably equate capitalism with democracy and socialism with totalitarianism— equations that would have been incomprehensible or a deliberate obfuscation to Wilde (nineteenth-century socialists used the terms *socialist* and *democrat* interchangeably).

Because Dollimore is more concerned with postmodern theory than modernist practice, and because Hitchens's essay is far too brief, I want to conclude this section with a few more reflections on "The Soul of Man under Socialism." "The Soul of Man" is an essay for our time, for it confronts Western democratic, or liberal, thought, allegedly committed to social and religious tolerance and the procedural freedoms of speech, dissent, and the vote, with its limitations under a free-market system that does not promote actual access to these freedoms. Actual access, the essay argues, is possible only by coupling substantive freedoms—the freedom from starvation, sickness, homelessness, ignorance, and so on—with procedural freedoms. It is possible, in short, only by coupling some form of social welfare with liberal democracy. Material well-being and availability of opportunity for self-development for all members of a society are thus the *precondition* of individualism. Only under such "socialism" will the rich stop sacrificing themselves to philanthropy and confusing their development with the accumulation of property, and will the poor *in fact,* rather than in theory, have access to the democratic processes that Western democracies claim they value.

Wilde's argument in "The Soul of Man" is clearly within the mainstream tradition of socialist thought (if not practice), but less recognized is its consistency with a long tradition of socialist aesthetics. In his *Letters on the Aesthetic Education of Man* (1795), Schiller tried to rectify the Kantian reduction of aesthetics to art by reestablishing the connections among pleasure, sensuousness, beauty, truth, and freedom. Schiller's aesthetic quest was for the solution of a political problem: the liberation of all human faculties as a critique of instrumentalization and rationalization under the industrial revolution, of the increasing subjection of humankind to the atomization of the marketplace. In Schiller's aesthetic, once humankind had achieved the conquest of scarcity, toil or labor would be transformed into play and repressive productivity would be transformed into "display," defined as "the free manifestation of potentialities."[7] Later, Marx and Engels wrote in *The German Ideology* (1846): "With a communist organization of society, there disappears the subordination of the artist to local and national narrowness . . . and also the subordination of the individual to some definite art, making him exclusively a painter, sculptor, etc. . . . In a communist society there are no painters but only people who engage in painting among other activities."[8] Often called the first English Marxist, Wilde's friend William Morris wrote in one of his finest political essays, "How We Live and How We Might Live" (1884), that under socialism "people would rather be anxious to seek work than to avoid it. . . . Then would come the time for the new birth of art, so much talked of, so long deferred. . . . The workshop would once more be a school of art, whose influence no one could escape from."[9] In "Revolutionary and Socialist Art," Trotsky wrote that under socialism it would "be the aesthetic schools around which 'parties' will collect, that is, associations of temperaments, of tastes and of moods. . . . In truth, we have no reason to fear that there will be a decline of individuality or an impoverishment of art in a Socialist society."[10] In 1924 Trotsky concluded *Literature and Revolution* with an aesthetic dialectic he called "the cultural construction and self-education of Communist man," in which human faculties no longer apportioned as in the division of labor between mind and body, reason and sensuousness, mental and manual are transformed and perfected in particularly Wildean terms: "Man will become immeasurably stronger, wiser and subtler; his body will become more harmonized, his movements more rhythmic, his voice more musical. The forms of life will become dynamically dramatic" (Trotsky, 256). In 1941 Herbert Marcuse concluded "Some Social Implications of Modern Technology" with, "The less time and energy man has to expend in maintaining his life and that of society, the greater the possibility that he can 'individualize' the sphere of his human realization. Beyond the realm of necessity, the essential differences between men could unfold themselves: everyone could think and act by himself, speak his own language, have his own emotions and follow his own passions. No longer chained to competitive efficiency, the self could grow in the realm of satisfaction."[11] Except for the transcendent connotations of "Man," this freedom from competitive efficiency is what Wilde meant by individualism.

It is worth emphasizing how Wilde's dialectically materialist aesthetic—socialism giving rise to individuals who then build the first genuinely flourishing society—differs from recent poststructuralist "aestheticizing of life." In his last interviews Foucault began to speak nostalgically of an aestheticized subject he had derived from the Hellenic "care of the self," "the idea of a self that had to be created as a work of art":

> We have hardly any remnant of the idea in our society, that the principal work of art which one has to take care of, the main area to which one must apply aesthetic values, is oneself, one's life, one's existence. We find this in the Renaissance, but in a slightly academic form, and yet again in nineteenth-century dandyism, but those were only episodes. . . . What strikes me is the fact that in our society, art has become something which is related only to projects and not to individuals, or to life. That art is something which is specialized or which is done by experts who are artists. But couldn't everyone's life become a work of art? Why should the lamp or the house be an art object, but not our life?"[12]

Both Wilde's and Foucault's respective aestheticizings of the self reject the autonomous, authentic self. Yet Foucault's regime of self-regulation differs in important ways from Wilde and the socialists' aestheticizing of the self. The earlier authors predicated the free manifestation of potentialities on a humane socialism. What remains a possibility under socialism appears under current conditions (i.e., Foucault's) as mere nostalgia for an autonomous community of honorable men or the private luxury of a life freed from necessity. "Why couldn't everyone's life become a work of art?" Wilde had answered this question in 1891 in the last lines of "The Soul of Man": because the Greeks had slaves and fed them and the Renaissance had slaves and starved them. For the socialists, life as art was an image of possibility predicated on the abolition of exploitation and scarcity (as Hitchens says, a solidarity that recognized mutual interest); for Foucault, it was an apparently autonomous regime of self-regulation in a finely "disciplined" world, a highly individualistic project reminiscent of Pater's stoic epicureanism. Unlike both liberal and poststructural accounts of subjectivity, aesthetic subjectivity as the free manifestation of potentialities of mind and body under the conditions of socialism has all but disappeared. It reminds us, however, of what a really radical aesthetic, a socialist aesthetic, looks like: it is an aesthetic not reduced to artworks, an aesthetic of the everyday rather than the extraordinary, of the many rather than the few. I suspect that this critical aesthetic explains the fact that although "The Soul of Man" is Wilde's best-known work in the world at large, it is the least discussed of all his works in the Anglo-American literary community.

WILDEAN WIT:
THE IMPORTANCE OF BEING EARNEST

A windy brawler in a world of words
I never met so eloquent a fool.
—*A Florentine Tragedy*

In focusing on Wilde's identifying characteristic, his wit, the contributors in this section turn their attention to his most popular play, *The Importance of Being Earnest*. Each, however, analyzes the wit in the play differently: in relation to a self-contained text or system of language, to the hierarchy of philosophy and literature, to the subversiveness of puns, or to the subversion of genre.

After the Hitchens essay, Camille A. Paglia's chic and elegant "Oscar Wilde and the English Epicene" (*Raritan*, 1985) may come as something of a surprise. Paglia sees Wilde's language in *The Importance of Being Earnest* as an aristocratic sequestration, a mode of hierarchical positioning; the play itself as "a reactionary political poem" displaying Wilde's love of aristocratic hierarchy, order, and manners for their own sake; and Wilde himself as the definitive amoralizer. Paglia does, however, grant that such allegedly reactionary tendencies eventually led to certain conflicts for "a suffering homosexual in a Christian society." In her account of the androgynes, epicenes, and even androids in *Earnest*, Paglia says much descriptively true of the play; she differs from many other contemporary Wildeans only by not seeing Wilde as critical of the society he is representing. By limiting her assessment of Wilde to his method in *Earnest*, she rightly shows how Wilde's comedy transforms content into form, soul into surface, but does not allow that elsewhere Wilde's technique is not "hard," without metaphor, or syntactically simple. More important, in overly schematizing androgynes, epicenes, and androids, Paglia falls into the error of essentializing wit as an autonomous linguistic system independent of particular audiences or social situation: one might counter, with Dollimore, that wit cannot guarantee, a priori, any effect, conservative or otherwise.

A similar attempt has been made by Richard Pine to distinguish between dandies like Wilde and heralds like Marx and Engels. Beginning with the sensible hypothesis that dandies were concerned with "the accomplishment of manners, the aristocracy of taste," with, in short, ego, and heralds with "an accomplishment of mind and morals," or social purpose, Pine is eventually driven to compromise figures like heraldic dandies, aesthete-rebels, rogue-criminals, naif-fantasists, and naif-chivalrics.[13] For one who knows the range of their work, it is hard not to see that Wilde was sometimes, as in "The Soul of Man," a herald, and that Marx and Engels were often dandies. See, for example, such witticisms, precisely comparable in form to Wildean wit, as "the arm of criticism cannot replace the criticism of arms" and "in monarchy we have the people of the constitution, in democracy we have the constitution of the people" (*Critique of Hegel's Philosophy of Right*). Marx was the heraldic dandy who responded to a book called *The Philosophy of Poverty* with *The Poverty of Philosophy;* who seized on the revolutionary value of the early Christian paradoxes "blessed are the poor" and "the wisdom of this world is foolishness"; and who, anticipating Wilde's notorious attack on bourgeois law in "Pen, Pencil, and Poison," wrote about the "stimulus to the productive forces" bestowed on society by the criminal: "A philosopher produces ideas, a poet poems, a clergyman sermons, a professor compendia and so on. A criminal produces crimes . . . also criminal law . . . moreover the whole of the police and of criminal justice, constables, judges, hangmen, juries . . . also art, *belles-lettres,* novels, and even tragedies. . . . Crime constantly calls into being new methods of defense, and so is as productive as strikes for the invention of machines. . . . Would the world-market ever have come into being but for national crime? Would even the nations have arisen?" (Compare Wilde's "charity creates a multitude of sins," "in the interest of the rich we must get rid of private property," and "disobedience is man's original virtue" in "The Soul of Man.")[14]

Yet if Paglia's essay first overgeneralizes and then essentializes Wilde's technique, it also reminds us of one persistent response to *Earnest*. From Shaw's judgment that the play was "heartless" to Mary McCarthy's moralistic outrage against Wilde's alleged selfishness and *superbia,* critics who do not see Wildean wit as critical see Wildean Society as atomistic and asocial.[15]

The essay by the late Joel Fineman, "The Significance of Literature: *The Importance of Being Earnest"* (*October* 1980), is little more than an informal MLA talk with some appended footnotes on Anglo-American philosophy of language, but its suggestiveness for other critics, such as Christopher Craft in this volume, and its relative inaccessibility in the back issues of *October* have merited its inclusion here. Fineman initially contrasts literary language as exemplified in *Earnest,* a language that exhibits the alternation and oscillation of the subject ("Bunburyism"), with language as conceived by the philosophy of language from Plato to John Searle. Fineman, however, sees twentieth-century developments in analytic philosophy of language dovetailing with recent critiques from the so-called Continental tradition: "The history of philosophy of language should be of special interest to students of literature, for in many ways the progressive and increasingly dogmatic subordination by philosophy of nominal reference, first to extension, then to expression, then to intention, and finally to a historicity that postpones its temporality, in many ways parallels the development and eventual demise of an aesthetics of representation." In note 7 Fineman presents his account of the history of the philosophy of names, and in note 5 he describes the theory of the established hierarchy of literary forms that derives from the "heterological" prejudice, or dominant philosophical theory of reference. Thus tragedy is the highest form, as it imitates an action, and farce (like *Earnest*) the lowest, being merely the action of imitation, or even the imitation of imitation—that is, farce imitates, or parodies, other literature or genres. (See Kerry Powell's essay and my remarks on it later in this section.) Congruent with the theory of reference that subordinates farce is, of course, the dominant theory of the subject that elevates tragedy: tragedy presents us with a unified, authentic subject; farce, with a stock caricature. In contrasting the seriousness of tragedy and philosophy with the triviality of farce and literature, Fineman returns to the subject of *Earnest,* now representing the free play of the subject in writing, or the literary subject par excellence. Jack-Ernest is thus the ideal image of the relation of the self not to itself but to writing. Fineman at least partly worked out his theory of genres in relation to subjectivity in his *Shakespeare's Perjured Eye* (1986); his illness prevented him from completing his work on Wilde's contribution to the demise of an aesthetics of representation.

Fineman's challenge to see Wilde in relation to the philosophy of names has been partly met by the work of Linda Dowling, whose *Language and Decadence* (1986) situates late Victorian aesthetics in relation to contemporary philology and linguistics, in which the possibilities of language as an autonomous, self-reflexive system were being formulated.[16] Unfortunately, Dowling believes that her most recent work specifically on Wilde is not detachable from her wider argument, and thus it cannot be represented here. Others, developing the elusive concluding suggestions in Fineman's essay, have focused rather on *Earnest's* literary "erotics" and their manifestation in puns. Fineman calls Bunbury the only "naturally motivated," or referential, name in the play, expressing a desire "to bury in the bun."

In "Alias Bunbury: Desire and Termination in *The Importance of Being Earnest*" (*Representations* 1990), Christopher Craft follows Fineman and Dollimore in claiming that Wilde delegitimates the claims of ontological authority (with *Earnest's* "origins in terminuses") and natural reference (Jack-Ernest) and grounds experience and identity not in nature but in representation. Like Cohen and Dollimore, Craft wants to discern the homosexual countervalences in Wilde's apparently heterosexual texts. In the third and fourth parts of his essay, which are reprinted here, he pursues Fineman's suggestion and examines a sequence of puns and textual events in which Wilde lifts to liminality a specific subcultural knowledge of the desire "to bury in the bun." In Wilde's deconstruction of the language of sex, or, more precisely, of the integral and heterosexual male subject, Craft finds the erotics, or, more specifically, the homoerotics, of punning, in which "difference vanishes in the ear." Craft's essay is exemplary of its genre of literary (homo)erotics, a genre that elsewhere has interpreted *The Ballad of Reading Gaol* as about "reading" or "Mr. W. H." 's Erskine as "kin of the Erse and of the arse" (i.e., Irish and homosexual), or Wilde himself. This way of reading has also been called "grammatological"—after Derridean reading practices as well as after Cyril Graham in "Mr. W. H."[17] Such work is typically so heteronomously motivated that it makes little sense to point out that, technically speaking, Wilde rarely made puns. On the other hand, as the next section, on Wilde's criticism, indicates, many modern readers trace the genealogy of such "creative criticism" to Wilde's own time. One could certainly argue that "The Portrait of Mr. W. H." or some of the contemporary burlesques of late Victorian Shakespearean criticism anticipated some of our own critical punsters.[18]

Kerry Powell's impressive scholarship on late Victorian farce in "Algernon's Other Brothers" (from his *Oscar Wilde and the Theatre of the 1890s,* 1990) shows that if critics are right in discerning the homosexual countervalences in *Earnest,* Wilde refashioned them from their tamer instantiations in the work of his contemporaries, for the tropes, figures, and plots themselves were, as Powell demonstrates conclusively, stock elements of farce in the 1890s. Well before *Earnest,* late Victorian farce used to dramatic effect objects lost and found in railway terminals; the double life of bunburying and even the character Bunbury himself; the imaginary brother named Ernest; foundlings in search of parents, christening, and personal identity; mistaken identities; sexual revolutionaries; the subversion of domesticity; gluttony; and imaginary lovers. Yet while establishing incontrovertibly the extreme derivativeness of Wilde's farce, Powell claims for Wilde more rather than less originality. For Powell, Wildean wit is most subversive in its macrorelations with its genre, the play's unlikely critical intelligence distinguishing it from less self-conscious exempla of its kind. Moreover, when Powell considers, in *Oscar Wilde and the Theatre of the 1890s,* the range of Wilde's drama, he shows that Wilde's dramatic stereotypes and conventions consistently subverted the Victorian stereotypes and conventions they imitated. If Wilde shamelessly plagiarized entire, detailed plots from his colleagues, he did so with the inversion that his women did not repent, his errant mothers did not reclaim their children, and his ideal husbands rejected the conventional constraints of masculinity. Such a wit defied both the literary and the social status quo.

WILDEAN CRITIQUE

In "The Critical Legacy of Oscar Wilde" (*Texas Studies in Literature and Language,* 1988), Zhang Longxi cites Max Beerbohm's judgment of Wilde's significance: "In point of fact, wit was the least important of his gifts. Primarily, he was a poet, with a life-long passion for beauty; and a philosopher, with a life-long passion for thought." The contributors to this section illustrate an increasing willingness on the part of critics to take Wilde seriously as a philosopher of aesthetics.

Zhang recounts René Wellek's disapproval in 1965 of Wilde's "creative criticism." It went "beyond the demands of sympathy," confused criticism with creation, and misled the critic into "irresponsible subjectivity." In the 1960s, however, Wellek reassured his audience that a takeover by such "creative criticism" was "no present danger." By 1983, he was writing in the *New Criterion* of the destruction of literary studies, meaning deconstruction, *Rezeptionsästhetik,* and reader-response theory. Zhang's goal, like that of another recent critic of Wilde, Bruce Bashford, is to show how Wilde's art and literary criticism anticipates much of our own contemporary theory, tracing his lineage from Vico to Barthes, Said, Bloom, and Hartman.[19] Zhang also reminds us that, before Dollimore, Dowling, and Fineman, Northrop Frye saw Wilde as "turning away from the descriptive use of language and the correspondence form of truth." Yet Zhang is careful not to elide, in an overzealous spirit of relevance, Wilde's difference from more recent critics: whereas Hartman appreciates criticism as a form of power *over* others, Wilde, according to Zhang, saw it more benignly as a form of cosmopolitanism, implying communication and tolerance. Wilde wrote in "The Decay of Lying" that criticism "treats the work of art simply as a starting point for a new creation," yet he also made stringent demands on the critic's self-discipline, claiming, in the same essay, that "criticism demands infinitely more cultivation than creation does" or (in "The Critic as Artist") "an appreciation of Milton is . . . the reward of consummate scholarship."

In "Semiotics and Oscar Wilde's Accounts of Art" (*British Journal of Aesthetics,* 1985), Ian Small also resists the dualistic approach to art, often attributed to Wilde, as representational or self-reflexive by introducing a third term—*cultural*—by which he means an account of art's place in a system of values. After the semioticians Charles Morris and Umberto Eco, Small is interested in both how different cultures construct conceptions of the natural and how social practices determine a work's cultural significance. He finds both of these accounts in Wilde's aesthetics. Gerhard Joseph's "Framing Wilde" (*Victorian Newsletter,* 1987) uses "The Portrait of Mr. W. H." to explore both textual and extratextual interpretive framing in Wilde, thus bringing another approach to the problems of representation, self-reflexivity or autonomy, and cultural politics that Wilde has come to stand for. A good companion piece to Joseph's postmodern concern with framing and Patrice Hannon's "Aesthetic Criticism, Useless Art: Wilde, Zola, and 'The Portrait of Mr. W. H.'" is Horst Schroeder's *Oscar Wilde, "The Portrait of Mr. W. H."—Its Composition, Publication and Reception* (1984). As aesthetic theorists, Joseph and Hannon are preoccupied with the theoretical implications of Wilde's narrative framing devices. As a meticulous historical and bibliographic scholar, Schroeder demonstrates how insignificant Wilde's framing was to his contemporaries.

"Mr. W. H." was received by its first readers in *Blackwood's Edinburgh Magazine* (July 1889) as an attempt to contribute to Shakespearean criticism; even when it was rejected, the theory of Shakespeare's sonnets was treated favorably as an amusing piece of critical ingenuity. None of Wilde's reviewers, however, was interested in Wilde's elaborate narrative framing of Cyril, Erskine, and the narrator. One reviewer said the frame could have been "spared." Many years later, Alfred Douglas himself called the frame "silly": "Wilde's theory is so good and so ingenious that it is a thousand pities that he did not write it and put it forth as a theory and nothing else. Instead of this he wrapped round the theory what I can only describe as a very foolish and unconvincing story. . . . The result of all this silliness is that the excellence of the theory is obscured, and Wilde himself . . . leaves his readers in doubt as to whether he is really advancing a serious theory or simply indulging in a piece of clever 'leg-pulling' " (Schroeder, 54). The dramatic shift in critics' appreciation of "Mr. W. H." illustrates Small's cultural aesthetics.

Hannon also uses "The Portrait of Mr. W. H." to contrast Wildean aestheticism, with its values of empathy and toleration, with Zola's scientism (in "The Experimental Novel" [1880]), with its project of social control. Although one could argue that comparison of Wilde and Zola would be valuable in showing how two contemporary and powerful social critics developed different programs for progressive ends, Hannon does not emphasize this aspect of the pairing. Rather, she insists on keeping Wilde determinedly "aesthetic" in the limited sense of the term. In claiming that Wildean theory (e.g., of Shakespeare's sonnets) is "useless," Hannon means that it has use value only for the mind that creates it: the critical process itself is its own end. Unlike Zola's social engineering, Wildean critique for Hannon has no exchange value, cannot be used for heteronomous ends.

Critics who do make a persuasive case for Wilde's historical connections with, and commitment to, progressive ends are Philip E. Smith II and Michael S. Helfand in their commentary to Wilde's *Oxford Notebooks* (1989), one of the most significant works of scholarship in late Victorian studies to date.[20] Briefly, Smith and Helfand argue, with much evidence from the *Notebooks,* that Wildean critique was a systematic synthesis of Hegelian idealism and evolutionary theory. They demonstrate Wilde's intellectual embeddedness in social evolutionism of various stripes—radical Darwinism, socialist eugenics, educational theory, and critiques of liberalism. For those of us who take "The Soul of Man under Socialism" seriously, it is gratifying to read the authors' conclusion that "by allowing all individuals to take their physical subsistence for granted, that is, to live aesthetically, Wilde wished to free those humane qualities which, like sexual selection, would give new forms, variety, and progress to life and so allow mankind to evolve naturally toward humane individualism" (*Notebooks,* 84). Smith and Helfand's commentaries go far to clarify one of Wilde's most significant and least recognized metaphors, in "The

Critic as Artist"—that aesthetics are to ethics "in the sphere of conscious civilisation" what sexual is to natural selection in the natural world: "Ethics, like natural selection, make existence possible. Aesthetics, like sexual selection, make life lovely and wonderful, fill it with new forms, and give it progress, and variety and change." Although the analogy underestimates the progressive force of ethics and natural selection, placing it, as Smith and Helfand do, within specific and differentiated traditions of social evolutionism enables one to see the noble social function that Wilde attributed to aesthetics. The commentary offers an invaluable intellectual history of the late Victorian period and Wilde in particular, especially in social theory. For example, in the *Notebooks,* following William Kingdon Clifford's critique of Mill's "individualistic empiricism" and "atomistic society," Wilde wrote that individualism and its outgrowths, "private property and a private conscience," are not fundamental to human ethical nature (*Notebooks,* 30, 129). Another example is Wilde's views on education. Opposed to Arnold's centralized education, Wilde saw, presciently, that it could lead to a mass society; rather, he opted for autodidacticism and individual development predicated on socially guaranteed access to opportunity.

Smith and Helfand "take Wilde seriously as a theoretician with a system" (*Notebooks,* 59) and so make his critical work from "The Rise of Historical Criticism" (1879) through *Intentions* (1891) more coherent and consistent than scholars have hitherto understood. Given the accessibility of the *Oxford Notebooks,* I am here including some of Smith's continuing work, "Protoplasmic Hierarchy and Philosophical Harmony: Science and Hegelian Aesthetics in Oscar Wilde's Notebooks" (*Victorian Newsletter,* 1988), which addresses itself specifically to Wilde's interest in contemporary debates in the natural sciences. Many readers, however, will continue to prefer Hannon's graceful, ludic Wilde to Smith and Helfand's monumentally consistent Hegelian dialectician.

WILDE AND SUFFERING, OR UNIVERSALITY

You came to me to learn the Pleasure of Life and the Pleasure of Art. Perhaps I am chosen to teach you something much more wonderful, the meaning of Sorrow, and its beauty.

—*De Profundis*

There is some concern today in the popular press and pedagogical literature about Americans' increasing inability to comprehend irony. Television scriptwriters and talk-show hosts are aware of it. Educators notice it while they are lecturing. If this trend continues, it is likely that *Earnest* will cease to be Wilde's most visible work. Going on the principle articulated in Wilde's prose poem "The Artist," that only sorrow endures forever, it may be that the works with longevity will be those that speak of suffering: *De Profundis, The Ballad of Reading Gaol,* the prose poems, and some of the stories. The final group of contributors addresses these works, or Wilde and suffering.

Leonard Nathan's "The Ballads of Reading Gaol: At the Limits of the Lyric" is the only contribution by a practicing poet, and it duly begins with the craft of poetry, the problems a poet faces in making. *The Ballad of Reading Gaol* was motivated in part by personal anguish and in part by social protest: how was Wilde to reconcile his own assumptions about poetry—that is, a late romantic poetics—with a public project? Nathan is an experienced rhetorician as well as a poet, and his inquiry into the crafting of *The Ballad* raises the most important issues in poetics since the romantics: the problem of a public poetry in a lyric, romantic—or, in social terms, atomistic and privatized—age; the relative strengths of lyric and argument; the poet-as-social-critic's desire for adversarial ends without adversarial means. The limits of lyric in the modern world are at the heart of not only *The Ballad* but every poet who dreams, if not of being a legislator of the world, then at least of being read in modern, or postmodern, society. Nathan targets romantic authenticity in considering poetry's lack of public position; like many feminist poets, or poets within revolutionary societies, Nathan views a plastic notion of self as the sine qua non of a public poetics, a poetics that aims to change the world precisely because the world, like the self, is changeable.

The lyric/propaganda crux in *The Ballad,* the modern problematics of private desire and political danger, libidinal and political economies, and public and private agency pervade Wilde's work. In "Wilde and Huysmans: Autonomy, Reference, and the Myth of Expiation," the comparatist James Winchell eloquently treats *Dorian Gray* and *De Profundis*'s dialectics of individuality and universality, autonomy and responsibility, aestheticism and expiation for community, and the subject-as-spectator and the subject-as-object. Well-versed in modern theories of mimesis and sacrifice, Winchell transforms—via Wilde, Huysmans, and an astonishing painting by Rops—what are elsewhere abstract structural dualisms into dynamic human struggles.

Most lovers of Wilde from Yeats to the present have been struck by the hermetic beauty of the poems in prose—those narratives, as legend has it, that were all the more haunting when Wilde himself narrated them to friends "spontaneously" in café bars. Lovers of Wilde must also be struck by the prose poems' apparent immunity from critical commentary. Yet Winchell's approach would be fruitful here, for the theme of the prose poems is the paradoxes of individuality and universality, autonomy and responsibility, self and other.[21] "The Doer of Good" tries autonomously to do good, but objective conditions invert his intentions. In "The Disciple," as Narcissus saw but his own beauty in the pool's reflection, so the pool saw only its own beauty in the reflection of Narcissus's eyes. "The Master" imitates Christ in all things and weeps because the world has not crucified him. In "The House of Judgment" God cannot cast Man into Hell for he has lived there always; nor can He send Man to Heaven, for he cannot imagine it. God is appalled by Man's subjectivity: his own mind is hell. Finally, "The Teacher of Wisdom" gives up his perfect knowledge of God—God as his object—only to receive by his sacrifice the perfect love of God—the gift of himself as a subject of God's love.

In 1962 G. Wilson Knight published a famous essay on Christ and Wilde in *The Christian Renaissance*. Now a new generation of Wildeans can take up this aspect of the 1890s in which sacrificial figures are as at home as Bunbury—are indeed Bunbury's tragic doubles. Some sophistication and much sensitivity in dealing with such material would enrich our understanding not only of Wilde and Huysmans but also of many other writers of the spiritual (if not literal) 1890s: my own candidate would be the heretofore critically ignored Frederick Rolfe, alias Baron Corvo, whose *Desire and Pursuit of the Whole: A Romance of Modern Venice* (1909) is perhaps the strangest and most moving novel in the English language; it is certainly the nakedest.

In "The Christ of Oscar Wilde" (*American Benedictine Review,* 1988) John Albert, O.C.S.O., sees agons of self and other, autonomy and sacrifice, throughout Wilde's works. Brother John Albert is a solemnly professed Trappist monk. With his essay he intended "to provide the reader with ample texts from Oscar Wilde, which will allow the richness of his thought and style to emerge," and he hoped "to provide material for the monastic exercise of *lectio* that leads to meditation, prayer and contemplation." Having taken the vows of silence and monasticism, he has had limited access to critical work on Wilde, and his scholarship is dated. Yet I have included his work here in accordance with a lesson I learned while writing about *De Profundis:* that by far Wilde's largest audience is not academic and not primarily concerned with his wit or his supersubtle subversions of the status quo. Wilde saw in Jesus Christ the Man of Sorrows "who made of himself the mouthpiece of those who are dumb under oppression," and many readers go to Wilde for the same reason. Although criticism, after Auden, found the bits about Christ in *De Profundis* "tedious," I have learned that prisoners and prisoners of war do not. Time after time, as I lectured on the letter from prison, prisoners and former prisoners taught me new levels of appreciation of its accuracy of emotional description in the precise conditions of solitary confinement and mass convict labor under a strong centralized prison system. Despite the postmodern critiques that throughout this volume have appealed to Wilde as a precursor, I have been haunted by Wilde's own realist statement to Robert Ross from prison: "In point of fact, Robbie, prison life makes one see people and things as they really are." If from a certain standpoint—that of the outcast—one can in fact see the mainstream or center as it really is, more people will soon be enlightened. In *Idylls of the Marketplace* I wrote that *De Profundis* resisted modern consumption, that its extreme isolation and material conditions unknown to most of us made it unassimilable in the complacent consumption of art commodities in mass society. Now, as the United States has taken the lead of all nations in the proportion of its citizens incarcerated, as our number of prisoners has exceeded

1 million, as more and more Americans fall through the proverbial safety net, become homeless, and, as homeless, are incarcerated, *De Profundis* becomes more assimilable, the conditions of its production more familiar.

I have included two sections from "The Christ of Oscar Wilde" as a reminder that Wilde's largest, if most submerged, audience reads him for his articulateness during suffering, for the comfort he can give. After a century of critical dismissals of Wilde's early poetry, Brother John Albert reminds us that faithful and generous readers still find in Wilde's putatively derivative and undistinguished poems faith and generosity. What I like about John Albert's work is the way he contextualizes in an aura of care and kindness quotations from Wilde that have in the work of other critics ceased to sound compelling. It is perhaps another example of creative criticism.

Notes

1. Richard Ellmann, *Oscar Wilde* (London: Hamish Hamilton, 1987), 553.

2. J. A. Barbey d'Aurevilly, *Of Dandyism and of George Brummell*, trans. Douglas Ainslie (London: J. M. Dent, 1897), 102.

3. Charles Baudelaire, *The Painter of Modern Life and Other Essays*, trans. Jonathan Mayne (London: Phaidon Press, 1964), 28–29; hereafter cited in text.

4. Charles Robert Maturin, *Melmoth the Wanderer* (London: Oxford University Press, 1968), 540.

5. Max Beerbohm, *Zuleika Dobson* (New York: 1952), 206.

6. Eve Kosofsky Sedgwick, *Between Men: English Literature and Male Homosocial Desire* (New York: Columbia University Press, 1985).

7. Friedrich Schiller, *On the Aesthetic Education of Man* (New York: Ungar, 1965); see also Herbert Marcuse on Schiller in *One Dimensional Man* (Boston: Beacon Press, 1964).

8. Karl Marx and Friedrich Engels, *On Literature and Art* (Moscow: Progress Publishers, 1976), 179; hereafter cited in text.

9. William Morris, *Political Writings*, ed. A. L. Morton (New York: International Publishers, 1979), 153.

10. Leon Trotsky, *Literature and Revolution* (Ann Arbor: University of Michigan Press, 1960), 230–32; hereafter cited in text.

11. Andrew Arato and Eike Gebhart, eds., *The Essential Frankfurt School Reader* (New York: Continuum, 1985), 161.

12. Michel Foucault, *The Foucault Reader*, ed. Paul Rabinow (New York: Pantheon, 1984), 350–62.

13. Richard Pine, *The Dandy and the Herald: Manners, Mind and Morals from Brummell to Durrell* (New York: St. Martin's Press, 1988), esp. 12–13.

14. For more on this topic, one can await the appearance of Terry Eagleton's novel and play about Wilde, in which, Eagleton has said, he "explores the link between wit and commitment." See Peter Snow, "Oxford English Limited," *Oxford Today* 2, no. 3 (Trinity Issue 1990): 8.

15. For Shaw, see *Saturday Review*, 23 February 1895, pp. 249–50. McCarthy's original essay is reprinted as "The Unimportance of Being Oscar," in *Oscar Wilde: A Collection of Critical Essays*, ed. Richard Ellman (Englewood Cliffs, N.J.: Prentice-Hall, 1969), 107–10. In Harold Bloom's collection of essays on *The Importance of Being Earnest* (New York: Chelsea House, 1988), McCarthy's essay remains that which is most cited by contributors.

16. Linda Dowling, *Language and Decadence* (Princeton, N.J.: Princeton University Press, 1986).

17. Wayne Koestenbaum gave the "reading" interpretation of *The Ballad* at the annual MLA meeting 1988, New Orleans. For the puns on Graham and Erskine, see William A. Cohen, "Willie and Wilde: Reading *The Portrait of Mr. W. H.*" *South Atlantic Quarterly* 88, no. 1 (Winter 1989): 227, 230–31; the special issue is entitled *Displacing Homophobia.* For other appearances of Erskine in Wilde's works, see Horst Schroeder, *Annotations to Oscar Wilde, The Portrait of Mr. W. H.* (Braunschweig, Germany: privately printed, 1986), 3.

18. See Horst Schroeder, *Oscar Wilde, The Portrait of Mr. W. H.—Its Composition, Publication and Reception* (Braunschweiger Anglistische Arbeiten, Heft 9, 1984), 16–18.

19. See also Bruce Bashford, "Oscar Wilde, His Criticism and His Critics," *English Literature in Transition* 20, no. 3 (1977): 181–87; "Oscar Wilde and Subjectivist Criticism," *ELT* 21, no. 4 (1978): 218–34: and "Oscar Wilde," a review of Peter Raby's *Oscar Wilde* in *ELT* 32, no. 3 (1989): 338, in which Bashford calls Wilde the herald of postmodernism.

20. *Oscar Wilde's Oxford Notebooks: A Portrait of Mind in the Making,* ed. with a commentary by Philip E. Smith II and Michael S. Helfand (New York: Oxford University Press, 1989); hereafter cited in text as *Notebooks.*

21. For the prose poems, see *The Complete Shorter Fiction of Oscar Wilde,* ed. Isobel Murray (Oxford: Oxford University Press, 1979), 253–63.

PART 1
WILDE AND SOCIETY
◆

Sexuality, the Public, and the Art World

REGENIA GAGNIER

Until 1895 a relatively isolated art world in Britain held two views of aestheticism. For Wilde aestheticism was "a mode of acting, an attempt to realize one's own personality on some imaginative plane out of reach of the trammeling accidents and limitations of real life" ("The Portrait of Mr. W. H."). Its political goal was to enable its proponents to "know the meanings of the words, and realise them in free, beautiful lives" ("The Soul of Man Under Socialism"). For others it meant a heightened perception through the senses. This last was certainly the view held by J. A. Symonds when he wrote to members of his set describing his hypersensitivity to beauty, whether the beauty of Italian architecture, of the perfect proportions of the male form, or of male comradeship.[1] Both views resisted the Victorian values of utility, rationality, scientific factuality, and technological progress. In Wilde's trials in 1895, his perceived position as both spokesperson for art and example of sexual deviant resulted in a remarkable elision in the public domain of art and sexuality and thus in the creation of a new category of aestheticism.

As the press reported it from the trials, Wilde's life—the most prominent elements of which appeared to be young men of aristocratic and unemployed status—exhibited the same lack of conformity to middle-class norms as had *Dorian Gray*. As his works were given equal time with his sexual practices during the trial, aestheticism came to represent a distinct and private realm of art and sexuality. Wilde's trials confronted the public with an art that refused to say nothing but the truth, that refused to take its interrogation solemnly, and a sexuality outside of the rational demands of reproduction. Thus aestheticism came to mean the irrational in both productive (art) and reproductive (sexuality) realms: an indication of the art world's divorce from middle-class life.

In the art world, Wilde's homosexuality, contrary to mainstream notions of "productive" or "purposive" sexuality, likewise contributed to his particular formulation of aestheticism, including his explicit rejections of Victorian notions of the natural (as in "Nature imitates art"), of the purposive (as in his

Reprinted from *Idylls of the Marketplace: Oscar Wilde and the Victorian Public*, 139–76. © 1986 by the Board of Trustees of the Leland Stanford Junior University, Stanford University Press, 1986.

stance of idleness), and of the productive (as in "art for art's sake"). The genesis of his formulations may be traced in the homosexual literature of the period; they reached their culmination in *Salome* and *The Ballad of Reading Gaol*. Had it been performed, a play like *Salome* would have confronted Victorian audiences with a spectacle of purposeless, "unnatural," unproductive, and uncensored art and desire. In the same lush language that had spoken all along to a community of men, *Salome* attempted to seduce a broader audience into an awareness of its suppressed longings. *The Ballad of Reading Gaol*, a tribute to that original community of men—by 1898 dispersed throughout Europe— provided the spectacle of their banishment from polite society. *Reading Gaol* provided an image of the separation of art and middle-class life, a separation enforced as much by life as by art. This [essay] will trace that separation and conclude with the two works that were respectively an attempt to heal it and a monument to the failure to effect that healing.

A note of caution, however, is in order: the separation of art and illegitimate sexualities from middle-class life was neither simple nor total. When I use the term "homosexual" in this [essay] I do so for the sake of brevity and with the following qualifications. Before his conviction, Wilde was a married man and father who also engaged in same-sex practices and frequented the society of men who engaged in same-sex practices. Although his imaginative life was male-centered, he materially inhabited a genuinely double life and lived before a time when sexual preference had become an identity. I shall cite evidence that a community of men engaged in homosexual practices cautiously with respect to the larger society while many of its members worked publicly for political reform. This community was coherent insofar as its members were aware of its oppression and, in some cases, repression in the larger society. Nonetheless, homosexual identity as opposed to homosexual practice is, as Foucault suggests in his *History of Sexuality*, a possibility that was only coming into being in the 1890's in England. Wilde did not, properly speaking, enjoy a gay identity.[2]

On the other hand, in addition to the identity of the oppressed, we should remember that the other consistent manifestation of this male community was an evident male consumerism, from pornography to a specialized tourism. The brave critiques of sexual oppression discussed in this [essay] were to some extent already co-opted by bourgeois consumerist practices: a "life-style"—the neologism has come to represent precisely the convergence of such phenomena —of identifiable costume and predictable presents (cigarette cases, sleevelinks, etc.), holidays (in Paris, Monte Carlo, Naples, etc.), and ostentatious dining out at all hours (at the Café Royal, Willis's, Savoy, etc.). All this suggests that the "idleness" of these men was not simply a protest against an ethos of productivity or reproduction but was also another form of conspicuous consumption, in this case the consumption of time as "leisure." . . . As Foucault has suggested, what could not be integrated into the circuits of production could be assimilated into the circulation of profit. This is the other side of Salome's spectacle, its integration or sameness in society, which should not be forgotten as, in this [essay], the discussion takes up difference.

Before examining the attacks on the homosexual Cause in the press, popular criminology, and even in the work of other artists (who called themselves counterdecadents), it is worth situating them in the gender confusion of the times. Like the dandies and public schoolmen treated earlier, the historical tradition of aestheticism in England was burdened with such confusion. In 1895, the members of the Rhymers Club were stunned by the craven, or commercially shrewd, defection of Wilde's erstwhile publisher John Lane.[3] Lane, the leading publisher of the early 1890's, whose firm, the Bodley Head, was known for its poetry and belles lettres, banished Aubrey Beardsley from the art editorship and pages of the year-old *Yellow Book*. When Beardsley, Max Beerbohm, Charles Conder, Joseph Conrad, Ernest Dowson, Havelock Ellis, Lionel Johnson, Bernard Shaw, and Arthur Symons linked up with Leonard Smithers in 1896, some thought that they had, like Melmoth, sold their souls to the devil. Smithers was one of what Chesterton called "the decadent publishers," who had promised to "publish anything that the others [were] afraid of." He was also, as Wilde said, "the most learned erotomaniac in Europe," loaning to young Beardsley his *Gamiani ou deux nuits d'excès* and *Priapeia,* translated in collaboration with Sir Richard Burton.[4] As in most bargains with the devil, the association with Smithers was, for a time, lucrative. The new magazine the *Savoy* and Smithers' publications more or less sustained Beardsley, Dowson, and Wilde for the few remaining years of their lives.

Sometime during the early 1890's, Madame Blavatsky told Yeats why people sold their souls to the devil: "they do it to have somebody on their side."[5] In *The Trembling of the Veil* Yeats talks about the members of the Rhymers Club, who were paralyzed (and polarized) by the moral posturing and public poetry of the middle classes. Yeats apologizes that they were poor men, but too rich in Paterian perfectionism to sell out to the vulgar demands for art. Consequently they were too poor for taking on a wife and domicile, and Yeats describes them seeking beauty in classical scholarship and Roman Catholicism. Less of a perfectionist and more ambitious, Wilde conceded to the popular tastes and sought beauty in the members of the Rhymers Club. (Among them was John Gray, probably the visual inspiration for *Dorian Gray,* who became a priest at St. Peter's in Edinburgh—the church built for him by his friend Marc-André Raffalovich, the author of *L'Affaire Oscar Wilde* [1895] and the Catholic apologetic for homosexuality *Uranisme et unisexualité* [1896].[6] Raffalovich, a wealthy Russian Jew from Paris who converted to Catholicism in 1896, was largely responsible for Beardsley's conversion the year before he died.) Unlike the Rhymers, Yeats wrote, Wilde was a public man who needed a crowd; since the Victorian crowd, according to Yeats, lacked heroism and nobility, Wilde's talents were wasted in idle performances: "He must humor and cajole and pose, take worn-out stage situations, for he knows that he may be as romantic as he please, so long as he does not believe in his romance, and all that he may get their ears for a few strokes of contemptuous wit in which he does believe."[7]

But although Wilde's superior "true thought," as Yeats put it, may have been closer to the Rhymers' than to that of the public, there is a key difference between him and "the tragic generation": the Rhymers treated their marginality with sentiment. With the exceptions of Yeats and Beardsley, the Rhymers were for the most part Oxford men; their immediate artistic tradition included the Pre-Raphaelites and Pater. While Tennyson was composing the treacheries and betrayals of *The Idylls of the King,* the Pre-Raphaelites and their associates were eluding typical versions of Victorian domesticity and transforming the problems of their eccentric ménages in their art and poetry. They found that if one were to marry a working woman, specifically a model, she could as easily sit for one artist as another. William Morris, aware of the growing love in his house between his wife Jane and Dante Gabriel Rossetti, ran off to write *The Earthly Paradise*—in Iceland. Rossetti, in turn, kept his wife Elizabeth locked up in a decrepit house on the river and shared his income with an amiable mistress, Fanny. Meanwhile their defender, John Ruskin, was losing his wife to the renegade from the Brotherhood who had turned from Mantegna to advertising, John Millais. (With his customary oblique insight, Ruskin accused Millais's painting of infidelity.) And Swinburne, while multiplying praise upon praise of Venus in terms of classical erudition, was receiving drawings from Simeon Solomon of boys being flogged by schoolmasters and was himself habitually flagellated at a brothel in Regent's Park. Swinburne's contributions to the large body of Victorian flagellation literature, like his images of the hermaphrodite, contain the typical elements of the genre: male submissiveness and instability of identity—the direct antithesis of the gentleman's ideals of manliness, solidity, certitude of self, and singleness of purpose.[8]

Behind all these figures is the astonishingly erudite and exotically inclined Sir Richard Burton, whom the Pre-Raphaelites universally admired and whose material in his sixteen-volume translation of *The Book of the Thousand Nights and a Night* (1885) necessitated, he felt, the inclusion of a "Terminal Essay" on the history of pederasty all over the world up to the year of writing. The "Terminal Essay" was published during the same year as the passage of section xi of the Criminal Law Amendment Act, which related to the commission of homosexual practices among consenting adults in private and under which Wilde was sentenced to two years' imprisonment with hard labor. The advertisements for Burton's "Arabian Nights" emphasized that they were not for women or children and were available only by subscription; yet Swinburne publicly praised them in a poem in the *Athenaeum* on 6 February 1886 and treated Captain Burton, who resembled Errol Flynn, as a sublime Melmoth in his "Memorial Verses on the Death of Richard Burton." In one of her last letters to Smithers, Isabel Burton, who resembled the elderly Queen Victoria, prayed for her husband's tortured soul in purgatory. In an earlier letter to Smithers from the Mid-East, Burton had prayed for the poor and for women who were trapped in the purgatory of London.[9]

The Rhymers were caught between this half of their tradition and Pater. Despite the vividness of desire, often of orgiastic violence, in Pater's *Renaissance* and *Imaginary Portraits,* the Oxford don's life was so uneventful that today the thought of his biography, even after several have been written, seems excessive. His followers, on the other hand, were left to bear the implications of his prose. Although scholars today assure us that in the "Conclusion" to *The Renaissance* Pater "intended" a refined, intellectual aestheticism, the Rhymers found that to some extent it was false to pretend that the "passion" for and "impressions" of paintings in the Louvre could be restricted to museums, as if passion in life always led one way and passion in art always led nowhere.

It was probably just this sort of betrayal that led to Richard C. Jackson's celebratory poem of Pater's suppressed eroticism, "Joy Standeth on the Threshold: A Reverie of Walter Pater" (c. 1887–89),[10] and to Lionel Johnson's two vastly different tributes to Wilde. Johnson's first tribute, "In Honorem Doriani Creatorisque Eius," was in Latin, "modo modulans Romano / Laudes dignas Doriano" thanking Wilde, "qui tanta cernis," in a language worthy of his Dorian, for perceiving so much. The second, "The Destroyer of a Soul," was composed after Johnson had introduced Alfred Douglas to Wilde in 1891. Although Yeats tells us that the Rhymers were always unerringly polite, something went awry in the aftereffects of this particular introduction. The poem begins "with a necessary hate" directed toward one who has corrupted a friend with "the soul of a saint." The poem ends, "Call you this thing my friend? this nameless thing? This living body, hiding its dead soul?" Johnson had fallen in love with Douglas at Winchester.

The Rhymers' emotional crux between Paterian idealism and their own desires is apparent in their pathetically confused lives. Yeats tells us that Lionel Johnson, who lectured Dowson from the Church Fathers on chastity, was discovered at his autopsy "never to have grown, except in the brain, after his fifteenth year." Dowson dedicated all his poems to Adelaide Foltinowicz, the teenage daughter of a restaurateur. Upon reading a newspaper account of a courageous girl's indictment of her abductor, Dowson began to fear that his intentions would be misunderstood and delayed proposing. Adelaide married someone else and died as a result of complications from an abortion in 1903.[11] In volume III of the *Yellow Book,* Dowson published a story entitled "Apple Blossom in Brittany" in which a Jamesian literary gentleman encourages the young girl he loves to enter a convent. Beardsley, whose drawings after Wilde's trial were attacked as "sexless" and "asexual," meaning too erotic, and "unclean," died penitent, "like a saint." His sister, on the other hand, who cared for him as Pater's sisters had cared for their brother, continued her career on stage long after she married in 1902.[12] Yeats himself has best described his own sexual frustrations, including his relationship to the dynamic and public figure Maud Gonne. In his draft *Autobiography* he recounts their mystical consummation, "the initiation of the spear": in a double vision Maud Gonne is "a great stone statue through which passed flame." Yeats, of course, found himself "becoming flame and mounting up through and looking out of the eyes of a great stone Minerva." Shortly after the double vision, she told Yeats that she had a horror and terror of physical love.[13]

The "tragic generation" of men were either cared for by sisters, intimidated by New Women, or like Johnson, after "four or five glasses of wine," denied "that a gelded man lost anything of intellectual power." Whereas the Victorian organization of gender deserted them in their romance and pain, Wilde was supported by a "modern" (their term) homosexual community, a community candid in its pleasures and unified in its protectiveness. Despite a critical tradition that has taken for granted a radical disjunction between Wilde's pre-prison and post-conviction work and an assumption, following Wilde's early biographers, that prison was psychologically and literarily good for Wilde, Wilde's position as a practicing homosexual leading a "double life" in society contributed to the peculiar form of witty paradoxes in the pre-prison work and to the paradoxical themes of the later material. The paradox and epigram, which criticized society by turning its own language curtly on its head, and the double-edged critical impetus of Wilde's comedies were particularly appropriate techniques for a homosexual Irishman with socialist sympathies in nineteenth-century Britain.

For the difference between the pre- and post-prison work is that at first Wilde lived the contradictions with a sense of amused and proud superiority, with the added *frisson* of danger, and that later the contradictions surfaced as an allegiance to a loved community that conflicted with an equal desire to be an accepted member of the larger society. After prison Wilde was free to love the way he wished, but for this freedom he had forfeited his social position and economic security as well as the personal affection of many former friends and his right to see his two young sons. The distinction, therefore, between the so-called "trivial" paradoxes of the pre-prison work, for which Wilde's wit was so well known, and the "profound" paradoxes of the later work, like the *felix culpa* and joy in suffering in *De Profundis,* has nothing to do with an alleged "redemption" on Wilde's part, but is rather a light versus a more solemn treatment of the politics of inside/outside social relations.[14] Although he treated it with varying degrees of levity, this political problem was a consistent one for Wilde and is a persistent element in his works. Unlike most of his confused and tragic generation, Wilde saw the problem as political and treated it as such.

During the three trials, which terminated with Wilde's and Alfred Taylor's sentencing, with the exception of one daily and one weekly journal (the

Daily Chronicle and *Reynolds's Newspaper)*, the London press was uniformly hostile to Wilde; and frequently its hostility was directed toward art, education, and "idleness" as well as toward homosexuality. After the conviction the *Daily Telegraph* wrote that "No sterner rebuke could well have been inflicted on some of the artistic tendencies of the time than the condemnation of Oscar Wilde at the Central Criminal Court. . . . The man has now suffered the penalties of his career, and may well be allowed to pass from that platform of publicity which he loved into the limbo of disrepute and oblivion which is his due. The grave of contemptuous oblivion may rest on his foolish ostentation, his empty paradoxes, his incurable vanity." Through the press, the middle class complacently chastened the "upper sections of society" in which Wilde had "enjoyed a certain popularity." The article continues, "Young men at the universities, silly women who lend an ear to any chatter which is petulant and vivacious, novelists who have sought to imitate the style of paradox and unreality, poets who have lisped the language of nerveless and effeminate libertinage—these are the persons who should ponder with themselves the doctrines and the career of the man who has now to undergo the righteous sentence of the law." The *Evening News* attacked the Aesthetic school, "a centre of intellectual corruption," and called for the corrective of public opinion to terminate the fashion of conceding immoral license to men of genius. The editor also imitated Wilde's legal prosecutors in his rebuke to the lower-class young men who had crossed the boundaries of class and intellectual pretense in their association with artists: "Light has been let in upon them now in a very decisive fashion, and we venture to hope that the conviction of Wilde for these abominable vices, which were the natural outcome of his diseased intellectual condition, will be a salutary warning to the unhealthy boys who posed as sharers of his culture." The *Echo* wrote: "The best thing for everybody now is to forget all about Oscar Wilde, his perpetual posings, his aesthetical teachings and his theatrical productions. Let him go into silence, and be heard no more."[15]

During the trials not only were Wilde's own works, particularly *The Picture of Dorian Gray* and "Phrases and Philosophies for the Use of the Young," used as evidence against him, but he was also called to answer for the alleged immorality of others' works, like "The Priest and the Acolyte," *A Rebours,* and Alfred Douglas's sonnets.[16] In the first trial, which terminated with the prosecution's admission of justified libel in order to avert Queensberry's witnesses against Wilde, the defense played to the jury with such statements as Edward Carson's insult to Wilde, "I do not profess to be an artist; and when I hear you give evidence, I am glad I am not."[17] In Carson's opening speech for the defense he emphasized the confluence of art, crime, and the lower classes in Taylor's establishment: "Taylor has in fact been the right-hand man of Mr. Wilde in all the orgies in which artists and valets have taken part." Carson mocked the highbrow artist whose standard for his readers seemed to be at odds with that for his companions: "[Wilde] took up with Charles Parker, a gentleman's servant, whose brother was a gentleman's servant; with young Alphonse Conway, who sold papers on the pier at Worthing; and with Scarfe, also a gentleman's servant. Then his excuse was no longer that he was dwelling in regions of art but that he had such a noble, such a democratic soul [laughter in the court], that he drew no social distinctions, and that it was quite as much pleasure to have the sweeping boy from the streets to lunch or dine with him as the greatest *literateur* [*sic*] or artist."[18]

Throughout the second and third trials, in which Alfred Taylor was Wilde's co-defendant, the counsel for the Crown, first Charles Frederick Gill and then Frank Lockwood, the solicitor-general, attempted to get extended mileage out of Taylor's having independent means, frequently stating that his habitual mode of living was "idle" and "extravagant." In the third trial the verdict of guilty for Taylor preceded Wilde's trial but the sentencing was deferred until after the verdict on Wilde had been reached. During the cross-examination the solicitor-general asked Taylor how he had met the Parker brothers. Taylor replied that he was having a drink after the theater. "Following your usual custom of doing nothing?" Lockwood demanded. "Yes, if that's what you call doing nothing," Taylor replied.

Although the prosecution and press overgeneralized and put to execrable use their association of art and "crime," it should be noted that two of the leading artistic journals of the time had openly contributed to the pro-homosexual literature of the period. *The Artist and Journal of Home Culture,* under the editorship of Charles Kains-Jackson from 1888 through 1894, and *The Studio,* under that of his friend Joseph Gleeson White in 1893, were the vehicles of polemical and research articles on homosexuality as well as a good deal of homosexual poetry and fiction. Until 1895 contributors to these two journals formed an informal, migratory artistic coterie, first at Christchurch, then in Chiswick, then in London. At these locations visitors met other visitors of similar tastes, two of which were a love of arts and the Greek philosophical tradition of pederasty.[19] At Oxford, such grown-up journals were imitated by the undergraduate *Chameleon* and *Spirit Lamp.* On 19 November 1894 John Francis Bloxam wrote from Exeter College to Kains-Jackson that he had discussed the founding of the *Chameleon* with Wilde and George Ives at Ives's home, where Wilde promised him aphorisms.[20] Under the editorship of Alfred Douglas, the *Spirit Lamp* was advertised as for "all who are interested in modern life and the new culture"—the new culture being one coterie's term for homosexuality.

Like the prosecution and hostile press, popular criminology also linked crime and art—thereby conditioning middle-class suspicion of art and encouraging their divorce; and today it is impossible to know who took the vocabulary of disease, degeneration, and genius from whom. Several books by the Italian criminologist Cesare Lombroso (1836–1909) had been translated into English and were popular enough that in prison Wilde cited Lombroso's theories on "the intimate connection between madness and the literary and artistic temperament" in his appeal to the Home Secretary for an attenuated sentence.[21]

Lombroso's *Man of Genius,* included in the Contemporary Science Series edited by Havelock Ellis, specifically addressed itself to the connection between education, superior intelligence, art, and crime. His enumeration of symptoms of insanity reads like a checklist of the elements of Wilde's style, literary and personal: "In literature and science, a tendency to puns and plays upon words, an excessive fondness for systems, a tendency to speak of one's self, and substitute epigram for logic, an extreme predilection for the rhythm and assonances of verse in prose writing, even an exaggerated degree of originality may be considered as morbid phenomena. So also is the mania of writing in Biblical form, in detached verses, and with special favourite words, which are underlined, or repeated many times, and a certain graphic symbolism." Lombroso urged that students, and especially politicians, beware lest "geniuses" usurp power over the "true normal man, the man who works and eats." Signs of the imminence of such a crisis are the proliferation of abstract systems for social reform, systems particularly containing "declamation, assonances, paradoxes, and conceptions often original, but always incomplete and contradictory," systems, that is, which "take the place of calm reasoning based on a minute and unprejudiced study of facts."[22]

In Lombroso's *Crime: Its Causes and Remedies,* sexual crimes and crimes of fraud are "the specific crimes of advanced civilization." Regarding the former, he wrote, "It seems that the more a man's psychic activity increases, the more the number of his needs and tastes for pleasures grows, especially when his mind is not occupied with great scientific and humanitarian ideas, and when his wealth permits an over-abundant diet. Of all these, the sexual need is certainly that which is most keenly felt, and this is that which, throughout the whole animal world, is in the closest connection with the cerebral system."[23] Journalists, too, perceived the connection between sex and cerebration, not only in *The Artist* and *The Studio,* but in the traditions of Oxford. Brian Reade has traced the beginnings of the enormous increase in male romantic-erotic literature between 1850 and 1895 to the writings and all-male community of the Tractarians, particularly Newman, his close friend Richard Hurrell Froude, and his intensely devoted Frederick William Faber.[24] The term "pervert," which, as Lombroso might have said, was a special favorite, underlined and repeated so many times in the press and popular criminology, had been once reserved for the Oxford converts to Roman Catholicism; genius, mysticism, and surreptitious sexuality formed another notorious triad in representations of colleges as well as those of monasteries and convents in gothic novels. By the 1890's, the *Spirit Lamp,* to which Wilde contributed, and the *Chameleon,* which included "The Priest and the Acolyte," the two poems by Douglas that elicited such scrutiny during the trials, and Wilde's "Phrases and Philosophies for the Use of the Young," seemed to indicate to the middle classes that the products of "genius" and "education" required some immediate control.

As preventatives of such "sexual excesses" as adultery and pederasty, Lombroso recommended greater facility of divorce and "the diffusion of prostitution in the agricultural districts, and especially in localities where there are a large number of sailors, soldiers, and laborers. It is especially necessary to make sexual intercourse accessible to all dissolute-minded young men."[25] Although Lombroso did not hesitate to suggest the indenture of women to cure the excesses of heterosexual men, he made no similar provisions for men who could not be redirected toward women. Occasional ("criminaloid") offenders needed only sustain "a conditional punishment," for once out of barracks and colleges they would revert to legitimate sexual access. "Born" offenders, on the other hand, "who manifest their evil propensities from childhood without being determined by special causes," should "be confined from their youth, for they are a source of contagion and cause a great number of occasional criminals."[26]

In addition to Lombroso's recommendations for jurists in *Crime: Its Causes and Remedies,* in the conclusion of *The Man of Genius* he set down principles of literary criticism: "What I have hitherto written may, I hope (while remaining within the limits of psychological observation), afford an experimental starting-point for a criticism of artistic and literary, sometimes also of scientific, creations." The most explicit attack on artists as criminals duly came from his pupil and friend—their books are dedicated to each other—Max Nordau. This attack was entitled *Entartung* (1893) and was translated into English as *Degeneration* in 1895. Wilde also referred to Nordau's chapter on "Oscar Wilde" in his petition to the Home Office, while Bernard Shaw, in less personal jeopardy, answered Nordau in the American paper *Liberty* (1895) and later republished his essay for the New Age Press (1908) under the title *The Sanity of Art: An Exposure of the Current Nonsense About Artists Being Degenerate.*[27]

As Shaw succinctly put it, the message of Nordau's massive, very popular text was "that all our characteristically modern works of art are symptoms of disease in the artists, and that these diseased artists are themselves symptoms of the nervous exhaustion of the race by overwork." The point of Book I ("Fin-de-Siècle") of *Degeneration* was that the upper classes of European civilization were exhausted and deranged due to the rapid expansion of technology. There Nordau noted the deleterious effects of "railway spine" and "railway brain" as well as those of the press and postal systems. (Later in the book he would paradoxically argue that the symbolists' critique of science and Mallarmé's hesitancy to publish were also signs of degeneracy.) In his exposé of artists as carriers of the hereditary symptoms of the "fin-de-race" disease, Nordau not only finds all the French writers whom Arthur Symons heralded in *The Symbolist Movement in Literature* to be "imbeciles" and "idiots," but he includes chapters on Tolstoy and Wagner ("mystics" nostalgic for the "dark ages"), Whitman (a "vagabond," "reprobate rake," and "erotomaniac"), Ibsen, Wilde, and Nietzsche ("ego-maniacs" who are directly contrary in their views to Nordau's ideal of "altruism"), and all French and German proponents of "realism" and "naturalism" (translated as the degenerate tendencies of "pessimism" and "obscenity").

Nordau, himself a novelist as well as a practicing physician, advocated the ordered progress of the community through the potentialities of the natural sciences. He saw the "style" and "word games" of much modern literature as elitist and detrimental to the social function of art. (His own positivist attitude toward language was indicated in his changing his name from Südfeld—southern field—to Nordau—northern meadow—when he broke from his Hungarian rabbinical family to enter the profession of journalism in Germany.)[28] Lombroso allowed that "the frequency of genius among lunatics and of madmen among men of genius explains the fact that the destiny of nations has often been in the hands of the insane; and shows how the latter have been able to contribute so much to the progress of mankind." Nordau, however, who had patience with nothing but normality and middle-class values like discipline and materialistic science, had no sympathy with any extraordinary attitudes or practices, including those of artists who felt themselves estranged from the larger work force.

Thus Nordau's critique of Wilde stems from the latter's dress and his criticism. (Wilde's literary works, says Nordau, are mere imitations of the degenerate mystics Rossetti and Swinburne.) For Nordau, Wilde's egomania is apparent in his eccentric dress, in his "hatred" of nature (so different from Nordau's organic view of humanity in the world), in his ideal of inactivity, and in his admiration of crime and "sin." The social body has a necessary duty to expel the egomaniac, and Nordau stresses that degenerates in thought are no less virulent than active degenerates. In the last chapter of his book he calls on "sane" members of society to pull in their stomachs, tighten their belts, clear their minds, and act.

> Mystics, but especially ego-maniacs and filthy pseudo-realists, are enemies to society of the direst kind. Society must unconditionally defend itself against them. Whoever believes with me that society is the natural organic form of humanity, in which alone it can exist, prosper, and continue to develop itself to higher destinies; whoever looks upon civilization as a good, having value and deserving to be defended, must mercilessly crush under his thumb the anti-social vermin. To him, who with Nietzsche, is enthusiastic over the "freely-roving, lusting beast of prey," we cry, "Get you gone from civilization! . . . Our streets and our houses are not built for you; our looms have no stuffs for you; our fields are not tilled for you. All our labour is performed by men who esteem each other, have consideration for each other, mutually aid each other, and know how to curb their selfishness for the general good. There is no place among us for the lusting beast of prey; and if you dare return to us, we will pitilessly beat you to death with clubs."[29]

Here, as throughout his book, one can see why later socialists, and specifically advocates of socialist realism, could find sympathy with Nordau's views on art and society. (When Nordau died, the French Communist newspaper *Humanité* praised his "noble love for mankind" and hatred of bourgeois ideals.)[30] The apparent paradox of the bourgeois par excellence hailed as a hater of bourgeois ideals is explained by the fact that Nordau's 1895 attack on the effete upper classes with their hereditary degeneracy was later duplicated in the socialist attack on the effete, complacent bourgeoisie. Even Shaw admitted that in the course of his attack on art Nordau had incidentally said "many more true and important things than most of the counsel on the other side were capable of."[31]

After 1895 all Nordau's books as well as his activities in Paris were extensively covered by the British press. On one occasion, the entire front page of the Sunday Edition of the *Weekly Sun* reviewed *Degeneration* as book of the week (16 June 1895). The reviewer quotes Nordau at length and recommends the book with the greatest approbation "to the admiration of every honest, pure, and manly man." In a biographical sketch of Nordau on pages one and two of the *Westminster,* Wilde's biographer and devoted friend Robert Sherard interviewed Nordau, who was fulsome on his own achievements and industriousness. Since genius and disease were equated in his system, the physician was paradoxically proud that he had not healed himself: about one of his plays, *Der Krugel,* he observed that critics in Berlin "wrote that no such filth had ever been served up on the German stage before." Sherard concluded that Nordau was an example of industry, "indeed his only pleasure in life is in hard work. He has fully deserved all his success."[32]

A few critics exploited Nordau's middle-class conservatism for humorous effect. The *Daily Chronicle* (8 May 1896) cited Nordau's *Paradoxes* of 1885 to criticize his tendency toward generalization and his irritating ability to dictate on any subject whatsoever. If you know one woman, Nordau had claimed, you know them all, with but few exceptions. Be particularly wary of "the original woman," "for deviation from the type is in woman, in eighty cases out of the hundred, significant of disease." Finally even Lombroso had to criticize *Degeneration* in the pages of the *Century* for Nordau's exaggeration and misinterpretation of data. In *La Revue Blanche* (1 June 1896) Alfred Douglas lamented that "even that superior (although unconscious) humorist, Max Nordau, has great difficulty in discovering . . . symptoms of degeneracy" in Douglas's poems: "I say it with regret, for who would not wish to be a degenerate in company with Verlaine, Rossetti, Oscar Wilde and so many others?" A few weeks after Wilde left prison, a journalist in Paris asked his opinion on "Nordau's firm belief that all men of genius were mad." "I quite agree," the exile reportedly said, "with Dr. Nordau's assertion that all men of genius are insane, but Dr. Nordau forgets that all sane people are idiots."[33]

Although he could joke about Nordau, Wilde, like the most politically active among the homosexual circles, continued to be interested in the growing dissemination of sociological and criminological literature. In prison he had also requested William Douglas Morrison's *Criminology Series,* which included Lombroso's *Female Offender* and *Criminal Sociology* by Enrico Ferri, who was greatly influenced by Lombroso. Wilde had admired the prolific work on prison reform by Morrison, who was a chaplain at Wandsworth as well as a recognized criminologist, and he sent him a personal copy of *The Ballad of Reading Gaol.*

Nor were the less flamboyant scientists of the time able to ignore the work of Lombroso and Nordau. Francis Galton, who is recognized as the founder of eugenics, had published *Hereditary Genius: An Inquiry into Its Laws and Consequences* in 1869. He studied lines of descent of genius from 1660 to 1865 according to the reputations of British judges, statesmen, Peers, commanders, literary men, men of science, poets, musicians, painters, divines, and senior classics of Cambridge; he included oarsmen and wrestlers of the north country as examples of inherited muscle and concluded with a chapter entitled "The Comparative Worth of Different Races." In his prefatory chapter to the edition of 1892, Galton acknowledged where Lombroso's, Nordau's, and his own findings converged:

> The relation between genius in its technical sense . . . and insanity had been much insisted upon by Lombroso and others, whose views of the closeness of the connection between the two are so pronounced that it would hardly be surprising if one of their more enthusiastic followers were to remark that so-and-so cannot be a genius, because he has never been mad nor is there a single lunatic in his family. I cannot go nearly so far as they, nor accept a moiety of their data. . . . Still, there is a large residuum of evidence which points to a painfully close relation between the two, and I must add that my own later observations have tended in the same direction, for I have been surprised at finding how often insanity or idiocy has appeared among the near relatives of exceptionally able men.[34]

The most disastrous abuse of such medical and psychological theorizing occurred in the notorious Pemberton-Billing libel trials of 1918. The internationally renowned dancer Maud Allan and J. T. Grein on behalf of the Independent Theatre jointly sued Noel Pemberton-Billing, a zealous, vice-crusading M.P., for publishing a libelous article on Grein's production of Wilde's *Salome.* The article, for which Pemberton-Billing took full responsibility, linked Allan, the Theatre, and its subscribers with "the Cult of the Clitoris." During the two trials, spanning three months, Pemberton-Billing conducted his own defense and called no fewer than fourteen witnesses, including Alfred Douglas, minor dramatic critics, and doctors of psychology. Pemberton-Billing justified his libel by claiming that "the exhibition of an overpowering but unnatural passion of a child of tender years for the prophet . . . culminating . . . in the presentation of a physical orgasm, is calculated to attract moral perverts who . . . seek sexual satisfaction in the watching of this exhibition by others. . . . *Salome* is calculated to do . . . harm not only to the young men and the young women, but to all who see it, by undermining them, even more than a German army itself."[35]

One Dr. Serrell Cooke, a witness for the defense and authority on psychosexual pathology, testified that *Salome* "was quite likely to light up dormant perversion in men who did not even know they possessed it, and in women." The same psychologist had become interested in the case upon reading in the press Grein's first testimony, largely in support of *Salome* as a work of art. Cooke said that he "came to the conclusion that [Grein] had some mental aberration from the peculiar way he replied to questions." (Grein's testimony exhibited shades of dandiacal wit.) It was the doctor's opinion, solicited by Pemberton-Billing's examination, that Grein should be "locked up." The dramatic critic from the *Morning Post* testified that *Salome* was "a drama of disease"; the part of the actress, "sadistic"; and that Herod was "suffering from erotomania." The judge advised that the jury take such "sworn evidence" very seriously, and the jury duly bowed to the opinions of these experts when it acquitted Pemberton-Billing.

So much for literary psychologizing. Regarding heredity, in an act of zeal and cruelty Pemberton-Billing stunned the entire courtroom by confronting Allan with newspaper clippings of her brother's execution in San Francisco for murdering two young girls. When the stricken dancer admitted the kinship, Pemberton-Billing asked her if her brother had not defiled the bodies, explaining to the objecting judge that he was trying to prove that sadism was hereditary. The case grew to outrageous proportions, including allegations of German plots that implicated Asquith and the very judge hearing the trial, and recent histories have linked it with a generals' plot to bring down Lloyd George's coalition government. . . .

Unfortunately for many writers at the turn of the century, attacks on art were not perpetrated solely by megalomaniacal physicians and legislators encouraged by the press. Richard Le Gallienne, the major reader for the Bodley Head, and William Watson, a major contributor to the *Yellow Book,* called themselves counterdecadents and stolidly upheld a romantic-Victorian tradition in the face of what they considered the French-inspired impressionism of the likes of Wilde, Arthur Symons, and John Gray. The colored impressions of the so-called decadents exhibited "merely limited thinking" at best and unhealthy effeminacy at worst.[36] In his preface to Alfred Austin's *English Lyrics* (1890), Watson wrote:

> If poetry is not to sink altogether under the lethargy of an emasculate euphuism, and finally to die surfeited with unwholesome sweetmeats, crushed under a load of redundant ornament and smothered in artificial rose-leaves, the strenuous and virile temper which animates this volume must come to be more and more the temper of English song. . . . If we be wise we shall turn more and more to whatsoever singer scents his pages, not with livid and obnoxious *Fleurs du Mal,*

but with the blossoms which English children gather in their aprons, and with the candid breath of our hearty English sky.

In Le Gallienne's "To the Reader" of his own *English Poems,* he emphasized, as did all the counterdecadents, the Englishness of his work and lamented that the temple of English art had become "a lazar-house of leprous men."[37] Since Le Gallienne had long befriended Wilde in his private life and had written numerous, indeed generous, appreciations of his and other "decadent" work, such rallying around the temple must be taken as less inspired by purity than politics and profit.

Only the subtlest authors could employ the decadent themes of the time and remain above suspicion. In the first entry of the first *Yellow Book,* "The Death of the Lion," Henry James included all the elements of decadence: a "fantastic book," a male narrator in love with a male literary lion, nominal sex changes in profusion, and the fall of an artist to publicity and an unworthy public. Yet the discreet James was responsible for no more than upholding the dignity of art and poking fun at authors who, like Mary Chavelita Dunne ("George Egerton"), masculinized their names so as to be better able to express the "larger view" on the New Woman and relationships between the sexes.

Amid such liberal, and illiberal, debate, several groups of men, a number of whom were included on either Nordau's or Watson's blacklist (or on both), were writing and publishing their own sexual manifestos. At the same time that Wilde was posing in the dominant society, the meaning and significance of his works and actions were interpreted differently by members of the homosexual community. As the literary skit *The Green Carnation* (1894) by Robert Hichens goes to great lengths to suggest, by putting Wilde's words in the mouth of the great aesthete Esmé Amarinth and Alfred Douglas's form and attitudes in the character of Lord Reggie Hastings, the unnatural flower that the uninitiated thought merely symbolic of an aesthetic school served also as a secret sign among men who loved men. In defending the "unnatural" flower to a lady who speaks of herself as the "superior officer" to her pubescent "soldier" son, Esmé paraphrases Wilde on the term "natural":

How I hate that word natural. . . . To me it means all that is middle-class, all that is of the essence of jingoism. . . . It might be a beautiful word, but it is the most debased coin in the currency of language. Certain things are classed as natural, and certain things are classed as unnatural—for all the people born into the world. Individualism is not allowed to enter into the matter. A child is unnatural if it hates its mother. A mother is unnatural if she does not wish to have children. A man is unnatural if he never falls in love with a woman. A boy is unnatural if he prefers looking at pictures to playing cricket, or dreaming over the white naked beauty of a Greek statue to a game of football under Rugby rules. . . . [Yet] it is natural to one man to live like Charles Kingsley, to preach gentleness, and love sport; it is natural to another to dream away his life on the narrow couch of an opium den, with his head between a fellow-sinner's feet. I love what are called warped minds, and deformed natures. . . . There are only a few people in the world who dare to defy the grotesque code of rules that has been drawn up by that fashionable mother, Nature, and they defy—as many women drink, and many men are vicious—in secret, with the door locked and the key in their pockets. And what is life to them? They can always hear the footsteps of the detective in the street outside.[38]

We know that Wilde approved of *The Green Carnation,* for he advertised it in the original four-act version of *The Importance of Being Earnest.* In the search for his father's name, Jack mistakenly gives Lady Bracknell the novel rather than the *Army Lists* of the preceding 40 years, telling her to "bring [her] masculine mind to bear on this subject." True to the intentional confusion of gender roles in the quotation on the natural above, and to Lady Bracknell's "masculine" mind, Lady Bracknell responds that the "culture of exotics" in the novel seems to preclude the masculine military type: "This treatise, the 'Green Carnation,' as I see it is called, seems to be a book about the culture of exotics. It contains no reference to Generals in it."

Wilde was not the only writer of the period whose devaluation of nature (as in "nature imitates art") and the natural derived from sexual pleasures that were viewed by society as "unnatural." In his impassioned plea for the amendment of homosexual laws and the termination of social persecution of "urnings," "A Problem in Modern Ethics" (1891), J. A. Symonds, poet, literary critic, and collaborator with Havelock Ellis, repeatedly criticized the term "unnatural." It was precisely his discomfort with terms like "unnatural," "perverse," even the medical "invert" that resulted in his comically elaborate adaptations of K. H. Ulrich's categories of male sexuality: dioning, uraniaster, urning, mannling, weibling, zwischen-urning, virilized urning, uranodioning. Such a vocabulary produced rather bizarre English sentences like "Headmasters know how many Uraniasters they have dealt with, what excellent Dionings they become, and how comparatively rare, and yet how incorrigibly steadfast, are the genuine Urnings in their flock."[39] (Translation: Headmasters know how many occasional homosexuals they have dealt with, what excellent heterosexuals they become, and how comparatively rare, and yet how incorrigibly steadfast, are the genuine homosexuals in their flock.) Trying to distance himself from the prejudicial vocabulary of his times, Symonds found that his Germano-scientific vocabulary had the added advantage of distancing him from his own very anguished emotions. His multiplied, multiform vocabulary, like Wilde's epigrams and paradoxes, also sought to break down the conventional dualist vocabulary of natural/unnatural, normal/abnormal. Similarly, by 1913 Kains-Jackson was able to outline to Ross a personalized vocabulary that relieved the individual body of normative definitions altogether: "If instead of harping on the word 'abnormal' [the Psychiatry Committee of England] takes up the sound *physical* line that the normal is what to that person is normal, it will do much good."[40]

The more enthusiastic of Victorian heterosexuals also had to reconstruct nature. Although the official Victorian view of female sexuality was that it did not exist except for purposes of procreation, Victorian pornographers, who fought their own battles against current views of the natural, viewed nature from rather un-Victorian prospects. Steven Marcus uses their own clichés to describe their "representation of nature": "It is usually seen at eye-level. In the middle distance there looms a large irregular shape. On the horizon swell two immense snowy white hillocks; these are capped by great, pink, and as it were prehensile peaks or tips—as if the rosy-fingered dawn itself were playing just behind them. The landscape then undulates gently down to a broad, smooth, swelling plain, its soft rolling curves broken only in the lower center by a small volcanic crater or omphalos."[41] The essential image of nature in the pornographic utopia, says Marcus, is this immense, supine, female form. And nature thus defined exists "for the sole purpose of confirming the existence of its creator." That is, the insatiable and eternally accessible woman exists as the dominion of the fruitful, replenishing penis: an Eden of natural surplus.

As our contemporary historians of homosexuality have shown, the works of Wilde and the humiliation of Wilde that began in 1895 were watched with great, if dismayed, interest by both practicing and nonpracticing homosexuals, from the socialist Edward Carpenter living in Sheffield to J. A. Symonds.[42] Although many of these preferred the manly homoeroticism that they discerned in Whitman's poetry to what Symonds called the "morbid and perfumed" manner of *Dorian Gray,* the very absence of the name of the sins in Wilde's stories and novel indicated to some men of the "modern" same-sex preference the presence of a like mind. That is, in the absence of named sins in *Dorian Gray* and the stories, the middle-class journalists found the presence of the sin they despised and the members of the homosexual community found the presence of the sin they loved.

In other ways, too, Wilde apparently signed to fellow homosexuals. In a surprising review of Whitman's *November Boughs,* the great aesthete praised Whitman for, in effect, artlessness.[43] As Jeffrey Weeks has shown, a great appreciation of Whitman was an explicit point of contact among homosexuals like Symonds, Carpenter, George Ives, and Laurence Housman, the two latter being founders of the secret homosexual society of the 1890's, the Order of Chaeronea, as well as friends of Wilde. Symonds included in "A Problem in Modern Ethics" Whitman's indignant denial that such a construction could be put on the "comradeship" described in "Calamus"—a denial that had exceedingly frustrated Symonds. But despite Whitman, Symonds cited long passages from the poem in question as "idealistic" sanctions of homosexual love. In 1889 Wilde had discerned in Whitman's views "a largeness of vision, a healthy sanity, and a fine ethical purpose." He found the value of Whitman's work "in its prophecy not in its performance," and he heralded Whitman as a "prelude" to "a new era," "a precursor of a fresh type," a "factor in the heroic and spiritual evolution of the human being." "If poetry has passed him by,"

Wilde concluded, "philosophy will take note of him." Such high praise succeeded a long quotation in which Whitman states that *Leaves of Grass* "is avowedly the song of Sex, and Amativeness, and even Animality."

In like manner the homoeroticism of "The Portrait of Mr. W. H.," the references to hermaphroditism in "Pen, Pencil, and Poison," and the double life of Bunburying in *The Importance of Being Earnest* must have represented to the subculture the "posing" and "double lives" to which homosexuals were accustomed until very recently. Indeed, in an unpublished introduction to Wilde's letters to Ives, Louis Marlow, a friend of Ives, claims that Ives served as Wilde's "Bunbury" on a trip to visit a friend at Cambridge.[44] Although within the circle Ives and Kains-Jackson were looked upon as authorities to help indiscreet men out of frays, Ives himself was so discreet that after prison Wilde repeatedly rebuked him for his lack of courage. At Posillippo near Naples with Wilde, Douglas wrote to Ives parodying his mysterious epistles:

> My dear G.,
> O showed me your letter. We are here at N or rather at P which is close to N. We met a charming fellow here yesterday. I wonder if you know him; his name is X and he lives at Z. He was obliged to leave R on account of a painful scandal connected with H and T. The weather here is D today but we hope it may soon be L again.
>
> Yours in strictest privacy,
> A.B.D.

A less discreet letter follows, and it concludes, doubtless to Ives's chagrin, "Oscar sends his love."[45]

In his double life, Wilde established a balanced economy that pervaded not only his view of nature but art and production as well. Like his redefinition of the natural and the dialectics of his paradoxes, his theory of art for art's sake was linked with sexual pleasures contrary to bourgeois notions of productive or purposive sex. In two of the most controversial chapters (22 and 23) of Frank Harris's biography of Wilde, Wilde and Harris debate the merits of homosexual versus heterosexual love. Wilde's basic argument is against the unaesthetic bodies of Victorian women, particularly when they are pregnant, and the fact that their function as producers of children has wrenched from women the possibility of so-called nonpurposive, that is merely pleasurable, passion; just as domestic servitude had deprived women of the opportunity to pursue merely pleasing intellectual study. This argument is so typical of the defenses of homosexuality in the period's literature, and so contrived a justification of sexual desire, that Harris's account need not be particularly credited. Yet the components, sex for sex's sake and intellectual study for its own sake, are entirely consistent with Wilde's view of art for art's sake. As in Nordau's projected expulsion of the lustful beast and Lombroso's herding of prostitutes to save society from dissolute-minded young men, the Victorians advocated sexuality for the state at the expense of the citizen's sexual freedom and pleasure. This sexuality for the state, in combination with the likes of Nordau's prescriptive views of art for society, made up an ethos of productivity for art and sexuality. And this ethos was directly contrary to art for art's sake and "nonpurposive" sex.

In fact, both sides of the Victorian debate on sex proffered implicit or explicit economic metaphors or theories of "production." Although today Marcus's primitive psychoanalytic framework for interpreting Victorian pornography is increasingly dubious and his Freudian attitude toward his material and sex in general is needlessly grim and depressing, he is nonetheless correct to discern that the official Victorian papers on sexuality calculated the expense of spirit on an economic model of scarcity.[46] Against this model, in which an ounce of semen meant more to a man's health and well-being than forty of blood, pornography—as we have seen in *Teleny*—presented worlds of infinite resources, both economic and sexual. Similarly, we need not read the eleven volumes of *My Secret Life* (c. 1890) to know that the anonymous author's emotional distance from his women partners was due to the Victorian economic and class structure that turned women into commodities: for woman-as-commodity is a figure pervading even the most respectable Victorian novels. And of course Victorian pornography itself is dominated by a kind of (male) consumerism.

That good women were no more than the means of reproduction was not only Wilde's alleged complaint to Harris but also the source of the antifeminist thread running through the polemical homosexual literature of the period. Foucault has posited this "hysterization of women's bodies" in the course of the eighteenth and nineteenth centuries, and we saw an example of it [earlier] in Baudelaire's treatment of George Sand. Foucault describes the process in terms of sexual politics:

> A *hysterization of women's bodies*: a threefold process whereby the feminine body was analyzed—qualified and disqualified—as being thoroughly saturated with sexuality; whereby it was integrated into the sphere of medical practices, by reason of a pathology intrinsic to it; whereby, finally, it was placed in organic communication with the social body (whose regulated fecundity it was supposed to ensure), the family space (of which it had to be a substantial and functional element), and the life of children (which it produced and had to guarantee, by virtue of a biologico-moral responsibility lasting through the entire period of the children's education); the Mother, with her negative image of "nervous woman," constituted the most visible form of this hysterization.[47]

In "The New Chivalry" (from *The Artist*, April 1894), Kains-Jackson argues that now that England is militarily stable, she need not concern herself with population; real "civilization" may consequently and finally flower under the "new chivalry" of more spiritual, more intellectual male love.[48] Part of the reason, of course, that love between males was more spiritual and more intellectual was that in many cases it was unconsummated. Many homosexual men of the time were so accustomed to frustration, through their own reticence or others', that they habitually valued contemplation (e.g., of the beloved) above activity, which was often associated with sex with a woman. Symonds wrote to his sister in disillusionment the morning after his wedding night. He had hoped that marriage would save him from his illicit desires. It did not. "So action is always less essential than contemplation," he writes. "But after it is done, a sense of inadequacy and incompleteness, proceeding from the contrast between the deed meditated and the deed accomplished, springs up."[49] Although Wilde was not one to be reticent, his comic insistence upon "the importance of doing nothing" may well have a similar source.

Certainly the association of activity and sex with women was as common in homosexual literature as that between material production and sex with women. In *Homogenic Love* (1894), even the mild, socialist Edward Carpenter says: "It may indeed be doubted whether the higher heroic and spiritual life of a nation is ever quite possible without the sanction of this attachment [that is, "Dorian" or homosexual love] in its institutions; and it is not unlikely that the markedly materialistic and commercial character of the last age of European civilized life is largely to be connected with the fact that the *only* form of love and love-union that is recognized has been one founded on the quite necessary but comparatively materialistic basis of matrimonial sex-intercourse and child-breeding."[50] And Marc-André Raffalovich's poem "Put on That Languor" contrasts the affectation of idleness characterizing some of the homosexuals of the time with the industrious activity of a materialistic age.[51] A later Uranian poet went so far as to claim that a boy lover was more economical than heterosexual procreation: for a boy could satisfy both sexual desire and a desire for children.[52]

From the argument that women were biologically materialist, it followed in the minds of such poets that women were industrious, and they were consequently lumped together with the distasteful aspects of an artificial industrial age. With them could thus be contrasted the beautiful young boy in nature or sport, as "Philebus" (John Leslie Barford) contrasted them in his pretty *Young Things:*

> Is it unnat'ral that I should joy
>   To join in the heart of natural things?
> To run and swim and ride with you, my boy?
>   To feel the thrill that sweating effort brings?
> To watch with envious love your limbs' display?
>   Or should I chase some chocolate-chewing girl?
> Pass in a cinema a sunny day
>   And nightly in a dusty dance-hall whirl?

That girls must be held in contempt for chewing chocolate is, however, forgotten in *Fantasies,* when a boy offers Philebus a morsel and the poet poignantly takes it all:

> If a boy all suddenly thrust in *your* hand
> Some chocolate, *you* would laugh
> And, failing entirely to understand
> His meaning, would give him half.
> Though loudly I laughed, yet a tear I hid,
> As *I* took the lot from the funny kid.

In the long run the sharpest among the proponents of these anti-action and anti-materialist arguments and metaphors were troubled by the contradiction that although the bodies of women were gross and produced gross, material fruits, the bodies of men and boys were themselves just as material. With the exception of one petition to the Home Office from prison, in which Wilde humbly repents and excuses his "vice" as "madness" (an obvious pose for obvious reasons), he insisted to the last that he did "not hold with the British view of morals that sets Messalina above Sporus";[53] yet in his post-conviction letters he does frequently regret his earlier "materialism." When homosexuals sought to defend themselves by way of critiques of materialism and consumerism they were caught in the most serious and pervasive contradiction of the age.

Here it need only be noted that in the rather extensive homosexual literature of the century—fiction, poetry, and polemic—a tradition Wilde participated in to a limited degree but knew fully, one finds some shame, more social persecution, but for the most part candor and affection on the parts of the writers. The tradition predominantly includes, that is, exactly what we might expect: a love literature for and about men, ranging from the idealistic and chivalric to the openly sexual. There is, for example, a quite distinct genre of encomia on boys bathing. It was probably the extent of this literature, and the support of the community that produced it, that saved its members from the overwhelming guilt that the larger society expected of them. Homosexuals who felt guilt were probably too fearful to publish or to participate in the community in the first place.

Although 1895 began an enforced hiatus, unpublished correspondence of the early 1890's proves the community's political and polemical solidarity. In September 1893 the young Alfred Douglas very enthusiastically praised Kains-Jackson's "New Chivalry."[54] Answering a letter in which Kains-Jackson had criticized Wilde and his "jeweled" prose style, Douglas defended his friend and concluded, "Perhaps nobody knows as I do what he [i.e., Wilde] has done for the 'new culture,' the people he has pulled out of the fire, and 'seen through' things not only with money, but by sticking to them when other people wouldn't speak to them." Through his 1890's correspondence Douglas consistently agitated for homosexual rights and penal reform. He had tactfully done so in the pages of the *Spirit Lamp*. In an editorial "Memoriam" for Symonds, Douglas lamented that Symonds had died before completing his political and literary work: "there were chains he might have loosened, and burdens he might have lifted; chains on the limbs of lovers and burdens on the wings of poets."[55]

Douglas's largely suppressed and very forthright articles of outrage after Wilde's imprisonment, however much he falsified and repudiated them in his later Catholic and celibate life, remain testimony to the courage and precocity that Wilde must have loved in him. . . . In November 1894 Douglas wrote Ives concerning a suicide reported in the paper of an unnamed man of social position who had been charged with assault on one or more boys. Douglas wanted a full-scale scandal so as to educate the public and prevent cause for any more suicides. He also begged Ives to publicize in this connection an earlier death of an Oxford history professor under similar circumstances. In November 1894 Douglas wrote to Kains-Jackson asking legal advice or practical help for a man called Bernard awaiting trial for a similar offense. In April 1895, he scrawled distraught letters to Ives and Kains-Jackson for some help for Wilde. "Do you know no strong fearless man who will stand up?" he asked. Ives and Kains-Jackson did not, but there were a few. James H. Wilson, a Quaker, had written articles in *Reynolds's* on the blackmail industry of male prostitutes and reform of the law of 1885, and he wanted to publish attacks on the authorities during Wilde's trials throughout July–October 1895. Ross and More Adey, however, prevented him, feeling that such publicity would harm Wilde.

Yet until 1895 Wilde seems to have been amused by his ability to pose and pass, and consequently to get the best of both worlds. Take, for example, a real incident involving the green carnation. In *Salome*, the daughter of Herodias promised a young captain who was loved by a page a "little green flower" on the condition that he release to her John the Baptist. During Wilde's lifetime and in later criticism, this particular green flower, the green carnation, has been taken as a symbol of the aesthetic movement. It has been interpreted as a symbol of dandyism or decadence, of the triumph of the artificial over Nature and things called "natural." In W. Graham Robertson's account of the premiere of *Lady Windermere's Fan,* he discussed Wilde's plan for the flower, a plan that would turn the audience itself into an object of artifice, that would make the audience play a role, replete with props, in the theater—even though only an initiated few would be aware of the precise nature of the role. Wilde requested that Robertson wear a green carnation at the premiere and that he persuade as many men as he could to do likewise. Many others, Wilde told him, had already promised to do so. It would "annoy the public," Wilde said. "But why annoy the public?" Robertson asked. Wilde responded: "It likes to be annoyed. A young man on the stage will wear a green carnation; people will stare at it and wonder. Then they will look round the house and see every here and there more and more little specks of mystic green. 'This must be some secret symbol,' they will say. 'What on earth can it mean?' " "And what does it mean?" said Robertson. "Nothing whatever," said Wilde, "but that is just what nobody will guess."[56]

Wilde was disingenuous here, for although most English were unaware of it, he, like Robert Hichens, knew that the distinctive green carnation was the emblem worn by homosexuals in Paris.[57] By encouraging members of the audience to wear the flower, Wilde not only made them part of the performance, forcing them to regard themselves, but he also created an amusing drama for his own entertainment. If he was compelled to double as heterosexual, he had the pleasure at the premiere of watching straight men unwittingly bearing the emblem of homosexuality. When he strolled onto the stage with a cigarette and casually remarked upon the role of the audience in the performance—"I congratulate you on the *great* success of your performance"—he did not, of course, explain the particular joke that had contributed to his enjoyment of the show.

Such, then, was the social climate in which Wilde led his double life, and such was his attitude toward it. Two of his works directly and indirectly deal with his attitudes toward the body and toward the larger society that limited the body's activities. *Salome* was written in France just prior to the events (1892–93) for which Wilde was indicted three years later, that is, for his relations with young men, many of whom were associated with Alfred Taylor's rooms on Little College and Chapel streets. *The Ballad of Reading Gaol* was composed in 1897, just after Wilde's release from prison. *Salome* liberates and communicates physical desire; *Reading Gaol,* on the other hand, portrays the confinement and punishment of the bodies of men who are almost exclusively characterized as lovers. . . .

Notes

1. Grosskurth, *Symonds,* p. 271.

2. See John D'Emilio, "Capitalism and Gay Identity," in Snitow, Stansell, and Thompson, *Powers of Desire,* pp. 100–113; and Foucault, *History of Sexuality,* especially p. 4.

3. For the complicated events leading to Beardsley's dissociation from the *Yellow Book,* see Mix, *Study in Yellow,* ch. 15, pp. 140–47; and for the business aspects of the event, see the chapter "Poisonous Honey and English Blossoms" in Nelson, *Early Nineties,* especially p. 211.

4. Beardsley, *Letters,* p. 158.

5. Yeats, *Autobiography,* p. 121.

6. *L'Affaire Oscar Wilde* in Raffalovich, *Uranisme,* pp. 241–78.

7. Yeats, *Autobiography,* p. 195.

8. See Reade, *Sexual Heretics,* pp. 14–15, 18, 30–31; S. Marcus, *Other Victorians,* p. 263; and Jerry Palmer in Fletcher, *Decadence,* pp. 88–106.

9. For the "Terminal Essay" see Burton, *Thousand Nights,* vol. 10, pp. 63–302. Swinburne's "Memorial Verses" and Richard and Isabel Burton's correspondence with Smithers are in the Huntington Library.

10. In Reade, *Sexual Heretics,* p. 225.

11. Dowson, *Letters*, pp. 127–28, 378n.

12. Beardsley, *Letters*, pp. 58, 92, 394, 440.

13. Yeats, "Memoirs," p. 1956.

14. For the distinction between Wilde's trivial and profound paradoxes see Chamberlin, *Ripe Was the Drowsy Hour*, chs. 4–5. For discussions concerning the form and function of Wilde's epigrams and paradoxes, see (in Mikhail, *Wilde: Interviews*): Percival W.H. Almy, *The Theatre*, vol. 1, pp. 233–34; Coulson Kernahan, *In Good Company*, vol. 2, p. 312; Frank Harris, *Contemporary Portraits*, vol. 2, p. 389; Richard Le Gallienne, *The Romantic '90s*, vol. 2, p. 389; and Stuart Merrill, *Le Plume*, vol. 2, p. 466. Also Hough, *Last Romantics*, p. 203; George Woodcock, "The Social Rebel," in Ellmann, *Wilde: Critical Essays*, p. 152; San Juan, *Art of Wilde*, p. 201 and passim; Shewan, *Wilde: Art and Egotism*, p. 4; Dyson, *Crazy Fabric*, pp. 138–50; Ericksen, *Oscar Wilde*, pp. 78–81; and Jan Gordon, " 'Decadent Spaces': Notes for a Phenomenology of the *Fin de Siècle*," in Fletcher, *Decadence*, pp. 51–52.

15. Hyde, *Trials*, pp. 11–12, 64–75; and Holland, *Son of Oscar Wilde*, p. 268.

16. In "The Priest and the Acolyte," a priest and his altar boy commit suicide before their "perfect love" is degraded by the congregation that has found them out. The story, by John Francis Bloxam, is included in Reade, *Sexual Heretics*, pp. 342–60.

17. Hyde, *Trials*, p. 133.

18. Ibid., pp. 165–66.

19. See Reade, *Sexual Heretics*, pp. 40–48. Reade includes many publications from *The Artist* and *The Studio* in his anthology. For more on the "little" (art) magazines and homosexuality, see Fletcher's "Decadence and the Little Magazines," in Fletcher, *Decadence*.

20. Letter in the Clark Library.

21. Wilde, *Letters*, pp. 401–5.

22. Lombroso, *Genius*, pp. 359–61.

23. Lombroso, *Crime*, pt. II, ch. 2, pp. 255–61.

24. For further speculation on the historical alliance of Anglo-Catholicism and homosexuality, see Hilliard, "Un-English."

25. See Lombroso, *Crime*, pt. II, pp. 255–61. This type of sanctioned vice to remedy vice, heavily weighted against women, was the target of the middle-class feminists' campaign of the early 1870's against the English Contagious Disease Acts. To protect troops from venereal disease, women in certain garrison towns could be stopped by the police on suspicion of prostitution and had to submit to examination for sexually transmitted diseases or appear before a magistrate. Josephine Butler and her supporters objected to the Acts as an example of the double standard of sexual morality, which punished women and not men and which disregarded middle-class notions of social purity. See Rowbotham and Weeks, *Socialism*, p. 13.

26. Lombroso, *Crime*, pt. II, p. 418. Within Lombroso's biological tradition, both Richard von Krafft-Ebing in *Psychopathia Sexualis* (trans. Charles G. Chaddock, London, 1892) and Havelock Ellis in *Sexual Inversion* (Philadelphia, 1915) made the same distinction. Thus Ellis distinguished between occasional and circumstantial "homosexuality" (or "perversion") and "inversion," defined as a congenital condition.

27. Shaw's attack on Nordau uses the scientist/literary critic's weapons against him. Nordau claims that rhyme, poetic inconsistency, and repetition indicate general softening of the brain and body, and Shaw cites examples of Nordau's own echolalia (*Sanity of Art*, p. 80). Nordau denounces socialism and other forms of discontent and social critique in the arts as stigmata of degeneracy, and Shaw cites Nordau's own lengthy passages expressing dissatisfaction with the social order (*Sanity of Art*, pp. 94–97).

28. After personal contact with Theodor Herzl in 1895, Nordau reaffirmed his Jewish background and worked in the new Zionist movement. See George L. Mosse's Introduction to the 1968 edition of *Degeneration*.

29. Nordau, *Degeneration* (1920), p. 557.

30. Cited in Mosse's Introduction to *Degeneration* (1968), p. xxxii.

31. Shaw, *Sanity of Art*, p. 5.

32. These interviews and reviews are among the news clippings at the Clark Library.

33. Chris Healy, "Oscar Wilde and Zola," *Today*, 26 Nov. 1902, p. 145. In *Today* of 8 Oct. 1902, Healy had claimed that Wilde "was one of the direct instruments in freeing Alfred Dreyfus."

34. Galton, *Hereditary Genius*, p. ix.

35. The articles quoted here appeared in Pemberton-Billing's private subscription paper, the *Vigilante*, on 13 Apr. and 15 June 1918.

36. See Nelson, *Early Nineties*, pp. 211–16, 260–61.

37. For more appreciative reviews of the "decadents," see Le Gallienne, *Retrospective Reviews*.

38. Hichens, *Green Carnation*, pp. 109, 125–26.

39. In Reade, *Sexual Heretics*, pp. 248–85.

40. Letter of 4 September 1913 in the Clark Library.

41. S. Marcus, *Other Victorians*, pp. 271–72.

42. See Rowbotham and Weeks, *Socialism*, and Weeks, *Coming Out*.

43. *Pall Mall Gazette*, 25 Jan. 1889, p. 3; included in Wilde, *Artist as Critic*, pp. 121–25.

44. *Five Unknown Letters of Oscar Wilde to George Ives*, introduced by Louis Marlow (1950), in the Clark Library manuscript collection.

45. Letters of 22 October 1897 in the Clark Library.

46. S. Marcus, *Other Victorians*, ch. 1. Marcus does not discuss homosexual pornography, but see pp. 22 and 274. Marcus states that "inside of every pornographer there is an infant screaming for the breast from which he has been torn" (p. 274), and his general view of sex is that it is all a matter of grimness, sadness, and defeat, a matter of repetitious attempts to repossess a wholeness once lost. Such Freudian premises in conjunction with terms of condescension toward his material such as "disgusting" and "it is all rather like 'The Solitary Reaper' written in a sewer" (p. 102) may put off many present-day readers.

47. Foucault, *History of Sexuality*, p. 104.

48. In Reade, *Sexual Heretics*, pp. 313–19.

49. Grosskurth, *Symonds*, p. 95.

50. In Reade, *Sexual Heretics*, pp. 324–47.

51. In ibid., p. 226.

52. This and the poems that follow are cited in Smith, *Love in Earnest*, pp. 176–78.

53. Wilde, *Letters*, p. 621 and throughout.

54. This and the letters that follow are included in Alfred Douglas's wide correspondence at the Clark Library. Wilson's letters were addressed to More Adey.

55. *Spirit Lamp* 4, no. 1 (May 1893): 45.

56. Robertson, *Time Was*, pp. 130–38; also in Mikhail, *Wilde: Interviews*, vol. 1, p. 212.

57. Hyde, *Trials*, app. E, p. 370.

Different Desires: Subjectivity and Transgression in Wilde and Gide

JONATHAN DOLLIMORE

In Blidah, Algeria, in January 1895 André Gide is in the hall of a hotel, about to leave. His glance falls on the slate which announces the names of new guests: "suddenly my heart gave a leap; the two last names . . . were those of Oscar Wilde and Lord Alfred Douglas."[1] Acting on his first impulse, Gide "erases" his own name from the slate and leaves for the station. Twice thereafter Gide writes about the incident, unsure why he left so abruptly; first in his *Oscar Wilde* (1901), then in *Si le grain ne meurt* (*If It Die,* 1920, 1926). It may, he reflects, have been a feeling of *mauvaise honte* or of embarrassment: Wilde was becoming notorious and his company compromising. But also he was severely depressed, and at such times "I feel ashamed of myself, disown, repudiate myself."[2] Whatever the case, on his way to the station he decides that his leaving was cowardly and so returns. The consequent meeting with Wilde was to precipitate a transformation in Gide's life and subsequent writing.

Gide's reluctance to meet Wilde certainly had something to do with previous meetings in Paris four years earlier in 1891; they had seen a great deal of each other across several occasions, and biographers agree that this was one of the most important events in Gide's life. But these meetings had left Gide feeling ambivalent towards the older man, and it is interesting that not only does Gide say nothing in *If It Die* about Wilde's obvious and deep influence upon him in Paris in 1891, but, according to Jean Delay, in the manuscript of Gide's journal the pages corresponding to that period—November–December 1891—are torn out.[3]

Undoubtedly Gide was deeply disturbed by Wilde, and not surprisingly, since Gide's remarks in his letters of that time suggest that Wilde was intent on undermining the younger man's self-identity, rooted as it was in a Protestant ethic and high bourgeois moral rigour and repression that generated a kind of conformity to which Wilde was, notoriously, opposed. Wilde wanted to encourage Gide to transgress. It may be that he wanted to re-enact in Gide the creative liberation—which included strong criminal identification—which his

Reprinted from *Textual Practice* 1, no. 1 (Spring 1987): 48–67.

own exploration of transgressive desire had produced nine years earlier.
(Wilde's major writing, including that which constitutes his transgressive
aesthetic, dates from 1886 when, according to Robert Ross, he first practised
homosexuality.)[4] But first Wilde had to undermine that law-full sense of self
which kept Gide transfixed within the law. So Wilde tried to decentre or
demoralize Gide—"demoralize" in the sense of liberate from moral constraint
rather than to dispirit; or, rather, to dispirit precisely in the sense of to liberate
from a morality anchored in the very notion of spirit. ("Demoralize" was a
term Gide remembers Wilde using in just this sense, one which, for Gide,
recalled Flaubert.) Hence, perhaps, those most revealing of remarks by Gide to
Valéry at this time (4 December 1891): "Wilde is religiously contriving to kill
what remains of my soul, because he says that in order to know an essence, one
must eliminate it: he wants me to miss my soul. The measure of a thing is the
effort made to destroy it. Each thing is made up only of its emptiness." And in
another letter of the same month: "Please forgive my silence: since Wilde, I
hardly exist anymore."[5] And in unpublished notes for this time he declares that
Wilde was "always trying to instil into you *a sanction for evil.*"[6] So, despite his
intentions to the contrary, Wilde at that time seems indeed to have dispirited
Gide in the conventional sense. Yet perhaps the contrary intention was partly
successful; on 1 January 1892 Gide writes: "Wilde, I think, did me nothing
but harm. In his company I had lost the habit of thinking. I had more varied
emotions, but had forgotten how to bring order into them."[7] In fact, Gide
reacted, says Delay, in accordance with his Protestant instincts, reaffirming a
moral conviction inseparable from an essentialist conception of self (cf. *Journal,*
29 December 1891: "O Lord keep me from evil. May my soul again be
proud"). Even so, this meeting with Wilde is to be counted as one of the most
important events in Gide's life: "for the first time he found himself confronted
with a man who was able to bring about, within him, a transmutation of all
values—in other words, a revolution."[8] Richard Ellmann concurs with this
judgement, and suggests further that Wilde's attempt to "authorize evil" in
Gide supplies much of the subject of *The Immoralist* and *The Counterfeiters,* the
former work containing a character, Ménalque, who is based upon Wilde.[9]

It is against the background and the importance of that earlier meeting,
together with the ambivalence towards Wilde which it generated in Gide, that
we return to that further encounter in Algeria four years later. If anything, the
ambivalence seems even stronger; in a letter to his mother Gide describes
Wilde as a terrifying man, a "most dangerous product of modern civilization"
who had already depraved Douglas *"right down to the marrow."*[10] A few days
later Gide meets them again in Algiers, a city which Wilde declares his
intention to demoralize.[11] It is here that there occurs the event which was to
change Gide's life and radically influence his subsequent work, an event for
which the entire narrative of *If It Die* seems to have been preparing. He is taken
by Wilde to a café. It is there that "in the half-open doorway, there suddenly

appeared a marvellous youth. He stood there for a time, leaning with his raised elbow against the door-jamb, and outlined on the dark background of the night." The youth joins them; his name is Mohammed; he is a musician; he plays the flute. Listening to that music, "you forgot the time and place, and who you were."[12] This is not the first time Gide has experienced this sensation of forgetting. Africa increasingly attracts him in this respect;[13] there he feels liberated and the burden of an oppressive sense of self is dissolved: 'I laid aside anxieties, constraints, solicitudes, and as my will evaporated, I felt myself becoming porous as a beehive."[14] Now, as they leave the café, Wilde turns to Gide and asks him if he desires the musician. Gide writes: "how dark the alley was! I thought my heart would fail me; and what a dreadful effort of courage it needed to answer: 'yes,' and with what a choking voice!" (Delay points out that the word "courage" is here transvalued by Gide; earlier he had felt courage was needed for self-discipline, whereas now it is the strength to transgress.)[15]

Wilde arranges something with their guide, rejoins Gide and then begins laughing: "a resounding laugh, more of triumph than of pleasure, an interminable, uncontrollable, insolent laugh . . . it was the amusement of a child and a devil." Gide spends the night with Mohammed: "my joy was unbounded, and I cannot imagine it greater, even if love had been added." Though not his first homosexual experience, it confirmed his (homo)sexual "nature," what, he says, was "normal" for him. Even more defiantly Gide declares that, although he had achieved "the summit of pleasure five times" with Mohammed, "I revived my ecstasy many more times, and back in my hotel room I relived its echoes until morning"[16] (this passage was one of those omitted from some English editions). At this suitably climactic moment we postpone further consideration of Gide and turn to the anti-essentialist, transgressive aesthetic which Wilde was advocating and which played so important a part in Gide's liberation or corruption, depending on one's point of view. And I want to begin with an indispensable dimension of that aesthetic: one for which Wilde is yet hardly remembered—or, for some of his admirers, one which is actively forgotten—namely, his advocacy of socialism.

Wilde begins his *The Soul of Man under Socialism* (1891) by asserting that a socialism based on sympathy alone is useless; what is needed is to *"try and reconstruct society on such a basis that poverty will be impossible."* It is precisely because Christ made no attempt to reconstruct society that he had to resort to pain and suffering as the exemplary mode of self-realization. The alternative is the socialist commitment to transforming the material conditions which create and perpetuate suffering. One might add that, if the notion of redemption through suffering has been a familiar theme within English studies, this only goes to remind us of the extent to which, in the twentieth century, criticism has worked in effect as a displaced theology or as a vehicle for an acquiescent quasi-religious humanism. So Wilde's terse assertion in 1891 that "Pain is not the ultimate mode of perfection. It is merely provisional and a protest"[17] may still be an appropriate response to those who fetishize suffering in the name, not of Christ, but of the tragic vision and the human condition (sainthood without God, as Camus once put it).

Wilde also dismisses the related pieties, that humankind learns wisdom through suffering, and that suffering humanizes. On the contrary, "misery and poverty are so absolutely degrading, and exercise such a paralysing effect over the nature of men, that no class is ever really conscious of its suffering. They have to be told of it by other people, and they often entirely disbelieve them." Against those who were beginning to talk of the dignity of manual labour, Wilde insists that most of that too is absolutely degrading. Each of these repudiations suggests that Wilde was fully aware of how exploitation is crucially a question of ideological mystification as well as of outright coercion: "to the thinker, the most tragic fact in the whole of the French Revolution is not that Marie Antoinette was killed for being a queen, but that the starved peasant of the Vendée voluntarily went out to die for the hideous cause of feudalism." Ideology reaches into experience and identity, re-emerging as "voluntary" self-oppression. But it is also the ruling ideology which prevents the rulers themselves from seeing that it is not sin that produces crime but starvation, and that the punishment of the criminal escalates rather than diminishes crime and also brutalizes the society which administers it even more than the criminal who receives it.[18]

There is much more in this essay, but I have summarized enough to show that it exemplifies a tough materialism; in modern parlance one might call it anti-humanist, not least because for Wilde a radical socialist programme is inseparable from a critique of those ideologies of subjectivity which seek redemption in and through the individual. A case in point would be Dickens's treatment of Stephen Blackpool in *Hard Times* (Wilde made a point of disliking Dickens); another might be Arnold's assertion in *Culture and Anarchy*: "Religion says: *'The Kingdom of God is within you';* and culture, in like manner, places human perfection in an *internal* condition, in the growth and predominance of our humanity proper."[19] But isn't a category like anti-humanism entirely inappropriate, given Wilde's celebration of individualism? The term itself, anti-humanism, is not worth fighting over; I have introduced it only as a preliminary indication of just how different is Wilde's concept of the individual from that which has prevailed in idealist culture generally and English studies in particular. It is this difference which the next section considers.

INDIVIDUALISM

In Wilde's writing, individualism is less to do with a human essence, Arnold's inner condition, than a dynamic social potential, one which implies a radical possibility of freedom "latent and potential in mankind generally." Thus individualism as Wilde conceives it generates a "disobedience [which] in the eyes of anyone who has read history, is man's original virtue. It is through disobedience that progress has been made, through disobedience and through rebellion."[20] Under certain conditions there comes to be a close relationship between crime and individualism, the one generating the other.[21] Already, then, Wilde's notion of individualism is inseparable from transgressive desire and a transgressive aesthetic. Hence, of course, his attack on public opinion, mediocrity and conventional morality, all of which forbid both the desire and the aesthetic.[22]

The public which Wilde scorns is that which seeks to police culture; which is against cultural difference; which reacts to the aesthetically unconventional by charging it with being either grossly unintelligible or grossly immoral. Far from reflecting or prescribing for the true nature or essence of man, individualism will generate the cultural difference and diversity which conventional morality, orthodox opinion and essentialist ideology disavow. Wilde affirms the principle of differentiation to which all life grows and insists that selfishness is not living as one wishes to live, but asking others to live as one wishes to live, trying to create "an absolute uniformity of type." And unselfishness not only recognizes cultural diversity and difference but enjoys them. Individualism as an affirmation of cultural as well as personal difference is therefore fundamentally opposed to that "immoral ideal of uniformity of type and conformity to rule which is so prevalent everywhere, and is perhaps most obnoxious in England."[23]

Uniformity of type and conformity to rule: Wilde despises these imperatives not only in individuals but as attributes of class and ruling ideologies. Wilde's Irish identity is a crucial factor in his oppositional stances, and it is instructive to consider in this connection a piece written two years earlier, in 1889, where he addresses England's exploitation and repression of Ireland. "Mr. Froude's Blue Book" is a review of J. A. Froude's novel, *The Two Chiefs of Dunboy*. In the eighteenth century, says Wilde, England tried to rule Ireland "with an insolence that was intensified by race-hatred and religious prejudice"; in the nineteenth, with "a stupidity . . . aggravated by good intentions." Froude's picture of Ireland belongs to the earlier period, and yet to read Wilde's review now makes one wonder what if anything has changed in Tory "thinking" except that possibly now the one vision holds for both Ireland and the mainland:

Resolute government, that shallow shibboleth of those who do not understand how complex a thing the art of government is, is [Froude's] posthumous panacea for past evils. His hero, Colonel Goring, has the words Law and Order ever on his lips, meaning by the one the enforcement of unjust legislation, and implying by the other the suppression of every fine natural aspiration. That the government should enforce iniquity, and the governed submit to it, seems to be to Mr.

Froude, as it certainly is to many others, the true ideal of political science. . . . Colonel Goring . . . Mr. Froude's cure for Ireland . . . is a *"Police at any price"* man.[24]

Individualism joins with socialism to abolish other kinds of conformity, including, says Wilde, family life and marriage, each being unacceptable because rooted in and perpetuating the ideology of property.[25] Individualism is both desire for a radical personal freedom and a desire for society itself to be radically different, the first being inseparable from the second. So Wilde's concept of the individual is crucially different from that sense of the concept which signifies the private, experientially self-sufficient, autonomous, bourgeois subject; indeed, for Wilde, "Personal experience is a most vicious and limited circle" and "to know anything about oneself one must know all about others."[26] Typically, within idealist culture, the experience of an essential subjectivity is inseparable from knowledge of that notorious transhistorical category, human nature. This is Wilde on human nature: "the only thing that one really knows about human nature is that it changes. Change is the one quality we can predicate of it."[27] To those who then say that socialism is incompatible with human nature and therefore impractical, Wilde replies by rejecting practicality itself as presupposing and endorsing both the existing social conditions and the concept of human nature as fixed, each of which suppositions socialism would contest: "it is exactly the existing conditions that one objects to . . . [they] will be done away with, and human nature will change."[28] Elsewhere Wilde accepts that there is *something* like human nature, but, far from being the source of our most profound being, it is actually ordinary and boring, the least interesting thing about us. It is where we differ from each other that is of definitive value.[29]

ART VERSUS LIFE

The key concepts in Wilde's aesthetic are protean and shifting, not least because they are paradoxically and facetiously deployed. When, for example, he speaks of life—"poor, probable, uninteresting human life"[30]—or reality as that to which art is opposed, he means different things at different times. One of the most interesting and significant referents of concepts like life and reality, as Wilde uses them, is the prevailing social order. Even nature, conceived as the opposite of culture and art, retains a social dimension,[31] especially when it signifies ideological mystification of the social. That is why Wilde calls being natural a "pose," and an objectionable one at that, precisely because it seeks to mystify the social as natural.[32]

Nature and reality signify a prevailing order which art ignores and which the critic negates, subverts and transgresses. Thus, for example, the person of culture is concerned to give "an accurate description of what has never occurred," while the critic sees "the object as in itself it really is not"[33] (Wilde is here inverting the proposition which opens Arnold's famous essay "The function of criticism at the present time"). Not surprisingly, then, criticism and art are aligned with individualism against a prevailing social order; a passage which indicates this is also important in indicating the basis of Wilde's aesthetic of transgressive desire: "Art is Individualism and Individualism is *a disturbing and disintegrating force*. Therein lies its immense value. For what it seeks to disturb is monotony of type, slavery of custom, tyranny of habit."[34] Art is also self-conscious and critical; in fact, "self-consciousness and the critical spirit are one."[35] And art, like individualism, is oriented towards the realm of transgressive desire: "What is abnormal in Life stands in normal relations to Art. It is the only thing in Life that stands in normal relations to Art."[36] One who inhabits that realm, "the cultured and fascinating liar," is both an object and source of desire.[37] The liar is important because s/he contradicts not just conventional morality but its sustaining origin, "truth." So art runs to meet the liar, kissing his "false beautiful lips, knowing that he alone is in possession of the great secret of all her manifestations, the secret that Truth is entirely and absolutely a matter of style." Truth, the epistemological legitimation of the real, is rhetorically subordinated to its antitheses—appearance, style, the lie—and thereby simultaneously both appropriated and devalued. Reality, also necessarily devalued and demystified by the loss of truth, must imitate art, while life must meekly follow the liar.[38]

Further, life is at best an energy which can only find expression through the forms that art offers it. But form is another slippery and protean category in Wilde's aesthetic. In one sense Wilde is a proto-structuralist: "Form is the beginning of things. . . . The Creeds are believed, not because they are rational, but because they are repeated. . . . Form is everything. . . . Do you wish to love? Use Love's Litany, and the words will create the yearning from which the world fancies that they spring."[39] Here form is virtually synonymous with culture. Moreover, it is a passage in which Wilde recognizes the priority of the social and the cultural in determining meaning, even in determining desire. So for Wilde, although desire is deeply at odds with society in its existing forms, it does not exist as a pre-social authenticity; it is within and in-formed by the very culture which it also transgresses.

TRANSGRESSION AND THE SENSE OF SELF

Returning now to Gide, we are in a position to contrast his essentialism with Wilde's anti-essentialism, a contrast which epitomizes one of the most important differences within the modern history of transgression. In a way that perhaps corresponds to his ambivalence towards Wilde, Gide had both submitted to and resisted the latter's attempts to undermine his sense of self.

Both the submission and the resistance are crucial for Gide's subsequent development as a writer and, through Gide's influence, for modern literature. The submission is apparent enough in the confirmation of his homosexual desire and the way this alters his life and work. In 1924 he published *Corydon,* a courageous defence of homosexuality which he later declared to be his most important book (*Journal,* 19 October 1942). In *Corydon* he did not just demand tolerance for homosexuality but also insisted that it was not contrary to nature but intrinsically natural; that heterosexuality prevails merely because of convention; that historically homosexuality is associated with great artistic and intellectual achievement, while heterosexuality is indicative of decadence. About these provocative and suspect claims I have only the space to observe that the fury they generated in the majority of commentators is as significant as Gide's reasons for making them in the first place. Two years later Gide published the equally controversial commercial edition of *If It Die,* which, as already indicated, contained, for that time, astonishingly explicit accounts of his homosexuality, and for which, predictably, Gide was savagely castigated. Much later still, Gide was to write to Ramon Fernandez, confirming that "sexual non-conformity is the first key to my works"; the experience of his own deviant desire leads him first to attack sexual conformity and then "all other sphinxes of conformity," suspecting them to be "the brothers and cousins of the first."[40]

But Gide—having with Wilde both allowed and encouraged the subversion of an identity which had hitherto successfully, albeit precariously, repressed desire—does not then substitute for it the decentred subjectivity which animates Wilde's aesthetic; on the contrary, he reconstitutes himself as an essentially new self. Michel in *The Immoralist* (1902) corresponds in some measure to Gide in Algiers (while, as earlier remarked, another character in that novel, Ménalque, is probably based on Wilde). For Michel, as for Gide, transgression does not lead to a relinquishing of self but to a totally new sense of self. Michel throws off the culture and learning which up to that point had been his whole life, in order to find himself: that "authentic creature that had lain hidden beneath . . . whom the Gospel had repudiated, whom everything about me—books, masters, parents, and I myself had begun by attempting to suppress. . . . Thenceforward I despised the secondary creature, the creature who was due to teaching, whom education had painted on the surface." He composes a new series of lectures in which he shows "Culture, born of life, as the destroyer of life." The true value of life is bound up with individual uniqueness: "the part in each of us that we feel is different from other people is the part that is rare, the part that makes our special value."[41]

Whereas for Wilde transgressive desire leads to a relinquishing of the essential self, for Gide it leads to a discovery of the authentic self. As he writes in *If It Die,* it was at that time in Algiers that "I was beginning to discover myself—and in myself the tables of a new law."[42] And he writes to his mother on 2 February 1895: "I'm unable to write a line or a sentence so long as I'm not in *complete possession* (that is, WITH FULL KNOWLEDGE) of myself. I should like very submissively to follow nature—the unconscious, which is within myself and must be *true.*"[43] Here again there is the indirect yet passionate insistence on the naturalness, the authenticity of his deviant desire. With that wilful integrity—itself a kind of perversity?—rooted in Protestantism, Gide not only appropriates dominant concepts (the normal, the natural) to legitimate his own deviation, but goes so far as to claim a sanction for deviation in the teachings of Christ.[44] (In his journal for 1893 (detached pages) he wrote: "Christ's saying is just as true in art: 'Whoever will save his life (his personality) shall lose it.'" He later declared, after reading Nietzsche's *Thus Spake Zarathustra,* that it was to this that Protestantism led, "to the greatest liberation.")[45] Delay contends, plausibly, that some of the great Gidean themes, especially those entailing transgression, can be found in the rebellious letters that he wrote to his mother in March 1895, letters inspired by his self-affirmation as a homosexual.[46]

It would be difficult to overestimate the importance, in the recent history of Western culture, of transgression in the name of an essential self which is the origin and arbiter of the true, the real and the moral—that is, the three main domains of knowledge in Western culture: the epistemological, the ontological and the ethical. Its importance within the domain of sexuality and within discourses which intersect with sexuality is becoming increasingly apparent, but it has been central also in liberation movements which have not primarily been identified with either of these. This, finally, is Gide in 1921: "The borrowed truths are the ones to which one clings most tenaciously, and all the more so since they remain foreign to our intimate self. It takes much more precaution to deliver one's own message, much more boldness and prudence, than to sign up with and add one's voice to an already existing party. . . . I believed that it is above all to oneself that it is important to remain faithful."[47]

PARADOX AND PERVERSITY

The contrast between Gide and Wilde is striking: not only are Wilde's conceptions of subjectivity and desire anti-essentialist but so too—and consequently—is his advocacy of transgression. Deviant desire reacts against, disrupts and displaces from within; rather than seeking to escape the repressive ordering of sexuality, Wilde reinscribes himself within and relentlessly inverts the binaries upon which that ordering depends. Inversion, rather than Gide's escape into a pre- or trans-social reality, defines Wilde's transgressive aesthetic. In Gide, transgression is in the name of a desire and identity rooted in the natural, the sincere and the authentic; Wilde's transgressive aesthetic is the reverse: *in*sincerity, *in*authenticity and *un*naturalness become the liberating attributes of decentred identity and desire, and inversion becomes central to

Wilde's expression of this aesthetic, as can be seen from a selection of his *Phrases and Philosophies for the Use of the Young* (1894):

If one tells the truth, one is sure, sooner or later, to be found out.
Only the shallow know themselves.
To be premature is to be perfect.
It is only the superficial qualities that last. Man's deeper nature is soon found out.
To love oneself is the beginning of a lifelong romance.[48]

In Wilde's writings a non-centred or dispersed desire is both the impetus for a subversive inversion *and* what is released by it. Perhaps the most general inversion operating in his work reverses that most dominating of binaries, nature/culture; more specifically, the attributes on the left are substituted for those on the right:

X	for	Y
surface		depth
lying		truth
change		stasis
difference		essence
persona/role		essential self
abnormal		normal
insincerity		sincerity
style/artifice		authenticity
facetious		serious
narcissism		maturity

For Michel in *The Immoralist* and to an extent for Gide himself, desire may be proscribed, but this does not affect its authenticity; if anything, it confirms it. In a sense, then, deviant desire is legitimated in terms of culture's opposite, nature, or, in a different but related move, in terms of something which is pre-cultural or *always more than* cultural. Gide shares with the dominant culture an investment in the Y column above; he appropriates its categories *from* the dominant *for* the subordinate. In contrast, for Wilde transgressive desire is both rooted in culture and the impetus for affirming different/alternative kinds of culture. So what in Gide's conception of transgression might seem a limitation or even a confusion—namely, that the desire which culture outlaws is itself thoroughly cultural—in fact facilitates one of the most disturbing of all forms of transgression: the outlaw turns up as inlaw; more specifically, that which society forbids Wilde reinstates through and within some of its most cherished and central cultural categories—art, the aesthetic, art criticism, individualism. At the same time as he appropriates those categories he also transvalues them through inversion, thus making them now signify those binary exclusions (the

X column) by which the dominant culture knows itself (thus abnormality is not just the opposite, but *the necessarily always present* antithesis of normality). It is an uncompromising inversion, this being the (perversely) appropriate strategy for a transgressive desire which is of its "nature," according to this culture, an inversion.

But inversion has a specific as well as a general target: as can be seen from the *Phrases and Philosophies* just quoted, Wilde seeks to subvert those dominant categories which signify *subjective depth*. Such categories (the Y column) are precisely those which ideologically identify (interpellate?) the mature adult individual, which confer or ideologically coerce identity. And they too operate in terms of binary contrast: the individual knows what he—I choose the masculine pronoun deliberately[49]—is in contrast to what he definitely is not or should not be. In Wilde's inversions, the excluded inferior term returns as the *now superior* term of a related series of binaries. Some further examples of Wilde's subversion of subjective depth are:

A little sincerity is a dangerous thing, and a great deal is absolutely fatal.[50]

All bad poetry springs from genuine feeling.[51]

In matters of grave importance, style, not sincerity, is the *vital* thing.[52]

Only shallow people . . . do not judge by appearances.[53]

Insincerity . . . is merely a method by which we can multiply our personalities. Such . . . was Dorian Gray's opinion. He used to wonder at the shallow psychology of those who conceived the Ego in man as a thing simple, permanent, reliable, and of one essence. To him man was a being with myriad lives and myriad sensations, a complex, multiform creature.[54]

At work here is a transgressive desire which makes its opposition felt as a disruptive reaction upon, and inversion of, the categories of subjective depth which hold in place the dominant order which proscribes that desire.

THE DECENTRED SUBJECT AND THE QUESTION OF THE POSTMODERN

Wilde's transgressive aesthetic relates to at least three aspects of contemporary theoretical debates: first, the dispute about whether the inversion of binary opposites subverts or, on the contrary, reinforces the order which those binaries uphold; second, the political importance—or irrelevance—of decentring the subject; third, postmodernism and one of its more controversial criteria: the so-called disappearance of the depth model, especially the model of a deep human subjectivity. Since the three issues closely relate to each other, I shall take them together.

It might be said that Wildean inversion disturbed nothing; by merely reversing the terms of the binary, inversion remains within its limiting framework: the world turned upside down can only be righted, not changed. Moreover, the argument might continue, Wilde's paradoxes are superficial in the pejorative sense of being inconsequential, of making no difference. But we should remember that in the first of the three trials involving Wilde in 1895 he was cross-examined on his *Phrases and Philosophies,* the implication of opposing counsel being that they, along with *Dorian Gray,* were "calculated to subvert morality and encourage unnatural vice."[55] There is a sense in which evidence cannot get more material than this, and it remains so whatever our retrospective judgement about the crassness of the thinking behind such a view.

One of the many reasons why people thought as they did was to do with the perceived connections between Wilde's aesthetic transgression and his sexual transgression. It is not only that at this time the word "inversion" was being used for the first time to define a specific kind of deviant sexuality and deviant person (the two things now being indissociable), but also that, in producing the homosexual as a species of being rather than, as before, seeing sodomy as an aberration of behaviour,[56] society now regarded homosexuality as rooted in a person's identity; this sin might pervade all aspects of an individual's being, and its expression might become correspondingly the more insidious and subversive. Hence in part the animosity and hysteria directed at Wilde during and after his trial.

After he had been found guilty of homosexual offences and sentenced to two years' imprisonment with hard labour, the editorial of the London *Evening News* subjected him to a vicious and revealing homophobic attack. He had, it claimed, tried to subvert the "wholesome, manly, simple ideals of English life"; moreover, his "abominable vices . . . were the natural outcome of his diseased intellectual condition." The editorial also saw Wilde as the leader of a likeminded but younger subculture in London.[57] The view expressed here was, and indeed remains, for some, a commonplace: sexual deviation is symptomatic of a much wider cultural deterioration and/or subversion. There is an important sense in which Wilde confirmed and exploited this connection between discursive and sexual perversion: "What the paradox was to me in the sphere of thought, perversity became to me in the sphere of passion."[58] This feared crossover between discursive and sexual perversion has sanctioned terrible brutalities against homosexuals, at the same time, at least in this period, it was also becoming the medium for what Foucault calls a reverse or counter-discourse,[59] giving rise to what is being explored here in relation to Wilde—what might be called the politics of inversion/perversion (again crossing over and between the different senses of these words). Derrida has argued persuasively for binary inversion as a politically indispensable stage towards the eventual displacement of the binary itself.[60] The case of Wilde indicates, I think, that in actual historical instances of inversion—that is, inversion as a strategy of cultural struggle—it already constitutes a displacement, if not of the binary itself, then certainly of the moral and political norms which cluster dependently around its dominant pole.

We begin to see, then, why Wilde was hated with such an intensity, even though he rarely advocated in his published writings any explicitly immoral practice. What held those "wholesome, manly, simple ideals of English life" in place were traditional and conservative ideas of what constituted human nature and human subjectivity, and it was *these* that Wilde attacked: not so much conventional morality itself as the ideological anchor points for that morality, namely notions of identity as subjective depth, whose criteria appear in the Y column above. And so it might be said that here, generally, as he did with Gide more specifically, Wilde subverts the dominant categories of subjectivity which keep desire in subjection, and subverts the essentialist categories of identity which keep morality in place. Even though there may now be a temptation to patronize and indeed dismiss both the Victorians' "wholesome, manly, simple ideals of English life" and Wilde's inversion of them, the fact remains that, in successively reconstituted forms, those ideals, *together with* the subject positions which instantiate them, come to form the moral and ethical base of English studies in our own century, and, indeed, remain culturally central today.

I am thinking here not just of the organicist ideology so characteristic of an earlier phase of English studies, one that led, for example, to the celebration of Shakespeare's alleged "national culture, rooted in the soil and appealing to a multi-class audience," but more specifically and importantly of what Chris Baldick in his excellent study goes on to call its "subjective correlative," namely, the *"maintenance of the doctrine of psychic wholeness in and through literature as an analogue for a projected harmony and order in society."*[61] For I. A. Richards, all human problems (continues Baldick) become problems of mental health, with art as the cure, and literary criticism becomes "a question of attaining the right state of mind to judge other minds, according to their degree of immaturity, inhibition, or perversion." As Richards himself puts it, sincerity "is the quality we most insistently require in poetry. It is also the quality we most need as critics."[62] As a conception of both art and criticism, this is the reverse of Wilde's. Similarly with the Leavises, whose imperative concept was the related one of "maturity," one unhappy consequence of which was their promotion of the "fecund" D. H. Lawrence against the perverse W. H. Auden. As Baldick goes on to observe, "this line of critics is not only judicial in tone but positively inquisitorial, indulging in a kind of perversion-hunting" which is itself rooted in "a simple model of [pre- or anti-Freudian] normality and mental consistency."[63]

This tradition has, of course, been subjected to devastating critiques in recent years; in particular, its notions of subjective integration and psychic wholeness have been attacked by virtually all the major movements within contemporary critical theory including Marxism, structuralism, post-structuralism and psychoanalysis. Yet Wilde's subversion of these notions is still excluded from consideration, even though we now think we have passed beyond that heady and in many ways justified moment when it seemed that only Continental theory had the necessary force to displace the complacencies of our own tradition. The irony, of course, is that while looking to the Continent we failed to notice that Wilde has been and remains a very significant figure there. (And not only there: while the *Spectator* (February 1891) thought *The Soul of Man under Socialism* was a joke in bad taste, the essay soon became extremely successful in Russia, appearing in many successive editions across the next twenty years.) Perhaps, then, there exists or has existed a kind of "muscular theory," which shares with the critical movements it has displaced a significant blindness with regard to Wilde and what he represented. This almost certainly has something to do with the persistence of an earlier attempt to rid English studies of a perceived "feminized" identity.[64]

Recent critics of postmodernism, including Fredric Jameson, Ihab Hassan, Dan Latimer and Terry Eagleton,[65] have written intriguingly on one of its defining criteria: the disappearance of the depth model. In a recent essay, Eagleton offers an important and provocative critique of postmodernism: "confidently post-metaphysical [it] has outlived all that fantasy of interiority, that pathological itch to scratch surfaces for concealed depths." With the postmodern there is no longer any subject to be alienated and nothing to be alienated from, "authenticity having been less rejected than merely forgotten." The subject of postmodernist culture is "a dispersed, decentred network of libidinal attachments, emptied of ethical substance and psychical interiority, the ephemeral function of this or that act of consumption, media experience, sexual relationship, trend or fashion." Modernism, by contrast, is (or was) still preoccupied with the experience of alienation, with metaphysical depth and/or the psychic fragmentation and social wretchedness consequent upon the realization that there is no metaphysical depth or (this being its spiritual instantiation) authentic unified subject. As such, modernism is "embarrassingly enmortgaged to the very bourgeois humanism it otherwise seeks to subvert"; it is "a deviation still enthralled to a norm, parasitic on what it sets out to deconstruct." But, concludes Eagleton, the subject of late capitalism is actually neither the "self-regulating synthetic agent posited by classical humanist ideology, nor merely a decentred network of desire [as posited by post-modernism], but a contradictory amalgam of the two." If in one respect the decentred, dispersed subject of postmodernism is suspiciously convenient to our own phase of late capitalism, it follows that those post-structuralist theorists who stake all on the assumption that the unified subject is still integral to contemporary bourgeois ideology, and that it is always a politically radical act to decentre and deconstruct that subject, need to think again.[66]

Eagleton's argument can be endorsed with yet further important distinctions. First, even though the unified subject was indeed an integral part of an earlier phase of bourgeois ideology, the instance of Gide and the tradition he represents must indicate that it was never even then exclusively in the service of dominant ideologies. Indeed, to the extent that Gide's essentialist legitimation of homosexual desire was primarily an affirmation of his own nature as pederast or paedophile, some critics might usefully rethink their own assumption that essentialism is fundamentally and always a conservative philosophy. In Gide we find essentialism in the service of a radical sexual nonconformity which was and remains incompatible with conventional and dominant sexual ideologies, bourgeois and otherwise. Even a glance at the complex and often contradictory histories of sexual liberation movements in our own time shows that they have, as does Eagleton's contradictory subject of late capitalism, sometimes and necessarily embraced a radical essentialism with regard to their own identity, while simultaneously offering an equally radical anti-essentialist critique of the essentializing sexual ideologies responsible for their oppression.

This is important: the implication of Eagleton's argument is not just that we need to make our theories of subjectivity a little more sophisticated, but rather that we need to be more historical in our practice of theory. Only then can we see the dialectical complexities of social process and social struggle. We may see, for example, how the very centrality of an essentialist concept to the dominant ideology has made its appropriation by a subordinate culture seem indispensable in that culture's struggle for legitimacy; roughly speaking, this corresponds to Gide's position as I am representing it here. The kind of challenge represented by Gide—liberation in the name of authenticity—has been more or less central to many progressive cultural struggles since, though it has not, of course, guaranteed their success.[67] Conversely, we may also see how other subordinate cultures and voices seek not to appropriate dominant concepts and values so much as to sabotage and displace them. This is something we can observe in Wilde.

Whether the decentred subject of contemporary post-structuralism and postmodernism is subversive of, alternative to, or actually produced by late capitalism, there is no doubt that Wilde's exploration of decentred desire and identity scandalized bourgeois culture in the 1890s and in a sense cost him his life. The case of Wilde might lead us to rethink the antecedents of postmodernism and, indeed, of modernism as they figure in the current debate which Eagleton addresses. Wilde prefigures elements of each, while remaining importantly different from—and not just obviously prior to—both. If his transgressive aesthetic anticipates postmodernism to the extent that it suggests a culture of the surface and of difference, it also anticipates modernism in being not just hostile to but intently concerned with its opposite, the culture of depth and exclusive integration. Yet Wilde's transgressive aesthetic differs from some versions of the postmodern in that it includes an acute political awareness and often an uncompromising political commitment; and his critique of the depth model differs from the modernist in that it is accompanied not by *Angst* but by something utterly different, something reminiscent of Barthes's *jouissance,* or what Borges has perceptively called Wilde's "negligent glee . . . the funda-mental spirit of his work [being] joy."[68]

An anti-essentialist theory of subjectivity can in no way guarantee, *a priori,* any effect, radical or otherwise; nor, more generally, can any transgressive practice carry such a guarantee. But there is much to be learned retrospectively both from the effects of anti-essentialism and the practice of transgression, especially in the light of the currently felt need to develop new strategies and conceptions of resistance. Orthodox accounts of resistance have proved wanting, not least essentialist ideas of resistance in the name of the authentic self, and—in some ways the opposite—resistance in terms of and on behalf of mass movements working from outside and against the dominant powers. And so we have become acutely aware of the unavoidability of working from within the institutions that exist, adopting different strategies depending on where and who we are, or, in the case of the same individual, which subject positions s/he is occupying. But is this the new radicalism, or incorporation by another name?

It is in just these respects, and in relation to such pressing questions, that, far from finding them irrelevant—the one a *passé* wit and the other a *passé* moralist/essentialist—I remain intrigued with Wilde and Gide. In different ways their work explores what we are now beginning to attend to again: the complexities, the potential and the dangers of what it is to transgress, invert and displace *from within;*[69] the paradox of a marginality which is always interior to, or at least intimate with, the centre.

I began with their encounter in Algiers in 1895. Gide, dispirited in the sense of being depressed and unsure of himself, sees the names of Wilde and Douglas and erases his own name as a result, pre-empting perhaps the threat to his own identity, social and psychic, posed by Wilde's determination to demystify the normative ideologies regulating subjectivity, desire and the aesthetic. Nevertheless the meeting does occur, and Gide does indeed suffer an erasure of self, a decentring which is also the precondition for admitting transgressive desire, a depersonalization which is therefore also a liberation. Yet, for Gide, transgression is embraced with that same stubborn integrity which was to become the basis of his transgressive aesthetic, an aesthetic obviously indebted, yet also formed in reaction to, Wilde's own. Thus liberation from the self into desire is also to realize a new and deeper self, belief in which supports an oppositional stand not just on the question of deviant sexual desire, but on a whole range of other issues as well, cultural and political. Integrity here becomes an ethical sense inextricably bound up with and also binding up the (integral) unified self.[70] So the very categories of identity which, through transgression, Wilde subjects to inversion and displacement are reconstituted by Gide for a different transgressive aesthetic, or, as it might now more suitably be called in contradistinction to Wilde, a transgressive ethic: one which becomes central to the unorthodoxy which characterizes his life's work. In 1952, the year after his death, his entire works were entered in the Roman Catholic Index of Forbidden Books; six years earlier he had been awarded the Nobel Prize for Literature.

Wilde's fate was very different. Within weeks of returning from Algiers to London he was embroiled in the litigation against Queensberry which was to lead to his own imprisonment. He died in Paris in 1900, three years after his release. So, whereas Gide lived for fifty-seven years after that 1895 encounter, Wilde survived for only six. And yet it was also Wilde's fate to become a legend. Like many legendary figures, he needs to be rescued from most of his admirers and radically rethought by some, at least, of his critics.

Notes

Thanks to Joseph Bristow for his comments on an earlier draft of this paper.

1. André Gide, *If It Die* (1920; private edn. 1926), trans. Dorothy Bussy (Harmondsworth: Penguin, 1977), p. 271.

2. Ibid., pp. 271, 273.

3. Jean Delay, *The Youth of André Gide,* abridged and trans. J. Guicharnaud (Chicago and London: University of Chicago Press, 1956–7), p. 290.

4. Richard Ellmann (ed.), *The Artist as Critic: Critical Writings of Oscar Wilde* (1968; London: W. H. Allen, 1970), p. xviii. Those aspects of Wilde's transgressive aesthetic which concern me here derive mainly from work published across a relatively short period of time, the years 1889–91. My reading of Wilde is avowedly partial. There is, of course, more—much more—to be said; about these works, about different works not discussed here, about Wilde himself, especially about other of his ideas which intersect with and contradict the perspective explored here. My concern, though, is to address aspects of his work which have been largely ignored. What Richard Ellmann said of Wilde nearly twenty years ago is still true today: he "laid the basis for many critical positions which are still debated in much the same terms, and which we like to attribute to more ponderous names" (ibid., p. x). Thomas Mann compared Wilde with Nietzsche; Ellmann in 1968 added the name of Roland Barthes. In 1987 we could add several more; more constructive, though, will be the renewed interest in Wilde that is sure to be generated by the expected publication this year of Ellmann's major biography.

5. J. Guicharnaud (trans.), *Correspondence 1890–1942, André Gide—Paul Valéry* (1955), cited here from the abridged version, *Self-Portraits: The Gide/Valéry Letters* (Chicago and London: University of Chicago Press, 1966), pp. 90, 92.

6. Delay, op. cit., p. 291.

7. André Gide, *Journals,* 4 vols. (New York: Alfred A. Knopf, 1947–51).

8. Delay, op. cit., pp. 289, 90, 291, 295.

9. Richard Ellmann (ed.), *Oscar Wilde: A Collection of Critical Essays* (Englewood Cliffs, NJ: Prentice-Hall, 1969), p. 4.

10. Quoted from Delay, op. cit., p. 391 (my italics).

11. André Gide, *Oscar Wilde,* trans. Bernard Frechtman (New York: Philosophical Library, 1949).

12. Gide, *If It Die,* pp. 280, 281.

13. Ibid., pp. 236–7, 247–9, 251, 252, 255, 258–9.

14. Ibid., p. 264.

15. Delay, op. cit., p. 394.

16. Gide, *If It Die,* pp. 282, 284–5.

17. Oscar Wilde, *The Soul of Man under Socialism* (1891), reprinted in Ellmann (ed.), *The Artist as Critic,* pp. 256 (his italics), 286–8, 288.

18. Ibid., pp. 259, 268, 260, 267.

19. Matthew Arnold, *Culture and Anarchy* (1869; London: Smith Elder, 1891), p. 8.

20. Wilde, *The Soul of Man under Socialism,* pp. 261, 258.

21. Wilde reiterates this elsewhere: see Oscar Wilde, "Pen, pencil and poison" (1889), in Ellmann (ed.), *The Artist as Critic,* p. 338; "The critic as artist" (1890), in Ellmann (ed.), *The*

Artist as Critic, p. 360. Cf. Ellmann's formulation of Wilde's position: "since the established social structure confines the individual, the artist must of necessity ally himself with the criminal classes" (Ellmann (ed.), *Oscar Wilde*, p. 3).

22. See also Wilde, "The critic as artist," p. 341; Wilde, *The Soul of Man under Socialism*, pp. 271–4.

23. Wilde, *The Soul of Man under Socialism*, pp. 273, 284–5, 286.

24. Oscar Wilde, "Mr. Froude's Blue Book" (1889), in Ellmann (ed.), *The Artist as Critic*, pp. 136–7.

25. Wilde, *The Soul of Man under Socialism*, p. 265.

26. Oscar Wilde, "The decay of lying" (1889), in Ellmann (ed.), *The Artist as Critic*, p. 310, and "The critic as artist," p. 382.

27. Wilde, *The Soul of Man under Socialism*, p. 284.

28. Ibid., p. 284.

29. Wilde, "The decay of lying," p. 297.

30. Ibid., p. 305.

31. For example, Wilde, "The critic as artist," pp. 394, 399.

32. Oscar Wilde, *The Picture of Dorian Gray* (1890–1; Harmondsworth: Penguin, 1949), p. 10.

33. Wilde, "The critic as artist," pp. 343, 368.

34. Wilde, *The Soul of Man under Socialism*, p. 272 (my italics).

35. Wilde, "The critic as artist," p. 356.

36. Oscar Wilde, "A few maxims for the instruction of the overeducated," *The Complete Works*, with introduction by Vyvyan Holland (London and Glasgow: Collins, 1948), p. 1203.

37. Wilde, "The decay of lying," pp. 292 and 305.

38. Ibid., p. 305.

39. Wilde, "The critic as artist," p. 399.

40. Delay, op. cit., p. 438.

41. André Gide, *The Immoralist* (1902; Harmondsworth: Penguin, 1960), pp. 51, 90, 100.

42. Gide, *If It Die*, p. 298.

43. Delay, op. cit., p. 396.

44. Gide, *If It Die*, p. 299.

45. Delay, op. cit., p. 467.

46. Ibid., p. 407.

47. Gide, *Journals*, p. 338. Cf. ibid., pp. 371–6.

48. Oscar Wilde, *Phrases and Philosophies for the Use of the Young* (1894), in Ellmann (ed.), *The Artist as Critic*, pp. 433–4.

49. The attacks on Wilde after his trial frequently reveal that it is masculinity which felt most under threat from him, and which demanded revenge.

50. Wilde, "The critic as artist," p. 393.

51. Ibid., p. 398.

52. Oscar Wilde, *The Importance of Being Earnest* (1894–9), ed. R. Jackson (London: Ernest Benn, 1980), p. 83 (my italics).

53. Wilde, *The Picture of Dorian Gray*, p. 29.

54. Ibid., pp. 158–9.

55. H. M. Hyde, *Oscar Wilde: A Biography* (1976; London: Methuen, 1982), p. 271.

56. Michel Foucault, *The History of Sexuality*, vol. I: *An Introduction* (1978; New York: Vintage Books, 1980), p. 43.

57. H. M. Hyde, *The Trials of Oscar Wilde* (London: William Hodge, 1948), p. 12.

58. Oscar Wilde, *De Profundis* (1897), in *The Letters of Oscar Wilde* (London: Rupert Hart-Davis, 1962); cited from the abridged edition, *Selected Letters* (London: Oxford University Press, 1979), p. 194. In certain important respects, *De Profundis* is a conscious renunciation by

Wilde of his transgressive aesthetic. This is a work which registers many things, not least Wilde's courage and his despair during imprisonment. It also shows how he endured the intolerable by investing suffering with meaning, and this within a confessional narrative whose aim is a deepened self-awareness: "I could not bear [my sufferings] to be without meaning. Now I find hidden somewhere away in my nature something that tells me that nothing in the whole world is meaningless . . . that something . . . is Humility." Such knowledge and such humility, for Wilde (and still, for us now), is bought at the cost of fundamentally—deeply—renouncing difference and transgression and the challenge they present. In effect, Wilde repositions himself as the authentic, sincere subject which before he had subverted: "The supreme vice is shallowness," he says in this work, and he says it more than once. And later: "The moment of repentance is the moment of initiation" (ibid., pp. 195, 154, 215). This may be seen as that suffering into truth, that redemptive knowledge which points beyond the social to the transcendent realization of self, so cherished within idealist culture; those who see De Profundis as Wilde's most mature work often interpret it thus. I see it differently—as tragic, certainly, but tragic in the materialist sense of the word: a defeat of the marginal and the oppositional of a kind which only ideological domination can effect; a renunciation which is experienced as voluntary and self-confirming but which is in truth a self-defeat and a self-denial massively coerced through the imposition, by the dominant, of incarceration and suffering and their "natural" medium, confession. What Wilde says here of the law is true also of the dominant ideologies he transgressed: "I . . . found myself constrained to appeal to the very things against which I had always protested" (ibid., p. 221).

59. Foucault, op. cit., p. 101.

60. Jacques Derrida, *Positions* (London: 1981), pp. 41–2.

61. C. Baldick, *The Social Mission of English Criticism 1848–1932* (Oxford: Clarendon, 1983), pp. 213–18 (my italics).

62. I. A. Richards, quoted in ibid., p. 215.

63. Ibid., p. 217.

64. B. Doyle, "The hidden history of English studies," in Peter Widdowson (ed.), *Re-Reading English* (London: Methuen, 1982); Terry Eagleton, *Literary Theory: An Introduction* (Oxford: Blackwell, 1983); Baldick, op. cit. On Wilde in Germany see Manfred Pfister (ed.), Oscar Wilde, *The Picture of Dorian Gray* (München: Wilhelm Fink, 1986).

65. Fredric Jameson, "Postmodernism and consumer society," in H. Foster (ed.), *The Anti-Aesthetic: Essays on Postmodern Culture* (Washington, DC: Bay Press, 1983); Fredric Jameson, "Postmodernism, or the cultural logic of late capitalism," *New Left Review*, 146 (1984); Ihab Hassan, "Pluralism in postmodern perspective," *Critical Inquiry*, 12, 3 (1986), pp. 503–20; Dan Latimer, "Jameson and postmodernism," *New Left Review*, 148 (1984), pp. 116–28; Terry Eagleton, "Capitalism, modernism and postmodernism," in *Against the Grain* (London: Verso, 1986), pp. 131–47.

66. Eagleton, "Capitalism, modernism and postmodernism," pp. 143, 132, 145, 143–5.

67. M. Berman, *The Politics of Authenticity: Radical Individualism and the Emergence of Modern Society* (London: Allen & Unwin, 1971).

68. Ellmann (ed.), *Oscar Wilde*, p. 174.

69. See Jacques Derrida, *Of Grammatology* (1967), trans. Gayatri Spivak (Baltimore, Md., and London: Johns Hopkins University Press, 1976), pp. lxxvi–lxxviii; Derrida, *Positions*, pp. 41–2; R. Terdiman, *Discourse/Counter Discourse: Theory and Practice of Symbolic Resistance in Nineteenth-Century France* (Ithaca, NY: Cornell University Press, 1985), esp. Introduction. Some of the most informative work addressing inversion and transgression is historically grounded; I have in mind especially recent work on early modern England. See, for example, D. Kunzle, "World turned upside down: the iconography of a European broadsheet type," in Barbara Babcock (ed.), *The Reversible World: Symbolic Inversion in Art and Society* (Ithaca, NY, and London: Cornell University Press, 1978); Christopher Hill, *The World Turned Upside Down: Radical Ideas during the English Revolution* (Harmondsworth: Penguin, 1975); P. Stallybrass and A. White, *The Politics and Poetics of Transgression* (London: Methuen, 1986); S. Clark,

"Inversion, misrule and the meaning of witchcraft," *Past and Present*, 87 (1980), pp. 98–127. Kunzle, discussing the iconography of the world turned upside-down broadsheets, offers a conclusion which registers the complex potential of inversion and is, quite incidentally, nicely suggestive for understanding Wilde: "Revolution appears disarmed by playfulness, the playful bears the seed of revolution. 'Pure' formal fantasy and subversive desire, far from being mutually exclusive, are two sides of the same coin" (op. cit., p. 89). This is the appropriate point at which to note that the fuller study to which this article is a contribution will necessarily address other considerations in relation to transgression in Wilde and Gide, most especially those of class, race, and colonialism. A crucial text for the latter is Gide's *Travels in the Congo* (1927–8), trans. D. Bussy (Harmondsworth: Penguin, 1986). But see also Jean-Paul Sartre, *What is Literature?* (1948; London: Methuen, 1967), esp. pp. 52, 98–9, 133.

70.   It is instructive to see in Gide's writing how complex, vital and unconventional the existential and humanist commitment to sincerity of self could be, especially when contrasted with its facile counterpart in English studies, or indeed (a counter-image) the reductive ways in which it is sometimes represented in literary theory. See especially the following entries in Gide's *Journals:* 21 December and detached/recovered pages for 1923; January 1925; 7 October and 25 November 1927; 10 February (especially) and 8 December 1929; 5 August and September 1931; 27 June 1937.

Writing Gone Wilde:
Homoerotic Desire
in the Closet of Representation

ED COHEN

Oh! It is absurd to have a hard and fast rule about what one should read and what one shouldn't. More than half of modern culture depends on what one shouldn't read.

—Algy to Jack in *The Importance of Being Earnest*

. . . every reader of our columns, as he passed his eye over the report of Wilde's apology for his life at the Old Bailey, must have realized, with accumulating significance at each line, the terrible risk involved in certain artistic and literary phrases of the day. Art, we are told, has nothing to do with morality. But even if this doctrine were true it has long ago been perverted, under the treatment of the decadents, into a positive preference on the part of "Art" for the immoral, the morbid, and the maniacal. It is on this narrower issue that the proceedings of the last few days have thrown so lurid a light. . . . But this terrible case . . . may be the means of incalculable good if it burns in its lesson upon the literary and moral conscience of the present generation.

—The *Westminster Gazette* (6 Apr. 1895) assessing the Marquis of Queensbury's acquittal on charges of criminal libel.

PROLOGUE: A TRYING (CON)TEXT

During the late spring of 1895, the trials of Oscar Wilde erupted from the pages of every London newspaper. The sex scandal involving one of London's most renowned popular playwrights as well as one of the most eccentric members of the British aristocracy titillated popular opinion. And why not? For it had all the elements of a good drawing-room comedy—or, in Freudian terms, of a good family romance. The characters were exact: the neurotic but righteously outraged father (the Marquis of Queensbury), the prodigal and effeminate young son (Alfred Douglas), and the degenerate older man who came between them (Wilde). Wilde was portrayed as the corrupting artist who

Reprinted by permission of the Modern Language Association of America from *PMLA* 102 (October, 1987), 801–13.

dragged young Alfred Douglas away from the realm of paternal solicitude down into the London underworld, where homosexuality, blackmail, and male prostitution sucked the lifeblood of morality from his tender body. How could such a story have failed to engage the public imagination?

Yet the widespread fascination with Wilde's trials should not be viewed solely as the result of a prurient public interest, nor should it be seen only as the product of a virulent popular desire to eradicate "unnatural" sexual practices. Rather, the public response must be considered in the light of the Victorian bourgeoisie's larger efforts to legitimate certain limits for the sexual deployment of the male body and, in Foucault's terms, to define a "class body." The middle-aged, middle-class men who judged Wilde—both in the court and in the press—saw themselves as attempting not merely to control a "degenerate" form of male sexuality but also to ensure standards for the health of their children and their country.[1] To this end, the court proceedings against Wilde provided a perfect opportunity to define publicly the authorized and legal limits within which a man could "naturally" enjoy the pleasures of his body with another man. The trials, then, can be thought of as a spectacle in which the state, through the law and the press, delimited legitimate male sexual practices (defining them as "healthy," "natural," or "true") by proscribing expressions of male experience that transgressed these limits.[2] The legal proceedings against Wilde were therefore not anomalous; rather, they crystallized a variety of shifting sexual ideologies and practices. For what was at issue was not just the prosecution of homosexual acts per se or the delegitimating of homosexual meanings. At issue was the discursive production of "the homosexual" as the antithesis of the "true" bourgeois male.

In Britain during the late nineteenth century, "the homosexual" was emerging as a category for organizing male experience alongside other newly recognizable "types" ("the adolescent," "the criminal," "the delinquent," "the prostitute," "the housewife," etc.).[3] Coined by the Swiss physician Karoly Benkert in 1869 and popularized in the writings of the German sexologists, the word (along with its "normal" sibling, "the heterosexual") entered English usage when Krafft-Ebing's *Psychopathia Sexualis* was translated during the 1890s. The shift in the conception of male same-sex eroticism from certain proscribed *acts* (the earlier concepts "sodomite" and "bugger" were identified with specific legally punishable practices [see Trumbach; Gilbert]) to certain kinds of *actors* was part of an overall transformation in class and sex-gender ideologies (see Weeks, *Coming Out,* esp. chs. 1–3). If we think of the growth and consolidation of bourgeois hegemony in Victorian Britain as a process whereby diverse sets of material practices ("sex" and "class" among others) were organized into an effective unity (see Connell), then we can see that "the homosexual" crystallized as a distinct subset of male experience only in relation to prescribed embodiments of "manliness." This new conceptualization reproduced asymmetrical power relations by privileging the enactments of white middle-class, heterosexual men (see Cominos for the classic description of this privilege; see also Thomas).

In *Between Men: English Literature and Male Homosocial Desire,* Eve Kosofsky Sedgwick explores the range of "maleness" in English literature between the late eighteenth and early twentieth centuries and proposes that the normative structuring of relations between men established other male positionings within the larger sex-gender system.[4] Investigating the strategies whereby literary texts (primarily nineteenth-century novels) constructed a "continuum of homosocial desire," she illustrates that these texts articulate male sexuality in ways that also evoke asymmetrical power relations between men and women. Hence, she suggests that we must situate both the production and the consumption of literary representations depicting male interactions (whether overtly sexualized or not) within a larger social formation that circulates ideologies defining differences in power across sex and class.

This suggestion seems particularly applicable to Wilde's texts, which embody an especially contradictory nexus of class and sexual positionings. As the son of a noted Irish physician, Sir William Wilde, and a popular nationalist poet, Lady Jane Wilde (also called "Speranza"), Wilde was educated in a series of public schools and colleges before attending Oxford. After receiving a double "first" in 1879, Wilde "went down" to London, where, owing to his father's death and his family's insolvency, he was forced to earn his own income. From that time until his imprisonment in 1895, Wilde consciously constructed and marketed himself as a liminal figure within British class relations, straddling the lines between nobility, aristocracy, middle class, and—in his sexual encounters—working class. The styles and attitudes that he affected in his writing and his life creatively packaged these multiple positionings; "I have put all my genius into my life," Wilde observed in his famous remark to André Gide; "I have only put my talents into my work." Typically, literary critics have explained this overdetermined positioning by situating Wilde among the nineteenth-century manifestations of decadence and dandyism, thereby emphasizing that his aesthetic paradoxically signified his dependence on the prevailing bourgeois culture and his detachment from it.[5] Yet his literary and personal practices also embodied a more contradictory relation to sexual and class ideologies.

As Regenia Gagnier demonstrates, these contradictions became evident in the contemporary reviews of *The Picture of Dorian Gray:*

> One is struck by the profusion of such terms [in the reviews of *Dorian Gray*] as "unclean," "effeminate," "studied insincerity," "theatrical," "Wardour Street aestheticism," "obtrusively cheap scholarship," "vulgarity," "unnatural," "false," and "perverted": an odd mixture of the rumors of Wilde's homosexuality and of more overt criticism of Wilde as a social poseur and self-advertiser. Although the suggestion was couched in terms applying to the text, the reviews seemed to say that Wilde did not know his place, or—amounting to the same

thing—that he did know his place and it was not that of a middle-class gentleman. (59)

In Gagnier's analysis, the immediate critical response to *Dorian Gray* denounced the text's transgression of precisely those class and gender ideologies that sustained the "middle-class gentleman": the novel was seen as "decadent" both because of "its distance from and rejection of middle-class life" and because "it was not only dandiacal, it was 'feminine'" (65). Thus, the *Athenaeum* would refer to the book as "unmanly, sickening, vicious (although not exactly what is called 'improper'), and tedious and stupid" (Mason 200). And the *Scotts Observer* would remark: "Mr. Wilde has again been writing stuff that were better unwritten and while 'The Picture of Dorian Gray,' which he contributes to *Lippincott's,* is ingenious, interesting, full of cleverness, and plainly the work of a man of letters, it is false art—for its interest is medico-legal; it is false to human nature—for its hero is a devil; it is false to morality—for it is not made sufficiently clear that the writer does not prefer a course of unnatural iniquity to a life of cleanliness, health and sanity" (Mason 75–76). Emphasizing that Wilde's novel violated the standards of middle-class propriety, these characterizations illustrate the intersection of Victorian class and gender ideologies from which Wilde's status as the paradigmatic "homosexual" would emerge. For, in contrast to the "manly" middle-class male, Wilde would come to represent—through his writing and his trials—the "unmanly" social climber who threatened to upset the certainty of bourgeois categories.

To situate Wilde's emergence as "a homosexual" in late nineteenth-century literary (con)texts and thereby explore the ways that sex-gender ideologies shape specific literary works, I focus first on *Teleny,* a novel widely attributed to Wilde and one of the earliest examples of male homoerotic pornography, whose encoding of sexual practices between men moves athwart those ideologies that sought to "naturalize" male heterosexuality. Then by analyzing the better-known and yet manifestly "straight" text *The Picture of Dorian Gray,* I illustrate that even in the absence of explicit homosexual terminology or activity, a text can subvert the normative standards of male same-sex behavior. In considering how these works challenge the hegemonic representations of male homoerotic experience in late Victorian Britain, I suggest how textual depictions of male same-sex experience both reproduce and resist the dominant heterosexual ideologies and practices.

THROUGH THE REVOLVING DOOR: THE PORNOGRAPHIC REPRESENTATION OF THE HOMOEROTIC IN *TELENY*

In *The Other Victorians,* Steven Marcus states: "The view of human sexuality as it was represented in the [late Victorian] subculture of pornography and the view of sexuality held by the official culture were reversals, mirror images, negative analogies of each other. . . . In both the same set of anxieties are at work; in both the same obsessive ideas can be made out; and in both sexuality is conceived of at precisely the same degree of consciousness" (283–84). While Marcus's analysis suggestively projects the "pornotopia" as the underside of bourgeois society, it fails to consider the ways that Victorian pornography not only reflected but refracted—or perhaps, more specifically, *interrupted*—the assumptions and practices of the dominant culture.[6] In other words, since Marcus relates the production of the pornographic only to institutionally legitimated forms of the sexual and the literary, he obscures the degree to which such an unsanctioned (and hence uncanonized) genre could provide positive articulations of marginalized sexual practices and desires.

One such textual affirmation can be found in *Teleny: Or, The Reverse of the Medal: A Physiological Romance*. Written in 1890 (the same year "The Picture of Dorian Gray" appeared in *Lippincott's Monthly Magazine*), *Teleny* is reputed to be the serial work of several of Wilde's friends (who circulated the manuscript among themselves), with Wilde serving as general editor and coordinator.[7] Even if this genealogy proves apocryphal, the unevenness of its prose styles suggests that the novel was the collaboration of several authors and possibly a set of self-representations evolving out of the homosexual subculture in late Victorian London.

Chronicling the ill-fated love between two late nineteenth-century men, *Teleny* unfolds as a retrospective narrative told by the dying Camile Des Grieux to an unnamed interlocutor. Prompted by his questioner, Des Grieux unfolds a tale of seductions, sex (homo- and hetero-, oral and anal), orgies, incest, blackmail, rape, suicide, death, and love. Aroused by his passion for the beautiful—and well-endowed—young pianist René Teleny, Des Grieux opens himself to the varied possibilities of male sexual expression only to find himself drawn back again and again to a single object of desire: the male body of his beloved Teleny. Thus, Des Grieux's narrative represents an explicit set of strategies through which the male body is ensnared in the passions and excesses of homoerotic desire.

Introducing the image of its fatal conclusion, the novel's opening sentence directs us immediately to the body on which the narrative is inscribed: "A few days after my arrival in Nice, last winter, I encountered several times on the Promenade a young man, of dark complexion, thin, a little stooped, of pallid color, with eyes—beautiful blue eyes—ringed in black, of delicate features, but aged and emaciated by a profound ailment, which appeared to be both physical and moral" (21). The novel's conclusion can be initially "read off" from Des Grieux's degenerate condition only because his body serves as the "recording surface" for the story.[8] The narrator underscores this relation between body and narrative: "The account that follows is not, then, a novel. It is rather a true story: the dramatic adventures of two young and handsome human beings of refined temperament, high-strung, whose brief existence was cut short by death after flights of passion which will doubtless be misunderstood by the generality of men" (22). Here the generic "human beings" distinguishes the protagonists from the "generality of men" who will doubtlessly misunderstand them, introducing a fundamental opposition "fleshed out" in the text: by juxtaposing male same-sex passion with a cultural concept of "manliness" that seeks to exclude it, the novel deconstructs those definitions of human nature that deny the homoerotic as unnatural. Thus, even before its pornographic plot begins, the text attaches itself to the male body as the surface on which its markings will become legible and simultaneously undertakes to use this legibility to validate same-sex desire.

Within the novel's narrative logic, this validation derives from the irrationality of the attraction uniting Des Grieux and Teleny, in spite of their manifestly masculine (and hence ideologically rational) positioning. In the first chapter, positing their almost mystical affinity, Des Grieux recalls their "predestined" meeting at a London charity concert. On stage, Teleny, the pianist, senses the presence of a "sympathetic listener" who inspires him to incredible heights of virtuosity. In the audience, Des Grieux responds to Teleny's performance by visualizing a set of extravagant and exotic scenes—portraying classical European images of non-European sexualized otherness—which, we soon learn, are the same visions that Teleny conjures as he plays. Indeed, these images are so distinct that Des Grieux experiences them physically: "a heavy hand [that] seemed to be laid on my lap, something was bent and clasped and grasped, which made me faint with lust" (27). In the midst of this masturbatory incantation, Des Grieux succumbs to the novel's first stirrings of priapic ecstasy. Thus, when the young men meet and their first touch (a properly masculine handshake) "reawakens Priapus," Des Grieux feels that he has been "taken possession of" (29). The ensuing conversation leads the men to recognize their affinity and, at the same time, foregrounds the irrationality underlying their erotic connection. Describing the music that has brought them together as the product of a "madman," Teleny hints at "insanity" and "possession," enmeshing the two in a web of superstition and "unreason." By violating the dominant Victorian associations of masculinity with science and reason, the first encounter between the lovers casts their attraction as an implicit challenge to the normative ideologies for male behavior.

Following this initial highly charged meeting, the next four chapters elaborate the deferral of its sexual consummation, recounting Des Grieux's emotional turmoil as he comes to recognize, accept, and ultimately enjoy his physical desire for Teleny. The sexual content of this portion of the novel depicts primarily illicit—if not taboo—heterosexual practices. All these manifestly straight incidents, however, portray the heterosexual as a displacement of the true affection of one man for another; they juxtapose the universal acceptability and "naturalness" of heterosexual passion (even if accompanied by incest or violence) to the execration and "unnaturalness" of homoerotic desire.

As Des Grieux begins to make sense of his obsession with Teleny, he realizes that this natural-unnatural distinction is itself learned (i.e., cultural): ". . . I had been inculcated with all kinds of wrong ideas, so when I understood what my *natural* feelings for Teleny were I was staggered, horrified . . ." (63; my emphasis). This inverted use of the word *natural* deconstructs the mask of ideological neutrality and underscores the moral implications it attempts to conceal. Once he accepts that he "was born a sodomite," Des Grieux can remark that "I read all I could find about the love of one man for another, that loathsome crime against nature, taught to us not only by the very gods themselves, but by all of the greatest men of olden times. . . ." Thus the text mocks the culture's pretensions in defining as a "crime against nature" that which *his* nature demands and which the "very gods themselves" and the "greatest men of olden times" have practiced. By subverting the claims to "natural" (read "ideological") superiority by "honorable [heterosexual] men," the narrative's logic opens the possibility for a counterhegemonic representation of homoerotic desire.

The first sexual encounter between Des Grieux and Teleny inaugurates this new representation of same-sex desire by reviving the "fatedness" of their relationship. As Des Grieux, convinced of the hopelessness of his passion for a man, stands on a bridge over the Thames and contemplates "the forgetfulness of those Stygian waters," he is grabbed from behind by the strong arms of his beloved Teleny, who is drawn to the spot by supernatural premonition (explained by Teleny's "gypsy blood"). This charmed meeting culminates in a scene of extravagant and abandoned lovemaking through which the two men form an inseparable bond that sustains them for many climaxes and an unforgettable orgy. The charm is broken, however, when Teleny—through a combination of boredom, irrepressible lust, and economic necessity—is led into an affair with Des Grieux's mother. The shock of discovering that his mother has usurped his place in Teleny's bed sends Des Grieux into a decline from which he never recovers, and the shock of being found out causes Teleny to take his own life.

This summary can only hint at the profusion of sexual representation the novel engenders. Despite its tragic ending, its depiction of male homoerotic desire and practice insists on not only the possibility but the naturalness of same-sex eroticism. Thus, in reflecting on the story of his first night with Teleny, Des Grieux offers one of the most articulate defenses of same-sex love to be found in late Victorian fiction. Responding to his interlocutor's question, "Still, I had thought, on the morrow—the intoxication passed—you would have shuddered at the thought of having a man for a lover?" Des Grieux asks:

Why? Had I committed a crime against nature when my own nature found peace and happiness thereby? If I was thus, surely it was the fault of my blood, not myself. Who had planted nettles in my garden? Not I. They had grown there unawares from my very childhood. I began to feel their carnal sting long before I could understand what conclusion they imported. When I had tried to bridle my lust, was it my fault if the scale of reason was far too light to balance that of sensuality? Was I to blame if I could not argue down my raging motion? Fate, Iago-like, had clearly shewed me that if I would damn myself, I could do so in a more delicate way than drowning. I yielded to my destiny and encompassed my joy. (119)

By juxtaposing his homoerotic "nature" to a Victorian definition that criminalized it, Des Grieux's statement foregrounds the moral-ideological concerns implied in this naturalizing terminology. In so doing, he articulates a theory of "innate difference" similar to the third-sex theories first proposed by the late nineteenth-century apologists for same-sex desire (Edward Carpenter, J. A. Symonds, and Havelock Ellis).[9] Since these formulations assume the opposition between intellect and passion—or between male and female— found elsewhere in late Victorian discourse, they necessarily encode the implicit bias on which these dichotomies depend. Here, however, the polarities are resolved through an alternative outlet, physical and moral: joy. In affirming the naturalness of Des Grieux's homoerotic experience, this new joyous possibility undermines the monovocalizing strategies the bourgeois heterosexual culture used to ensure the reproduction of its dominance and thus opens up the possibility of representing a plurality of male sexualities.

Behind the Closet Door: The Representation of Homoerotic Desire in *The Picture of Dorian Gray*

What if someone wrote a novel about homosexuality and no body came? To what extent is *The Picture of Dorian Gray* this book? And what does it mean to say that a text is "about" homosexuality anyway?

While *The Picture of Dorian Gray* has generated much speculation and innuendo concerning its author's sexual preferences, the aftermath of Wilde's trials has left no doubt in the critical mind that the "immorality" of Wilde's text paralleled that of his life. Yet this critical reflection has never directly addressed the question of how Wilde's "obviously" homoerotic text signifies its "deviant" concerns while never explicitly violating the dominant norms for heterosexuality. That Wilde's novel encodes traces of male homoerotic desire seems to be ubiquitously, though tacitly, affirmed. Why this general affirmation exists has never been addressed. To understand how "everyone knows" what lurks behind Wilde's manifestly straight language (i.e., without descending to a crude biographical explanation), we must examine the ways that Wilde's novel moves both with and athwart the late Victorian ideological practices that naturalized male heterosexuality.[10]

The Picture of Dorian Gray narrates the development of male identity within a milieu that actively subverts the traditional bourgeois representations of appropriate male behavior. While it portrays a sphere of art and leisure in which male friendships assume primary emotional importance and in which traditional male values (industry, earnestness, morality) are abjured in favor of the aesthetic, it makes no explicit disjunction between these two models of masculinity; rather, it formally opposes an aesthetic representation of the male body and the material, emotional, sexual male body itself. In other words, *The Picture of Dorian Gray* juxtaposes an aesthetic ideology that foregrounds representation with an eroticized milieu that inscribes the male body within circuits of male desire. To understand how this opposition operates, we must first consider the components of the male friendships in the novel.

The text of *Dorian Gray* develops around a constellation of three characters—Lord Henry Wotton, Basil Hallward, and Dorian Gray—who challenge the Victorian standards of "true male" identity. Freed from the activities and responsibilities that typically consumed the energies of middle-class men, they circulate freely within an aestheticized social space that they collectively define. As inhabitants of a subculture, however, they still use a public language that has no explicit forms to represent (either to themselves or to one another) their involvements; hence, they must produce new discursive strategies to express concerns unvoiced within the dominant culture. In producing these strategies, the novel posits its moral and aesthetic interests. By projecting the revelation, growth, and demise of Dorian's "personality" onto an aesthetic consideration of artistic creation, Wilde demonstrates how the psychosexual development of an individual gives rise to the "double conscious-ness" of a marginalized group.[11] Dorian Gray is to some extent born of the conjunction between Basil's visual embodiment of his erotic desire for Dorian and Lord Henry's verbal sublimation of such desire. From this nexus of competing representational modes, Dorian Gray constitutes his own representa-tions of identity. But who then is Dorian Gray?

Within the narrative structure, Dorian is an image—a space for the constitution of male desire. From the time he enters the novel as the subject of Basil's portrait until the moment Wilde has him kill himself into art, Dorian Gray provides the surface on which the characters project their self-representations. His is the body on which Basil's and Lord Henry's desires are inscribed. Beginning with an interview between these two characters, the novel constructs Dorian as a template of desire by thematizing the relation between the inspiration derived from Dorian's "personality" and the resulting aesthetic products. For Basil, Dorian appears as an "ideal," as the motivation for "an entirely new manner in art, an entirely new mode of style." Dorian's mere "visible presence" enables Basil to represent emotions and feelings that he found inexpressible through traditional methods and themes: "I see things differently now. I think of them differently. I can recreate life in a way that was hidden from me before" (150).

But what gives Basil's relation to Dorian this transformative power? In describing his friendship with Dorian to Lord Harry, Basil narrates the story of their meeting: "I turned halfway round, and saw Dorian Gray for the first time. When our eyes met I felt I was growing pale. A curious sensation of terror came over me. I knew I had come face to face with someone whose mere personality was so fascinating, that if I allowed it to do so it would absorb my whole nature, my very art itself. . . . Something seemed to tell me that I was on the verge of a terrible crisis in my life. I had a strange feeling that fate had in store for me exquisite joys and exquisite sorrows" (146). Dorian's "personality" enchants Basil and throws him back upon himself, evoking a physical response that is then translated into a psychic, verbally encoded interpretation. As an artist, Basil resolves this crisis by experientially and aesthetically transforming his representations of this experience. His fascination with Dorian leads him to foreground their erotic connection ("We were quite close, almost touching. Our eyes met again." [147]) and at the same time to legitimate it in the sublimated language of aesthetic ideals ("Dorian Gray is to me simply a motive in art." [151]).

This symbolic displacement of the erotic onto the aesthetic is reiterated by the absent presence of the "picture" within the novel. While homoerotic desire must be muted in a literary text that overtly conforms to dominant codes for writing—which have historically excluded same-sex desires as unrepresentable —it is nevertheless metonymically suggested by a verbally unrepresentable medium, the painting, whose linguistic incommensurability deconstructs the apparent self-sufficiency of these representational codes. Since the portrait stands outside the text and evokes an eroticized tableau transgressing the limits of verbal representation, it establishes a gap whereby unverbalized meaning can enter the text. In particular, its visual eroticism suffuses the dynamic between Dorian and Basil, thereby foregrounding the male body as the source of both aesthetic and erotic pleasure. The portrait provides the space within which, in contemporary psychoanalytic terminology, the phallic activity of "the gaze" encroaches on the dominant linguistic unrepresentability of male same-sex eroticism.[12] Thus, the picture's absent presence (which motivates the narrative development) interrupts the novel's overt representational limits by introducing a visual, extraverbal component of male same-sex desire.

Since Wilde defines painting as an active expression of personal meanings, Basil's "secret" infuses Dorian's picture with a vitality and passion that fundamentally change its "mode of style." Yet this secret does not lie in the work of art itself but rather grows out of Basil's emotional and erotic involvement with Dorian Gray, thereby establishing a new relation between the artist and his subject. As Basil eventually explains to Dorian: ". . . from the moment I met you, your personality had the most extraordinary influence over me. I was dominated soul, brain, and power by you. You became to me the visible incarnation of that unseen ideal whose memory haunts us artists like an exquisite dream. I worshipped you. I grew jealous of everyone to whom you spoke. I wanted to have you all to myself. I was only happy when I was with you. When you were away from me you were still present in my art" (267–68).

The emotional intensity with which Wilde describes Basil's passion for Dorian belies the Platonic invocation of "the visible incarnation of that unseen ideal," since this verbal interpretation merely echoes the available public forms of expression. That Wilde displaces Basil's physical domination onto a dream (albeit exquisite) indicates that there is no publicly validated visible reality to express male homoerotic desire. But because painting can only occur in the nonlinear, and hence extralinguistic, space where Basil synthesizes the visual elements of his emotional and aesthetic inspiration, this visual expression and its verbal analogue are necessarily disjunct. Thus, although Basil's painting is entirely exterior to the text, it provides the reference point for a mode of representation that admits the visible, erotic presence of the male body.

Nowhere is this disjunction made more obvious than in Wilde's distinction between Basil's visual and physical involvement with Dorian and Lord Henry's detached, ironic, and self-conscious verbal stance. In contrast to Basil, who has surrendered his "whole nature," his "whole soul," his "very heart itself," to the immediacy of Dorian Gray, Lord Henry first becomes interested in Dorian through the story of Basil's passion. As a consummate aesthete, Lord Henry derives his passions not from direct engagement with his object but through mediated representations. By separating "one's own soul" from the "passions of one's friends" (153), Wilde opposes Lord Henry's self-objectifying archness to Basil's passionate engagement with his inspiration's embodiment. To the extent that Basil, as a painter, seeks to create a spatialized frame that synthetically mirrors his emotional and erotic reality, Lord Henry, as a conversationalist, segments this aesthetic space into the paradoxes and conundrums that characterize his linguistic style. Basil himself exposes the logic behind this verbal analytics when he says to Lord Henry: "You are an extraordinary fellow. You never say a moral thing and you never do a wrong thing. Your cynicism is simply a pose" (144). It is precisely this cynical posture that distinguishes the two modes of representation the characters engender. For while Basil registers his passion in expressive forms, Lord Henry maintains an autonomous "pose" by detaching himself from his own passions. He never does a wrong thing because he distances himself from the material world of activity by representing reality, both to himself and to others, as an ongoing conversation in which he never says a moral thing. This discursive maneuver, which collapses the physical plenitude of bodily reality into abstract conceptualization, interrupts the visual inscription of Basil's picture and thereby opens the space from which "Dorian Gray" emerges.[13]

Chronologically, this emergence coincides with Basil and Lord Harry's rivalry for Dorian's attention. In recounting his story to Lord Harry, Basil initially hesitates to introduce Dorian's name for fear of violating his "secret." He pleads with Lord Henry not to "take away from me the one person who gives my art whatever charm it possesses," yet his plea merely confirms their competition for the same "wonderfully handsome young man." Though the motives behind this competition are left unspoken, it unfolds during Dorian's final sitting for his portrait. Here, in Basil's studio, the conflict plays itself out as a seduction: Lord Henry woos Dorian away from the adoring gaze of the painter to awaken him to a new, symbolic order of desire—an order at the very heart of the narrative.

Responding to Dorian's complaint that Basil never speaks while painting, Basil allows Lord Henry to stay and entertain Dorian. While Basil puts the finishing touches on the canvas, Lord Henry charms Dorian with a discussion of morality:

> The aim of life is self-development. To realize one's nature perfectly—that is what each of us is here for. People are afraid of themselves nowadays. They have forgotten the highest of all duties is the duty that one owes to oneself. Of course they are charitable. They feed the hungry and clothe the beggar. But their souls starve and are naked. Courage has gone out of our race. Perhaps we never really had it. The terror of society, which is the basis of morals, and the terror of God, which is the secret of religion—these are the two things that govern us. (158)

As Lord Henry's words provide Dorian with new vistas on the moral prejudices of their era, his "low musical voice" seduces the younger man, who becomes transfigured: ". . . a look came into the lad's face . . . never seen there before." Simultaneously, Basil inscribes this "look"—the object of both his artistic and erotic gaze—onto the canvas, thus doubly imbuing his aesthetic image with the representations of male homoerotic desire.

By dialectically transforming Lord Henry's verbal and Basil's visual representations, Dorian enters into the circuits of male desire through which these characters play out their sexual identities. He inspires both Basil and Lord Henry to new heights of expression, but only by internalizing and modifying images through which the older men would have themselves seen. Thus, the development of Dorian's "perfect nature" underscores the disjunction between male homoerotic experience and the historical means of expressing it, so that his strategic mediation between them enables desire to enter the novel explicitly. Lord Henry continues his moral panegyric, once again voicing the problem: "The body sins once and has done with sin, for action is a mode of purification. Nothing remains then but the recollection of a pleasure, or the luxury of a regret. The only way to get rid of a temptation is to yield to it. Resist it, and your soul grows sick with longing for those things it has forbidden to itself, with desire for what its monstrous laws have made monstrous and unlawful" (159). Temptation resisted, Lord Henry suggests, gives rise to the image of a desired yet forbidden object. This overdetermined representation, in turn, mediates between the active body and the reflective mind by forbidding those desires that the soul's monstrous laws proscribe. Thus, these laws—the social representations of self-denial—separate the body as a source of pleasure from the interpretation of that pleasure as sin. By negating pleasure, the natural expression of the body, society (introjected here as "soul") inhibits the body's sensuous potential and circumscribes feeling within established moral codes.

Responding passionately to Lord Henry's critique of this interdictive morality, Dorian senses "entirely fresh influences . . . at work within him [that] really seemed to have come from himself." Since the older man's words counterpose the social to the personal, the desiring associated with self-development to the interdictions of culture, his influence on Dorian emphasizes the sensual as a strategy for resisting society's limitations. "Nothing can cure the soul but the senses, just as nothing can cure the senses but the soul." Although Lord Henry speaks only of the body's sensual possibilities, Dorian uses these words to formulate a new self-image: "The few words that Basil's friend had said to him—words spoken by chance, no doubt, and with willful paradox in them—had touched some secret chord that had never been touched before, but that he felt was now vibrating and throbbing to curious pulses" (160). By defining Dorian's formerly inchoate feelings and sensations, Lord Henry's language creates a new reality for Dorian (". . . mere words. Was there anything so real as words"), and Basil's canvas records Dorian's changing self-image—but only as expressed through Basil's desire. The rivalry between the two older friends for Dorian's affection vitalizes the surface of Basil's painting by attributing an erotic charge to Dorian's body itself. And as this body becomes the object of male attention and representation, the young man's concept of his own material being is transformed—he is "revealed to himself."

Looking on his completed portrait for the first time, Dorian encounters himself as reflected in the "magical mirror" of Basil's desire. This image organizes the disparate perceptions of his body into an apparently self-contained whole and reorients Dorian in relation both to his own identity and to his social context. He begins to conceive of his beauty as his own, failing to understand it as the product of the images that Basil and Lord Harry dialectically provide for him. Wilde describes this change as a physical response, thereby foregrounding the connection between psychic representation and somatic perception while indicating that this seemingly coherent internal representation synthesizes a complex nexus of social relationships. Hence, Dorian's identification with the painted image constitutes a misrecognition as much as a recognition, leading him to confuse an overdetermined set of representations with the "truth" of his experience.

Within these (mis)representations Dorian comes to view his body as distinct from his soul and misrecognizes the certainty of his aging and death. Splitting his self-image into two, Basil's visual representation and Lord Henry's verbal portrait, Dorian internalizes an identity that excites his body only to make it vulnerable to the passage of time. The transitiveness of this new self-recognition manifests itself as physical experience: "As he thought of it [his body's aging] a sharp pang of pain struck through him like a knife and made each delicate fibre of his nature quiver" (167). To avoid aging, Dorian inverts the imaginary and the real and thus conceptualizes the painful disjunction between the image of his body and his body itself as a form of jealousy: "How sad it is! I shall grow old, and horrible, and dreadful. But this picture will always remain young. It will never be older than this particular day of June. . . . If it were only the other way! If it were I who was to be always young, and the picture that was to grow old! For that—for that—I would give everything. Yes there is nothing in the world I would not give! I would give my soul for that" (168). In voicing this statement, Dorian executes a linguistic schism—dividing the "I" against itself—which repositions him within the narrative flow. As the "I" of the speaking character is projected against the visual image of the "I," his body is evacuated and thereby removed from the flow of time.

Dorian stakes his soul for the preservation of his physical beauty, of his body image, and Wilde makes the motive for this wager clear: Dorian fears that time will rob him of the youth that makes him the object of male desire: " 'Yes,' he continued [to Basil], 'I am less to you than your ivory Hermes or your silver faun. You will like them always. How long will you like me? Til I have my first wrinkle, I suppose. I know now, that when one loses one's good looks, whatever they may be, one loses everything. Your picture has taught me that' " (168–69). In portraying Dorian's self-perception as a function of Basil's erotic and aesthetic appreciation, Wilde fuses the artifacts of homoerotic desire and the representations that Dorian uses to constitute his identity. The classical images of male beauty and eroticism make Dorian jealous because he fails to understand that the body can have simultaneous aesthetic and erotic appeal. His focus on visual and sexual desirability emphasizes the importance that culturally produced representations have in the construction of male identity.

In describing Dorian's identity as a product of aesthetic and erotic images, Wilde locates "the problem" of male homoerotic desire on the terrain of representation itself. Since his characters encounter one another at the limits of heterosexual forms, they produce multiple positionings for articulating different desires, evoking possibilities for male same-sex eroticism without explicitly voicing them. Instead, Wilde posits many uncovered secrets (Basil's "secret," Dorian's "secrets," Lord Henry's continual revelation of the "secrets of life," even the absent portrait itself), thereby creating a logic of displacement that culminates in Dorian's prayer for eternal youth. Standing outside the text and yet initiating all further narrative development, the prayer is marked only by a caesura that transforms the relation between representation and desire. In a moment of textual silence, Dorian—misperceiving the true object of Basil's feeling—defends his idealized self-image by invoking the magical aspects of utterance. To maintain his identity as the object of another man's desire, he prays to exchange the temporality of his existence for the stasis of an erotically charged visual representation. Inasmuch as Basil's secret—his "worship with far more romance than a man usually gives a friend" (in the 1890 edition)—radiates from the canvas reflecting its subject's beauty, Dorian's profession, "I am in love with it, Basil. It is part of myself. I feel that," underscores the degree to which his male self-image reverberates with the passion of same-sex desire. And this passionate attachment inspires the supplication that makes his portrait perhaps the most well-known nonexistent painting in Western culture.

Not coincidentally, then, the famous reversal between the character and his portrait first appears to stem from the failure of the novel's only explicitly heterosexual element. By introducing the feminine into a world that systematically denies it, Dorian's attraction to the young actress Sibyl Vane (a vain portent?) seems to violate the male-identified world in which Basil and Lord Henry have "revealed [Dorian] to himself." Yet, Sibyl's presence can never actually disturb the novel's male logic, for her appearance merely shows how much an overtly heterosexual discourse depends on male-defined representations of female experience. For Dorian, Sibyl exists only in the drama. Offstage, he imbues her with an aesthetic excess, so that her reality never pierces his fantasy. His remarks to Lord Henry demonstrate that Dorian's passion is the passion of the voyeur, whose desiring gaze distances the viewer from the possibility (necessity?) of physical consummation:

"Tonight she is Imogen," [Dorian] answered, "and tomorrow she will be Juliet."
"When is she Sibyl Vane?"
"Never." (200)

When Dorian impassions Sibyl with a single kiss (the only physical [sexual?] expression that evades his aesthetic voyeurism), her own real passion renders her incapable of making a male-defined representation of female passion "real." Thus she fails to achieve the aesthetic standard he expects of her in the role of Juliet, and Dorian—unable to sustain his heterosexual fantasy—abandons her.[14]

This abandonment leads Sibyl to suicide and introduces the disjunction between Dorian and his portrait. Returning home after his final scene with her, Dorian finds the picture changed, marked by "lines of cruelty around his mouth as clearly as if he had been looking into a mirror after he had done some dreadful thing" (240). He senses anew that this representation "held the secret of his life, and told *his story*" (242; my emphasis). Where once the painting had been confined to the atemporality of the aesthetic moment, it now becomes the surface that records the narrative of his life, not only serving as a static reflection of the interiority of his soul but also telling his soul's story. A "magical mirror," it turns Dorian into a "spectator of [his] own life," thus creating a divided consciousness that initiates the remaining action in the novel.

As Dorian realizes the separation between self-representation and self-image, his behavior becomes ominous and degenerate. He enters into a world of self-abuse and destruction, through which he effects the downfall of many innocent men and women, and yet his body shows no sign of these activities.

Only the picture—now locked away in an inaccessible room—reveals the depths to which he has descended. For, as the portrait tells his story, it graphically reveals the details of all he does. In time, the portrait's increasing grotesqueness begins to haunt Dorian. His awareness of the terrifying gap between the man whom others see and the representation that only he may view serves as the limit against which he conceives of his existence. He immerses himself in the life of the senses to test the absoluteness of this limit but finds that he cannot break through it. So long as he remains inscribed within the network of representations—both verbal and visual—that the painting constructs, he can only embody the agonizing dichotomy that it engenders.

Ultimately, seeking to free himself from the images that have ensnared and "destroyed" him, Dorian kills the man who "authored" the "fatal portrait." This murder removes the one person to whom Dorian could impute responsibility for the portrait. The picture, which now also depicts the horror of Basil's death, remains only to remind Dorian of the monstrosity of his life. In the final pages of the novel, Dorian resolves to destroy the image. Standing before it, he faces both the material representation of his existence and the distance between that representation and himself. As he plunges the knife into the canvas that reveals his secret, he rends this disjunction, finally breaking free of its absolute limit. Yet, since the price of this freedom is the destruction of the complex configuration of images that motivate both the character and the narrative, the act that concludes the novel does so only by killing Dorian into art.

As his death brings the interplay between representation and the body full circle, the images that Dorian had reflected through his entry into the male-defined world presented by Basil Hallward and Lord Henry Wotton are once again inscribed on his body. And so, in the end, Dorian's corpse becomes the surface that records his narrative, liberating Dorian in death from the consciousness divided between experience and representation that had marked his life.

CODA: OUT OF THE THEORETICAL CLOSET

To the extent that Wilde and contemporaries like him were beginning to articulate strategies to communicate—both to themselves and to others—the experience of homoerotic desire, their texts enact and virtually embody this desire. But since these men were also writing within a larger culture that not only denied but actively prosecuted such embodiments, they were forced to devise ways to mediate their expressions of passion. While in certain uncanonized genres, like pornography and to some extent poetry (e.g., the "Uranian" poets), relatively explicit statements of same-sex eroticism were possible, these statements were still posed in relation to the social norms that enjoined them. Thus, although *Teleny* explicitly represents sexual practices between men for an audience who either enjoyed or at least sympathized with such practices, it still reinscribes these representations within the (hetero)sexual symbolic order that it sought to interrupt. In a more canonized work, such as *The Picture of Dorian Gray*, the mediations are necessarily more complex. Wilde's text doubly displaces male homoerotic desire, thematizing it through the aesthetic production of a medium that the novel cannot represent. Basil's portrait of Dorian can embody his desire for the eponymous character, and yet male homoerotic passion remains, in the dominant representational codes of the period, *peccatum illude horribile non nominandum inter christanos*—or, in a bad paraphrase of Lord Alfred Douglas, a love whose name the text dare not speak. In *The Picture of Dorian Gray*, Wilde problematizes representation per se to move athwart the historical limitations that define male homosexuality as "unnameable," thereby creating one of the most lasting icons of male homoerotic desire.

By approaching *Teleny* and *The Picture of Dorian Gray* as complex cultural artifacts, we recognize them not just as texts but as contexts. For, as Raymond Williams says, "If art is a part of the society, there is no solid whole, outside it, to which by the form of our question, we concede priority" (45). Instead of seeing these literary works as ideological reflections of an already existing reality, we must consider them elements in the production of this reality. In analyzing the textual strategies through which these two novels put male desire for other men into discourse, we begin to understand some of the historical forms that such relations between men took and thereby begin to suggest others that they can take.[15]

Notes

1. Press reports of the trials note that court attendance was exclusively male. The defendant, the prosecution, all the court officials, as well as the audience and press, were also male; hence all that transpired and all that was reported occurred within an entirely male-defined social space for the benefit of a male public.

2. For the theoretical underpinnings of this argument see Michel Foucault's *History of Sexuality*. Here Foucault counters the post-Freudian notion that Victorian practice repressed natural sexuality and, instead, considers the positive strategies that enveloped the body within particular historical discursive apparatuses. He suggests that the bourgeoisie's concern with regulating its own sexual practices stemmed not from an interdictive moral ideology but rather from an attempt to define its materiality—its body—as a class: "The emphasis on the body should undoubtedly be linked to the process of growth and establishment of bourgeois hegemony: not, however, because of the market value assumed by labor capacity, but because of what the 'cultivation' of its own body could represent politically, economically, and historically for the present and the future of the bourgeoisie" (125–26).

3. That "homosexuality" stood in a negative relation to "heterosexuality" is metaphorically indicated by the term *invert*, which historically preceded *homosexual* and often served as a synonym (see Chauncey for a more precise explanation of these two terms). Since this essay attempts to explore two particular textual negotiations of the emerging heterosexual-homosexual

opposition, the use of both these terms here seems anachronistic. Thus, I use them advisedly and often quarantine them between quotation marks to indicate that I am quoting from the larger cultural (con)text in which they have become commonplace. In a recent article Tim Calligan, Bob Connell, and John Lee note the enduring effects of this opposition (587). For details of the development of "the adolescent," see Ariès; Gillis, *Youth;* Gorham; and Donzelot. On "the criminal," see Lombroso's *Criminal Man* and *The Female Offender.* Judith Walkowitz details the emergence of "the prostitute." For "the delinquent" see Foucault, *Discipline,* and Gillis, "Evolution." On "the homosexual" see Weeks, *Coming Out;* Plummer; Faderman; Katz; and Chauncey.

4. The term belongs to Gayle Rubin, who initially defined it as "the set of arrangements by which a society transforms biological sexuality into products of human activity and in which these transformed sexual needs are satisfied" (159).

5. For a comprehensive survey of the critical appraisal of Wilde as "decadent" and "dandy," see Gagnier, especially ch. 2, "Dandies and Gentlemen."

6. I take the concept "interruption" from David Silverman and Brian Torode, who define it as a practice that "seeks not to impose a language of its own but to enter critically into existing linguistic configurations, and to re-open the closed structures into which they have ossified" (6). This notion of interruption as a critical refiguring of ossified linguistic structures—itself a wonderful metaphor for ideological attempts to petrify historically constructed, hegemonically organized semiotic equivalences into timeless, natural usages—provides an excellent analytical tool for examining subcultural discourses that challenge a dominant culture's monovocalizing practices. I apply it to resistant or counterhegemonic textual strategies that reopen the polyvalence of linguistic practices—here specifically the homoerotic challenge to the conception of heterosexuality as natural.

7. This account is paraphrased from Winston Leyland's introduction to the Gay Sunshine reprint of *Teleny.* Leyland takes most of his information from H. M. Hyde's introduction to the 1966 British edition, which Hyde derives in part from the introduction of a 1934 French translation written by Leonard Hirsch, the London bookseller whose shop was supposedly the transfer point for the various authors.

8. This terminology, which is implicit throughout my essay, derives from Gilles Deleuze and Félix Guattari. They develop the metaphors of "marking the body" and "recording surfaces of desire" to elaborate the mechanisms through which desire invests somatic experience as well as to consider the ways in which the socius "codes" the body. See especially their part 3, "Savages, Barbarians, Civilized Men."

9. For a discussion of these initial apologies for homoerotic behavior see Jeffrey Weeks, *Coming Out* and *Sexuality and Its Discontents.* On the body-mind dichotomy in nineteenth-century discourse, see Rosalind Coward.

10. For a selection of articles showing how the contemporary press responded to *Dorian Gray,* along with Wilde's replies to these criticisms, see Stuart Mason. Later explanations of the relation between Wilde's personal and textual sexuality include G. Wilson Knight's "Christ and Wilde," which attributes Wilde's "perverse pleasures" (138, quoting Wilde's *De Profundis*) to his "mother fixation," to his mother's having "dressed him as a girl until he was nine," and to his "love of flowers and of male and female dress." Knight reads *Dorian Gray* as the "subtlest critique of the Platonic Eros ever penned" (143)—without stooping to textual exegesis—and then justifies Wilde's "homosexual engagements" as "a martyrdom, a crucifixion, a self-exhibition in agony and shame" deriving from both "the instinct . . . to plunge low when disparity between near-integrated self and the community becomes unbearable" and "a genuine liking for the lower orders of society" (144–45). Richard Ellmann informs us that Wilde changes the date of Dorian's murder of Basil Hallward from "the eve of his own thirty-second birthday" in the original Lippincott's version to "the eve of his own thirty-eighth birthday" in the bound edition to mask the reference to his first sexual experience with Robbie Ross, which—according to a mathematical extrapolation from Ross's memoirs—must have occurred during Wilde's

thirty-second year (11). Other critical works that acknowledge Wilde's homosexuality without analyzing the "homotextual problematic" include those by Philip Cohen, Jeffrey Meyers, and Christopher Nassaar. Meyers is especially interesting, given his explicit project of examining the homosexual "in" literature, but unfortunately his eclectic methodology quickly descends into the biographical and associational strategies that characterize most criticism on *Dorian Gray*.

11. My use of "double consciousness" derives largely from Jack Winkler's article relating the work of Sappho as a lesbian poet to the public discourse of the Greek polis. Winkler develops a concept reminiscent of W. E. B. Du Bois's notion of the "twoness" of the Afro-American experience (16–17) to refer to the overdetermined conditions of Sappho's representations. Because of her "double consciousness," Winkler suggests, the marginalized poet can speak and write in the dominant discourse but subvert its monolithic truth claims by recasting them in the light of personal, subcultural experience: "This amounts to a reinterpretation of the kinds of meaning previous claims had, rather than a mere contest of claimants for supremacy in a category whose meaning is agreed upon" (73). Applying this theory of "reinterpretation," I conclude that Wilde repeatedly deals with heterosexual morality to deconstruct its social force through wit and witticism.

12. On the connections between the construction of male sexual identity, visual eroticism, and desire see Jane Gallop's discussion of French feminist theory. Also see Toril Moi's suggestion, in her discussion of the readings of Freud in the texts of Luce Irigaray, that "the gaze [is] a phallic activity linked to anal desire for the sadistic mastery of the object" (134).

13. Gallop connects "phallic suppression" and the evacuation of the body (67).

14. Many of Sibyl's roles involve her cross-dressing as a boy, which further complicates the problematic construction of heterosexual desire within the novel. For example, playing Rosalind dressed as a boy, she stirs the desire of Orlando, who is saved from the "horror" of this same-sex passion by the underlying premise that the boy is indeed a girl. (Of course, in Shakespearean theater, where boys played the female characters, the complexities were redoubled.) Dorian's remark on Sibyl's "perfection" in boy's clothes and *Portrait of Mr. W. H.*, which argues for the homoerotic inspiration of Shakespeare's sonnets, would both indicate that Wilde intended this resonance.

15. I wish to express my gratitude to all those who have commented on the numerous successive versions of this article. I especially wish to thank Regenia Gagnier, whose enthusiasm and support have encouraged me to persevere; Mary Pratt, who has taught me by her example that care and concern are the most essential elements of good scholarship; and Mark Frankel, at whose desk in Lytton basement this essay was first begun and to whom it is dedicated.

Works Cited

Ariès, P. *Centuries of Childhood*. Trans. Robert Baldick. London: Cape, 1962.

Calligan, Tim, Bob Connell, and John Lee. "Towards a New Sociology of Masculinity." *Theory and Society* 14.5 (1985): 551–604.

Chauncey, George. "From Sexual Inversion to Homosexuality." *Salmagundi* 58–59 (1982–83): 114–46.

Cohen, Philip. *The Moral Vision of Oscar Wilde*. London: Fairleigh Dickinson UP, 1978.

Cominos, P. "Late Victorian Sexual Respectability and the Social System." *International Review of Social History* 8 (1963): 18–48, 216–50.

Connell, R. W. "Class, Patriarchy and Sartre's Theory of Practice." *Theory and Society* 11 (1982): 305–20.

Coward, Rosalind. *Patriarchal Precedents*. London: Routledge, 1983.

Deleuze, Gilles, and Félix Guattari. *Anti-Oedipus: Capitalism and Schizophrenia*. Trans. Robert Hurley, Mark Seem, and Helen R. Lane. New York: Viking, 1977.

Donzelot, Jacques. *The Policing of Families.* Trans. Robert Hurley. New York: Pantheon, 1979.

Du Bois, W. E. B. *The Soul of Black Folks.* Greenwich: Fawcett, 1961.

Ellmann, Richard. "The Critic as Artist as Wilde." *Wilde and the Nineties.* Ed. Charles Ryskamp. Princeton: Princeton U Library, 1966. 1–20.

Faderman, Lillian. *Surpassing the Love of Men.* New York: Morrow, 1981.

Foucault, Michel. *Discipline and Punish.* Trans. Alan Sheridan. New York: Vintage, 1979.

———. *The History of Sexuality.* Vol. 1. New York: Vintage, 1980.

Gagnier, Regenia. *Idylls of the Marketplace: Oscar Wilde and the Victorian Public.* Stanford: Stanford UP, 1986.

Gallop, Jane. *The Daughter's Seduction: Feminism and Psychoanalysis.* Ithaca: Cornell UP, 1982.

Gilbert, Arthur. "Buggery and the British Navy, 1700–1861." *Journal of Social History* 10.1 (1976): 72–97.

Gillis, John. "The Evolution of Delinquency, 1890–1914." *Past and Present* 67 (1975): 96–126.

———. *Youth and History.* New York: Academic, 1974.

Gorham, Deborah. *The Victorian Girl and the Feminine Ideal.* Bloomington: Indiana UP, 1982.

Hyde, H. Montgomery. *The Trials of Oscar Wilde.* London: Hodge, 1948.

Katz, Jonathan. *Gay/Lesbian Almanac.* New York: Harper, 1983.

Knight, G. Wilson. "Christ and Wilde." *Oscar Wilde: A Collection of Critical Essays.* Ed. Richard Ellmann. Englewood Cliffs: Prentice, 1969. 138–50.

Leyland, Winston. Introduction. Wilde, *Teleny* 5–19.

Lombroso, Caesar. *Criminal Man.* London, 1875.

———. *The Female Offender.* New York, 1897.

Marcus, Steven. *The Other Victorians.* New York: Basic, 1964.

Mason, Stuart. *Oscar Wilde: Art and Morality.* New York: Haskell, 1971.

Meyers, Jeffrey. *Homosexuality and Literature.* London: Athlone, 1977.

Moi, Toril. *Sexual/Textual Politics: Feminist Literary Theory.* New York: Methuen, 1985.

Nassaar, Christopher. *Into the Demon Universe.* New Haven: Yale UP, 1974.

Plummer, Kenneth, ed. *The Making of the Modern Homosexual.* London: Hutchinson, 1981.

Rubin, Gayle. "The Traffic in Women." *Towards an Anthropology of Women.* Ed. Rayna Reiter. New York: Monthly Review, 1975. 157–210.

Sedgwick, Eve Kosofsky. *Between Men: English Literature and Male Homosocial Desire.* New York: Columbia UP, 1985.

Silverman, David, and Brian Torode. *The Material World.* London: Routledge, 1980.

Thomas, Keith. "The Double Standard." *Journal of the History of Ideas* 20.2 (1959): 195–216.

Trumbach, Randolph. "London's Sodomites: Homosexual Behavior and Western Culture in the 18th Century." *Journal of Social History* 11.1 (1977): 1–33.

Walkowitz, Judith. *Prostitution and Victorian Society.* New York: Cambridge UP, 1980.

Weeks, Jeffrey. *Coming Out: Homosexual Politics in Britain from the Nineteenth Century to the Present.* New York: Quartet, 1977.

———. *Sexuality and Its Discontents.* London: Routledge, 1985.

Wilde, Oscar. "The Picture of Dorian Gray." *Lippincott's Monthly Magazine* July 1890: 3–100.

———. *The Picture of Dorian Gray. The Portable Oscar Wilde.* Ed. R. Aldington and S. Weintraub. New York: Viking, 1974.

———. *Teleny.* San Francisco: Gay Sunshine, 1984.

Williams, Raymond. *The Long Revolution.* London: Chatto, 1961.

Winkler, Jack. "Garden of Nymphs: Public and Private in Sappho's Lyrics." *Women's Studies* 8 (1981): 65–91.

[Style and Socialism]

CHRISTOPHER HITCHENS

In England prisoners are detained "at Her Majesty's pleasure" and are therefore often ironically termed "guests of Her Majesty." After his years in Reading Gaol, during which he was witness to the flogging of a mentally deficient inmate and the dismissal of a warder who showed kindness to a child locked up for poaching rabbits, Oscar Wilde observed, "If this is how Her Majesty treats them, then she doesn't deserve to *have* any prisoners." I could not find this biting comment in Richard Ellmann's voluminous new biography of Wilde, nor could I detect this aspect of Wilde from any of the book's flattering reviews, most of which have represented him as a sort of sumptuous fop, possessed of a dangerous vanity, whose tale may be told as an example of hubris.

Yet the salient point about Wilde was the economy and address of his wit. He did not froth with bons mots like some second-rate charmer. He was a tough and determined Irishman who more than once flattened bullies with his fist, and most of the time—if we exempt pardonable and tempting sallies about blue china and decorative screens—his drawling remarks were not snobbish or mannered. I suppose that people need to see him as a species of languid dandy, which is why *The Soul of Man Under Socialism* is almost never discussed when dear Oscar's name comes up.

Try to find that essay in any of the current anthologies of Wilde. First published in 1891, it was geldingly retitled *The Soul of Man* while Wilde was in prison. It expressed the sensibility that had impelled him to take the side of the Irish rebels and, in particular, to oppose the British government's attempted frame-up of Charles Stewart Parnell, who, like Wilde, was destroyed on a charge of immorality when all else had failed. It gave Wilde the same distinction as that which he acquired by being the only writer in London to sign George Bernard Shaw's petition for the Haymarket martyrs. And it contains the following imperishable sentence: "The chief advantage that would result from the establishment of Socialism is, undoubtedly, the fact that Socialism would relieve us from that sordid necessity of living for others which, in the present condition of things, presses so hardly upon almost everybody." This is not the

Reprinted from *The Nation* magazine February 20, 1988, "Minority Report," p. 223. Copyright *The Nation* magazine/The Nation Company, Inc., 1988.

flippant remark that philistines might take it to be. It is in fact what is truly meant by "compassion," a word now made to sound sickening in the mouths of Democratic hypocrites.

What those hypocrites mean when they intone the hack word "compassion" is that we should not forget the needy and the desperate as we pursue our glorious path of self-advancement. This is the rough equivalent of the older injunction that we should remember the wretched in our prayers. Wilde was proposing something infinitely more daring and intelligent—that we regard poverty, ugliness and the exploitation of others as something repulsive to ourselves. If we see a slum, a ghetto, a beggar, or an old person eating pet food, we should not waste pity on the victim. We should want the abolition of such conditions for our own sakes. The burden of enduring them is too much.

This is why early socialists were quite proud to be accused of spitting in the face of charity. The principle that an injury to one is an injury to all is not just talk; it is the expression of a solidarity that recognizes mutual interest. As Wilde also wrote, in his review of Edward Carpenter's *Chants of Labour,* "For to make men Socialists is nothing, but to make Socialism human is a great thing." His appreciation of paradox here makes an excellent match with his rejection of sentimentality.

There is another sense in which it would be nice to think that Wilde intended his insight about "living for others." In the great working-class novel *The Ragged Trousered Philanthropists* the laborer Robert Tressell describes the feelings of charity and gratitude that overwhelm the credulous, patriotic men who worked alongside him. They were content to spend their entire lives living for others—their betters—each of them confident of his own sturdy independence. This type did not disappear with the waning of the Industrial Revolution. You can meet him today, the despair of "progressive" intellectuals, as he bellies up to the bar with his "can't fool me" talk and proceeds to speak, sometimes using the very same phrases, in the tones of the President's last lying paean to native virtues. Praise for these philanthropists, especially at times when they are needed to be expended in war, is the only official rhetoric you hear that mentions the word "class." Almost the only place that class distinctions are stressed these days is at the Vietnam Veterans Memorial.

They deserve to be stressed more often. Society labors on, supporting both an enormously wealthy upper class, whose corporate holdings are frequently tax free or even tax subsidized, and a growing underclass, which is sporadically and pathetically cited as a spur to conscience. Never is it asked, What are these classes *for?*

A sort of moral blackmail is exerted from both poles. The underclass, one gathers, should be dulled with charity and welfare provision lest it turn nasty. The upper class must likewise be conciliated by vast handouts, lest it lose the "incentive" to go on generating wealth. A rising tide, as we have recently learned, does not lift all boats, nor does a falling tide sink them all. If people were to recognize that they are all in the same boat, they would take better care of its furnishings, its comfort and its general décor. This is what Wilde meant by the importance of the aesthetic.

Radicals have been taught to distrust any too-great display of individualism, and where they forget this lesson there are always conservatives to remind them (a madly sweet but slightly lugubrious example of this style appears in the current *New Criterion,* reprobating my good self). Wilde himself was haunted by a Podhoretz-like chaplain in prison, who reported that the cell reeked of semen. (How could he tell?) We are in the debt of the brave man who taught us to ask, of their majesties, whether they deserve us, or our continued amiable subservience.

PART 2
WILDEAN WIT:
THE IMPORTANCE OF
BEING EARNEST

◆

Oscar Wilde and the
English Epicene

Camille A. Paglia

Oscar Wilde is the premier documenter of a sexual persona which I call the Androgyne of Manners, embodied in Lord Henry Wotton of *The Picture of Dorian Gray* and in the four young lovers of *The Importance of Being Earnest*. The Androgyne of Manners inhabits the world of the drawing room and creates that world wherever it goes, through manner and mode of speech. The salon is an abstract circle in which male and female, like mathematical ciphers, are equal and interchangeable; personality becomes a sexually undifferentiated formal mask. Rousseau says severely of the eighteenth-century salon, "Every woman at Paris gathers in her apartment a harem of men more womanish than she." The salon is politics by coterie, a city-state or gated forum run on a barter economy of gender exchange.

Elegance, the ruling principle of the salon, dictates that all speech must be wit, in symmetrical pulses of repartee, a malicious stichomythia. Pope's complaint that Lady Mary Wortley Montagu and the epicene Lord Hervey had "too much wit" for him alludes to the icy cruelty of the beau monde, to which moral discourse is alien because it posits the superiority of the inner life to the outer. Sartre says of Genet, "Elegance: the quality of conduct which transforms the greatest quantity of being into appearing." The salon, like the object-realm venerated by the esthete, is a spectacle of dazzling surfaces—words, faces, and gestures exhibited in a blaze of hard glamour.

Occasionally, Pope was drawn to the idea of spiritual hermaphroditism. But he was deeply hostile to the Androgyne of Manners, whom he satirizes as the Amazonian belles and effeminate beaux of *The Rape of the Lock,* because this psychological type is ahistorical in its worship of the ephemeral. The salon is populated by sophisticates of a classical literacy, but its speed of dialogue inhibits deliberation and reflection, recklessly breaking with the past through fashionable irresponsibility. Pope might have said, had the word been available, that the salon was too chic. The Androgyne of Manners—the male feminine in his careless, lounging passivity, the female masculine in her brilliant, aggressive wit—has the profane sleekness of chic.

Reprinted by permission from *Raritan: A Quarterly Review* 4, no. 3 (Winter 1985): 85–109. © 1985 by *Raritan,* 165 College Avenue, New Brunswick, NJ 08903.

In the Decadent nineties, before his career abruptly ended in arrest and imprisonment, Wilde was moving towards an Art Nouveau esthetics. Art Nouveau, then at its height of decorative popularity, is a late phase in the history of style, in many ways analogous to Italian Mannerism. Kenneth Clark says of one of Giambologna's streamlined Mannerist bronzes:

> The goddess of mannerism is the eternal feminine of the fashion plate. A sociologist could no doubt give ready answers why embodiments of elegance should take this somewhat ridiculous shape—feet and hands too fine for honest work, bodies too thin for childbearing, and heads too small to contain a single thought. But elegant proportions may be found in many objects that are exempt from these materialist explanations—in architecture, pottery, or even handwriting. The human body is not the basis of these rhythms but their victim. Where the sense of chic originates, how it is controlled, by what inner pattern we unfailingly recognize it—all these are questions too large and too subtle for a parenthesis. One thing is certain. Chic is not natural. Congreve's Millamant or Baudelaire's dandy warns us how hateful, to serious votaries of chic, is everything that is implied by the word "nature."

Smoothness and elongation, the Mannerist figure is a series of polished ovoids hung on a mannequin's frame. Lord Henry Wotton, with his "long, nervous fingers," is an ectomorph, an undulating ribbon of Mannerist Art Nouveau. The ectomorphic line is a suave vertical, repudiating nature by its resistance to gravity, but the Mannerist figure, overcome by worldly fatigue, sinks back toward earth in languorous torsion. The Androgyne of Manners may be seen in complete effete collapse in Henry Lamb's painting of Lytton Strachey turning his back to a window, his long denatured limbs draped over an armchair like wet noodles. Because of its swift verbal genius, however, the Androgyne of Manners is best represented as sleekness and speed. Count Robert de Montesquiou, the decadent model for Huysmans's Des Esseintes and Proust's Charlus, was once described as a "greyhound in evening dress," a phrase we might readily apply to Lord Henry Wotton.

Sleekness in a male is usually a hermaphroditic motive. Cinema, the cardinal medium of modern sexual representation, evokes this theme in its topos of the well-bred English "gentleman," a word of such special connotations that it cannot be perfectly translated into any other language. From the thirties through the fifties, movies used actors of this type to illustrate a singular male beauty, witty and polished, uniting sensitivity of response to intense heterosexual glamour: Leslie Howard, Rex Harrison, Cary Grant, David Niven, Michael Wilding, Fred Astaire. The idiomatic representational qualities here are smoothness and elongation, smooth both in manner and appearance, long in ectomorphic height and cranial contour. I think, for instance, of the astounding narrowness of Cary Grant's shiny black evening pumps in *Indiscreet*. The smoothness and elongation of figure are best shown off by a gleaming tuxedo, which signifies a renunciation of masculine hirsutism. The cinematic "gentle-man" is always prematurely balding, with swept-back hair at the temples. His receding hairline is sexually expressive, suggesting hermaphroditic gentility, a grace of intellect and emotion. His sleek head is a promise of candor and courtesy, of eroticism without ambivalence or suffering. Smoothness always has an exclusively social meaning: it is nature subdued by the civil made second nature.

In *The Importance of Being Earnest,* the English gentleman, in whom the crudely masculine has been moderated by courtesy, may be seen turning into the Androgyne of Manners, in whom smoothness has become the cold glossiness of a bronze surface, like the "armored look" (*Panzerhaft*) of Bronzino's Mannerist portraits. Meeting and finally mating with their counter-parts, the Art Nouveau androgynes of the play speak Wilde's characteristic language, the epicene witticism, analogous to their formal personae in its hardness, smoothness, and elongation. The Wildean epigram, like a Giambologna bronze, is immediately identifiable by a slim spareness, an imperious separateness, and a perverse elegance. Speech in Wilde is made as hard and glittering as possible; it follows the Wildean personality into the visual realm. Normally, it is pictorialism that gives literature a visual character. But there are few metaphors in Wilde and no complex syntactical units. Vocabulary and sentence structure are amazingly simple, arising from the vernacular of the accomplished raconteur. Yet Wilde's bon mots are so condensed that they become *things,* artifacts. Without metaphor, the language leaps into concreteness.

Language in Wilde aspires to an Apollonian hierarchism. His epigrams turn language from the Dionysian Many into the Apollonian One, for as an aphoristic phrase form and conversation stopper, the epigram thwarts real dialogue, cutting itself off from a past and a future in its immediate social context and glorying in its aristocratic solitude. It is the language of the Apollonian lawgiver, arbitrarily assigning form, proportion, and measure. A character in Wilde's *An Ideal Husband* declares, "Women are never disarmed by compliments. Men always are. That is the difference between the sexes." The iron rod of classification is thrust before us—even if it does not fall where expected. In form and in content, the Wildean epigram is a triumph of rhetorical self-containment. No one in English, or probably any other modern language, has produced a series of utterances more mysteriously delimited. The epigram, as practiced in the Renaissance, was a poem of sharply ironic or sententious concluding verses. But the *epigramma* of antiquity was literally an inscription, as on a tombstone. Wilde may therefore be said to have restored the epigram to its original representational character, for his language has a hieroglyphic exactitude and cold rhetorical stoniness, separating itself from its background by the Apollonian incised edge.

In *The Importance of Being Earnest* the courtship of youth and maiden, at the traditional heart of comedy, loses its emotional color in the Wildean transformation of content into form, of soul into surface. Jack Worthing and Algernon Moncrieff, idle gentlemen-about-town, and Gwendolen Fairfax and Cecily Cardew, the well-bred objects of their affections, are all Androgynes of Manners. They have no sex because they have no real sexual feelings. The interactions of the play are governed by the formalities of social life, which emerge with dancelike ritualism. The key phrase of the English fin de siècle was Lionel Johnson's axiom, "Life must be a ritual." In *The Picture of Dorian Gray* Wilde says: "The canons of good society are, or should be, the same as the canons of art. Form is absolutely essential to it. It should have the dignity of a ceremony, as well as its unreality." In *The Importance of Being Earnest* the ceremony of social form is stronger than gender, shaping the personae to its public purpose and turning the internal world into the external.

The play's supreme enforcer of form is Lady Bracknell, who remarks with satisfaction, "We live, I regret to say, in an age of surfaces." In a stage direction to another play, Wilde says of a lord's butler: "The distinction of Phipps is his impassivity. . . . He is a mask with a manner. Of his intellectual or emotional life, history knows nothing. He represents the dominance of form." An optimal performance of *The Importance of Being Earnest* would be a romance of surfaces, male and female alike wearing masks of superb impassivity. The Anthony Asquith film, made in 1952, though it shortens and questionably edits the text, comes close to achieving this. Joan Greenwood's entranced and nearly somnambulistic performance as Gwendolen—slow, stately, and ceremonious —is the brilliant realization of the Wildean esthetic. But the effort to make Dorothy Tutin's Cecily sympathetic at Gwendolen's expense is sentimentally intrusive, a misreading of the play disordering the symmetry between the two young ladies, twin androgynes who fight each other to a standoff.

Productions of *The Importance of Being Earnest* are often weakened by flights of Forest of Arden lyricism which turn what is sexually ambiguous in Wilde into the conventionally heterosexual. The hieratic purity of the play could best be appreciated if all the women's roles were taken by female impersonators. Language, personality, and behavior should be so hard that the play becomes a spectacle of visionary coldness. The faces should be like glass, without gender or humanity. *The Importance of Being Earnest* takes place in Spenser's Apollonian "world of glas," a realm of glittering, sharp-edged objects. Chapman says of the goddess Ceremony, "all her bodie was / Cleere and transparent as the purest glasse." Gwendolen and Cecily are the goddess Ceremony conversing with herself, her body transparent because she is without an inner life. That Wilde may well have thought of his characters in such terms is suggested in *The Picture of Dorian Gray,* where Lord Henry Wotton longs for "a mask of glass" to shield one from the "sulphurous fumes" of life.

Gwendolen is the first of the women to enact a drama of form. Soliciting Jack to propose to her, she announces in advance that she will accept him but still insists that her bewildered suitor perform the traditional ritual, on his knees. Gwendolen's thoughts never stray from the world of appearances. At the climax of their romantic interlude, she says to Jack, "I hope you will always look at me just like that, especially when there are other people present." This voyeuristic series of observers is a psychosexual topos of Decadent Late Romanticism, first occurring in 1835 in Gautier's *Mademoiselle de Maupin*. Gwendolen imagines Jack looking at her while she looks at others looking at *them*. As a worshipper of form, Gwendolen craves not emotion but display, the theater of social life.

Gwendolen's self-observing detachment is exhibited by Cecily in precisely the same situation. When Algernon ardently declares his love for her, Cecily replies, "If you will allow me, I will copy your remarks into my diary." Emotion is immediately dispatched into a self-reflexive Mannerist torsion. Going to her writing table, Cecily exhorts her suitor to continue his protestations: "I delight in taking down from dictation." Intimacy is swelled into oratory, and poor Algernon is like Alice grown suddenly too big for the White Rabbit's house. Despite their impending marriage, Cecily declares it quite out of the question for Algernon to see her diary. Nevertheless, it is "meant for publication": "When it appears in volume form I hope you will order a copy." The Sibylline archivist, with professional impartiality, grants no special privileges to her sources of data.

Never for a moment in the play are Gwendolen and Cecily persuasively "female." They are creatures of indeterminate sex who take up the mask of femininity to play a new and provocative role. The dandified Algernon and Jack are simply supporting actors whom the women boldly stage manage. Gwendolen and Cecily are adepts of a dramaturgical alchemy: they are Cerberuses on constant guard to defend the play against encroachment by the internal, which they magically transform into the external. *The Importance of Being Earnest* is one long process of crystallization of the immaterial into the material, of emotion into self-conscious personae. In Shakespeare's volatile Rosalind and Cleopatra, automanipulation of personae arises from a Renaissance abundance of emotion, which flows into a multiplicity of psychodramatic forms. But Wilde's Gwendolen and Cecily inhabit a far more stringently demarcated world, the salon of the Androgyne of Manners, and their personae are radically despiritualized, efflorescences not of psyche but of couture.

Lady Bracknell, too, ruthlessly subordinates persons to form. If Algernon does not come to dinner, "It would put my table completely out," and Lord Bracknell will be exiled upstairs. In one of Wilde's most wonderful lines, Lady Bracknell rebukes Jack for being an orphan: "To lose one parent, Mr. Worthing, may be regarded as a misfortune; to lose both looks like carelessness." Matters of form are uppermost, in death as in life. The emotional intensities of Victorian bereavement are cancelled. Nothing is of interest but the public impression. Once again there is the Late Romantic stress upon visual cognition: "may be *regarded* as a misfortune;" "*looks* like carelessness." Every event occurs with naked visibility on a vast, flat expanse; life is a play scrutinized by a ring of appraising eyes. This illustrates one of Wilde's central principles, as cited by Dorian Gray: "To become the spectator of one's own life is to escape the suffering of life." Late Romantic spectatorship is an escape from suffering because all affect is transferred from the emotional and tangible into the visual: no wounds can pierce the glassy body of the Wildean androgyne. The self is without a biological or historical identity. Self-originating, it has no filial indebtedness. A parent is merely a detail of social heraldry. To lose both parents, therefore, is not tragedy but negligence, like tipping the tea service into the trashbin.

The liturgy of the religion of form of which Lady Bracknell is a communicant, and in which she has instructed her daughter Gwendolen, is determined by fashion, whose bible is any one of "the more expensive monthly magazines." Lady Bracknell declares, "Style largely depends on the way the chin is worn. They are worn very high, just at present." The chin is imperiously "worn" like an article of clothing because the human figure is merely decorative, like the mummy's foot which serves as a paperweight in a Gautier tale. There is a latent surrealism here, for once the chin, like the eyebrow of Gautier's hieratic Cleopatra, has been detached from the body by Decadent partition, there is no reason why it cannot be worn elsewhere—on the shoulder, perhaps, or hip. Gwendolen, requesting Cecily's permission to examine her through a lorgnette (Cecily graciously makes the expected Late Romantic reply, "I am very fond of being looked at"), boasts that her mother "has brought me up to be extremely short-sighted." The body is sculpted at the whim of fashion, responding to its commands with plastic ductility.

At the tea table, Gwendolen declines Cecily's offer of sugar: "No, thank you. Sugar is not fashionable any more." To the choice of cake or bread and butter, she replies ("in a bored manner"), "Bread and butter, please. Cake is rarely seen at the best houses nowadays." For Gwendolen, tastiness is irrelevant, since the body has no needs in the world of form. Sugar and cake are items of decor, marks of caste by which one group separates itself from a lower group. Personal preference is renounced for hierarchical conformity. And note that cake is "rarely *seen*," not eaten—its status is visual and not gustatory. Gwendolen is an Androgyne of Manners rapidly approaching the android. She is so completely the product of fashion that she is a machine, seeing myopically by maternal edict, eating, drinking, hearing, thinking, and speaking by preprogrammed desire. Mallarmé says, "Fashion is the goddess of appearances." Fashion is the divinity of this world of form, which Lady Bracknell and Gwendolen uphold with apostolic fervor.

The literary term "high comedy" is often rather loosely applied to any comedy of manners that does not descend to broad verbal or physical humor. I would argue that the most advanced high comedy is a ceremoniously mannered "presentation of self," the style of *The Importance of Being Earnest,* as most splendidly exemplified by Gwendolen. Indeed, in Gwendolen Fairfax, Wilde has reached the generic limit of high comedy. Gwendolen's self-hierarchization is so extreme that other characters are virtually dispensable, for they impinge on her only feebly and peripherally. But without at least two characters, drama as a genre cannot exist. When Gwendolen speaks it is not to others as much as to herself or to some abstract choir of celestial observers. Like the picture of Dorian Gray, which is not content to remain in its assigned place and rejects its entelechy, she seems ready to abandon drama for some extrageneric destination. Here is Wilde's greatest departure from the Restoration dramatists, for he detaches the witticism from repartee, that is, from social relationship. The Wildean witticism is a Romantic phenomenon in its proud isolationism. In this mode of high comedy there is an elaborately formal or ritualistic display of the persona, indeed a brandishing of it, like an aegis. The practitioner is in a double relation to the self, acting and also observing. But more importantly, there is a distinct trace of Late Romantic "connoisseurship": the self is the subject of Decadent studiousness and scholarship.

Let us examine several of Gwendolen's incomparable utterances, with their unyielding uniformity of tone. Late in the play she says, "I never change, except in my affections." This could serve as a darkly ironic caption to Walter Pater's Decadent "Mona Lisa." But what Gwendolen means is that, just as one might expect, she is rigidly punctilious in formal and external matters, while emotional events are beneath notice, flotsam and jetsam aimlessly adrift. Observe how she "brandishes" her personality, flaunting her faults with triumphant self-love. Her speech always has a hard, even, relentless, and yet rhetorically circumscribed character, as in her first words in the play:

ALGERNON: Dear me, you are smart!

GWENDOLEN: I am always smart! Am I not, Mr. Worthing?

JACK: You're quite perfect, Miss Fairfax.

GWENDOLEN: Oh! I hope I am not that. It would leave no room for developments, and I intend to develop in many directions.

If we were to speak of a psychodramatic "music," then in this last clause we are hearing the monody of a Gautierian contralto, the husky self-pleasuring of hermaphrodite autonomy. Identical intonations are present in two other of Gwendolen's remarks. At one point she gratuitously informs her suitor, "In fact, I am never wrong." And in the last act, as Jack struggles to regain her alienated affections, she says to him, "I have the gravest doubts upon the subject. But I intend to crush them." Such lines must be properly read—with slow, resonant measure—in order to appreciate their intractable severity. "I intend to develop in many directions": there is an extraordinarily distinctive sound to this in British diction, flat, formal, and sonorous, forbidding with self-command. Note the way personality is *distributed* throughout the sentence, filling the narrow channel of its syntax with a dense silvery fluid, acrid and opaque. Gwendolen's willful, elegantly linear sentences fit her like a glove. Smooth with Mannerist spareness, they carry not an extra ounce of rhetorical avoirdupois. There is no Paterian mistiness in Gwendolen. She overtly relishes her personality, caressing its hard edges, which are echoed in the brazen contours of her sentences. In this doyenne of Art Nouveau worldliness, Wilde has created a definitively modern selfhood, exposed, limited, and unsentimental, cold as urban geometry.

Above all his characters, it is Gwendolen whom Wilde has charged with creating an Apollonian dramatic language. Her speech, like Wilde's epicene witticisms, has a metallic self-enclosed terseness. She spends her words with haughty frugality for the same reason that Spenser's Belphoebe dashes off in the middle of sentences: the Apollonian is a mode of self-sequestration. The bon mot in general is jealous of its means, prizing brevity above all. It is a kind of sacramental display, permitting the self to be seen only in epiphanic flashes, like the winking of a camera shutter. These spasms of delimitation are attempts to defy the temporal character of speech or narrative, turning sequences of words into discrete *objets*. Ideas are never developed in the Apollonian style because of its antipathy to internality. Instead, as we find in Gwendolen and in the classic maliciously witty Androgyne of Manners of the salon, language is used confrontationally, as a distancing weapon, like a flaming sword. Gwendolen's self-exhibiting utterances follow the principle of *frontality* in painting and sculpture, which, as Arnold Hauser observes, is intrinsic to "all courtly and courteous art." Abjuring the modesty of the unmarried maiden, the potent Gwendolen turns herself full-face to her suitor, bathing him with a rain of hierarchical emissions.

Admiration of *The Importance of Being Earnest* is widespread, but discussion of the play is scarce and slight. Critics seem to have accepted Wilde's own description of it—"exquisitely trivial, a delicate bubble of fancy." Scholarship has never distinguished itself in studying this kind of high comedy, with its elusive "sophistication." Frye-style myth criticism, for example, can do little with *The Importance of Being Earnest*. From the point of view of Decadent Late Romanticism, however, there is scarcely a line in the play which fails to yield rich implications.

Here are two examples. In the midst of her dispute with Cecily, Gwendolen declares, "I never travel without my diary. One should always have something sensational to read in the train." The latter sentence comes as a surprise, for ordinarily one travels with a diary not to read but to write in it. Gwendolen, however, as an Apollonian androgyne, does not keep a journal for self-examination—inwardness always being distasteful—but for self-display. To read one's diary as if it were a novel is to regard one's life as spectacle, which Wilde of course advocates. Gwendolen contemplates her life with appreciative detachment, acting both as objet d'art and Late Romantic connoisseur. Reading is normally a medium of expansion of personal experience; one reads to learn what one does not know. Here, however, reading is an act of Romantic solipsism: Gwendolen reads not to enlarge but to condense herself. Far from Emily Dickinson's mobile frigate, a book has become a mirror in which one sees only one's own face. The diary is a self-portrait. Hence Gwendolen reading her diary in a train compartment is exactly like Dorian Gray standing before his picture in the locked room. Both are performing their devotions to the hierarchized self.

The life which this diary records is, according to Gwendolen, "sensational," a source of public scandal and eroticized fascination. But to find one's own life sensational is to be aroused by oneself. The eyes, as always in Late Romanticism, are sexual agents: Gwendolen reading her diary is lost in autoerotic skeptophilia, a titillation of the eye. If books can corrupt, and we know from *The Picture of Dorian Gray* that they can, then it is possible to be corrupted by one's own diary. To be corrupted by oneself is a perfect pattern of sexual solipsism, like Goethe's twisting Venetian acrobat Bettina, self-delectating and self-devirginizing. Gwendolen is an uroboros of amorous self-study, an Art Nouveau serpent devouring herself. Train reading is casual reading, a way to pass time with minimal effort. The life recorded and contemplated in the diary is therefore reduced in significance, trivialized: it is simply a series of sensational incidents without moral meaning.

Reading one's diary like a novel implies that one has forgotten what is in it. It demonstrates a lack of moral memory characteristic of the Decadent in general. In Wilde's *A Woman of No Importance,* Lord Illingworth declares, "No woman should have a memory. Memory in a woman is the beginning of dowdiness." The internal erodes the perfection of surfaces. In *An Ideal Husband,* Sir Robert Chiltern says of an antagonist, "She looks like a woman with a past," to which Lord Goring replies, "Most pretty women do." But as we see from Gwendolen's relations with her diary, the person with a past has no past. The self is a tabula rasa open only to sensationalized Paterian "impressions." There is no moral incrementation; experience corrupts, but it does not instruct. In *The Picture of Dorian Gray* Lord Henry Wotton reflects, "Experience was of no ethical value. It was merely the name men gave to their mistakes." Reading one's diary is a diversion of the "late" phase of culture. Memory is inhibited precisely because one has done *too much,* like Pater's "Mona Lisa," fatigued by history. Her information retrieval system blocked by sensory overload, the robotlike Gwendolen is a stranger to herself, a stranger-lover.

Gwendolen never travels without her diary because it is her familiar, the inseparable escort which enables her to keep herself in a state of externalization. This is one of many traits she shares with Cecily, who uses her diary to similar effect, as we saw in the proposal scene, where Cecily instantly petrifies Algernon's sentiments midair, as if engraving them upon stone tablets. Gwendolen's diary, again like the picture of Dorian Gray, is a repository of the soul which she is able to carry about with her like a hatbox, preserving her soulless Apollonian purity. The diary is also a chronicle, the testament of her cult of the self. For both the High and Late Romantic, a diary is a personal cosmogony, a book of first and last things.

Hence it can be seen that Wilde's witticisms contain a wealth of unsuspected meaning. Even his most apparently nonsensical *boutades* are Late Romantic gestures. For example, Lady Bracknell attempts to terminate the stormy scene at the Manor House by declaring to Gwendolen, "Come, dear, we have already missed five, if not six, trains. To miss any more might expose us to comment on the platform." These bizarre lines have that air of skewed lunatic certainty we know from Lewis Carroll, who I believe strongly influenced Wilde. What is Lady Bracknell saying? Missing a train, even "five, if not six" (a studied Decadent enumeration) normally has only private and not public consequences. In the Looking-Glass world of form, however, failure to adhere to plan is an affront to natural law, bringing murmurs of complaint from passersby. But how do others learn of one's deviation from a train schedule? Since everything is visible in this landscape of externals, and since the mental life of these androgynes, like their bodies, has a glassy transparency, their intention may be said to precede them, like a town crier, alerting the populace to their tardiness. In its visionary materialism, *The Importance of Being Earnest* reverts to the Homeric world of allegorized psychic phenomena, in which the enraged Achilles feels Athena tugging at his hair. If we characterized Lady Bracknell's remark in naturalistic terms, we would have to speak of a megalomaniacal paranoia: she imagines a general consciousness of their every move; everyone knows what they are doing and thinking. But this is a development of aristocratic worldliness. Fashionable life, as Proust attests, does indeed take place before the unblinking eyes of *le tout Paris*.

"To miss any more might expose us to comment on the platform": Lady Bracknell exists in a force field of visual sightlines. Like Gautier's chaste Queen Nyssia, tainted by the gaze of another, Lady Bracknell fears being "exposed" to infection, in this case an infection of words. Barthes says of the sadomasochistic relations in Sade's novels, "The master is he who speaks . . . ; the object is he who is silent." Lady Bracknell will lose caste if she is subject to public "comment." Her hierarchical dominance will drain from her, like divine ichor. The scene of shame which she envisions on the railway platform is one of ritual exposure, like Hawthorne's Hester Prynne braving public scorn on the town scaffold. In Wilde's world, of course, crime is not sin but bad form.

The Importance of Being Earnest was the last thing Wilde wrote before his fall. Its opening night coincided with the initiation of the Marquess of Queensberry's most virulent campaign against him, and the play continued to be performed, to great acclaim, during his two trials. Now it is a strange fact that Wilde's passage to prison was a terrible fulfillment of this remark by Lady Bracknell. In *De Profundis*, written in Reading Gaol, Wilde recalls:

> On November 13th, 1895, I was brought down here from London. From two o'clock till half-past two on that day I had to stand on the centre platform of Clapham Junction in convict dress, and handcuffed, for the world to look at. . . . When people saw me they laughed. Each train as it came up swelled the

audience. Nothing could exceed their amusement. That was, of course, before they knew who I was. As soon as they had been informed they laughed still more. For half an hour I stood there in the grey November rain surrounded by a jeering mob.

For a year after that was done to me I wept every day at the same hour and for the same space of time.

Lady Bracknell's railway platform was to be the site of Wilde's greatest humiliation. Who can doubt that the imagination can shape reality to its will? So close are these two scenes of ritual exposure that one wonders whether Wilde's memory of Clapham Junction was not a hallucination, a variation on a fictive theme in the solitude and squalor of prison. But granting its truth, it is another example of Wilde's shamanistic power to bring his own imaginative projections into being. Publication of *The Picture of Dorian Gray* produced Lord Alfred Douglas, the beautiful boy as destroyer, who brought Wilde to his ruin. Clapham Junction came as the agonizing materialization of Wilde's principle of life as "spectacle." The entire Late Romantic tradition of concentrated visual experience reaches a disastrous climax on that railway platform, and it ends there, with Wilde the dizzy center of the visible world, like the Ancient Mariner the focus of cosmic wrath, here taking the unbearable form of laughter. The comedian, losing control of his genre, is devoured by the audience.

The epicene witticism has received little attention partly because it is sexually heterodox and partly because it does not fit into received critical categories. Thus Wilde's plays are suitable for explication while his conversation is not. But the Androgyne of Manners, of which Wilde was his own best example, makes an art of the spoken word. With his radical formalism, Wilde created an original language which I will call the *monologue extérieur.*

The salon dialogue of the Androgyne of Manners is a duel of "cutting" remarks. Language is used aggressively as an instrument of masculine warfare designed to slash, stab, pierce, and penetrate. Dorian Gray says to Lord Henry Wotton, "You cut life to pieces with your epigrams." It is no coincidence that terms describing a witty exchange—thrust, parry, riposte, repartee—are drawn from swordplay. The close interrelations of language and martial contention in Western culture are demonstrated by fencing parlance which speaks of a "conversation" or "phrase" of action. In other words, a fencing match is imagined as a sequence of competitive speech. It is plain how a woman of the salon who commands this sharp, challenging rhetoric is masculinized into an Androgyne of Manners. The male Androgyne of Manners achieves his hermaphroditism by combining aggressive language with a feminine manner, graceful and languid, archly flirtatious and provocative. The persona which Wilde projects in his epicene witticisms is a conflation of masculine intimidation and attack with feminine seduction and allure.

To "cut" someone is to wound him, but it is also to sever social connections with him. This duality is the subject of a pun by Lewis Carroll, when Alice is introduced to the leg of mutton:

> "May I give you a slice?" she said, taking up the knife and fork, and looking from one Queen to the other.
> "Certainly not," the Red Queen said, very decidedly: "it isn't etiquette to cut any one you've been introduced to. Remove the joint!"

Wilde's witticisms operate by a systematic "cutting," separating the self from communality and withdrawing it into an aristocratic sequestration. In *The Importance of Being Earnest* Wilde makes language into a mode of hierarchical placement. It is a series of psychodramatic gestures, each remark asserting a caste location with regard to some other person or class of person. The speakers are constantly positioning themselves at fixed distances from others. This even occurs, as we have seen, in the marriage proposals, where the heroines of the play befuddle the heroes by ceremonial demarcations, exclamatory bulletins of incipient intimacy, which they narrate like play-by-play sportscasters. To paraphrase: "We will shortly be intimate"; "We are now being intimate"; "Pray continue to be intimate." The Wildean heroine is a hierarchical commentator, plotting the relations of personae upon a mental map.

The use of language as signs of placement is often overt, as in the tea table dispute between the young ladies.

CECILY: When I see a spade I call it a spade.

GWENDOLEN: [*satirically*] I am glad to say that I have never seen a spade. It is obvious that our social spheres have been widely different.

In this literalization of metaphor, a characteristic Wildean materialization, a spade becomes, like sugar or cake, a calibrator of caste. Gwendolen glories in her self-expanded hierarchical distance from Cecily. Such language appears everywhere in *The Importance of Being Earnest*. For example, the play opens with Algernon playing the piano: "I don't play accurately—anyone can play accurately—but I play with wonderful expression." "Anyone can play accurately": this self-absolving and demonstrably untrue premise, like a ladder leaned against a wall, stretches a great chain of being before our eyes, with Algernon exulting over the mass of the many from a topmost rung of esthetical "sensibility." The technique is used throughout Wilde. His polemical spokesman in *The Critic as Artist* says, "When people agree with me I always feel that I must be wrong." And a character in *An Ideal Husband* says, "Only dull people are brilliant at breakfast." Rhetorical energy is entirely directed toward social differentiation and segregation. Wilde was committed to an Apollonian enterprise—to create hierarchy through wit, ennobling himself, like the self-naming Balzac, through a magisterial persona construction. . . .

It is the ancient history of manners as articulations of power which energizes the climactic confrontation between Gwendolen and Cecily, the center not only of *The Importance of Being Earnest* but probably of Wilde's entire oeuvre. In a tableau of brilliant formal beauty, a tea table is made the scene of a ferocious wargame, with manners the medium of ritual advance and retreat. Gwendolen and Cecily manipulate their personae with chill virtuosity. Nowhere else in the play is it more evident that the gender of the Androgyne of Manners is purely artificial, that "femininity" in the salon is simply a principle of decorum shared equally by male and female. The escalating emotion of the conversation between Gwendolen and Cecily is entirely absorbed by the ceremonial framework and by the formality of their social masks.

> CECILY: [*rather shy and confidingly*] Dearest Gwendolen, there is no reason why I should make a secret of it to you. Our little county newspaper is sure to chronicle the fact next week. Mr. Ernest Worthing and I are engaged to be married.
>
> GWENDOLEN: [*quite politely, rising*] My darling Cecily, I think there must be some slight error. Mr. Ernest Worthing is engaged to me. The announcement will appear in the *Morning Post* on Saturday at the latest.
>
> CECILY: [*very politely, rising*] I am afraid you must be under some misconception. Ernest proposed to me exactly ten minutes ago. [*Shows diary.*]
>
> GWENDOLEN: [*examines diary through her lorgnette carefully*] It is very curious, for he asked me to be his wife yesterday afternoon at 5:30. If you would care to verify the incident, pray do so. [*Produces diary of her own.*]

Each gesture, each rhetorical movement is answered by a symmetrical countermovement of balletic grandeur. Language becomes increasingly elaborate, in baroque convolutions of ironic restraint: "It would distress me more than I can tell you, dear Gwendolen, if it caused you any mental or physical anguish, but I feel bound to point out that since Ernest proposed to you he clearly has changed his mind." There is no hysteria, or even excitement. The immovable wills of the two young women press so fiercely against the social limits of the moment that the hierarchical structure of manners leaps into visibility, another of Wilde's characteristic materializations. Stylization and ritualism approach the Oriental. The scene is a Japanese tea ceremony in which gracious self-removal has yielded to barely concealed Achillean strife.

It was Lewis Carroll who made this greatest of Wildean episodes possible. In Carroll, manners and social laws are disconnected from humane or "civilizing" values. They have a mathematical beauty but no moral meaning: they are absurd. But this absurdity is predicated not on some democratic notion of their relativism but on their arbitrary, divine incomprehensibility. In the *Alice* books, manners are meaningless, but they still retain their hierarchical force; they are Veblen's "pantomime" of mastery and subservience. Wilde, influenced by Carroll, appropriates his view of the mechanisms of social power and sets it into a much larger system of aristocratic presuppositions derived partly from his self-identification as a Baudelairean Late Romantic (always reactionary and antiliberal) and partly from his reading of English drama, in which aristocracy is one of the leading moral "ideas."

In the century of the middle class, Wilde reaffirms aristocratic *virtù*, fabricating it out of its accumulated meanings in English literature. *The Importance of Being Earnest* is a reactionary political poem which takes aristocratic style as the supreme embodiment of life as art. Through its masquelike use of manners as social spectacle, the play seeks out the crystallized idea or Platonic form of aristocracy, which resides in rank, in the ascending gradations of the great chain of being. Wilde's bon mots bring an Apollonian world into being: language and ceremony unite to take the hierarchical to its farthest dazzling point, until it appears as form without content, like the icy latticework of a snowflake. Thus it is that the characters of *The Importance of Being Earnest,* and especially the women, have abnormal attitudes, reactions, and customs and embark upon sequences of apparently irrational thought, for they are a strange hierarchical race, the *aristoi*.

Wilde's play is inspired by the glamour of aristocracy alone, divorced from social function. In this it is quite unlike Augustan literature, which celebrates Queen Anne for her wisdom and stability of rule. In Wilde no collective benefits flow from throne or court, where the upper class is preoccupied with fashionable diversions. No contemporary regime is eulogized, no past one nostalgically commemorated. Indeed, social order has no legal, economic, or military aspects whatever; it is entirely divorced from practical reality. Class structure in Wilde exists as *art,* as pure form. This markedly contrasts with Ulysses's sermon on "degree" in Shakespeare's *Troilus and Cressida:* in *The Importance of Being Earnest* order is admired not because it is right or just but because it is beautiful. In fact, order here makes no intellectual sense at all; in Carrollian terms, it is absurd. Hence it is an error, and a common one, to say that Wilde is "satirizing" Lady Bracknell, making her ridiculous in her haughty presumptions. Lady Bracknell is beautiful *because* she is absurd. Aristocracy in *The Importance of Being Earnest* satisfies esthetic and not moral demands. The world of the play is *kosmios,* well-ordered and comely. And that it is ruled by the chic makes perfect sense when one realizes that the etymological descent of this word resembles that of *cosmetic* from *cosmos,* for the French *chic* is apparently a version of the German *schick,* meaning taste, elegance, and order.

Outside his art, Wilde found himself in the same quandary as Coleridge and Swinburne, anxiously attempting apologia and moral revision of their daemonic poems. Thus Wilde declares in *The Soul of Man Under Socialism:* "All authority is quite degrading. It degrades those who exercise it, and it degrades those over whom it is exercised." Wilde was torn between his instinctive hierarchism as an Apollonian idealist and the liberalism to which he was impelled by the miseries of being homosexual in a Christian society. This led him into glaring self-contradictions, as in the testimony at his two trials.

The Wildean epicene unites the great English dramatic theme of aristocracy with Late Romantic Estheticism and Decadence. The first step in this process is Wilde's severance of the hierarchical social values of the eighteenth century and Jane Austen from the ideal of commonweal. The second step is his sexual volatilization of English wit. The bantering rhetoric of the celibate Jane Austen and Lewis Carroll becomes epicene in Wilde because of his sexual experience, with its shift into decadence. Works of epicene wit are typically dominated by image—a tyranny of the visual—and by scandal and gossip. There is little scandal or gossip in Lewis Carroll because the *Alice* books have no sexual "free energy": Carroll is an annalist of aggression but not of eroticism. In Wilde, however, gossip is a primary force, intensifying the aura of glamour by which prestige is measured in the salon. The erotic excitation of scandal and gossip produces the volatility of Wildean wit, aiding its transformation into the epicene. Words cast off their moral meanings and escape into the sexually transcendental, leaving only vapor trails of flirtation and frivolity.

The Significance of Literature:
The Importance of Being Earnest

JOEL FINEMAN

Man, poor, awkward, reliable, necessary man belongs to a sex that has been rational for millions and millions of years. He can't help himself. It is in his race. The History of Women is very different. We have always been picturesque protests against the mere existence of common sense. We saw its dangers from the first.

—*A Woman of No Importance*

What I am outlining here summarizes portions of a longer essay I have been writing on Oscar Wilde's *The Importance of Being Earnest*. For the most part, I will forego discussion of the play and focus on the way in which Wilde's farce precisely figures the problem of "The Self in Writing."[1] You will perhaps recall that Jack-Ernest, the hero of the play, discovers the unity of his duplicity when he learns that as an infant he was quite literally exchanged for writing in the cloakroom of Victoria Station, his absent-minded governess having substituted for his person the manuscript of a three-volume novel which is described as being "of more than usually repulsive sentimentality." As a result, because Jack-Ernest is in this way so uniquely and definitively committed to literature, with literature thus registered as his alter-ego, he is one of those few selves or subjects whose very existence, as it is given to us, is specifically literary, an ego-ideal of literature, as it were, whose form is so intimately immanent in his content as to collapse the distinction between a name and that which it bespeaks, and whose temporal destiny is so harmoniously organic a whole as to make it a matter of natural fact that his end be in his beginning—for Ernest is indeed, as Lady Bracknell puts it, paraphrasing traditional definitions of allegory, one whose origins are in a terminus.

Yet if Jack-Ernest is thus an ideal image of the relation of the self to writing, he is nevertheless himself a piece of literature, and therefore but a literary representation of the self's relation to literature, a fiction, therefore, if not necessarily a farce, and for this reason not to be trusted. This is the difficulty, I take it, that our forum has been established to address, recognizing that while the self and writing are surely implicated each in the other, perhaps

Reprinted by permission of the author, October Magazine Ltd., and the Massachusetts Institute of Technology, from *October* 15 (Winter 1980): 77–90.

even reciprocally constitutive each *of* the other, they are so in a way that at the same time undermines the integrity and the stability of both. This we can see even in the delicate phrasing of our forum's title, where the vagueness of the preposition, the problematic and diffusive metaphoricity of its innocuous "in"—"The Self *in* Writing"—testifies to the fact that the Self *and* Writing, as literal categories with their own propriety, can only be linked together in a figural discourse, which, even as it is spoken, calls the specificity and the literality of its terms into question. Strictly speaking, of course, "The Self in Writing" is an impossible locution, for in writing we do not find the self but, at best, only its representation, and it is only because *in* literature, in a literary mode, we characteristically, if illegitimately, rush to collate a word both with its sense and with its referent that we are, even momentarily, tempted to forget or to suspend the originary and intrinsic difference between, on the one hand, the self who reads, and, on the other, the literary revision of that self who is read.

This is to insist upon the fact that the self's relation to literature is not itself a literary relation, and that only a sentimental and literary reading will obsessively identify a thing with its word, a signified with its signifier, or the self with its literary image. This is also to avoid simplistic dialectical accounts of the act of reading—either identificatory or implicative—whose mechanical symmetries programmatically reduce the self to its idealization: the so-called "ideal reader" of whom we hear a great deal of late. Instead, this is to recognize that if we are to speak of the relation of the self to the writing in which it finds itself written, or, stylizing this familiar topos, if we are to speak of the relation of the self to the language in which it finds itself bespoken, then we must do so in terms of a critical discourse that registers the disjunction and the discrepancy between being and meaning, thing and word, and which therefore locates the self who is committed to language in its experience of the slippage between its immediate presence to itself and its mediated representation of itself in a symbolic system. Moreover, since Being, to be thought, must be thought as Meaning, even this self-presence of the self to itself will emerge only in retrospect as loss, with the self discovering itself in its own meaningful aftermath, just as Being can only be spoken in its own effacement, as Heidegger—not Derrida—has taught us.[2]

As is well known, it is thanks to the patient, painstaking, and rigorous labors of the tradition of psychoanalysis—a tradition that begins with Freud and which probably concludes with Lacan—that we possess a theoretical vocabulary sufficiently supple to capture this subject born in the split between self-presence and the representation of self. The insights of this tradition, however perfunctorily and schematically I refer to them here, are what enable us to situate the self of "The Self in Writing" in the metaphorical *in* whose very figurality is what allows us to articulate the problem in the first place, which is to say, in the same displacing place that Wilde—whose play will thematize this very problem of the place of the subject—places *Being,* midway between the import of *Importance* and a specifically literary pun on *Earnest*—the importance of *being Earnest*—as though the indeterminacy of meaning in turn determined *Being* as its own rueful double entendre.

What I should like to do here, however, recognizing, with some regret, that both the theory and the vocabulary of this psychoanalytic tradition are for many people both irritating and opaque, is translate its discourse into the more accessible and familiar terms of what today we will parochially call the Anglo-American speculative tradition. To that end, in an effort to sketch out the necessary contours of any psychoanalysis of what we can now identify as the "subject of literature," I would like to rehearse a rather well known paradox of logical reference, first formulated in 1908 by Kurt Grelling, but of interest to philosophy from Russell at least through Quine.

The paradox itself is relatively straightforward. Let us say, says the paradox, that there is a set of words that describe themselves. For example, *polysyllabic,* the word, is itself polysyllabic, *short* is itself short, and *English* is itself English, an English word. Let us call such self-descriptive words autological, because they speak about themselves. In addition, let us further say that there is another set of words that do not describe themselves. For example, *monosyllabic,* the word, is not itself monosyllabic, *long* is not itself long, *French* is not itself French. Let us now agree to call this second set of words heterological, because these are words that speak about things besides themselves— allegorical words, because they speak about the Other (*allos,* other; *agoreuein,* to speak), a *logos* of the *heteros,* or, in Lacan's phrase, a discourse of the Other. Having stipulated these two sets, the autological and the heterological, the question then emerges: is the word *heterological* itself autological or heterological? And here we discover the paradox, for simply asking the question forces upon us the odd conclusion that if *heterological,* the word, is itself heterological, then it is autological, whereas, in some kind of contrast, if it is autological, then it is heterological. That is to say, given the definitions and a classical system of logic, the heterological can only be what it is on condition that it is what it is not, and it can only be what it is not on condition that it is what it is.

Thus formulated, the paradox possesses both an elegance and a banality, and in proportions that rather directly correspond to the brittle yet mandarin tenor and texture we associate with Wilde's farce. So too, the paradox very neatly summarizes the plot of *The Importance of Being Earnest,* since Ernest will himself be earnest only when he isn't, just as he will not be earnest only when he is. This paradoxical alternation and oscillation of the subject, a phenomenon to which the play gives the general label Bunburyism, but which Lacan would call *auto-différence,* is resolved at the end of the play when Ernest consults the book of the name of the fathers and discovers that his name "naturally is Ernest," and that therefore to his surprise, "all his life he has been speaking nothing but the truth."[3] Were there time, we would want at this point to conduct both a phonological and a phenomenological analysis so as to explain why all the names of the fathers in the list that Ernest reads begin with the name of the mother, "Ma"—Mallam, Maxbohm, Magley, Markby, Migsby, Mobbs, Moncrieff—and we would want also to know why this enumeration of nasal consonants not only spells an end to the labial phonemics of *Bunbury,* but also marks the moment when denomination lapses into description, when use turns into mention, and when Truth itself arrives after the fact to validate what it succeeds.[4] Even putting these important questions to the side, however, we can see that the intention of the farce is to resolve the paradox of autology and heterology by enacting it through to its absurd reduction, to the point, that is, where Ernest becomes, literally becomes, his name.

Again, we might want to take this revival of the tradition of Paracelsian signatures, this coordination of signifier and signified, as indicative of the literary *per se.* But we can do so only if we recognize the specific twist or trope that literature gives to this semiotics of correspondence. For Ernest only becomes earnest when he recognizes in the heterology of words the paradoxical representationality of language, and thus discovers *in* the difference between a name and its thing the paradoxical difference *between* himself and his name. Ernest therefore inherits his name only to the extent that its significance is restricted or promoted to its nominality, only to the extent, that is to say, that it becomes a signifier of itself *as* a signifier, not a signified. This is indeed a paradigm of literary language, of language that calls attention to itself as language, just as the pun on *Earnest* in the title possesses its literary effect precisely because it *doesn't* mean its double-meaning and thereby forces us to register the word as just a word, significant of just itself, with no meaning beyond its palpability as a signifier. This is also why Wilde's play or farce on names is itself so important, for we may say that the special propriety of a proper name with respect to common nouns corresponds precisely to the specialized charge of literature with respect to so-called ordinary language— "so-called" because there could no more be an ordinary language without its fictive complement than there could be a natural language bereft of its fantasy of the propriety of proper names.[5]

Yet if this is a small-scale model, however general, of the literary, of language which stresses its literality, its letters, it is of course profoundly unlike the kind of ordinary language that philosophy, as opposed to literature, would instead prefer to speak—which is why where literature depends upon the paradox of heterology philosophy instead prohibits it, with the notion of "metalanguage," which keeps the orders of reference in their hierarchical place. Logicians are of course entitled to introduce whatever constraints might be required to maintain the coherence of their artificial systems, but this remains a merely logical, not a psychological, necessity, which is why Lacan, recognizing the fact that a subject of discourse might at any moment stumble into heterology, says that there is no such thing as "metalanguage."[6] This is not the place to make the point in any detail, but I would want to argue that philosophy of language has always been autological, and that this can be precisely documented by tracing its attitude towards proper names, from *The*

Cratylus, where a name will imitate its thing, through the epoch of representation, where a name will uncomplicatedly point to its thing, through Russell and Frege, where the immediate relation of a word to its referent is replaced by the equally immediate relation of a word to its sense, through to speech act theory, where a word uncomplicatedly reflects its speaker's intention. Of late, there are signs that this realism of nominalism has begun to lose its philosophical prestige, for example, Saul Kripke's devastating critique of Searle's theory of nominality, a critique whose account of reference constitutes the exact inverse of Derrida's equally devastating critique of Searle's hypothesis of expressable intention. On the assumption that the enemy of my enemy is my friend, it seems possible that continental and Anglo-American philosophy might eventually meet in the course of these complementary examinations of the propriety or impropriety of names. Leaving these relatively recent indications to the side, however, we may say that the perennial philosophical dream of true language, of language that always means what it says, stands in marked contrast to literary language which can never mean what it says because it never means anything except the fact that it is saying something that it does not mean.[7]

This traditional difference is worth developing, for it allows us to define the self of "The Self in Writing" as both the cause and the consequence of the paradox subtending the autological and the heterological. That is to say, the self becomes the difference between a discourse of things and a discourse of words, a subject situated midway between the subject of philosophy and the subject of literature, between ordinary and extraordinary language, in short, again, between *Importance* and *Earnest.* Where philosophy self-importantly commits itself to autology so as to make of language a transparent vehicle for the signifieds of which it speaks, literature, in contrast, "Earnestly" forswears signifieds altogether for the sake of the heterological materiality of its signifiers. The self between them constitutes the necessity of their difference, so that the ancient quarrel between philosophy and literature thus takes place over the body of the self in writing, with philosophy wanting to do with its signifieds what literature wants to do with its signifiers, and with the self in writing testifying to the fact that neither can do either. A signifier, says Lacan, is what represents a subject to another signifier. Literature and philosophy are thus the signifiers of each other, names, in this sense, whose "sense," or let us say significance, is what their readers are.

Situated thus, as both elision and bar between these two equally inhuman desires, the self in writing finds his own human desire strictly circumscribed, a desire that we might characterize as a lusting of the autological for the heterological, a desire that leaves something to be desired. "My ideal has always been to love someone of the name of Ernest," but "Bunbury is dead." In psychoanalytic terms this would correspond to the transition from narcissistic to anaclitic object choice, or to the difference between the self before and after what psychoanalysis thematizes as his accession to speech. If we recall, though, that desire too is an effect of the language, that Eros is the consequence of Logos, then our paradox will produce the appropriate Freudian paradigm without recourse to the Freudian lexicon. For now, remembering their etymology, we may rechristen the autological as the autosexual, or rather, the homosexual, and we may equally revalue the heterological as the heterosexual. This leaves us with the psychoanalytic conclusion that the fundamental desire of the reader of literature is the desire of the homosexual for the heterosexual, or rather, substituting the appropriate figurative embodiments of these abstractions, the desire of the man to be sodomized by the woman. This is a specifically obsessional desire, but it is one that Freud luridly locates at the center of his three major case histories: Ratman, Wolfman, Schreber. This would also explain why the only word that ends up being naturally motivated in *The Importance of Being Earnest* is not *Earnest* but *Bunbury* itself, which was not only British slang for a male brothel, but is also a collection of signifiers that straightforwardly express their desire to bury in the bun.[8]

With this cryptographic reference to the death that we always find buried in the logos of desire we are very close to the impulse to death that Freud assimilated to the wanderings of Eros. There is no time to pursue this connection further, but I would like in conclusion at least to draw the moral. In our literature the heterological is the trope of the autological, just as the heterosexual is the trope of the homosexual, just as woman is the trope of man. This accounts, respectively, for the semiotics, the syntax, and the semantics of our literature. So too does it account for its ethics. Asked to summarize her novel, the novel whose loss is responsible for the subject of the play, Miss Prism, the governess, says, "The good ended happily, and the bad unhappily. That is what Fiction means." So it does, but this embedding of the moral in a necessarily fictive register equally measures the cost of what we must therefore call the fiction of meaning, at least for so long as both the Self and Writing are accorded an authority that even Wilde's farce thus fails to deconstruct.[9]

Notes

1. This paper was delivered at the 1979 convention of the Modern Language Association, at one of the several panels associated with the forum on "The Self in Writing." The essay on *The Importance of Being Earnest* has now grown into a chapter on Wilde which will take its place in a projected book on literary names. The notes have been added for this publication.

2. See, for example, *The Question of Being*, or "The Temporality of Discourse" in *Being and Time* (IV, 68, d). Derrida's project is effectively to apply Heidegger's critique of Western metaphysics to Heidegger himself (e.g., "Ousia and Grammè: A Note to a Footnote in *Being and Time*," in *Phenomenology in Perspective*, ed. F. J. Smith, The Hague, Martinus Nijhoff, 1970; also, "The Ends of Man," *Philosophy and Phenomenological Research*, 30, No. 1 (1969), also in *Marges de la philosophie*, Paris, Minuit, 1972), so as to show that even Heidegger repeats, rather than revises, traditional metaphysical assumptions. For this reason, Derrida argues, even Heidegger's Being must be put under further erasure as part of an ongoing, ever-vigilant, vaguely messianic, deconstructive Puritanism. There is no doubt that Derrida makes this point persuasively; the

question is whether this measures a blindness or an insight on Heidegger's part, for what is important to Heidegger is the specificity of his history of Western philosophical speculation. What for Derrida is the mark of Heidegger's failure is also a measure, or so Heidegger would no doubt respond, of *necessary* metaphysical limits, a determination of the way it is and is not, or, more modestly and historically, the way it has always been and seems still to be. I am here assuming, following Derrida himself, that it is one of Western metaphysics' special and perennial pleasures to have itself deconstructed, and that for this reason we must register Derrida's always already predetermined *différance* within the horizon of its always eventual determinate recuperation. This is not a static balance: it has a direction, from pre-beginning to end, and this directionality also has its obvious metaphysical—not to mention its more obvious psychological —consequences.

3. See "Le clivage du sujet et son identification," *Scilicet*, Nos. 2, 3, Paris, Editions du Seuil, 1970, p. 127. Note that the fracture is imaginary, not symbolic.

4. I have elsewhere argued that the first phonemes, labial /papa/ or /baba/ and nasal /mama/, are acquired in accordance with a structure that determines specific literary themes. See "The Structure of Allegorical Desire," *October*, 12 (Spring 1980), 47–66. This "Pa/Ma" model phonologically instantiates what Heidegger describes more generally in terms of the question whose asking renders metaphysics possible: "In the service of thought we are trying precisely to penetrate the source from which the essence of thinking is determined, namely *alētheia* and *physis*, being as unconcealment, the very thing that has been lost by 'logic' " (*An Introduction to Metaphysics*, trans. R. Manheim, New York, Anchor Books, 1961, p. 102). In the same way that Heidegger's *alētheia* is forsworn by *logos*, the babbling /papa/ through which speech is thought is irrevocably lost at the first moment of its meaningful articulation. So too, as Heidegger predicts, the hidden unconcealment of truth always reemerges in literature as death, farcically so in *The Importance of Being Earnest*: "Bunbury is dead. . . . The doctors found out that Bunbury could not live, that is what I mean—so Bunbury died." This has ramifications for the metaphorics of literary sexuality, a point to which I refer briefly above.

5. I am assuming here Jakobson's "structuralist" definition of the literary function as that message which stresses itself as merely message, and I am assimilating this, for reasons discussed in the next footnote, to proper names, for these are nominal only because they stress their nominality. The opposition of meaningful words to meaningless proper nouns is therefore one instance of a more general system of opposition in *The Importance of Being Earnest* that manages consistently to juxtapose the serious against the trivial in such a way as to destabilize the integrity of meaningful binary antithesis. This is an obvious theme of *The Importance of Being Earnest*, which Wilde subtitled *A Trivial Comedy for Serious People* so as to make the very fact of farce a problem for whatever might be understood to be its opposite. In this way, by mentioning itself, Wilde's theme defends its own expression by referring the formal force of farce to an ongoing repetition internal to itself. This is, as it were, the asymptotic height of farce, which, because it is the genre that, as Marx suggested, imitates or repeats tragedy, is therefore the genre whose literary self-consciousness is formally most acute because thematically most empty.

The generic point is important because it shows us in what sense Wilde took his play seriously. For Aristotle, as for the serious literary tradition that succeeds him, tragedy is the imitation of a logically unified action, with the result that the hero of tragedy, his character subjected to his destiny, becomes a subjectivity as unified as the action he enacts. Hence Oedipus, whether Sophocles' or Aristotle's or Freud's, and the necessity historically attaching to the coherence of his person. It is this unity that makes tragedy, for Aristotle, the most important (and therefore the most "philosophical," see *Poetics,* chs. 9 and 26) of literary genres, just as this unity explains why, for Aristotle, Oedipus is both the perfect tragic object and the perfect tragic subject. In contrast, farce presents itself as the imitation of tragic imitation, as the action of imitation rather than an imitation of action, and the result of this double doubling is that the unifying logic of tragedy, which depends on imitation, is put into question by its own duplication. This sounds paradoxical, but it simply characterizes (1) the literary function as Jakobson describes it theoretically, i.e., the essential structural feature of literature, its recursive reflexivity, (2) the actual historical practice of a literary tradition that unfolds towards increasingly self-conscious forms and themes, i.e., the mocking mechanism, usually mimetic, by means of which literature regularly revives itself by calling attention to its conventions, for example, the way *The Importance of Being Earnest* (as do most of Wilde's plays) parodies what were in Wilde's theater established proprieties of stock and pointed melodrama (the crossed lovers, the bastard child, the discovery of origins that predetermine ends). On the one hand, this explains why farce is, again according to the tradition, of all poetic genres least important, for where tragedy is serious because it imitates something, farce is trivial because it imitates imitation (literature or literariness), which is nothing. (This is the case even if another principle of aesthetic meaning is substituted for imitation, for any notion of importance will be undone when it remarks itself.) But this is also why, on the other hand, because his play makes fun *of* tragedy, the farcically divided Jack-Ernest constitutes the most serious possible critique of Aristotle's tragically unified Oedipus, which explains why a critical tradition dominated by Aristotle and by Oedipus finds nothing funny in the play's humor—Shaw, for example, who hated the play because he thought its wit was unimportant—or, more generally, the way the play is labeled marginal *because* the perfect farce.

As serious tragedy to trivial farce, so philosophy to literature, and for the same reasons. We know that this is historically the case if we recall that Plato condemns sophistic rhetoric for the way it mimes philosophy, or the way Plato objects to literature for being but an imitation of a more substantial truth. Again the same problem: if any given tragedy might be a perfect farce, how does philosophy defend itself from what would be its perfect imitation, for example Gorgias's parody of Parmenides, which "proves" through nominal negative existentials that "nothing exists." In this paper, therefore, I am not simply assuming that Wilde's farce reenacts, or represents within a literary mode, the traditional quarrel of literature with philosophy. More specifically, I am arguing, first, that Wilde's play on names, the play's thematic matter, is the objectification of its parodic manner; second, that it is by a commitment to the propriety of names that philosophy has historically defended itself against the possibility that it is its own dissimulation—a weak defense, given the historical failure, to this day, of the philosophy of proper names. Gorgias's onto-logical name-play is what makes rhetoric a *necessary* mockery of philosophy (as Gorgias describes it in one of the few surviving fragments)—"to destroy an opponent's seriousness by laughter and his laughter by seriousness"—just as it is the earnestness of "Earnest" that makes Wilde's "philosophy of the trivial" serious (as Wilde described it in an interview just prior to the play's premiere):

What sort of play are we to expect?
It is exquisitely trivial, a delicate bubble of fancy and it has its philosophy.
Its philosophy?
That we should treat all the trivial things of life seriously, and all the serious things of life with sincere and studied triviality.

The relevant contemporary example is Derrida's parody, iteration, citation, quotation of Searle's defense of Austin (see "Limited Inc," *Glyph*, 2, Baltimore, Johns Hopkins University Press, 1977). Derrida not only makes fun of Searle's speech act theory and its notion of "copyrightable" proper names (for naively supposing some innocent principle of difference with which to distinguish a serious legitimate utterance from its nonserious illegitimate repetition); he also "proves" the point by making fun—a serious joke about corporeal anonymity—of "Searle-Sarl's" name itself.

6. See "D'une question préliminaire à tout traitement possible de la psychose," in *Ecrits,* Paris, Editions du Seuil, 1966, p. 538. See also, Jacques-Alain Miller, "U ou 'Il n'y a pas de meta-langage,'" *Ornicar?,* 5 (1975–1976), 67–72.

7. Gwendolen and Cecily both give voice to this philosophical-philological, idealist

dream of a true word: "My ideal has always been to love someone of the name of Ernest. There is something in that name that inspires absolute confidence." Or, "You must not laugh at me, darling, but it had always been a girlish dream of mine to love someone whose name was Ernest. There is something in that name that inspires absolute confidence." Here we can only briefly allude to the complications that make this confidence problematic. The traditional account of names—as formulated, for example, in Mill—is that a proper name has a denotation but not a connotation, in contrast to common nouns which have both. This is a muted version of Socrates' original philosophical desire for a language, whose words would necessarily metaphysically correspond with things, a language, as it were, where words literally *are* the things they speak, for example the way *R,* as Socrates says in *The Cratylus,* is the letter of motion. The history of philosophy of names—from Aristotle's *Categories* on, through Stoic grammar, through medieval sign theory (via the incipient nominalism of Abelard, the modified realism of Aquinas, the straightforward nominalism of Ockham)—is a continual attempt somehow to nourish and to satisfy this initial philosophical desire for true language (for a truth *of* language, an *etymos* of *logos*) by lowering the ontological stakes to something merely nominal, for example, Mill's denotation theory where names merely indicate the things that formerly they were. The covert metaphysical assumptions embedded even in so modest a claim as Mill's were brought out by Frege and Russell in their well-known criticisms of denotation theory, first, with the instance of negative existentials, where there is no referent to which a name might point (Odysseus, golden mountains, etc.), second, with the instance of identity propositions, which give off information even though the names they contain share the same referent (e.g., "The Morning Star is the Evening Star," "Cicero is Tully"—these being the traditional examples, as though philosophy can only think the problem under the aegis of the queen of desire, Venus, and the king of rhetoric, Cicero). For these reasons, lest language call things into being simply by denominating them, Frege and Russell, in somewhat different ways, introduced between a name and its referent a third term which is its "sense," arguing that while a name must have a sense in order to refer, it need not have a referent in order to make sense. As a result, no longer the essence of things, names now will merely mean them; they are truncated definite descriptions, to use Russell's phrase, and so not really names at all, but abbreviated bundles of meaning which are only contingently related to a referent.

There are several difficulties with this account of names which understands them to refer by means of what and how they mean. (Neither does such an account eliminate metaphysics by transferring its claims to the register of meaning. Cf. Quine: "Meaning is what essence becomes when it is divorced from the object of reference and married to the word," in "Two Dogmas of Empiricism," in *From a Logical Point of View,* Cambridge, Mass., Harvard University Press, 1961, p. 21.) First of all, it must be decided which aspects of nominal sense will be essential in determining a name's referent, for two people might well have entirely different senses of "Aristotle" and yet surely refer to the same person when they use his name (my "Aristotle" may only have written the *Poetics* whereas yours may have only tutored Alexander, and the real Aristotle might in fact have done neither). So too, there is an intuitive difficulty that comes of thinking names like *John* or *X* in fact possess a sense; this is to truncate description to a grotesque degree. These difficulties are not resolved even when the Russell-Frege account is "loosened up," as it is by Searle when, following Wittgenstein, he collates description and identification in a speech act theory of names. (See J. Searle, "Proper Names," *Mind,* 67 [1958]; see also the criticism of this in S. Kripke, "Naming and Necessity," in *Semantics of Natural Language,* eds. D. Davidson and G. Harman, Dordrecht, D. Reidel, 1972; also K. Donellan, "Speaking of Nothing," *The Philosophical Review,* 83 [1974]. Searle's essay should be read so as to notice the continuity subtending speculation about names in philosophy's *démarche* or retreat from ontology to psychology: first, names are the things to which they refer, then they imitate them, then they point to them, then they mean them, and then, in speech act theory, they "intend" them.) These difficulties, and others associated with them, have been much discussed in recent Anglo-American philosophy of language, by, amongst others, Donellan, Putnam, and, most influentially, Kripke. There is a good introduction to the topic, with bibliography, in *Naming, Necessity, and Natural Kinds,* ed. S. Schwartz, Ithaca, Cornell University Press, 1977. We cannot here discuss the technical issues involved, which begin, primarily with the way names rigidly designate the same thing in all possible worlds (e.g., "The author of the *Iliad* might not have been born and might not have been the author of the Iliad" makes sense, but, substituting a name for the description, as in "Homer might not have been born and might not have been Homer" does not), but the force of this recent theory is to oblige philosophy, for the most part, to give up a strong sense theory of nominal reference. Instead, as a possible alternative, Kripke proposes to explain nominal reference by appealing to history, relating every use of every name to a series of hypothetical causal chains which reach back to every name's original moment of ostensive baptism. The consequences of Kripke's novel account are subtle and far-reaching, and they remain important even though, still more recently, their argument has itself run into difficulties. Here we must be content simply to allude to the problem, and to mention these two points relevant to our discussion above.

First, though Kripke can demonstrate that a name cannot have a sense in a strong way such that it determines its referent, he must still account for the information we receive in identity propositions. Here, as N. Salmon suggests, the only sense a name conveys is of itself as a name. See Salmon's review of L. Linsky's *Names and Descriptions,* in *The Journal of Philosophy,* 76, No. 8 (1979). This is why I feel justified in assimilating proper names to Jakobson's account of literariness.

Second, Kripke has recently discovered a paradox built into his theory of causal chains, for he imagines a situation in which a single origin legitimately produces a divided name. See "A Puzzle about Belief," in *Meaning and Use,* ed. A. Margalit, Dordrecht, D. Reidel, 1979. Kripke confesses himself unable to resolve the paradox even though it calls his entire account of proper names into question (and, as Putnam points out, the paradox also infects a theory of natural kinds; see Putnam's "Comment" on Kripke's puzzle, also in *Meaning and Use*). Kripke's puzzle is an inversion of Derrida's differentiated, reiterated origin, which is why I suggest in this paper that the two philosophers, though neither speaks to or of the other, share a common criticism of Searle, and also why I say that Anglo-American philosophy of language and continental phenomenology are now drawing together in their discovery of the impropriety of proper names. This is also why they both share an interest in the ontological status of the fictive. This is a point to be developed elsewhere. The history of philosophy of names should, however, be of special interest to students of literature, for in many ways the progressive and increasingly dogmatic subordination by philosophy of nominal reference, first to extension, then to expression, then to intention, and finally to a historicity that postpones its temporality, in many ways parallels the development and eventual demise of an aesthetics of representation. That is to say, the perennial awkwardness philosophy discloses in the collation of word and thing is closely related to the uneasy relation our literary tradition regularly discovers when it connects literal to figurative literary meaning. So too, there is an obvious affinity between what are the topoi of a long philosophical meditation on names—e.g., the integrity of a clear-cut distinction between analytic and synthetic propositions, or the possibility of an overlap between *de dictu* intensional meanings and *de re* extensional truth values—and what are the corresponding chestnuts of hermeneutic concern—e.g., the relation of an autonomous text to its external context, or the imbrication of form with content, or medium with message. In this paper, however, I am more concerned with the difference, rather than the similarity, between philosophical and literary names, for this difference possesses a specificity of its own, and it can be identified, as I say above, with the significance (which is to be distinguished from the meaning) of literature. We assume (with De Man) that all literary texts share the same indeterminate meaning, but we further argue (with Lacan) that this indeterminacy of meaning in turn determines a specific literary significance.

8.   Again we cannot develop the point adequately, but we would begin our psychoanalytic account with Freud's essay on "The Uncanny" (which concludes, by the way, with a reference to Wilde), and we would conclude it with Lacan's discovery that there is no such thing as woman.

See "Aristotle et Freud: L'autre satisfaction," also "Dieu et la jouissance de la femme," in *Le Seminaire, Livre XX, Encore: 1972–1973,* Paris, Editions du Seuil, 1975. We thus assume, in traditional psychoanalytic fashion, that the subject of Western literature is male, that its object, which exists only as an effect which puts existence into question (in the same way that Wilde gives us *Being* flanked by punning), is female, and that its project is therefore the representation of desire. We deal here with the metaphorics of literary sexuality, with the way the male is historically a subject undone by its female sub-version. Hence our epigraph, or the way Wilde's farce repeats the erotic melodrama through which it is thought: "It is called *Lady Lancing* on the cover: but the real title is *The Importance of Being Earnest,*" letter to George Alexander, October 1894, printed in *The Letters of Oscar Wilde,* ed. R. Hart-Davis, New York, Harcourt, Brace, and World, 1962, pp. 375–376. For a summary of the proposed *Lady Lancing,* a cuckoldry plot which Wilde describes as "A sheer flame of love between a man and a woman," see the letter to Alexander, August 1894, *The Letters of Oscar Wilde,* pp. 360–362.

9.   Because the moral is imaginary it has that much more force. This speaks to an old psychoanalytic ambiguity, that the precursor of the super-ego is the ego-ideal. This raises a problem for Lacan's psychoanalytic topography, suggesting the possibility that Lacan's "Symbolic" is itself "Imaginary," the last lure of the "Imaginary." To discuss this problem properly we would necessarily consider a different literary genre: romance, which is not tragedy and is not farce, neither Oedipus nor his courtly derision.

Alias Bunbury:
Desire and Termination in
The Importance of Being Earnest

CHRISTOPHER CRAFT

Like all works of art, [*The Importance of Being Earnest*] drew its sustenance from life, and, speaking for myself, whenever I see or read the play I always wish I did not know what I do about Wilde's life at the time he was writing it—that when, for instance, John Worthing talks of going Bunburying, I did not immediately visualize Alfred Taylor's establishment. On rereading it after his release, Wilde said, "It was extraordinary reading the play over. How I used to toy with that tiger Life." At its conclusion, I find myself imagining a sort of nightmare Pantomime Transformation Scene in which, at the touch of the magician's wand, instead of the workday world's turning into fairyland, the country house in a never-never Hertfordshire turns into the Old Bailey, the features of Lady Bracknell into those of Mr. Justice Wills. Still, it is a masterpiece, and on account of it Wilde will always enjoy the impersonal fame of an artist as well as the notoriety of his personal legend.

—W. H. Auden, "An Improbable Life"[1]

As a character "always somewhere else at present," as a figure thus *sans figure,* Bunbury had been devised by Wilde to inhabit the erotic interstices of the double bind here represented by Auden's *volonté d'oublier,* his drive to forget: "I always wish I did not know what I do." The subtle instruction of such a double bind is not so much that knowledge be voided as that knowledge perform its work along self-blinded paths of "ignorance," nonrecognition, and misidentification. "In this light," as D. A. Miller writes, "it becomes clear that the social function of secrecy"—and Bunbury is the secret subject of an open secret—"is not to conceal knowledge so much as to conceal knowledge of the knowledge. . . . Secrecy would thus be the subjective practice in which the oppositions of private/public, inside/outside, subject/object are established, and the sanctity of their first term kept inviolate."[2] As Wilde's sly figure for this regime of knowing and unknowing, of knowing through unknowing, Bunbury remains a being or subject always otherwise and elsewhere; he appears nowhere on stage, and wherever his name is present he is not. Appeals to Bunbury yield

Reprinted in part from *Representations* 31 (Summer 1990): 19–46. © 1990, THE REGENTS OF THE UNIVERSITY OF CALIFORNIA.

only his absence: "Bunbury doesn't live here. Bunbury is somewhere else at present." But if Bunbury has been banished from the precincts of heterosexual representation, the need to frequent his secrecy has not, as Algy explains to Jack: "Nothing will induce me to part with Bunbury, and if you ever get married, which seems to me extremely problematic, you will be very glad to know Bunbury. A man who marries without knowing Bunbury has a very tedious time of it." Bunbury thus operates within the heterosexual order as its hidden but irreducible supplement, the fictive and pseudonymous brother whose erotic "excesses" will be manifested only by continual allusion to their absence.

Of course the gay specificity of such allusiveness was technically unspeakable: *non nominandum inter Christianos*. Refusing to chafe under this proscription, Wilde inverts it by inserting Bunbury into the text behind the ostentatious materiality of an empty signifier, a punning alias whose strategic equivocation between allusion and elision had already announced, a century before Foucault's formulation, "that the world of speech and desires has known invasions, struggles, plunderings, disguises, ploys."[3] Speaking strictly, *Earnest* cannot admit or acknowledge the erotic force of the gay male body, which must therefore be staged as an atopic body, a body constitutively "somewhere else at present." Hence the flickering present-absence of the play's homosexual desire, as the materiality of the flesh is retracted into the sumptuousness of the signifier, whether in the "labial phonemics" of Bunbury,[4] all asmack with death and kisses, or in the duplicitous precincts of the play's most proper and improper name, *Earnest*: a name at once splayed by a pun and doubly referential, pointing with one hand to the open secret of the double life and with the other to the brittle posturings of the Name of the Father—a figure whose delicate transmissibility has always required the strictest of heterosexual propaedeutics.

What then, more specifically, are the disguises and ploys of "serious Bunburyism"? Or, in Jack's more exasperated intonation: "Bunburyist? What on earth do you mean by a Bunburyist?" But the hermeneutical rage of a Jack must be a little undone by the interpretive insouciance of an Algy: "Now produce your explanation, and pray make it remarkable. The bore about most explanations is that they are never half so remarkable as the things they try to explain." In this spirit, I offer some explanations. Bunbury represents or disseminates the following: 1) an actual person of no historical importance, Henry Shirley Bunbury, a hypochondriacal acquaintance of Wilde's Dublin youth;[5] 2) a village in Cheshire that, appropriately enough, "does not even appear on most maps";[6] 3) a tongue-in-cheek allusion to Wilde's illegal "sodomitical" practices—"not only," as Fineman puts it, "British slang for a male brothel, but . . . also a collection of signifiers that straightforwardly express their desire to bury in the bun";[7] 4) a parody of the contemporaneous medicalization of homosexual desire ("Nor do I," says Lady Bracknell of Algy's visits to Bunbury, "in any way approve of the modern sympathy with invalids.

I consider it morbid. Illness of any kind is hardly a thing to be encouraged in others. Health is the primary duty of life"); 5) a sly, even chipper, allusion to the thanatopolitics of homophobia, whose severest directives against disclosure ensure that what finally gets disclosed will be, as in *Dorian Gray,* a corpse, homicide or suicide, upon whose cold or cooling flesh the now obvious text is for the first time made legible; 6) a pragmatics of gay misrepresentation, a nuanced and motile doublespeak, driven both by pleasure and, as Gide put it, "by the need of self-protection";[8] and, as we shall see before we end, 7) a pseudonym or alias for the erotic oscillation within the male subject, his fundamental waffling between Jack and Ernest.

But more crucially than any of these, Bunbury insists upon his "own" difference from himself and from whatever signification (as above) he may, by caprice or compulsion, assume. From his prone position just offstage (to know Bunbury is "to sit by a bed of pain"), *Bunbury* performs enormous representational work, but only by way of a disseminal passage whose first effect is to expel the referent from the neighborhood of the sign: where *Bunbury* is, Bunbury is not. It is typical of Wilde's inverting wit that he should stage this expulsion as an act of ingestion, as a buttered and material pun on Bunbury's cryptographic name. I mean the "luxurious and indolent" gluttony that, by axiomatically transposing sexual and gustatory pleasures (cucumber sand- wiches, muffins, breads: buns—Banbury or Bunbury—everywhere),[9] operates as a screen metaphor for otherwise unspeakable pleasures: "There can be little good in any young man who eats so much, or so often."[10] In this displacement, the obscene becomes the scenic, as that which must not be spoken is consumed, before an audience, with incomparable relish and finesse. "Well, I can't eat muffins in an agitated manner. The butter would probably get on my cuffs. One should always eat muffins quite calmly. It is the only way to eat them." The fastidious allusion to Wilde's sexual practice here is exact—from hand to mouth: as H. Montgomery Hyde reports, fondling "would be followed by some form of mutual masturbation or intercrural intercourse. . . . Finally, oral copulation would be practiced, with Wilde as the active agent [*sic*], though this role was occasionally reversed. It gave him inspiration, he said."[11] Inspirited by "reversed" practices and reversible tropes, Wilde adopts a polite decorum (no danger to Algy's cuffs) in order to display and displace a desire to bury in the bun. In this way, serious Bunburyism releases a polytropic sexuality so mobile, so evanescent in speed and turn, that it traverses, Ariel-like, a fugitive path through oral, genital, and anal ports until it expends itself in and as the displacements of language. It was Wilde's extraordinary gift to return this vertigo of substitution and repetition to his audience. The inspiration he derived from fellatio he then redisseminated, usually *sotto voce,* through the actor's mouth. "The ejaculation," says Lady Bracknell in a line that did not survive the revisor's knife, "has reached my ears more than once."[12]

Oscillating between verbal and seminal emissions, Lady Bracknell's pun enacts the rhetorical equivocation essential to serious Bunburyism: an "illicit" signification is broadcast into the text even as it is also withdrawn under the cover of a licit one. In this way, Wilde duplicitously introduced into *Earnest* a parodic account of his own double life (the public thumbing of a private nose) as well as a trenchant critique of the heterosexist presumption requiring, here statutorily, that such a life be both double and duplicitous. And that *Earnest* is a text sliding deviously between exposé and critique, a text saturating its reader/viewer with blinding disseminal effusions, is simply a fact whose closeting or imprisonment we must tolerate no longer. To substantiate this claim, I adduce below a brief series of discrete indiscretions in which *Earnest* "goes Bunburying"—in which, that is, Wilde lifts to liminality his subcultural knowledge of "the terrible pleasures of double life."[13] In providing these few examples (others are adduced in a longer version of the present essay), I have drawn freely from both the three- and four-act versions of the play.[14]

1) "It is a very ungentlemanly thing to read a private cigarette case" (act 1, in both three- and four-act versions). In the trials of April–May 1895, Wilde would be compelled to submit again and again to "ungentlemanly" exegesis. Cigarette cases, usually silver ones purchased in Bond Street, were part (along with cash, other jewelry, food, and drink) of Wilde's payment to the male prostitutes he frequented. As the most durable material trace of Wilde's illegal sexual practice, these cigarette cases (replete with inscriptions such as "To X from O. W.") would be repeatedly introduced into evidence by the prosecution throughout the second and third trials. Consider the following exchange between Solicitor General Frank Lockwood, prosecutor at the third trial, and the defendant:

> Did you ever give one [a cigarette case] to Charles Parker also?—Yes, but I am afraid it cost only £1.
> Silver?—Well, yes. I have a great fancy for giving cigarette cases.
> To young men?—Yes.
> How many have you given?—I might have given seven or eight in 1892 or 1893.[15]

These cigarette cases are remarkably rich metonyms of Wilde's sexual practice. Literally inscribed with the condescension implicit in Wilde's cross-class and cross-generational sexual activity, they suggest his ambivalent relation to the prostitution he repeatedly enjoyed: he preferred to think of the cases as "gifts" not necessarily related to the sexual services they nonetheless purchased. As evidenciary deposits purchased and distributed by a "first-class misdemeanant," as Jack describes Ernest, they also bespeak a contradictory emotionality compounded of defiance, foolhardiness, and, it would seem, a certain desire to be caught. And finally, they insistently point to the orality that was both Wilde's sexual preference and *Earnest's* primary trope of displacement. Henry Wotton, after all, had already explicated for Dorian Gray the evanescent perfection of a good smoke ("You must have a cigarette. A cigarette is the perfect type of a perfect pleasure. It is exquisite, and it leaves one unsatisfied. What more can one want?"); and Edward Shelley, one of Wilde's lovers, testified that he "had received a letter from Mr. Wilde inviting him to 'come smoke a cigarette' with him."[16] Furthermore, while reporting the events of the first (that is, the libel) trial, the London daily *Evening News* (5 April 1895) printed the following: "The Old Bailey recoiled with loathing from the long ordeal of terrible suggestions that occupied the whole of yesterday when the cross-examination left the literary plane and penetrated the dim-lit perfumed rooms where the poet of the beautiful joined with valets and grooms *in the bond of silver cigarette cases*" (italics added).[17] As the affective verso to the recto of *Earnest*'s gay gaming with cigarette cases, the "recoil[ing]" and "loathing" specified in these lines indicate the precarious volatility of the Victorian male bonds so deftly manipulated by Wilde on "the literary plane." A gentleman might offer his peer, or even his inferior in age or class, the benefit of a good smoke or the gratuity of a cigarette case, but only so long as the gift did not suggest a bond more intimate than "proper" gentlemanly relation or condescension. The performative success of *Earnest*'s oral insouciance lay in its capacity to tease the limit of the proper without seeming to violate it seriously. Prosecutor Lockwood's "very ungentlemanly" reading of private cigarette cases reversed this rhetorical strategy by transforming the *glissando* of Wildean wit into that "long ordeal of terrible suggestion."

2) "Fathers are certainly not popular just at present. . . . At present fathers are at a terrible discount. They are like those chaps, the minor poets. They are never even quoted" (act 1 in the four-act versions). Spoken by Algy, these lines point underhandedly to the escalating filial warfare between the Marquess of Queensberry and Lord Alfred Douglas. This triangular narrative is too familiar to require recapitulation here, except to say that the battle was being engaged even as Wilde was composing *Earnest* and that Wilde's failure to manage the situation adroitly precipitated the debacle of the trials, during which Queensberry's charge that Wilde had been "posing as a somdomite [*sic*]" would find a decisive institutional context in which to be "quoted," at length and in detail. At the conclusion of the libel trial, the jury determined that Queensberry's charge of sodomitical "posing" had been proved and that his "Plea of Justification" elaborating this charge had been "published for the public benefit."

3) Canon Chasuble in response to Jack's concern that he is "a little too old now" to be rechristened as Ernest:

Oh, I am not by any means a bigoted Paedobaptist. . . . You need have no apprehensions [about immersion]. . . . Sprinkling is all that is necessary, or indeed, I think, advisable. . . . I have two similar ceremonies to perform. . . . A case of twins that occurred recently in one of the outlying cottages on your estate. . . . I don't know, however, if you would care to join them at the Font. Personally I do not approve myself of the obliteration of class-distinctions. (Act 2 in the four-act versions; a truncated version of these lines, without "Paedobaptist" and "the obliteration of class-distinctions," appears in the three-act version)

The always serious Canon Chasuble repeatedly falls into oblique and unwilling licentious allusion, as in these lines, which insinuate an outrageous chain of gay metonyms: "Paedobaptist," "sprinkling is all that is necessary," "in one of the outlying cottages," "if you would care to join them at the Font," "the obliteration of class-distinctions." If "Paedobaptist" (or "sprinkler of boys") was too blatantly obscene to survive revision, then the more subtly insinuated "outlying cottages" was not: only an elite audience would have known that by the late nineteenth century *cottage* had currency as a camp signifier for a trysting site, usually a public urinal. The word also had a more personal reference; Queensberry's Plea of Justification claimed that Oscar Wilde "in the year of our Lord One thousand eight hundred and ninety-three [a year before the composition of *Earnest*] at a house called 'The Cottage' at Goring . . . did solicit and incite . . . the said . . . acts of gross indecency."[18] Once these Bunburied significations are allowed to resonate through the passage, once we recognize with Canon Chasuble that "corrupt readings seem to have crept into the text," the references to "sprinkling" and "join[ing] them at the Font" assume an "obscene" valence. Similarly with "the obliteration of class-distinctions," which boisterously points to the almost pederastic, cross-class prostitution Wilde enjoyed. Just a few lines earlier, Jack had the effrontery to say, "I am very fond of children," a sentence definitely courting the bourgeois outrage of the thus "discounted" fathers who pursued Wilde through the court and into prison.

4) "The next time I see you I hope you will be Parker" (act 3 in the four-act versions). As has been "public knowledge" (however inert) for some thirty years, the most substantial revision of *Earnest* was the deletion (demanded by George Alexander, who produced the play, and unhappily submitted to by Wilde) of an entire scene in which Algy, Bunburying as Ernest, is almost arrested for dining expenses incurred by Jack, or rather Ernest, at the Savoy Hotel, the site of both Jack/Ernest's "grossly materialistic" gluttony and some of Wilde's sexual encounters. Jack, delighted that Algy should suffer for extravagances that can only be correctly charged to Ernest, counsels his younger brother "that incarceration would do you a great deal of good." Algy understandably protests: "Well, I really am not going to be imprisoned in the suburbs for having dined in the West End. It is perfectly ridiculous." Ridiculous or not, Wilde would very soon suffer an analogous imprisonment, but in "never-never Hertfordshire" (as Auden called it) this end is happily remitted when Jack, his "generosity misplaced," "pay[s] this monstrous bill for my brother."

Two aspects of this scene merit emphasis. First, Algy's pseudo-arrest for serious overeating strengthens my argument that in *Earnest* "luxurious and indolent" gluttony operates as a jubilant screen metaphor for otherwise unrepresentable pleasures. This cathexis of extravagant dining and sexual transgression refers directly to Wilde's double life; it was his regular practice to dine luxuriously with his lovers prior to sex, thereby enjoying *in camera* the same metaphor he would display on stage in *Earnest*. Often meeting his assignations in the private chambers of public restaurants (Willis's or the Solferino or elsewhere), he would dazzle them with opulence, language, and alcohol. Here is the testimony of one prostitute:

> He [i.e., Alfred Taylor, Wilde's procurer] took us to a restaurant in Rupert Street. I think it was the Solferino. We were shown upstairs to a private room, in which there was a dinner-table laid for four. After a while Wilde came in. I had never seen him before, but I had heard of him. We dined about eight o'clock. We all four sat down to dinner, Wilde sitting on my left.
> Was the dinner a good dinner?—Yes. The table was lighted with red-shaded candles. We had champagne with our dinner, and brandy and coffee afterwards. Wilde paid for the dinner. Subsequently Wilde said to me, "This is the boy for me—will you go to the Savoy Hotel with me?" I consented, and Wilde drove me in a cab to the hotel. He took me first into a sitting-room on the second floor, where he ordered some more drink—whiskey and soda. Wilde then asked me to go into his bedroom with him.
> Witness here described certain acts of indecency which he alleged took place in the bedroom.[19]

The witness in this exchange is Charles Parker, a sometime valet, whose testimony against Wilde seems alternately to have been purchased and coerced. It is the name *Parker* that brings us to the last point regarding the deleted arrest scene. The scene commences with the delivery of a calling card, which Algy reads: " 'Parker and Gribsby, Solicitors.' I don't know anything about them. Who are they?" After taking and reading the card, Jack facetiously speculates: "I wonder who they can be. I expect, Ernest, they have come about some business for your friend Bunbury. Perhaps Bunbury wants to make his will, and wishes you to be executor." With these intimations of Algy's forthcoming execution of Bunbury lingering in the air, Messrs. Parker and Gribsby are shown in by Merriman, the butler. But "they," it turns out, are not exactly a they but a he ("There is only one gentleman in the hall, sir," Merriman informs Jack), and the one gentleman is Gribsby "himself," come either to collect the debt or "remove" Ernest to Holloway Prison, one of those "suburb[an]" facilities through which Wilde would be funneled on his way to ignominy: "The surroundings, I admit, are middle class; but the gaol itself is fashionable and well-aired." (From the other side of the bars Wilde would not find it so.) As these threats of incarceration and death are being ventilated in the text, Jack first teases Algy for his (that is, Jack's) profligacy and then "generously" pays Ernest's debt, thereby forestalling the correction that would, Jack says, have done Algy "a great deal of good." Having dispatched his serious problem, Jack then luxuriates in a little trivial banter:

JACK: You are Gribsby, aren't you? What is Parker like?

GRIBSBY: I am both, sir. Gribsby when I am on unpleasant business, Parker on occasions of a less serious kind.

JACK: The next time I see you I hope you will be Parker.

("After all," Wilde writes in a letter, "the only proper intoxication is conversation.")[20] Unfortunately, the next time Wilde saw "Parker," Parker would be "on [the] unpleasant business" of a reverse, or disciplinary, Bunbury. Appearing in the Central Criminal Court under the guise of *Gribsby,* appearing, that is, as an agent of the law, Parker would testify to "acts of gross indecency" committed with Wilde in 1893 while Gribsby, apparently, was otherwise and elsewhere engaged.

It could have come as no surprise to the creator of "Parker and Gribsby, Solicitors" that he should find himself prosecuted for the same sexual practices he had been (con)celebrating just beneath the lovely pellucid "heterosexual" skin of *Earnest.* That, quite literally, his dirty linen should be "well-aired" in court he had already anticipated in this deleted arrest scene, which I have only begun to discuss here. Conversely and symmetrically, the extensive newspaper coverage of April–May 1895 would guarantee the dissemination of Lady Bracknell's also deleted line: a (somewhat expurgated) narrative of his "ejaculation[s]" would indeed reach respectable English "ears more than once." But there is nothing uncanny in any of this. No mere prognosticator foretelling the doom that was about to settle around him, Wilde was instead a prevaricator of genius, a polymath of the pleasurable lie. As a person committed to homosexual practice, he was compelled *by law* to inhabit the oscillating and nonidentical identity structure of "Parker and Gribsby, Solicitors": a structure in which transgression and law, homosexual delight and its arrest, are produced and reproduced as interlocked versions and inversions of each other.

Writing from this ambivalent and endangered position, Wilde stated with a parodist's clarity and a criminal's obscurity that the importance of being was neither X nor Y, male nor female, homosexual nor heterosexual, Parker nor Gribsby, Jack nor Ernest. Being will not be disclosed by the descent of an apt and singular signifier, a proper name naturally congruent with the object it seeks to denominate. In contrast to H. C.'s essentialist move, Wilde never heralds "a true inversion" that "respond[s] finally to a stimulus strong and prolonged enough, as a man awakens when he is loudly called." Belying such notions of true being, Wilde suggests instead that identity has always already been mislaid somewhere between such culturally "productive" binarisms as those listed above. Homosexual or heterosexual? Parker or Gribsby? Jack or

Ernest? Which name should be "loudly called"? "I am both, sir." (Both indeed, and therefore not quite either: Wilde emphatically does *not* imply recourse to the compromise formation of bisexuality or, in Ellis's telling contemporaneous phrase, "psychosexual hermaphroditism"; for this formation leaves undisturbed the conveniently bifurcated gender assumptions that it only seemingly fuses. The component desires that, when added together, comprise the "bi" remain after all quite distinct: shot with the masculine *or* feminine through and through.) Wildean doubling indicates instead a strategy of lexical or nominal traversal, a skidding within the code and between its semantic poles. In this vertiginous shuttle, being itself must slip on a name, or two. "But what own are you?" Gwen astutely asks of Jack just as he is about to become Ernest John. "What is your Christian name, now that you have become someone else?"

I love the last words of anything: the end of art is the beginning.
—Oscar Wilde

Child! You seem to me to use words without understanding their proper meaning.
—Jack to Cecily in the four-act *Earnest*

In lieu of "serious" closure, and as if to deride even the possibility of formal solution to the fugitivity of Bunburying desire, Wilde terminates his play, farcically and famously, with an impudent iteration of his farce's "trivial" but crucial pun; here, finally, "the confusion of tongues is no longer a punishment."[21] For *Earnest* may close only when Jack, in a sly parody of tragic *anagnorisis,* "realizes for the first time in [his] life the vital Importance of Being Earnest." At this moment, as the last words of the play swallow the first words of its title, its origin therefore dutifully assimilated to its terminus, Jack "realizes" himself in and as his "own" *double entendre:* in and as, that is, the difference between 1) himself and himself and 2) himself and the symbolic system that seeks to determine his "proper" name. Jack's punning "being," such as it is, is thus located and dislocated—located *as* dislocated—in an experience of radical *méconnaissance,* of verbal and ontological slippage, that in turn fortifies his already supercharged "perception of the extravagance of the signifier."[22] As he celebrates the "vital importance" of being his own pun, so does Jack embrace, even as he is embraced by, the signifier's power of perverse subsumption—by the delight it gives and takes as it incorporates "deviant" vectors under its nominally proper head.

This extravagance constitutes both the subject and the subjectivity of the play, their very sound and sense; the plot is so devised that the play closes only when Jack's "being" is absurdly assimilated to his, or rather his father's, name, a requirement that enables Wilde both to acknowledge and to deride the oedipal force of prior inscriptions. In response to the pseudo-urgent question of

Jack's identity ("Lady Bracknell, I hate to seem inquisitive, but would you kindly inform me who I am?"), the play dutifully answers with the Name of the Father, but in doing so also insistently repeats its insistence upon the letter; in its expiring breath *Earnest* resounds with Jack's other double name and so closes with an openness to what Jonathan Culler calls "the call of the phoneme." Invoking the materiality of sound and its powers of startling conjunction, the pun's "echoes tell of wild realms beyond the [semantic] code and suggest new configurations of meaning."[23] In such wild realms, the pleasures of the homophone arrive just as the differentiae of the hetero dissolve into sound and same. Culler continues:

> Puns, like portmanteaux, limn for us a model of language where the word is derived rather than primary and combinations of letters suggest meanings while at the same time illustrating the instability of meanings, their as yet ungrasped or undefined relations to one another, relations which further discourse (further play of similarity and difference) can produce. When one thinks of how puns characteristically demonstrate the applicability of a single signifying sequence to two different contexts, with quite different meanings, one can see how puns both evoke prior formulations, with the meanings they have deployed, and demonstrate their instability, the mutability of meaning, the production of meaning by linguistic motivation. Puns present us with a model of language as phonemes or letters combining in various ways to evoke prior meaning and to produce effects of meaning—with a looseness, unpredictability, excessiveness, shall we say, that cannot but disrupt the model of language as nomenclature.[24]

Culler here efficiently formulates the duplicitous operations by which the pun opens in language a counterhegemonic or revisionary space, a plastic site in which received meanings ("language as nomenclature") may be perversely turned, strangely combined, or even emptied out. Because they "both evoke prior formulations, with the meanings they have deployed, and demonstrate their instability, the mutability of meaning," puns discover in prior formulations the horizon of a fresh possibility. As a figure that itself limns the liminal, sporting on the hazy border where tongues of sound and sense intermingle as in a kiss, the pun broadcasts a faintly scandalous erotic power, a power of phonemic blending and semantic bending, whose feinting extensions Reason always does its best to rein in; as when, for instance, Samuel Johnson famously quibbles with punning Shakespeare: "A quibble is the golden apple for which he will always turn aside from his career, or stoop from his elevation. A quibble, poor and barren as it is, gave him such delight, that he was content to purchase it by the sacrifice of reason, propriety, and truth. A quibble was to him the fatal *Cleopatra* for which he lost the world, and was content to lose it."[25] Wilde's genius implicitly submits Johnson's critique to a dizzying inversion. Earnestly "sacrific[ing] reason, propriety, and truth," Wilde works his trade, transcoding golden apples into cucumber sandwiches and fatal Cleopatra into vital Ernest. (Indeed, gender transposition of the objects of male desire was Wilde's characteristic mode of gay figuration: "I do not interest myself in that British view of morals that sets Messalina above Sporus."[26]

But it was not against just any gendered signifier that Wilde directed the splaying call of the phoneme. He expressly targets the most overdetermined of such signifiers—the Name of the Father, here Ernest John Moncrieff—upon whose lips (if we may borrow a figure from the good Canon Chasuble) a whole cultural disposition is hung: the distribution of women and (as) property, the heterosexist configuration of eros, the genealogy of the "legitimate" male subject, and so on. Closing with a farcical pun on the father's name, Wilde discloses, in a single double stroke, the ironic cathexis (and the sometimes murderous double binding) by which the homosexual possibility is formally terminated or "exploded" ("Oh," says Algy "airily," "I killed Bunbury this afternoon") in order that a familiar heterosexualizing machinery may be installed, axiomatically and absurdly, "at last." So decisive is the descent of the father's name, so swift its powers of compulsion and organization, that (at least seemingly) it subdues the oscillations of identity, straightens the byways of desire, and completes—*voilà!*—the marital teleology of the comic text. All three couples, "after all," are swept away ("At last!" "At last!") in the heady and "natural" rush toward presumptive conjugal bliss: a rush so heady that it peremptorily dismisses, for instance, both Cecily's exigent desire for an "Ernest" and Algy's own earlier caution against the exclusionary erotics of heterosexist integration: "Nothing will induce me to part with Bunbury, and if you [i.e., Jack] ever get married, which seems to me extremely problematic, you will be very glad to know Bunbury. A man who marries without knowing Bunbury has a very tedious time of it." Forgetting this brief dissertation on interminable Bunburyism, Algy fairly leaps toward marriage, thereby fulfilling, as if by amnesia, the comic topos which dictates that marital conjunction, or its proleptic image, shall close the otherwise open circuits of desire.

And yet the closural efficacy of this compulsory heterosexual sweep, especially any gesture it might make in the direction of the "natural" ("I mean it naturally is Ernest," as Jack assures Gwen), is rendered instantly absurd—or, as Algy puts it, "extremely problematic"—by, first, its hypertrophic textuality and, second, by Wilde's insistence upon both the sovereignty of the signifier over its signified and the signifier's "liability" to indiscreet slippage, its exorbitant appetite for signifieds. Not only must Jack seek his "natural" or "proper" identity in an antic succession of texts (he *rushes to bookcase and tears the books out,*" reads the stage direction), but in an earlier version this scene of frantic reading had included, besides "the Army Lists of the last forty years," an allusion to Robert Hichens's *The Green Carnation* (1894), a contemporaneous parody of Wilde's affair with Douglas.[27] Perusing this text from her unimpeachable altitude, Lady Bracknell emits an evaluation: "This treatise, the 'Green Carnation,' as I see it is called, seems to be a book about the culture of exotics. It contains no reference to Generals in it. It seems a morbid and middle-class affair."[28] After this and other preposterous citations (Canon

Chasuble, for instance, is handed a Bradshaw railway guide "of 1869, I observe"), it is of course the book with the "reference to Generals in it" that brings home the prize and so surprises Jack with his now naturally punning self.

In any case, the paternally sanctioned "being" that Jack's reading hereby secures entails a literal reinscription of the same pseudo-opposition (*Jack* versus *Ernest* or *Ernest John*) under which his double life had all along been conducted, except that the order of the terms has been inverted: where cognomen was, there pseudonym shall be. In this inversion, the closural move that would repair Jack's splayed identity and terminate the shuttle and slide of Bunburying desire discloses again, discloses "at last," neither the deep truth of essential being nor the foundational monad of a "real" sexuality. In contrast, for instance, to the memoirs of H. C., whose sexual identity is definitively secured once he is "loudly called" by his "true inversion," *Earnest* deploys inversion as a tropological machine, as a mode of erotic mobility, evasion, play. Hence Wilde terminates his farce with terminological play on the terms-in-us: with a punning recognition of, on the one hand, the determinative force of prior inscriptions and, on the other, the transvaluing power of substitution. Thus *Earnest* does not terminate at all but insistently relays and repeats the irreducible oscillations, back and forth, froth and buck, of very much the same erotic binarism that would soon be definitely consolidated in the violent counterframing of homo- and heterosexualities (two terms that, by the way, appear nowhere in Wilde's lexicon).

But Wilde's is a crucial, a crux-making, repetition—crucial not merely because he deploys repetition to *make* a difference, but also because the difference he makes he then *makes audible* in and as the disseminal excess with which he laves his pun, and through his pun, his audience, his readers. At once titular and closural, originary and terminal, Wilde's pun practices the erotics of repetition that Barthes, collating Sade and Freud, would later theorize so compactly: "Repetition itself creates bliss . . . to repeat excessively is to enter into loss, into the zero of the signified."[29] Because in *Earnest* the object of this zero targeting, the site of this obsessional emptying, is nothing less than the marriageable male subject (let us say, anachronistically, the integral and heterosexual male subject) whose strength and legitimacy are sanctioned by the frail transmissibility of his father's empowering names, Wilde effectively empties both name and subject of their natural content and naturalizing force. In doing so he reopens *within both* an erotic space that had been prematurely closed—foreclosed, precisely, as *non nominandum*.

Wilde opens this space through a subtle dilation upon the irreducibly ambivalent erotics of the pun. On the semantic level, puns work precisely because they presuppose and reaffirm a *received difference* between (at least) two objects, concepts, or meanings; "evok[ing] prior formulations, with the meanings they have deployed" (Culler), puns operate as the semantic conservators of the hetero; in this sense, they police the borders of difference. (It is, for instance, only because *ejaculation* may mean abruptly emitted speech that Lady Bracknell may properly ejaculate on the subject of ejaculations.) But on the phonemic level this work of differentiation is quite undone. When referred to the ear, to the waiting body of the reader/listener, punning becomes homoerotic because homophonic. Aurally enacting a drive toward the same, the pun's sound cunningly erases, or momentarily suspends, the semantic differences by which the hetero is both made to appear and made to appear natural, lucid, self-evident. Difference is repeated until difference vanishes in the ear. (The ejaculation, Lady Bracknell is right to insist, *"has* reached [our] ears more than once"; repetition guarantees a certain saturation.) And when difference vanishes the result is a correlative plosion at the mouth, the peal of laughter marking precisely the vanishing point at which good sense collapses into melting pleasure, or even bliss. This explains in part the distaste with which a homophobic critical tradition has regarded puns, an affect usually attributed to the "cheapness" of the thrills they so dearly provide. (In and out of school, it seems, serious pleasure requires still harder exactions.) No surprise, then, that heterocentric culture should disdain the linguistic process by which the very power of the hetero—the power to differentiate among signifieds, objects, beings—is, on the phonemic level at least, so laughingly disdained.

Understanding all of this precisely, Wilde harnessed the erotic ambivalence of the pun for the affined purposes of pleasure, transvaluation, critique. "I am sending you, of course, a copy of my book," Wilde wrote to a friend in 1899 after Sebastian Melmoth had received copies of *Earnest*'s first pressings. "How I used to toy with that tiger Life! I hope you will find a place for me amongst your nicest books. . . . I should like it to be within speaking distance of *Dorian Gray*."[30] "Amongst your nicest books" but still "within speaking distance of *Dorian Gray*": this ironic juxtaposition very nicely glosses the urbane duplicity with which Wilde insinuated the revisionary discourse of an "Urning"—the term of gay self-reference devised by Karl Heinrich Ulrichs some thirty years before, a term of which Wilde was very well aware—into his critical pun on Earnest, and through this pun, into the "nicest" of his texts. The intrinsic cross-switching within the pun of hetero- and homosexualizing impulsions provided Wilde with the perfect instrument for negotiating an impossibly difficult discursive situation. Writing "at large" for a respectably straight (not to say heterosexist) audience whose sensibilities he could afford to tease but not transgress, Wilde necessarily penned to a double measure. While mimicking the dramatic conventions of heterosexual triumph, he inserted within them the "unspeakable" traces of homosexual delight: inserted them where they would be least welcome—in the vocables of the paternal signifier, itself the guarantor of heterophallic order. The *Urning*, to put it wildly, would hide in *Ernest*, thereby pun-burying and Bunburying at the same time. ("Everything," Derrida says, "comes down to the ear you hear me with.")[31]

Of course, as Wilde insisted, his titular pun is "trivial," and it is so in the technical, etymological—and punning—sense of the word. *Trivial* not only marks what is "common," "ordinary," and "of small account" but indicates as well a crossroads or terminus "placed where three roads meet" (*OED*).[32] Etymologically speaking, the trivial is the locus of a common or everyday convergence: a site where paths (of meaning, of motion, of identity) cross and switch, a pivot in which vectors (and babies) enter in one direction and exit in another. The text represents this notion in two ways: materially and mechanically, in Victoria Station, the terminus where the "romantic story of [Jack's] origins" begins, where with a little help from Miss Prism (whose name, by the way, refracts an ocular version of the same idea) baby Jack enters as Ernest and exits as John; and, audibly and obsessively, in the pun on *e(a)rnest,* which operates exactly in the manner of a railway terminal. There should now be no difficulty in specifying the three paths that cross and merge here to such preposterous effect: 1) a plain and proper name (ultimately disclosed as the Name of the Father) that, for obscure reasons, "produces vibrations"; 2) the esteemed high Victorian quality of moral earnestness, of serious fidelity to truth, an attribute specifically gendered as "manly" and repeatedly derided by Wilde; 3) a pun-buried and coded allusion (and here two tongues, German and English, mingle) to a specifically homosexual thematics, to the practices and discourses of the "Urning" and of "Uranian love." (That Wilde was familiar with the specialized vocabulary of the "Urning" is beyond dispute: "A patriot put in prison for loving his country loves his country, and a poet put in prison for loving boys loves boys. To have altered my life would have been to have admitted that Uranian love is ignoble. I hold it to be noble—more noble than other forms.")[33] In this laughing inversion of propriety and authority, Wilde puts the intrinsically homophilic impulsion of the pun (its drive, at the phonemic level, toward the erasure of difference) to historically specific uses; not until the 1890s would the term *Urning* have been sufficiently diffused into English to operate within Wilde's punning trivium.[34]

Thus submitting his play to the delirium of the signifier, Wilde manages to achieve what Barthes would later call *subtle subversion,* by which he means that which "is not directly concerned with destruction, evades the paradigm, and seeks some *other* term: a third term, which is not, however, a synthesizing term but an eccentric, extraordinary term."[35] In *The Importance of Being Earnest,* I am arguing, Wilde invents just such an extraordinary term: a third, ternary, and trivial term in which oppositional meanings are not synthesized or sublated so much as they are exchanged, accelerated, derailed, terminated, cross-switched. Indeed, he invents this term twice over, invents it in duplicate, so that it emerges only under alias, submitted to an originary masquerade of two farcical pseudonyms. The first of these is Bunbury, the second is Ernest John. The interchangeability of these two terms (in exile Wilde even referred to *Earnest* as *Bunbury*) suggests an irreducible isomorphism between the technically unspeakable homoerotics of interminable Bunburyism and the structural bifurcation of the nominally heterosexual male subject, a point upon which Algy exuberantly insists when he explains to Jack why "I was quite right in saying you were a Bunburyist": "You have invented a very useful younger brother called Ernest, in order that you may be able to come up to town as often as you like. I have invented an invaluable permanent invalid called Bunbury, in order that I may be able to go down into the country whenever I choose. Bunbury is perfectly invaluable." In the four-act version Algy is even more concise; responding to Cecily's claim that Uncle Jack "has got such strict principles about everything. He is not like you," Algy disagrees: "Oh. I am bound to say that I think Jack and I are very like each other. I really do not see much difference between us."[36] Given this invincible parallelism, and the obviously reversible erotics of "coming up" and "going down," Jack fully qualifies as "one of the most advanced Bunburyists I know."

And yet we recall that the hetero-closure of the plot is predicated upon the formal expulsion of Bunbury, who is consequently "quite exploded" at play's end. But even as Bunbury is eliminated from the text, his (non)being thereby formally remanded to the closet from which at least his name had emerged, so also is he posthumously disseminated into the redoubled being of Wilde's earnest hero, in whose equivocal name Bunbury may be said to succeed his own surcease. Passing away only to be passed on, Bunbury is buried, and buried alive, within the duplicitous precincts of the titularly "natural" male subject. With this irreducibly ambivalent movement—partly homicidal, partly carceral, partly liberatory—Wilde closes his great farce, submitting to the heterocentric conventions that his pun thereafter continues to exceed and deride. That pun, with its gay shuttling, constitutes Wilde's bequest to a posterity that is only now learning how to receive so rare a gift: one whose power of posthumous critique is conveyed in and as an excess of signification, pleasure, even bliss. In *Earnest,* this excess is never laid to rest. Not every explosion, however terminal, implies a death. In Bunbury's end is Ernest John's beginning. . . .

Notes

1. W. H. Auden, "An Improbable Life," in *Forewords and Afterwords* (New York, 1973), 323. This essay, a review of Hart-Davis's edition of Wilde's letters, appeared originally in the *New Yorker,* 9 March 1963; it is also available in Richard Ellmann, ed., *Oscar Wilde: A Collection of Critical Essays* (Englewood Cliffs, N.J., 1969), 116–37.

2. D. A. Miller, *The Novel and the Police* (Berkeley, 1988), 207. Miller's landmark essay "Secret Subjects, Open Secrets," from which I quote here, has informed my thinking throughout these pages.

3. Michel Foucault, "Nietzsche, Genealogy, History," in *The Foucault Reader,* ed. Paul Rabinow (New York, 1984), 76.

4. Joel Fineman, "The Significance of Literature: *The Importance of Being Earnest,*" *October* 15 (1980): 83.

5. For more on Henry Shirley Bunbury, see William Green, "Oscar Wilde and the Bunburys," *Modern Drama* 21, no. 1 (1978): 67–80. I disagree with Green emphatically on the importance and function of Bunbury, to wit: "Even allowing for the possibility that the term may have existed in the form of a private joke, Wilde had ample opportunity to avoid using it in the play if he suspected it had any homosexual connotations which might have drawn attention to him. . . . Wilde could have substituted another name for Bunbury."

6. Ibid., 71. The English colloquialism for buttocks is of course not *bun* but *bum,* but the frail consonantal difference distinguishing the two terms remains always liable to elision, especially in performance, whether in a slip of the actor's tongue or in the labyrinth of the auditor's ear. *Bun,* as I argue above, points immediately to Algy's serious overeating and mediately to Wilde's sexual practice, which, his biographers agree, was primarily oral. In this regard we should remember that Wilde was not, as is often assumed, convicted of sodomy; rather he was prosecuted and convicted under section 11 of the Criminal Law Amendment Act of 1885, which criminalized all "acts of gross indecency" committed between males, whether in public or private. For an analysis of the conceptual shifts entailed by this legislation, see Ed Cohen, "From Sodomy to Gross Indecency," *South Atlantic Quarterly* 88, no. 1 (Winter 1989): 181–217.

7. Fineman, "Significance of Literature," 89.

8. André Gide, *The Journals of André Gide,* trans. Justin O'Brien, 3 vols. (New York, 1948). 2:410.

9. The *OED* citation for *Banbury* reads: "A town in Oxfordshire, England, formerly noted for the number and zeal of its Puritan inhabitants, still for its cakes." Cf. also the Mother Goose nursery rhyme, "Ride a cock-horse to Banbury Cross." The phonemic and imagistic affinities between *Bunbury* and *Banbury* proved too much for at least one of the typists working from Wilde's handwritten manuscripts. In a typescript of the play dated "19 Sep. 94" by Mrs. Marshall's Type Writing Office, *Bunbury* repeatedly appears as *Banbury.* Wilde, whose careless, looping handwriting no doubt encouraged the error, patiently restored the *us.*

10. This line, spoken by Miss Prism about Ernest (whom, of course, she has not met), does not appear in the three-act *Earnest* with which most readers are familiar, but can be found in the various manuscript and typescript drafts of the so-called "original" four-act version. A brief explanation of the textual confusion surrounding *Earnest* is in order. When in 1898, *après le deluge,* M. Melmoth sought to publish Mr. Wilde's farce, his only recourse to "the play itself" was to a truncated copy text, George Alexander's prompt copy, that had provided the basis for the short-lived 1895 production. Since Wilde's own drafts and copies of *Earnest* had been auctioned off in the bankruptcy proceedings following his imprisonment, "Alexander's manuscript," as Wilde called it, was for all purposes the only extant text upon which to base the published version of 1899. The problem with Alexander's typescript is that it contained substantial cuts, some authorial and some not, including, most famously, the excision of an entire scene in which Algy is almost arrested for Ernest's outstanding debts; this cut was essential to the structural reorganization of four acts into three. That Alexander's emendations were significant there can be no doubt; upon seeing the play on opening night, Wilde (whom Alexander had dismissed from rehearsals) is reported to have remarked: "My dear Aleck, it was charming, quite charming. And, do you know, from time to time I was reminded of a play I once wrote myself, called THE IMPORTANCE OF BEING EARNEST"; quoted in A. E. W. Mason, *Sir George Alexander and the St. James Theatre* (New York, 1969), 79. Not until the 1950s would the various working manuscripts and typescripts of the "original" four-act versions begin to surface, so that, by way of a temporal inversion that Wilde surely would have delectated, *Earnest* is a work whose lost origins *post*date its publication by some fifty years. Throughout this essay I refer both to the familiar three-act version and to the antecedent four-act versions without worrying the issue of textual authority. Unless otherwise specified all references here to the four-act version are to *The Importance of Being Earnest: A Trivial Comedy for Serious People in Four Acts as Originally*

Written by Oscar Wilde, ed. Sarah Augusta Dickson, 2 vols. (New York, 1955); Miss Prism's line as quoted above can be found in Dickson, *Earnest,* 1:77. See also *The Definitive Four-Act Version of The Importance of Being Earnest,* ed. Ruth Berggren (New York, 1987), 23–41.

11. H. Montgomery Hyde, *Oscar Wilde* (New York, 1975), 187.

12. Dickson, *Earnest,* 1:146. This line occurs during a wonderful bit of stage business in which, while Jack and Lady Brancaster (as she is called in the four-act versions) are discussing "the painful circumstances of [Jack's] origin," Algy and Cecily are hiding "behind [a] screen . . . whispering and laughing." As the good lady speaks, Algy's attempts to silence or "hush" Cecily interrupt her discourse; annoyed by these intrusions, Lady Brancaster complains: "It is clear that there is someone who says 'Hush' concealed in this apartment. The ejaculation has reached my ears more than once. It is not at any time a very refined expression, and its use, when I am talking, is extremely vulgar, and indeed insolent. I suspect it to have proceeded from the lips of someone who is of more than usually low origin." In this sadly excised tableau, Wilde compactly stages the sociopolitical operations of Bunburying representation, in which a discourse of social rectitude is interrupted by an "ejaculation" that can be heard but not seen. As the screen behind which Cecily and Algy are sporting very nicely materializes the strategy of visual occlusion, so does the transposition of "hush" and "ejaculation" make audible, as laughter, the Bunburying operations by which a secret erotics may be mouthed but not quite bespoken. We should note in passing, too, that Wilde here anticipates the more-than-audible ejaculation with which Roland Barthes closes *The Pleasure of the Text,* trans. Richard Miller (New York, 1975). Cinema, Barthes writes, "succeed[s] in shifting the signified a great distance and in throwing, so to speak, the anonymous body of the actor into my ear: it granulates, it crackles, it caresses, it grates, it cuts, it comes: that is bliss" (67).

13. Oscar Wilde, *The Picture of Dorian Gray* (Oxford, 1981), 79.

14. See note 10 above.

15. Anonymous, *Oscar Wilde: Three Times Tried,* 2 vols. ("Paris," n.d.), 389 (the two volumes are consecutively paginated). This text, which appears to be a pirated edition of another book issued anonymously under the same title by the Ferrestone Press (London, 1912), claims to be the most "complete and accurate account of this long and complicated case. Special care, it will be seen, has been devoted to the elucidation of abstruse legal points. . . . The evidence of witnesses, together with the prolonged cross-examination of Wilde in each of the three trials, is given as fully as possible, with due regard to discretion."

16. *Three Times Tried,* 355.

17. I encountered this passage while reading Ed Cohen's *Talk on the Wilde Side: Toward a Genealogy of the Discourse on Male Sexuality* (Ph.D. diss., Stanford University, 1988), to which I remain indebted. I quote with permission of the author.

18. Queensberry's "Plea of Justification" is reprinted as appendix A in H. Montgomery Hyde, *The Trials of Oscar Wilde* (New York, 1962), 323–27. The 1843 Criminal Libel Act, the statute under which Wilde sued Queensberry for accusing him of "posing as a somdomite [*sic*]," permitted the defendant (i.e., Queensberry) to place before the court a document, or "Plea of Justification," supporting the allegation for which the libel suit was being prosecuted.

19. *Three Times Tried,* 191.

20. Oscar Wilde, *The Letters of Oscar Wilde,* ed. Rupert Hart-Davis (New York, 1962), 749. *Conversation* is itself a pun, referring doubly to interlocution and intercourse.

21. Barthes, *Pleasure,* 4.

22. Ibid., 65.

23. Jonathan Culler, "The Call of the Phoneme," in Culler, ed., *On Puns: The Foundation of Letters* (New York, 1988), 3.

24. Ibid., 14.

25. Samuel Johnson, "Preface to Shakespeare," in *Poetry and Prose,* ed. Mona Wilson (London, 1970), 500; quoted in Culler, "Call of the Phoneme," 6–7.

26. Wilde, *Letters,* 594.

27. Robert Hichens's travesty of the Wilde-Douglas affair was originally published anonymously (London, 1894); for Wilde's bemused response to *The Green Carnation*, see *Letters*, 373.

28. Dickson, *Earnest*, vol. 2, facsimile typescript of act 4, p. 34; also Berggren, *Earnest*, 190.

29. Barthes, *Pleasure*, 41.

30. Wilde, *Letters*, 778.

31. Jacques Derrida, "Otobiographies: The Teaching of Nietzsche and the Politics of the Proper Name," in *The Ear of the Other*, ed. Christie McDonald (Lincoln, Neb., 1988), 4.

32. The pun thus also slyly alludes to our culture's paradigmatic instance of "trivial" meeting: the terminal convergence of father and son at the crossroads called Phokis, where Oedipus meets his father and his fate. "If I understand you," says a darkening Oedipus to his mother Jocasta, "Laios was killed / At a place where three roads meet." Trivial indeed. Against the background of these tragic resonances, we may read Wilde's earnest *and* trivial pun as a gay countersign to the murderous seriousness of oedipal heterosexuality; Sophocles, *Oedipus Rex*, trans. Dudley Fitts and Robert Fitzgerald (New York, 1969), 37.

33. Wilde, *Letters*, 705.

34. It is crucial to note here that the *Ernest/Earnest/Urning* pun did not originate with Wilde; it made its literary debut two years before Wilde began work on *Earnest*, and Wilde stole—or, as literary critics like to say, "appropriated"—the pun for the transvaluing purposes of his own genius. More than a merely private joke, the wordplay first appeared in a volume of poetry called *Love in Earnest* (London, 1892) by the Uranian writer John Gambril Nicholson. A collection of sonnets, ballads, and lyrics, *Love in Earnest* included a poem of pederastic devotion entitled "Of Boys' Names":

> Old memories of the Table Round
>   In Percival and Lancelot dwell,
> Clement and Bernard bring the sound
>   Of anthems in the cloister-cell,
>   And Leonard vies with Lionel
> In stately step and kingly frame,
>   And Kenneth speaks of field and fell,
> And Ernest sets my heart a-flame.
>
> One name can make my pulses bound,
>   No peer it owns, nor parallel,
> By it is Vivian's sweetness drowned,
>   And Roland, full as organ-swell;
>   Though Frank may ring like silver bell,
> And Cecil softer music claim,
>   They cannot work the miracle,—
> 'Tis Ernest sets my heart a-flame.
>
> Cyril is lordly, Stephen crowned
>   With deathless wreaths of asphodel,
> Oliver whispers peace profound,
>   Herbert takes arms his foes to quell,
>   Eustace with sheaves is laden well,
> Christopher has a nobler fame,
>   And Michael storms the gates of Hell,
> But Ernest sets my heart a-flame.

ENVOY.
My little Prince, Love's mystic spell
Lights all the letters of your name,
And you, if no one else, can tell
Why Ernest sets my heart a-flame.

Quoted from Timothy d'Arch Smith, *Love in Earnest* (London, 1970), xviii; Smith's book, a study of the Uranian poets, derives its title from Nicholson's.

Nicholson's book did not go unnoticed among gay readers and interlocutors. I think it self-evident that Wilde knew of it; the joke quoted above about "those chaps, the minor poets [who] are never even quoted" is likely Wilde's oblique acknowledgement of Nicholson's priority, although no doubt Wilde would have happily expatiated upon the (merely belated) originality of his own deployment of the pun. And certainly John Addington Symonds, who died a year *before* Wilde began composing his farce, caught the pun's gay valence. In a letter of 2 July 1892 Symonds wrote to a friend: "Have you read a volume of sonnets called 'Love in Earnest'? It is written by a Schoolmaster in love with a boy called Ernest." That "Wilde's" pun predates his own use of it would thus seem incontrovertible.

35. Barthes, *Pleasure*, 51.
36. Dickson, *Earnest*, 1:111.

Algernon's Other Brothers

KERRY POWELL

Our farcical comedies are all modelled on much the same lines, we are beginning
to perceive, and novelty in their plot is becoming a rare quality.
—From the *Era's* review of the Parisian farce *Les Ricochets de l'amour,*
5 January 1895

It has often been suggested that this play forms a genre in itself.
—Epifanio San Juan, Jr., in *The Art of Oscar Wilde*
commenting on *The Importance of Being Earnest*

I

On the one hand unique, "a genre in itself," on the other *The Importance of
Being Earnest* is a shameless ingathering of devices which characterized
Victorian farce, especially as it came to be written and staged in the 1890s. A
month after the *Era's* theatre critic announced he was "beginning to perceive" a
disturbing sameness in current farces, along came *Earnest* as if to prove his
point. But it is a point difficult to substantiate today, for the farces of this
period—although frequently zesty, readable, and spontaneously funny—are
with few exceptions hopelessly obscure. Few were ever printed, despite great
success on stage in some cases, and as a result even the names of most go
unrecorded in literary history.

   Like its hero, therefore, *The Importance of Being Earnest* can be said to have
lost its "parents"—those forgotten farces which in a real sense gave birth to
Wilde's play. In these unpretentious works, one can trace the genetic heritage
with which *The Importance of Being Earnest* is endowed. W. Lestocq and E. M.
Robson's *The Foundling,* which opened at Terry's theatre a half-year before the
first performance of *Earnest,* contains the dramatic basis of Wilde's play—the
story of a twenty-five-year-old foundling in search of the parents he "lost." But
what about the imaginary invalid named Bunbury, and the imaginary brother
named Ernest? These cannot be discovered in *The Foundling*—but they appear

Reprinted, with permission of Cambridge University Press, from *Oscar Wilde and the Theatre of the 1890s*
(Cambridge, England: Cambridge University Press, 1990), 124–39.

in the manuscript of an unpublished farce called *Godpapa,* which amused audiences at the Court Theatre for four months in 1891–2.

Wilde could not have written *The Importance of Being Earnest* without a thorough, practical knowledge of what was being done in the lowly theatrical genre of farce in the 1890s. He would have had, without the example of his obscure forerunners, little or nothing to say. Yet *Earnest* has survived, while nearly all the others perished utterly after their moment in the footlights. What distinguished Wilde's play—besides its publication as a book—was an undercurrent of seriousness which was mostly absent among other farces of the day.

Nothing could be more mistaken than the popular and traditional view of Wilde's play as a wisp of fantasy, void of significance and unconnected even to reality.[1] As Richard Ellmann has pointed out, *Earnest* resembles Wilde's earlier work in leading toward a ceremonial unmasking, its characters, like their creator, craving to show what they are.[2] In addition to serving as a staging ground for identity, the play's concern with appearances (Algy "has nothing but he looks everything" [p. 92]) may be, in part, Wilde's comment on a society of spectacle in which "all that mattered was the authority of the participants' poses and the glitter of their props."[3] Wilde's subjects, as Eric Bentley observes, are death, money, marriage, sociology, economics, and the class system, and his "flippancies repeated, developed, and, so to say, elaborated almost into a system amount of something in the end—and thereby cease to be flippant."[4] Katharine Worth finds in *Earnest* Wilde's "supreme demolition of late nineteenth-century social and moral attitudes, the triumphal conclusion to his career as revolutionary moralist."[5] It is highly ironic that Wilde achieved such effects in *Earnest* by using the mechanisms he had employed in the society dramas, with their almost fatal hesitations between sentimental morality and the dandy's world of pure form. Here again are women with a past, "ideal" yet guilty males, motifs of hidden parentage and mistaken identity, and the pivotal plot-object (handbag rather than fan). These similarities illustrate the close relation of farce and melodrama, as Worth has shown, but also the difference between the two forms.[6] Once out of melodrama, Wilde could dissolve in the dandy's laughter the notions of sin and guilt that were so potent, and disruptive, in his previous works.

II

Affording a holiday from earnest reality, Victorian farces appropriately find their setting in a vacation resort by the sea or some other hideaway where the routine and even the values of ordinary life can be suspended.[7] Thus W. E. Suter's popular farce *The Lost Child* (1863) is set in a "garden of a Seaside Hotel at . . . ," and the scene of *Tom, Dick, and Harry* (1893) is laid at the "Sea View

Hotel."[8] *The Foundling* takes place at the resort town of Brighton, after its orphaned hero "lost" his parents at another coastal watering place—Margate.[9] Its predecessor, *An Innocent Abroad*—performed in January 1895—depicts a sober broker forsaking his wife and City respectability for a card-playing lark in Brighton.[10] In *The Importance of Being Earnest,* which opened the next month, Jack Worthing's name derives from a seacoast resort in Sussex, and his problematic identity is linked curiously with luggage mislaid in Victoria Station—"the Brighton line" (p. 31).

In fact 1890s farce is obsessed with travel, whether to the sea in *An Innocent Abroad,* to foreign parts in Fred Horner's *The Late Lamented,* or to a country house in *The Importance of Being Earnest.* Occasionally a Jack Worthing visits London to escape tedium elsewhere, but more common is an Algernon Moncrieff who departs town to seek adventure at the seashore or in the country. Remarkable prominence is given to railway stations and luggage. A character in *Godpapa,* preparing to leave from Euston Station, stuffs his suitcase so full of mustard leaves and hot-water bottles that he cannot force it shut. In *Mr. Boodle's Predicament* (1890) comic mixups ensue when a lady novelist finds a handbag with her initials on it in Queensborough Station. In *The Importance of Being Earnest* confusion arises when another lady novelist *loses* a handbag with her initials on it in Victoria Station. And in *Mr. Boodle's Predicament* Theresa Babbacombe carries her manuscripts in the luggage, just as Laetitia Prism meant to do in *Earnest*—before she absent-mindedly put the draft of her novel in a bassinette and laid the baby Ernest in her handbag.[11]

En route to or from a railway terminal, carrying luggage or looking for lost bags, these travelers are in flight not only from their place, but also from their identity in time. Repeatedly they shed adulthood and revert, in one way or other, to the condition of children. Thus Wilde's young men find a way out of their romantic difficulties when they determine to get christened, as Jack says, like "other babies" (p. 54). In *Crime & Christening* (1891), a farce by two dramatists calling themselves Richard Henry, some of the incongruous humor arises from the notion that aging Uncle Gribble is about to undergo baptism.[12] In *Adoption* (1890), by the same authors, an engaged couple without income advertises in the *Times* for "any wealthy bachelor or spinster who would adopt them."[13] *The Magistrate* (1885), by Arthur Wing Pinero, presents a youth whom everyone believes to be fourteen, but is actually nineteen years old, displaying an unseasonable interest in liquor and sex.[14] In Arthur Law's *The New Boy* (1894), one of the biggest hits of the mid-1890s, a grown man mistaken for a schoolboy goes about smoking, ordering whiskey, and muttering "I'm damned!!!!"[15] Adults masquerade as children, and the chasm which opens between appearance and truth forms the basis for laughter. But the prominence of christening and other infantile imagery makes sense, too, in its kinship with the impulse by which these characters become ardent travelers and vacationers. Beginning the world again in a comic fantasy of childhood is one way they gratify the need to be somewhere else, somebody else. Without being self-consciously thematic, these farces make life a seaside holiday in which adult cares and duties can be postponed or set aside as characters become, in effect, perpetual children.

Escapes into childhood, to the seacoast, and to the country are inseparable in late Victorian farce from what Algernon Moncrieff calls "Bunburying." His creation of an imaginary "dreadful invalid" enables Algy to plead the excuse of visiting a sick friend in order to evade responsibility and do as he likes. "If it wasn't for Bunbury's extraordinary bad health," he explains to Jack, "I wouldn't be able to dine with you at Willis's to-night, for I have been really engaged to Aunt Augusta for more than a week" (p. 15). The concept of Bunburying—and its name—could have been suggested to Wilde by the recent success of *Godpapa,* a farce at the Comedy Theatre in which young Reggie describes the imaginary ailment of an acquaintance named Bunbury in order to indulge his own whims without interference: "The fact is he's under the slavery of drink just now. It's something he's read about in the papers and he's trying it as an experiment."[16] Not only does Bunbury's affliction enable the hero to conceal a disreputable double life, as in *Earnest,* but there is an absurdly premeditated quality about the illness in both plays. In *Godpapa* Bunbury— played by Charles H. E. Brookfield—becomes a drunk because "it's something he's read about in the papers," while in *Earnest,* as Algy says, "The doctors found out that Bunbury could not live . . . so Bunbury died" (p. 87). One Bunbury shows unusual reliance on journalism in health matters, while the other, as Lady Bracknell sardonically observes, "seems to have had great confidence in the opinion of his physicians" (p. 87).

But Bunburying, if not the name itself, is highly characteristic of late-century farce. Characters form imaginary identities or engage in fictitious activities which enable them to invigorate their respectable but humdrum lives. In the country, in his position as guardian to Cecily, Jack Worthing must "adopt a very high moral tone on all subjects"—so he invents a disreputable brother Ernest whose "dreadful scrapes" give him an excuse to escape to London as often as he wishes (p. 14). The successful farce *Jane* (1890), by W. Lestocq and Harry Nicholls, features a hero who creates a mythical spouse and uses her supposed extravagance as the pretext for extracting money from a wealthy relative.[17] Pinero's *The Schoolmistress* (1886) has a prim heroine who leads a double life as a music-hall singer, leaving her husband every night on the excuse "that I am visiting a clergyman's wife at Hereford."[18]

But in one of the rare farces by a woman, the popular *Our Flat* (1893) by Mrs. Musgrave, a wife decides she has "no genius for the domestic arts" and decides to enter the masculine world of play writing. "I'll not act in a play but I'll *write* one," Margery Sylvester determines, thus entering secretly into competition with her husband, a struggling writer of melodramas.[19] Her play, a farcical comedy written from her own life, becomes a huge success, with the result that thereafter she and her husband will collaborate on joint productions. "Bunburying" in *Our Flat* is more, therefore, than an essentially harmless lark.

In this play written by a woman it becomes, as it would in *Earnest,* a means of developing alternatives to the stifling roles that society imposes on individuals. Margery writes her way to a new and unconventional identity as feminine playwright, the equal of her husband, and thus at the curtain, not unlike *Earnest,* the creatively fashioned *alter ego* dissolves into the actual self of the Bunburyist.

The sheer illicit fun of the secret life is what most farces emphasize, and in these mostly male-written plays the "Bunbury" amounts to little more than a husband's philandering. Often the action centers round a shady hotel—the Hôtel Macotte in *A Night Out* (1896) or the Hôtel des Princes in *The Magistrate*—where the complications of a secret assignation were played out. In Fred Horner's farce *The Late Lamented* (1891), which ran for 230 performances, the late Godfrey Nicholson leaves *two* widows—one in London, one in Cyprus, where he visited regularly under the assumed name of "Mr. Webb," supposedly on business.[20] The hero of Sydney Grundy's *The Arabian Nights* (1887), desperate to evade his tyrannical mother-in-law, disguises himself as Caliph Haroun al Raschid and goes about London doing good deeds and ingratiating himself with pretty girls. The idea came to him when—"in order to escape that eye" of his wife's mother—he shut himself in his bedroom with a volume of *The Arabian Nights.* "My imagination was fired," explains Arthur Hummingtop. "I felt myself every inch a Caliph. In my excitement, I disguised myself."[21]

In addition to Bunbury himself, *Godpapa* introduces—nearly four years before Wilde's play—an evidently imaginary brother named "Ernest." In the farce of 1891 an ingenue makes observations of a very forward kind, but protects her feminine dignity by referring them to a "brother" who never appears or supplies any other token of existence. Thus, when she learns she is being wooed under false pretenses, Maria Browne comments: "Gentlemen & men of honour—don't assume—bogus names—when they go mashing—as my brother Ernest would say." Again, when Reggie Foster throws her over for another woman: "I am not by nature vindictive, but this young man has fairly given me the needle—as my feather-brained brother Ernest would say."[22] Like the brother Ernest imagined by Jack Worthing in Wilde's farce, Maria Browne's in *Godpapa* makes feasible an impropriety of expression or behavior at odds with the "high moral tone" expected of his creator. Thus Maria—and Jack, as Algy mischievously remarks—is a "serious Bunburyist," one who lies artfully to evade prevailing notions of responsibility and self-restraint. The young Oxonians in *Charley's Aunt* (1892) are serious Bunburyists, too, as is John Mags in Fred Horner's *Two Johnnies* (1893), who pretends to be his prosperous cousin in order to win the heart of Clara Bulman.

Characters in these plays not only sprout dual identities and fictitious relatives, they sometimes advance conflicting claims to a single name or personality. There are two persons calling themselves Ernest in Wilde's play, two Donna Lucias in *Charley's Aunt,* two John Magses in *Two Johnnies,* two William Joneses in *The Lost Child.* Frequently an absurd situation arises when a character's identity is misperceived by others rather than misrepresented by himself. In *Mistaken Identity* (1886), an unpublished farce by Alfred Murray, the hero calls upon the designated lover he has never met—only to be received as a valet looking for a place.[23] Carried to extremes, these mixups can be more bewildering than comic. The audience of *Cousin Jack* (1891)—written by Wilde's old elocution coach, the actor Hermann Vezin—would have had to take notes to be sure who is making love to whom. One vital distinction between Vezin's forgotten and unpublished play, which expired after one London performance, and *Charley's Aunt,* which ran four years, is that the successful farce confuses its characters without entirely baffling the audience.

Even when the audience escapes confusion, therefore, the *dramatis personae* assuredly do not. In many cases they virtually lose their grasp of self-identity, as if intoxicated by their own deceptions. This fundamental disorientation makes for one of the brightest moments in *Earnest*—when Jack Worthing asks: "Lady Bracknell, I hate to seem inquisitive, but would you kindly inform me who I am?" (p. 101). As Katherine Worth says, such a question looks forward to Pirandello and Beckett. At the same time, however, it looks backward to Wilde's immediate predecessors in farce. In *Charley's Aunt,* still playing to packed houses when *Earnest* made its debut, Lord Fancourt Babberley must pose questions of the same basic kind: "What did you say my name was? . . . What am I? Irish? . . . have I any children?"[24] In *Uncles and Aunts* (1888) a character complains: "You see I don't quite know who I am."[25] In W. S. Gilbert's *Tom Cobb* (1875): "I declare I don't know who I am."[26] In *The Foundling:* "I don't know who I am."[27] And in *Two Johnnies*:

CLARA: John, who are you?—Tell me.
JOHN: I don't know.[28]

The real answer to Jack's inquiry of Lady Bracknell—"would you kindly inform me who I am?"—is thus more complicated than audiences today can appreciate. His identity cannot be disentangled, any more than his language, from that of the stock hero of late Victorian farce whose holiday frolic leaves the customary verities in turmoil, not least his own sense of self.

Tokens of identity clutter the stage—the engraved cigarette case in *Earnest,* initialed bags in *Mr. Boodle's Predicament* and *Earnest,* handkerchiefs with names embroidered on them in *The Arabian Nights,* a portrait presiding enigmatically over the set of *The Late Lamented.* In Seymour Hicks's unpublished but spectacularly popular *A Night Out* (1896) an ebony brush initialed "H. P." encourages a character to believe, with comic results, that it belongs to the "Hotel Proprietor."[29] In Jerome K. Jerome's *New Lamps for Old*

(1890) an umbrella—"green alpaca, no ferrule, knobbly handle"—only seems to hold the key to one of the characters' secret life.[30] F. C. Burnand in *Mrs. Ponderbury's Past* (1895) provides a handkerchief "marked with an L in blue" to unlock the embarrassing history of his title character.[31] This was the age of Dorian Gray and Dr. Jekyll, and the plastic natures depicted in 1890s farce resemble them in more than a superficial way. An Algernon Moncrieff or Arthur Hummingtop becomes a comic Dorian, fashioning an alternative identity—a "double" within whose robes he can transgress accepted standards and satisfy desires which authority would restrain. Like the young people of *The Importance of Being Earnest*, the heroes of such plays seem always in conflict with their elders, who espouse conventional values and demand obedience. "I positively forbid you to aspire to the hand of my ward," the inflexible guardian tells the young man in *Tom, Dick, and Harry*.[32] This tone of absolute authority is adopted by Lady Bracknell in *Earnest*, by Hummingtop's mother-in-law in *The Arabian Nights*, and by many an eagle-eyed aunt, mother, father, and guardian in farces of the period. To evade these tyrants, the heroes conceive the importance of being someone else—they dress in costume, change their names—and so the masquerade and the mixups begin.

Thus the epidemic of mistaken identity in Victorian farces arises from a context of repression and revolt. The despotic parent is defied, and with him or her the constellation of authorized values in whose name obedience is exacted. In rebelling against Lady Bracknell in *Earnest*, for instance, the young people oppose custom itself as well as the stout woman who so brilliantly exacts conformity to it. Among the casualties of this conflict in Wilde's play is the Victorian ideal of the young girl—modest, unassertive, naive. Cecily Cardew and Gwendolen Fairfax become aggressors, capable of prodding an indecisive man through a marriage proposal or even writing his love letters for him. Cecily, indeed, goes so far as to fall in love and engage herself to a man she never met.

The two girls are sexual revolutionaries in the comic mode, but by 1895 their type had become a cliché in Victorian farce, influenced as it was by the topsy-turvydom of W. S. Gilbert. "How long you have been about it!" complains Gwendolen as Jack Worthing works his way nervously to an offer of marriage. "I am afraid you have had very little experience in how to propose" (p. 37). Her forwardness in matters romantic recalls an ingenue in Israel Zangwill's farce *Six Persons* (1893) who remarks after a similar occasion: "Even the way he proposed wasn't original. I've been proposed to far better."[33] In Pinero's *Dandy Dick* (1887) this exchange occurs when Darbey asks Sheba to marry him:

SHEBA: All I ask is time—time to ponder such a question, time to know myself better.

DARBEY: Certainly, how long?

SHEBA: Give me two or three minutes.[34]

Cecily Cardew in Wilde's play is no less bold, and in a sense no more original, than other young ladies of her type. She writes Ernest's love letters, just as in Sydney Grundy's *Man Proposes* (1878) the heroine dictates a marriage proposal from her young suitor to herself.[35] Enamored of a total stranger, Cecily becomes his fiancée before she meets him—a situation already presented in W. S. Gilbert's *Tom Cobb* (1875), and in *Two Johnnies,* in which Clara exclaims: "Do you know, darling, Father and I admired you oh, so much before we ever heard of you."[36] Propriety ordained a certain detachment of a young girl from her fiancé, as Lady Bracknell explains to Gwendolen—but not to know him at all was an absurd parody which turned Victorian reticence inside-out.

The obsession with engagements forms part of the domestic milieu of these farces. Even their titles announce with remarkable frequency an interest in family relations, from *Charley's Aunt* to *Uncle Jack* to *Uncles and Aunts.* Victorian farce, however, derives much of its humor from overturning current ideas of a wholesome domesticity. In marriage-proposal scenes, therefore, the women are predatory and the men yielding, almost feminine in the Victorian sense; indeed, Lord Fancourt in *Charley's Aunt* is dressed in drag. A man marries two women (in *The Late Lamented*) or a woman becomes engaged to two men (*Box and Cox*). Children not only defy their parents, they "lose" them like Jack Worthing in *Earnest* or Dick Pennell in *The Foundling.* As a character in *Godpapa* puts it: "I always think it's the first duty of a marriageable girl to lose her mother, to take her out and lose her altogether."[37] In *Jane,* Nicholls and Lestocq have fun with the related idea (as Wilde would in *Earnest*) of parents losing their children, even forgetting their existence. Shackleford can recall nothing about his supposed young son:

SHACKLEFORD: . . . I've forgotten all about it.

JANE: How old is it?

SHACKLEFORD: I don't know.

JANE: A boy or a girl?

SHACKLEFORD: That I can't tell you.[38]

Love, instead of being the lasting foundation upon which families are raised, is unstable and transient. Thus in *Adoption* a long engagement ends abruptly:

THEODOSIUS: I did love you fondly, nay, more so—until this morning.

CONSTANTIA: And I loved you with a devotion which mere words would but faintly express—until 10.15.[39]

This is the tone Wilde catches in Act III of *Earnest:*

CECILY: Algy, could you wait for me till I was thirty-five?
ALGERNON: Of course I could, Cecily. You know I could.
CECILY: Yes, I felt it instinctively, but I couldn't wait all that time. I hate waiting
            even five minutes for anybody. (pp. 94–5)

Similarly Gwendolen tells Jack that although "I may marry someone else, and marry often, nothing . . . can possibly . . . alter my eternal devotion to you" (p. 38).

The family ideal is conspicuous throughout Victorian literature, which indeed makes a special point of the homeless child—an Oliver Twist or Jane Eyre—whose difficulties are resolved by assimilation into a harmonious domestic circle. The unhappy waif typically finds a mother or father or in due time becomes a parent herself, establishing—like Esther Summerson in her tiny "Bleak House"—a shelter from the rough winds of the world outside. John Strange Winter's story *Bootle's Baby* (1885) was one such work which achieved spectacular success with the late Victorians. Oscar Wilde, like everyone else, had read it, and once remarked mockingly in a letter: "What a great passionate splendid writer John Strange Winter is! How little people understand her work! *Bootle's Baby* is *une oeuvre symboliste:* it is really only the style and the subject that are wrong. Pray never speak lightly of *Bootle's Baby*."[40] The victim of Wilde's irony was a story whose heroine, a little girl with "short golden curls" named Mignon, is left by her mother in the quarters of a captain of the Scarlet Lancers. He rears her as his own daughter and years later falls in love with the woman who turns out to be—who else?—Mignon's mother. They marry, and the foundling is reunited with the lost parent in a rapture of familial emotion. The novel was turned into what the *Times* called "a strong, pathetic play" in 1888, its success "attested by the applause of a crowded house."[41]

The great Victorian myth of the foundling assigns urgent significance to finding a home for the homeless child, for here, in the warmth of the fireside, humane values could prosper in a Darwinian world. Farce, however, mocks this ideal of domesticity and the foundling who is so integral a part of it. The "babies" become worldly Oxonians, as in *Charley's Aunt,* or twenty-five-year-old men about town, as in *The Importance of Being Earnest* and *The Foundling.* They desperately seek "one parent of either sex, before the season is quite over," but only to satisfy the punctilios of a Lady Bracknell or Mrs. Cotton about "blood."[42] Otherwise they seem comfortably reconciled to the loss of father and mother, and recovery of the lost parent does not bring the sacramental results that attend it elsewhere in Victorian literature. So the apocalyptic moment of the foundling myth is deflated—all the more so when the young hero cries

"Mamma!" or "Mother!" when embracing, as in *Charley's Aunt* or *The Foundling* or *Earnest*, a dignified woman of no relation to him. This is the distinctive tone of late Victorian farce, which—not unlike Ibsen's plays in this respect—treats all ideals, including that of domesticity, from the point of view of absurdity. But even an earlier work such as *The Lost Child* handles such materials irreverently. An anxious father in that mid-Victorian farce, having sought his missing child in vain, "starts up and stands paralyzed" when a waiter at a seaside hotel uncovers the cold-meat tray and rolls the lost infant onto the dinner table before him.[43]

To someone like Henry Arthur Jones, who hoped the theatre would take over the religious and moral functions of a dying English Church, it was disheartening that so many plays were content to be "foolishly dallying with the great issues of human life as with a child's box of wooden toy men."[44] Farcical playwrights, from Jones's viewpoint, neglected their sacerdotal duty when they brought up high ideals and great themes merely to insult them with giddy laughter. Their characters were invariably in flight from serious effort—vacationing, or Bunburying, or—like Jack in *The Importance of Being Earnest*—smoking cigarettes as their life's work. They respond to sublime crises—baptism, love, death—with commonplace physical hunger. "When I am in trouble," explains Algernon Moncrieff, feasting on muffins, "eating is the only thing that consoles me" (p. 79). Even love cannot quell an appetite for cucumber sandwiches in Wilde's play, but this was a trick Pinero had already played to perfection in *The Magistrate*, in a scene in which Captain Vale complains to Colonel Lukyn of a recent disappointment in romance:

LUKYN: Great loss—have a cigarette.

VALE: Parascho's?

LUKYN: Yes. Was she—full grown?

VALE: Just perfection. She rides eight stone fifteen, and I have lost her, Lukyn. Beautiful tobacco. . . . By Jove, it's broken my heart, old fellow. I'll go right on to the champagne, please.[45]

This flippant attitude in late-century farce suggests a disillusionment as profound, in its way, as that exhibited in the scabrous dramas of Ibsen. Playwrights were the heirs of priests, Henry Arthur Jones argued in the 1890s; but before English drama could fulfill its Arnoldian destiny as spiritual advisor to the nation, the twin evils of farce and Ibsenism would have to be outrooted.

Even when characters in these plays manifest some organizing focus in their lives, or some ideal, it is certain to be craven or absurd or both. This parody of purpose can be seen, for example, in *Two Johnnies* when the ingenue's father welcomes a new suitor, a grocer masquerading as a famous lawyer: "The dream of my life has been for my daughter to marry a celebrated man! Take her!

She's yours."[46] And in Pinero's *The Schoolmistress* the heroine's dream is fulfilled when she marries a broken-down aristocrat known as the Honourable Vere Queckett: "It had been a long-cherished ambition with me, if ever I married, to wed no one but a gentleman. I do not mean a gentleman in a mere parliamentary sense; I mean a man of birth, blood, and breeding."[47] The ideals so important to these characters are silly, but at least have a certain plausibility. In other plays, however, ideals are mere words emptied of content. Thus in Justin H. McCarthy's *Your Wife* (1890) a man is fanatically devoted to the idea that his infant nephew be christened "Livingston Burton Speke," after Africa's "most illustrious explorers."[48] In Wilde's play great urgency is attached to "being earnest"—but in name rather than fact. As Gwendolen explains it to her new fiancé: "My ideal has always been to love some one of the name of Ernest. There is something in that name that inspires absolute confidence. The moment Algernon first mentioned to me that he had a friend called Ernest, I knew I was destined to love you" (p. 23). As in *Your Wife,* furthermore, the dramatic crisis arises when it is learned that the person with the "ideal" name is really called Jack.

This mockery of official values—from male earnestness to modest femininity—is accompanied in many plays by a suggestion of outlawry and even revolution. Indeed the policeman is one of the stock characters of Victorian farce. In *The Magistrate* the first scene of Act III takes place in a police court, and in *Dandy Dick* the dean of a cathedral is jailed. Two leading characters are arrested by a bungling policeman in *Crime & Christening,* a curtain-raiser whose synoptic title captures the essence of 1890s farce. The title character of *Mr. Boodle's Predicament* is taken into custody when, by mistake, he claims a piece of luggage with an anarchist's bomb in it. And in *The Importance of Being Earnest*—in a scene eventually cut from the play—Algernon is threatened with imprisonment in connection with an unpaid bill for luxurious dinners in the West End. Most suggestively of all, Lady Bracknell, that fortress of convention-ality, discovers in the unorthodox young lovers "a contempt for the ordinary decencies of family life that reminds one of the worst excesses of the French Revolution" (pp. 32–2). She understood, and so did Oscar Wilde, that the upside-down attitudes of farcical characters were as much a threat to custom and authority as the dynamite of socialists.

III

If Wilde supplied himself with characters, situations, and speeches from the ample warehouse of *fin-de-siècle* farce, he also instilled his play with qualities which distinguish it from other comedies of the kind. *The Importance of Being Earnest* is characterized, above all, by an intellectual coherence and thematic solidity which are notably absent in its precursors. It is, as the playwright subtitled it, "A Trivial Comedy for Serious People."

By the 1890s the rough-and-tumble slapstick which typified older farces like *Box and Cox* (1847) and *The Lost Child* had abated considerably. Hurling chops across the stage and rolling infants off meat platters were devices too crude to suit the kind of play which drew large crowds to Terry's, the Court, the Criterion, and (in the case of *Earnest*) even the dignified St. James's. Pinero, however, was capable of having characters gorge themselves on jujubes and slip on a floor littered with nuts in *The Magistrate,* and even Wilde included the ritual food gags and suitcase business in *Earnest.* Boisterous farce in the tradition of *Box and Cox* continued to be written by playwrights like Mark Melford, who had a man run across the stage in his underwear in *A Screw Loose* (1893). In Melford's *Kleptomania* (1888) an agitated General Blair *"throws a book"* and *"smashes a vase"* before a general melee breaks out in the next act.[49] But by the late Victorian period, farce in general had become more verbal and less physical, finding its basis in the expression of an absurd idea more than in simple horseplay.[50] Humor sprang from the incongruity of a 25-year-old "baby" looking for his mother, a girl engaging herself to a stranger, a schoolmistress singing in the music halls, a young man mistakenly thinking himself a child. The knockabout style of *Box and Cox* was absent even from the most physical scenes of plays such as *Charley's Aunt* or *The Importance of Being Earnest.* Jack Worthing, it is true, dresses up in mourning garments, and Lord Fancourt Babberley dresses up in woman's clothing—but in both plays the Oxonian backgrounds and aristocratic eloquence of the characters prevent mere physical exuberance from taking command. The idea of the absurd is the keynote of 1890s farce, and often it finds expression in the ironic counterpointing of physical comedy (Jack in "mourning," Lord Fancourt in a dress) with the effete dignity of patrician drawing rooms.

The familiar judgment that *The Importance of Being Earnest* differs from other farces in being less "physical" is thus only partly true, for in de-emphasizing slapstick Wilde was unquestionably following recent trends in farcical drama. But he went further than his predecessors. Not only is Wilde's comedy more verbal than physical, it brings to the surface what was only incipient in the farces which preceded it. A cigar-smoking young man is made up as a woman, or girls comport themselves in the most outspoken fashion, but the typical farce only invites laughter at such disturbances of good order. Characters typically do not reflect upon the implications of their absurd behavior, and so the subversive possibilities of these plays—which derive their comedy from the discomposure of prevailing standards—remain for the most part latent. In *Earnest,* however, Wilde makes his characters think as well as act, with the result that absurdity becomes more than a theatrical style. An exchange between the two heroes at the end of Act I crystallizes the nihilism which lay just beneath the surface of late Victorian farce:

> JACK: If you don't take care, your friend Bunbury will get you into a serious scrape some day.

ALGERNON:　I love scrapes. They are the only things that are never serious.

JACK:　Oh, that's nonsense, Algy. You never talk anything but nonsense.

ALGERNON:　Nobody ever does. (p. 40)

Wilde's characters have serious views, if not actual philosophies, and from these their foolishness of word and deed develops. They generalize, and in doing so awaken to self-consciousness and the world outside the play. For Algy, therefore, Bunburying entails a critique of existence, but for the unreflecting Reggie in *Godpapa* it is simply an expedient to get what he wants.

In 1895, the year *Earnest* was staged, Henry Arthur Jones brought out *The Renascence of the English Drama,* admonishing playwrights to provide their audiences with an "interpretation of life" rather than merely "funny or sensational theatrical things."[51] Wilde's play satisfies this standard, although not in the way intended by Jones, who wished theatres to become the cathedrals of a secular age. Neither Jones himself, imbued with ideas of Arnoldian culture, nor the farcical dramatists who preceded Wilde would have permitted their heroes to assert, as Jack Worthing does, that "a high moral tone can hardly be said to conduce very much to either one's health or one's happiness" (p. 14). But it is language of this sort which makes *The Importance of Being Earnest* more than merely "funny." All through its dialogue runs a current of generalization which bestows upon the characters and their behavior a significance beyond themselves.

Cynical it may be, but what Jones would call an "interpretation of life" emerges from scene after scene in which the moral imperatives of Victorian society are reversed. "You musn't think that I am wicked," Algy assures Cecily in Act I—to which she replies: "If you are not, then you have certainly been deceiving us all in a very inexcusable manner. I hope you have not been leading a double life, pretending to be wicked and being really good all the time. That would be hypocrisy" (p. 46). Lady Bracknell, on the other hand, defends custom with a majesty of speech which makes her utterance almost theological. When Jack admits to smoking, for example, she is "glad to hear it," for "a man should always have an occupation of some kind" (p. 27). The tyrannical matriarch in *Earnest* becomes the embodiment of a system, and the contest between her and the young people is really a conflict between Victorian earnestness and conscious revolt against it. Mary Lydon's remark that in Wilde's work mothers are "monstrous" is true of *Earnest,* but in a sense equally true of *The Foundling* and other farces of the time.[52] Young people struggle to establish themselves against repression by the old, to clear a space for enactment of the self, even in the typical farce of the 1890s. The difference in Lady Bracknell resides in her speech—like much of Wilde's writing, "it is the language of the Apollonian law giver," withdrawn, as it were, into "aristocratic sequestration." The generalized formulations of Lady Bracknell, indeed of all the characters, provide not only magisterial personae for themselves (and indirectly for their author), but also make it necessary for them to think beyond themselves to the large issues of life beyond the play.[53] The power of generalization in *Earnest* is one of the qualities which most emphatically divides it from its farcical predecessors.

If the characters of Wilde's forerunners ever reflect on the significance of their tricks and disguises, it is done belatedly and with remorse. "Forgive me," pleads the forward young lady in *Man Proposes,* while in *Your Wife* the young people suddenly, near the end, become "very much ashamed of our deception."[54] Says a character in *A Night Out:* "This is a lesson for me. I'll never get myself into such a scrape again."[55] The hero in *Charley's Aunt* realizes just before the final curtain that his stratagems have been incompatible with the responsibilities of a sincere lover. But these characters have little to apologize for—at least in comparison with Jack Worthing and Algernon Moncrieff—for their revolt against authority has been unpremeditated, the product of high spirits rather than calculated defiance. Not only do Jack and Algernon understand their own positions from the beginning, they do not succumb to any sudden or improbable conversion at the end. Reproached by Lady Bracknell for displaying "signs of triviality," Jack replies in the last speech of the play: "On the contrary, Aunt Augusta, I've now realized for the first time in my life the vital Importance of Being Earnest" (pp. 104–5). It was common to end a farce with this kind of tag line, often a self-quotation of the play's title. But in a more conventional work such as the unpublished, anonymously written *Never Again* (1897), the tag speech confirms the characters' return to normative behavior. "But remember," says Vignon, just before the curtain falls. "I swear it," responds Ribot. "—Never again!"[56] Wilde's play concludes on the note of revolt with which it began, leaving its heroes in a state of clear-headedness which was unprecedented in such comedies.

The revolutionary use which Wilde made of farce does not answer the objection that too much of *Earnest* is not his own—a good deal less, in fact, than has been imagined by his harshest critics. Almost everything of importance came into the play ready-made, from Bunburying to the imaginary brother named Ernest to the comic idea of a grown man frantically seeking his mother and planning to be christened. *The Importance of Being Earnest,* from one point of view, provides the strongest evidence for the *Era's* complaint in early 1895 that originality in farces was "becoming a rare quality." Other English farceurs often modelled their plays on a single source—as Justin McCarthy adapted *Prête-moi ta femme* under the English title *Your Wife,* or Fred Horner made *The Late Lamented* out of Bisson's *Feu Topinel.* In *Earnest,* as in his other dramas, Wilde adapted not a particular play, but an entire genre—practically cataloguing its varied devices, yet somehow creating a fresh impression rather than only collocating what others had done before him. Absurdity is a wonderful joke for Wilde, but also a weapon of the critical intelligence. *The Importance of Being Earnest* resonates with significance, and it is this distinction more than anything else which divides it from the irreclaimable bog of its numerous but only "funny" precursors.

Notes

1. See, e.g., Edouard Roditi in *Oscar Wilde* (Norfolk, Conn.: New Directions, 1947), pp. 138–9; Shaw's review of *Earnest*, in *Saturday Review*, 23 February 1895, pp. 249–50; and Arthur Symons's "An Artist in Attitudes: Oscar Wilde" in *Studies in Prose and Verse* (London: Dent, [1904], pp. 124–8, which calls *Earnest* a "sublime" but "meaningless" farce. Mary McCarthy, "The Unimportance of Being Oscar," voices an influential complaint against *Earnest*'s alleged triviality (in Ellmann, ed., *Oscar Wilde: A Collection of Critical Essays*, pp. 107–10); Louis Kronenberger, *Oscar Wilde*, p. 140, offers a more tolerant view of the play as "proudly but unconquerably trivial."

2. Richard Ellmann, "Romantic Pantomime in Oscar Wilde," *Partisan Review*, 30 (1963), 342–55. James M. Ware finds Algernon to be an "artificer" whose "artifact" is his own life ("Algernon's Appetite: Oscar Wilde's Hero as Restoration Dandy," *English Literature in Transition 1880–1920*, 13 [1970], 17–26). Rodney Shewan notes that Jack and Algernon finally confront their *alter egos* in such a way as to unite them with their actual selves (*Oscar Wilde: Art and Egotism*, p. 187).

3. Gagnier, *Idylls of the Marketplace: Oscar Wilde and the Victorian Public*, p. 113.

4. Eric Bentley, *The Playwright as Thinker* in *Oscar Wilde: Modern Critical Views*, ed. Bloom, pp. 15–19.

5. Worth, *Oscar Wilde*, p. 155. Arthur Ganz stresses the subversiveness of Algernon in making ordinary morality seem ridiculous ("The Meaning of *The Importance of Being Earnest*," *Modern Drama*, 6 [1963], 42–52).

6. Worth, *Oscar Wilde*, p. 155.

7. For a discussion of the domestic nature of Victorian farce, see the introduction to *English Plays of the Nineteenth Century*, ed. Booth, vol. 4. Other useful discussions of Victorian farce include Martin Meisel, *Shaw and the Nineteenth-Century Theater*, chapter 10; and Jeffrey H. Huberman, *Late Victorian Farce* (Ann Arbor: UMI Research Press, 1986).

8. See W. E. Suter, *The Lost Child: or, Jones's Baby: An Original Farce in One Act* (London: French, n.d.), and Mrs. R. Pacheco, *Tom, Dick, and Harry: A Farcical Comedy* (London: French, n.d.), which ran for 105 performances at the Trafalgar Square Theatre in 1893–4.

9. Lestocq and Robson, *The Foundling: A Farce in Three Acts*, p. 4.

10. The typescript of *An Innocent Abroad*, by W. Stokes Craven, is in the Lord Chamberlain's collection of the British Library. The play had sixty-four performances at Terry's in 1895.

11. *Mr. Boodle's Predicament*, by C. J. Hamilton, was published in *Original Plays for the Drawing-Room* (London: Ward, Lock, 1890).

12. The typescript of *Crime & Christening: A Farce* is in the Lord Chamberlain's collection. Richard Henry was the pseudonym of Richard Butler and H. Chance Newton. The play had 112 performances at the Opera Comique, from October to July 1891.

13. Richard Henry's *Adoption: A Farce in One Act* (London: French, n.d.) ran for thirty-six performances at Toole's Theatre, and was revived for sixty more at the Prince of Wales's in 1893–4.

14. A. W. Pinero's *The Magistrate: A Farce in Three Acts* is reprinted in *English Plays of the Nineteenth Century*, ed. Booth, vol. 4. The play was revived in 1892 at Terry's, where it had fifty-three performances.

15. Arthur Law, *The New Boy: A Farcical Play in Three Acts* (New York: French, 1904), pp. 19, 25. The return to childhood was one of the devices of farcical comedy which Shaw

incorporated in *Mrs. Warren's Profession*. Bright but frivolous Frank Gardner, who expresses himself in baby talk to Vivie Warren, embodies the insubstantial cleverness so common in late Victorian farce, and for which Shaw expressed contempt.

16. F. C. Philips and Charles H. E. Brookfield, *Godpapa: A Farcical Comedy in Three Acts,* Act I, p. 30, is quoted from the typescript in the Lord Chamberlain's collection. The play, apparently never published, ran for seventy-two performances at the Comedy from October 1891 to January 1892. The hero's double life was an obsession, not an innovation, of late Victorian farce. It had been common in plays of an earlier time, from Etherege's *The Man of Mode* to Sheridan's *The Rivals*. Bunbury's name, like so many in Wilde's plays, is difficult to pin down in terms of its source. Names like Chiltern, Bracknell, Worthing, and even Bunbury are place-names, but reverberate with associations and meanings that have little to do with the map. On Bunbury's name, see William Green, "Wilde and the Bunburys," *Modern Drama*, 21 (1978), 67–80.

17. *Jane* ran for 191 performances at the Comedy in 1890–1. It was revived in 1892 at the same theatre, and in 1899 at Terry's.

18. A. W. Pinero, *The Schoolmistress: A Farce in Three Acts* (London: Heinemann, 1907), p. 23.

19. Mrs. H. Musgrave, *Our Flat: Farcical Comedy in 3 Acts,* is quoted from the first act of the Lord Chamberlain's manuscript. The play was performed at the Strand 118 times in 1894. I have been unable to determine Mrs. Musgrave's full name.

20. Fred Horner, *The Late Lamented,* an adaptation of Alexandre Bisson's *Feu Topinel,* remains unpublished, but the Lord Chamberlain's collection contains a typescript of the play. It ran for 230 performances at the Court and Strand in 1891–2.

21. Sydney Grundy, *The Arabian Nights: A Farcical Comedy in Three Acts* (Chicago: Dramatic Publishing, n.d.), p. 8. The play, founded on Gustav von Moser's *Haroun Alraschid,* was revived in 1892 at the Comedy and 1896 at the Novelty.

22. Philips and Brookfield, *Godpapa,* Act III, pp. 9, 15.

23. Alfred Murray's *Mistaken Identity* was never published; a typescript is in the Lord Chamberlain's collection. It was produced at the Gaiety.

24. Brandon Thomas, *Charley's Aunt: A Play in Three Acts* (London: French, 1962), pp. 49–50. The play had 1,469 performances at the Royalty and Globe Theatres 1892–6.

25. Walter Everard and W. Lestocq, *Uncles and Aunts: A Farcical Comedy in Three Acts,* played at the Comedy Theatre.

26. W. S. Gilbert, *Tom Cobb; or Fortune's Toy,* in *English Plays of the Nineteenth Century,* ed. Booth, vol. 4, p. 281.

27. Lestocq and Robson, *The Foundling,* p. 14.

28. Fred Horner's *Two Johnnies* was an adaptation of Albert Valabrègue and Maurice Ordonneau, *Durand et Durand.* Never published, it played the Trafalgar Square Theatre for a brief run in 1893.

29. Seymour Hicks, *A Night Out,* adapted from Maurice Desvallières and Georges Feydeau's *Hôtel du Libre Echange,* ran for 525 performances at the Vaudeville in 1896–7. The Lord Chamberlain's manuscript is quoted, Act II.

30. Jerome K. Jerome, *New Lamps for Old,* never published, ran for 160 performances at Terry's, from February to July 1890; p. 138 of the Lord Chamberlain's manuscript is quoted.

31. F. C. Burnand, *Mrs. Ponderbury's Past,* an adaptation of Ernest Blum and Raoul Touché's *Madame Mongodin,* played at the Avenue Theatre for ninety performances in 1895–6. The play, unpublished, is quoted from the Lord Chamberlain's manuscript, Act III, p. 24.

32. Pacheco, *Tom, Dick, and Harry,* p. 3.

33. Israel Zangwill, *Six Persons* (New York: French, 1898), p. 3. The play ran for ninety-two performances at the Haymarket in 1893–4.

34. A. W. Pinero, *Dandy Dick: A Farce in Three Acts* (London: Heinemann, 1906), p. 139.

35. Sydney Grundy, *Man Proposes: An Original Comedietta in One Act* (New York: French, n.d.), pp. 14–15. The play had 102 performances when it was revived at the Avenue Theatre in 1890–1. In Sheridan's *The Rivals* (1775) Lydia Languish provides an earlier instance of the heroine's writing romantic letters to herself.

36. Horner, *Two Johnnies*, Act I, p. 11.

37. Philips and Brookfield, *Godpapa*, Act I, p. 8.

38. Harry Nicholls and W. Lestocq, *Jane: A Farce in Three Acts* (New York: French, 1900), p. 43.

39. Richard Henry, *Adoption*, p. 19.

40. *Letters*, p. 586.

41. Review of *Bootle's Baby*, in the *Times*, 11 May 1888, p. 13.

42. Lestocq and Robson, *The Foundling*, p. 17.

43. Suter, *The Lost Child*, p. 15. By contrast, eighteenth-century comedies treat the foundling with an almost Dickensian respect. Not only is this true of *Tom Jones*, but also of such stage productions as Edward Moore's *The Foundling* and John O'Keefe's *Wild Oats*, revived in 1891 at the Criterion. In both plays the foundling's dilemma is made to seem pathetic, and resolved when his rightful parents are discovered. The mockery of family ties, so distinctive of 1890s farce, is absent.

44. Henry Arthur Jones, "Preface to *Saints and Sinners*" in *The Renascence of the English Drama*, p. 317.

45. Pinero, *The Magistrate*, pp. 333–4. The romantic mixups in the Hôtel des Princes in *The Magistrate* perhaps derive from James Albery's extremely popular *Pink Dominos* (1877; revived in 1892). The comedy of marital infidelity was often, like Albery's, adapted from a French model and considerably toned down (so that no adultery is ever committed, or seriously intended). See Jeffrey Huberman, *Late Victorian Farce*, chapter 2, for a good account of the heyday of French adaptation, 1875–83. Adaptation waned in popularity when copyright protection was extended in 1887 to foreign dramas.

46. Horner, *Two Johnnies*, Act I, p. 7.

47. Pinero, *The Schoolmistress*, p. 23.

48. J. H. McCarthy, *Your Wife*, is quoted from Act II, p. 6 of the Lord Chamberlain's typescript.

49. Mark Melford, *Kleptomania* (London: French, n.d.), pp. 15, 17.

50. By contrast, Pinero's farces dealt with deans, magistrates, and cabinet ministers, Brandon Thomas's with young Oxonians, and Wilde's with aristocratic dandies and their families. In this milieu, comic language was certain to prevail at the expense of slapstick gags. An interesting account of some alterations in class representation appears in Jeffrey Huberman, *Late Victorian Farce*, pp. 104–27.

51. Jones, "Relations of the Drama to Education" in *The Renascence of the English Drama*, p. 305.

52. "Myself and M/others," *Sub-stance*, no. 32 (1981), pp. 6–14.

53. See Camille A. Paglia, "Oscar Wilde and the English Epicene," *Raritan*, 4 (1985), 85–109, for a discussion of "the iron rod of classification" in Wilde's rhetoric.

54. Grundy, *Man Proposes*, p. 16; McCarthy, *Your Wife*, Act III, p. 23.

55. Hicks, *A Night Out*, Act II, p. 28.

56. *Never Again*, an anonymous adaptation of Maurice Desvallières and Anthony Mars's *Le Truc d'Arthur*, was licensed on 10 September 1897 and ran for 117 performances at the Vaudeville Theatre.

PART 3
WILDEAN CRITIQUE
◆

The Critical Legacy of Oscar Wilde

ZHANG LONGXI

Writing in *Vanity Fair,* 2 March 1905, Max Beerbohm noted the coincidence of an exhibition of Whistler's paintings and the publication of a book by Oscar Wilde in the previous week in London, and how suddenly everybody was talking about the greatness of these two men. "Whistler during the 'seventies and 'eighties," observes Beerbohm, "and Oscar Wilde during the 'eighties and early 'nineties, cut very prominent figures in London; and both were by the critics and the gossips regarded merely as clever *farceurs.* Both, apart from their prominence, were doing serious work; but neither was taken at all seriously."[1] The apostles of aestheticism struck most of their contemporaries as eccentric creatures, foppishly dressed, and ridiculously affected in their "medieval" manners, for which they were so effectively satirized in Gilbert and Sullivan's *Patience.* However, "if *Patience* exposed to Philistine laughter their obvious mannerism," as Jerome H. Buckley points out, "it left untouched the first principles of art for art's sake."[2]

Most critics and scholars have either overlooked those principles, brilliantly formulated in Wilde's critical essays in *Intentions,* looked upon them with deep suspicion, or regarded them with condescending tolerance. Even today, as Richard Ellmann remarks, the mere mention of the name of Oscar Wilde creates the anticipation that "what will be quoted as his will turn conventional solemnities to frivolous insights."[3] As a writer of witty, elegant, and truly delightful comedies and a number of charming fairy tales, Wilde is familiar to the public and the average reader, but as a most articulate and serious theoretician of aesthetic criticism, he has very seldom, until quite recently, been taken seriously.

It is the purpose of this essay to examine some responses to Oscar Wilde as a critic and some significant reevaluations of his critical theory in the perspective of contemporary criticism. No exhaustive survey has been attempted, but I hope to show that the critical legacy of Oscar Wilde, which has so long been unduly rejected or neglected, is more profound than has hitherto been recognized and deserves far more attention than it has yet received.

Reprinted from *Texas Studies in Literature and Language* 30, no. 1 (Spring 1988): 87–103, by permission of the author and the University of Texas Press.

René Wellek's *History of Modern Criticism* has a chapter on the "English Aesthetic Movement," in which he discusses Algernon Swinburne and Walter Pater, but not Wilde. The section on Wilde comes under the chapter heading of "Other English Critics," which includes, besides Wilde, J. A. Symonds, George Saintsbury, and G. B. Shaw. Wellek begins his discussion of Wilde with a kind of demythologization of Wilde's pathetic self-image, elaborately built up in *De Profundis,* as the crucified martyr of aestheticism. And yet, it is this "myth or legend," says Wellek, that "gives to Wilde's ideas on art and literature a historical position which they may not deserve in a history of criticism, apart from the personality and the pitiful fate of the man."[4] This highly patronizing note sets the tone of Wellek's discussion in a way that insufficiently acknowledges the independent value of Wilde's thought.

Wellek traces Wilde's ideas to Pater, Swinburne, Arnold, Gautier, Baudelaire, and Poe. He finds nothing original: even *Intentions,* the collection of Wilde's later dialogues and essays, "merely restates with greater brilliance and wit the main ideas he had absorbed from Pater."[5] Though Wellek concedes that Wilde's prose displays some solid brain-work, an ingenious play of mind, and a quick grasp of many verities, he blames Wilde for disconcertingly shifting "between three often divergent views: panaestheticism, the autonomy of art, and a decorative formalism. He does not hold his vision steady."[6] This shifting of views or inconsistency is nevertheless more a problem with Wellek the historian of criticism, who tries to characterize Wilde in terms of neatly defined categories within a coherent theoretical frame, than with Wilde himself, who protests, in his typically paradoxical way, "Who wants to be consistent? . . . Not I. Like Emerson, I write over the door of my library the word 'Whim.'" Wilde further insists "that each mode of criticism is, in its highest development, simply a mood, and that we are never more true to ourselves than when we are inconsistent."[7]

The real difficulty Wilde's ideas present to Wellek is the controversial notion of creative criticism that forms the center of Wilde's long essay, "The Critic as Artist." Wilde maintains that "the highest Criticism, being the purest form of personal impression, is in its way more creative than creation" (138); that it is "the only civilized form of autobiography" (139); and that "it treats the work of art simply as a starting point for a new creation" (142). In Wellek's eyes, however, this claim of higher creativity "goes beyond the demands of sympathy," for it confuses criticism with creation and misleads the critic "in the direction of irresponsible subjectivity."[8] He summarily dismisses all such criticism: "If we are concerned with criticism as organized knowledge, as interpretation and judgment of publicly verifiable objects, we must dismiss poetic criticism as an irrelevancy. Today the Mona Lisa passage in Pater, the ostentatious fireworks of Swinburne's eloquence, and even the charming reflections of Anatole France have lost their appeal and are no present danger."[9] However, "today" in this passage meant the 1960s and has now faded into a yesterday. In the 1970s and 1980s, much to his surprise and displeasure,

Wellek sees in the more recent trends of literary theory—deconstruction, *Rezeptionsästhetik,* and reader-response criticism—a dangerous revival of "the idea of 'creative criticism' propagated by Oscar Wilde," for they go even further to obliterate the distinction between criticism and fiction, turning everything into an irresponsible play of language, and finally "spell the breakdown or even the abolition of all traditional literary scholarship and teaching."[10]

This rather gloomy prognosis of the destruction of literary studies by contemporary criticism sounds ironically like Wilde's own prophecy perversely fulfilled. "It is to criticism that the future belongs," Wilde declares. "If creation is to last at all, it can only do so on the condition of becoming far more critical than it is at present" (206–07). Some critics lament that this is precisely what is happening today, that "a literal usurpation has begun which would depose literature and grant sovereign authority to one or more of several competing disciplines."[11] The crisis today concerns the very concept and nature of criticism, and the anger with which Wellek views much of contemporary theory comes presumably from his awareness that his own concept of criticism, which fifty years ago was regarded as so radical that it was attacked by traditionalists as the destruction of literary studies, is now regarded as old-fashioned by the younger generation of critics. "I sometimes feel guilty," says Wellek in a tone which sounds at once apologetic and complacent, "of having helped to propagate the theory of literature. Since my book, theory has triumphed in this country and has, possibly, triumphed with a vengeance."[12] However, Wellek's sense of guilt perhaps does not reveal so much the triumph of theory in general as the aging of a particular kind of theory that he has ironically helped to propagate.

Wellek is, of course, not alone in attacking creative criticism. It seems an idea long taken for granted, though logically not impeccable, that criticism as commentary or *explication de texte* arises after and because of the primary text of literature: *post hoc, ergo propter hoc.* Murray Krieger puts it clearly when he calls criticism a secondary art and asserts that the verbal artifact of the critics "finds its starting point where another verbal artifact has left off, and that the latter is prior both temporally and authoritatively to what they write *about* it."[13] Temporally, yes. But is the artist's verbal artifact also authoritatively prior to that of the critic? Wilde would certainly disagree. "I am always amused," says Wilde through his mouthpiece Gilbert, "by the silly vanity of those writers and artists of our day who seem to imagine that the primary function of the critic is to chatter about their second-rate work" (139). Of course, Krieger would contend that "I have deliberately overstated the case, using my rhetoric to urge the presence of a fetishizing motive for criticism as commentary on a sacred text, as allegory for an ultimately unspeakable symbol."[14] Nevertheless, the model of a sacred text's relation to its commentary is not fully relevant here. It would be rather naive to imagine that the power or authority of institutional-ized religion comes exclusively from the text of scripture, for the history of biblical interpretation shows that allegoresis as a method was taken over from the reading of literature, notably the Homeric epics, to the exegesis of the Bible, and that the authority of scripture is as much the authority of interpretation as that of the biblical text itself. Karlfried Froehlich argues convincingly that a careful study of patristic hermeneutics will show, "on the one hand, how biblical language determined theology and, on the other, how theological presuppositions shaped the reading of the Bible. It was in the hermeneutical circle of biblical text, tradition, and interpretation that Christian theology as a whole took shape."[15] In the history of religion as well as of literature, the canonicity of what Krieger calls "the original master text" is established by none other than the commentators, interpreters, and critics. It is the hermeneutical-critical tradition that has shaped the canon of texts as well as our understanding of it. As Wilde points out, "An appreciation of Milton is . . . the reward of consummate scholarship" (154). Now we can no longer believe in the myth of a self-sufficient text, and it is precisely a fruitful study of biblical hermeneutics and its implications for literary criticism that has contributed to the expansion of our horizon for looking at the complexity of textual meanings.

The essential problem with Wilde's critics, however, is condemnation of creative criticism without proper attention to Wilde's ideas and expositions. The dialogues on art and criticism in *Intentions* have a coherent and symmetrical structure. "The Decay of Lying" posits, among other things, the bold creed of the new aesthetics: that "Life imitates art far more than Art imitates life" (32); that "Life holds the Mirror up to Art, and either reproduces some strange type imagined by painter or sculptor, or realizes in fact what has been dreamed in fiction" (39). This not only refers to the fact that fashionable ladies in the 1880s tried to dress and look like the beautiful figures in the paintings of Rossetti or Burne-Jones, but to a far more profound truth that art helps to shape our own vision of the reality of life and nature and that we see things only as we have first created them. Wilde's discussion of landscape painting is quite illuminating, for where, if not in landscape paintings, in Rousseau and romantic literature, did Europe first discover the beauty of nature? "Where, if not from the Impressionists, do we get those wonderful brown fogs that come creeping down our streets, blurring the gas-lamps and changing the houses into monstrous shadows? To whom, if not to them and their master, do we owe the lovely silver mists that brood over our river, and turn to faint forms of fading grace curved bridge and swaying barge?" (40). When you come to the window and look at the glorious evening sky, what do you see but "a very second-rate Turner"? (42). Wilde further develops this paradoxical argument into an advocacy of form in "The Critic as Artist." He asserts that, from the artistic point of view, life is a failure, but art imposes form on the chaos of life and miraculously turns its raw material into things eternally beautiful.

This part of Wilde's argument is not so difficult for his critics to accept: Wellek does so by identifying it as "only an overstatement of old classical ideas on the function of art as idealization."[16] In this way he is able to reconcile it with the classical and more rational concept of art. Yet this reconciliation becomes problematic when we remember Wilde's remark that "all bad art comes from returning to Life and Nature, and elevating them into ideals" (54). It seems to me that Henri Peyre, though not so sympathetic with Wilde's views, understands Wilde more appropriately when he says that "Oscar Wilde's famous and easy paradox is at bottom truer than he himself suspected: literature seldom imitates life with serious profit, but life imitates literature. We see today with the eyes of Gauguin and Cézanne; we love like Proust's heroes (only a little more normally); we swear and drink like Hemingway's characters, and some of us perhaps eat like the heroes of Thomas Wolfe."[17] That may be a bit exaggerated, but it does share Wilde's idea that both our perception and conception of nature are shaped by what we have created in art.

Wilde takes Japan as an example and argues that Japan and the Japanese as presented in art are pure inventions; they are the effect of artistic representation. In this argument, Eugenio Donato finds some germs of the poststructuralist understanding that "representation cannot function without generating within itself the pseudopresence of an 'object.' This 'object,' however, is secondary and derived with respect to the play of representation." He compares this with Flaubert's realization that art is illusion and aligns Wilde with Alexandre Kojève, Roland Barthes, and Martin Heidegger, who all "make of Japan an allegory for the problematics of form in general."[18] Wilde is certainly not speaking only for the nineteenth century when he says that "things are because we see them, and what we see, and how we see it, depends on the Arts that have influenced us" (41).

Here a suggestion of the famous epistemological principle of Vico's *New Science,* that of *verum factum,* is quite irresistible, even though no connection whatever between Wilde and Vico could have existed. In his anti-Cartesian view of history, Vico maintains that our knowledge of history or the humanities is on a higher level than that of natural sciences, for we can only know what we have created, and we know history better because history is made by man. The criterion of truth, Vico argues, cannot be the Cartesian *cogito* but the convertibility of the true and the made. The founders of civilizations are called, in the Greek sense of the word "poets"; that is, makers of history and of human institutions, who are endowed with "poetic wisdom" and whose fables and myths register their knowledge in poetic forms no less accurately than does modern rational philosophy. Those "poets" create according to their experiences and ideas; "what Aristotle [*On the Soul* 432a 7f] said of the individual man is therefore true of the race in general: *Nihil est in intellectu quin prius fuerit in sensu.* That is, the human mind does not understand anything of which it has had no previous impression (which our modern metaphysicians call 'occasion') from the senses."[19] Therefore, nothing can be known to man unless it is experienced, and nothing makes sense unless it is accommodated to the shape of the human mind which, in its own way, is shaping the world and our experience of it. Needless to say, Wilde does not have, nor did he intend to propose, a systematic philosophical treatment, comparable with Vico's, of the relation between knowledge and creation. What is relevent here is just the indication of some similarity between Wilde's idea of creative criticism and Vico's fundamental idea of truth as our own making. Both of them emphasize that what we see as true has much to do with what we are and what we do, and that art plays a far more active role in shaping our mind and life than we usually think it does.

But Wilde calls art lying, not truth: "Lying and poetry are arts—arts, as Plato saw, not unconnected with each other" (9), and "Lying, the telling of beautiful untrue things, is the proper aim of Art" (55). We all know that Plato attacked poetry as untruth thrice removed from the reality of Ideas and that Sir Philip Sidney's and numerous other apologetics for poetry have striven for a defense since the Renaissance. Sidney's *Apology* is of special significance here because he, like Vico, emphasizes the meaning of poet as maker who creates, like God his own Maker, *ex nihilo*, "goeth hand in hand with nature, not enclosed within the narrow warrant of her gifts, but freely ranging only within the zodiac of his own wit."[20] To the charge of lying, Sidney rebuts that if to lie is to affirm as true what is actually false, then the poet "nothing affirms, and therefore never lieth"; he "never maketh any circles about your imagination to conjure you to believe for true what he writes," but overtly admits that he speaks "not affirmatively but allegorically and figuratively."[21] In other words, the overt fictionality of poetry is sufficient evidence to acquit the poet of any charge of lying.

It is quite characteristic of Wilde that, by deliberately calling the poet's overt fictionality lying, he joins Sidney in the long apologetic tradition in an ironical way, turning the opposition of truth and fiction into a paradox and an aphorism. There is perhaps something of an echo of Sidney in the preface to *The Picture of Dorian Gray* where Wilde asserts that "no artist desires to prove anything. Even things that are true can be proved." His idea of life imitating art does not necessarily mean a total rejection of the old Greek notion of mimesis: he is not contradicting Aristotle, but the kind of sterile realism or naturalism as exemplified by Zola's works. As John Allen Quintus argues, "Wilde appears to be countering nineteenth-century notions about art more than he is challenging or rethinking ancient formulations," though his celebration of art as "untruth" does attest to "Wilde's interest in overturning the ancient philosopher."[22] In any case, if literature is nothing but fiction and if a work of art does not refer to the outside world for verification, to call art lying would indeed be less puzzling than it seems. "After all, what is a fine lie?" asks Wilde, and he himself gives the answer, "Simply that which is its own evidence" (6).

If "The Decay of Lying" expounds the idea of life imitating art, this idea is then paralleled by that of creative criticism set forth in "The Critic as Artist" where Wilde maintains that if we understand nature and life through art, then we understand art through criticism. According to Wilde's argument, we learn to appreciate the glorious sky at sunset because of Turner, but we admire Turner because Ruskin has taught us how to understand his paintings; we adore the Italian beauty because of da Vinci, but we see Mona Lisa and the beauty of her mysterious smile because Pater's insight has opened our eyes. Just as life provides the artist with materials for creative work, so the work of art provides the critic with materials for a higher creation. We see life through art, and we see art through criticism. This double perspective certainly gives Wilde's argument a coherent and symmetrical structure, even though the argument may seem paradoxical, shocking, perverse or exasperating, depending on how you see it and where you stand. In this double perspective, Wilde is able to see criticism as "a creation within a creation" (138), for "the critic occupies the same relation to the work of art that he criticises as the artist does to the visible world of form and colour, or the unseen world of passion and of thought" (136–37). Wilde further argues that the mere creative instinct only reproduces, and it is criticism that best incarnates the creative spirit: "Creation is always behind the age. It is Criticism that leads us. The Critical Spirit and the World-Spirit are one" (215). No matter how pretentious this may sound, Wilde's argument is not without its rhyme and reason. As W. K. Wimsatt observes, this theory is "a logical enough outcome of the original paradox of art for art's sake," an inevitable result of Wilde's double perspective: "If nature, reversing our usual conceptions, is to imitate art, then art, continuing the direction of reference, may well imitate criticism."[23] As we shall see, this theory, which seemed too shocking to be taken seriously a hundred years ago, contains many ideas that are remarkably congenial to contemporary critical theories.

Northrop Frye regards *The Decay of Lying* as "the beginning of a new kind of criticism" and Wilde as "clearly the herald of a new age in literature" because, by calling art a form of lying, Wilde anticipates the modern awareness of imaginative literature as "turning away from the descriptive use of language and the correspondence form of truth."[24] Frye's *Anatomy of Criticism* is an attempt to establish criticism as a systematic and scientific study of literature within a specific conceptual framework, "a structure of thought and knowledge existing in its own right, with some measure of independence from the art it deals with."[25] Any claim of independence has of course to rest on the concept of autonomy, and both Wilde and Frye argue that criticism as systematic study of literature has to be distinguished from literature itself. Though Frye would reject the kind of impressionistic approach Wilde advocates, he certainly shares Wilde's idea that criticism should be independent not only of moral, political, and other imposed critical attitudes but of the work and its author. "Who cares whether Mr. Ruskin's views on Turner are sound or not? What does it matter?" asks Wilde rather bluntly (140). "Who, again, cares whether Mr. Pater has put into the portrait of Monna [*sic*] Lisa something that Lionardo [*sic*] never dreamed of?" (141). Criticism "treats the work of art simply as a starting point for a new creation. It does not confine itself—let us at least suppose so for the moment—to discovering the real intention of the artist and accepting that as final" (142).

Here Wilde clearly anticipates what Wimsatt and Beardsley later call the intentional fallacy, which confuses the poem with its origin and takes the *cause* of a poem for "a *standard* by which the critic is to judge the worth of the poet's performance."[26] Frye also dismisses authorial intention by arguing that only "criticism can talk, and all the arts are dumb": "not that the poet does not know what he is talking about, but that he cannot talk about what he knows."[27] The poet, Wilde says, cannot be a good critic because his artistic temperament is too strong to appreciate anything different from his own: "a really great artist can never judge of other people's work at all, and can hardly, in fact, judge his own" (204). Here again, we find him adumbrating Frye's argument that "what is true of the poet in relation to his own work is still more true of his opinion of other poets. It is hardly possible for the critical poet to avoid expanding his own tastes, which are intimately linked to his own practice, into a general law of literature."[28]

But Wilde's idea goes much further than the famous intentional fallacy of the New Critics and even further than Frye, for Wilde conceives of criticism as purely subjective, whereas Wimsatt and Beardsley are committed to the literary work as an ontological object and complain that, as a result of the intentional or the affective fallacy, "the poem itself, as an object of specifically critical judgment, tends to disappear."[29] For Wilde, however, the poem might as well profitably disappear in the critic's higher creation. He believes that Arnold's idea of the aim of criticism—to see the object as it really is—is "a very serious error," for it "takes no cognizance of Criticism's most perfect form, which is in its essence purely subjective" (140). Indeed, he goes even so far as to declare that the critic's work "need not necessarily bear any obvious resemblance to the thing it criticises" (145). In this unabashed plea for creative subjectivity, Wilde seems almost to lead to something like Roland Barthes's radical pronouncement of "the death of the Author," namely, that the liberated critic is engaged not in deciphering the authorial intention as the final signified but in working his or her own way in a "multi-dimensional space in which a variety of writings, none of them original, blend and clash."[30] Thus the critic participates in the traversing of that space with his or her own writing, which is no less original than that of the artist, producing a personal text as creative as literature itself.

Frye's mythological or archetypal criticism is based on the notion of literature as "a 'displaced' mythology," a structure of perennial and recurring myths, images, and archetypes that connect individual works with one another to form a tradition and help to "unify and integrate our literary experience."[31] The view that literature takes shape in the recurrence of archetypes inevitably lays special emphasis on the importance of form and the constitutive role of conventions. As Frye puts it, "Poetry can only be made out of other poems; novels out of other novels. Literature shapes itself, and is not shaped externally:

the *forms* of literature can no more exist outside literature than the forms of sonata and fugue and rondo can exist outside music."[32] In very much the same terms, Wilde talks about form and convention. He insists that art finds its perfection within, not outside itself, depending on the structural power of form: "Hers are the 'forms more real than living man,' and hers the great archetypes of which things that have existence are but unfinished copies" (31). It is with form that literature begins, and it is in the repetition of patterns and conventions that imagination operates, as imagination is "simply concentrated race-experience" (175). Form and convention, however, do not eliminate originality, for the making of literature is the working out of the dialectic relationship between convention and the departure from it, the speaking of a language at once conforming to and violating its grammar. "Each art has its grammar and its materials," observes Wilde, "but, while the laws upon which Art rests may be fixed and certain to find their true realization, they must be touched by the imagination into such beauty that they will seem an exception, each one of them" (205–06). It is surprising to find that these ideas in Wilde have so often been ignored, though they hardly contain anything at which critics now would raise their eyebrows. As Richard Ellmann points out, in arguing for the independence of criticism, "Wilde sounds like an ancestral Northrop Frye or Roland Barthes," and it can be urged that "for his own reasons and in his own way he laid the basis for many critical positions which are still debated in much the same terms, and which we like to attribute to more ponderous names."[33]

The idea of creative criticism, with which Wilde's name is so firmly connected, is being taken seriously by some critics today who give it a sophisticated elaboration in the context of contemporary literary theory. Edward Said, for whom Vico provides a most important guide in philosophy, readily accepts Wilde's idea of criticism as independent creation. In a discussion of contemporary criticism as represented or misrepresented in anthologies, Said discovers that "critical discourse is still ensnared by a simplistic opposition between originality and repetition, in which all literary texts worth studying are given the former classification, the latter being logically confined mainly to criticism and to what isn't worth studying." The opposition is simplistic and therefore false because, first of all, it mistakes "the regularity of most literary production for originality, while insisting that the relation between 'literature' and criticism is one of original to secondary," and then it overlooks "the profoundly important constitutive use of repetition" in the making of literature.[34] The critic understands the making of literature by tracing its genetic progress, by repeating the text from beginning to whole.

But the genetic hypotheses, Said emphasizes, "are not one-way referrals of 'a' work back to 'a' biography or society or whatever," but "include as part of the dialectic the critic's own shaping awareness of what he or she is doing."[35] Thus the critic is repeating the text in a way similar to the author's use of other texts as intertextual motifs and devices, and it is in this making or remaking as creation that true knowledge is obtained: "Only by reproducing can we know what was produced and what the meaning is of verbal production for a human being: this is the quintessential Vichian maxim. And it is no less valid for the literary critic for whom the genesis of a human work is as relevantly interesting as its being."[36] According to Said, it is Wilde and Nietzsche that first call our attention to the question of the role of criticism in the production of a literary work. In his study of the genesis or beginning of texts, Said points out the resemblance between "Nietzsche's division of Homer into two components" and "Oscar Wilde's fascination with the aesthetic powers of criticism to provide accurately inaccurate interpretations of creative energy," and he mentions Freud's Moses, Nietzsche's Dionysus, or Zarathustra as examples of such "inaccurate interpretations" or powerful misreadings.[37]

This leads us naturally to Harold Bloom's idea of creative misreading or "misprision" which comprises and blends both reading and writing, both poetry and criticism: "The influence-relation governs reading as it governs writing, and reading is therefore a miswriting just as writing is a misreading. As literary history lengthens, all poetry necessarily becomes verse-criticism, just as all criticism becomes prose-poetry."[38] Bloom's "revisionistic poetics" is mainly concerned with the problem of what he calls the "anxiety of influence," the desperate effort of the creative energy to break through the influence of previous writings into the space of creation. "Poetic history," says Bloom, "is held to be indistinguishable from poetic influence, since strong poets make that history by misreading one another, so as to clear imaginative space for themselves."[39] In Bloom's theory, the strong poet and the critic are not essentially different, since both are readers or misreaders wrestling with their strong precursors.

Bloom begins The Anxiety of Influence by citing Wilde as a perfect example of how devastating poetic influence can be, arguing that Wilde "had failed as a poet because he lacked strength to overcome his anxiety of influence" and demonstrating how that anxiety may become a recurrent theme in the self-conscious bitterness of the poet, as Wilde talks about influence as "transference of personality" in The Portrait of Mr. W. H., as a kind of immoral manipulation in The Picture of Dorian Gray, or self-deceptively denies the influence of his immediate precursor in his review of Pater's Appreciations by saying that Pater "has escaped disciples."[40] We may perhaps add yet another example from The Critic as Artist, where Gilbert suspects that Ernest has got his anticritical view from some older people and warns him that "that is a dangerous thing to do, and if you allow it to degenerate into a habit, you will find it absolutely fatal to any intellectual development" (109). As Ellmann remarks, "Wilde's mode was calculated juvenescence, and the characters in his books are always being warned by shrewder characters of the danger of listening to people older than themselves."[41] For Wilde then, influence seems to be the power of an older and stronger personality that hinders and even cripples the development of personality of the younger, hence a power either to be shunned or countervailed. We may even say that the idea of criticism as striving to overcome the influence of another personality is implicit in Wilde's argument that "it is only by intensifying his own personality that the critic can interpret the personality and work of others, and the more strongly this personality enters into the interpretation the more real the interpretation becomes, the more satisfying, the more convincing, and the more true" (156).

Frank Lentricchia deftly shows how Bloom's career, which is a prolonged warfare with his New Critical father figures, "is itself a complicated example of the theory of influence."[42] There are also quite remarkable traces of Wilde's influence in his "revisionistic poetics." In his "Manifesto for Antithetical Criticism," Bloom sounds just like Wilde, and the resemblance is quite unmistakable both in theme and style. Bloom characterizes his own theory of poetry as "a severe poem, reliant upon aphorism, apothegm, and a quite personal (though thoroughly traditional) mythic pattern."[43] One may want to apply that characterization quite justifiably to Wilde's criticism as well, to those brilliant and witty dialogues and essays so richly inlaid with aphorisms and apothegms, so memorably quotable. In the hand of the creative critic, that is, the critic as artist as Wilde conceives, or the critic as Bloom's prose-poet, criticism becomes at once a discursive writing and a form of literary expression. And that, as we have seen in the many recent efforts to question the distinction between literary and the nonliterary use of language and the kind of quasi-literary discourse like Jacques Derrida's *Glas,* is precisely one of the points the deconstructionists like very much to press home.

It seems that Geoffrey Hartman has made the most perspicuous deconstructive pronouncement on this subject. He claims that his *Criticism in the Wilderness* is an attempt to bring together his reading of criticism with reading of literature, "to view criticism, in fact, as within literature, not outside of it looking in."[44] He raises questions to challenge the traditional subjugation of criticism as a secondary and derivative text and argues for the "creative or insubordinate quality" of critical writing: "Ask a philosopher what he does and he will answer 'philosophy.' It could be argued, in the same spirit, that what a literary critic does is literature."[45] According to him, one of the central issues that affect literary studies today and concern the deconstructionists in particular is "the situation of criticism itself," and the solution to that issue would be to reconsider the traditional attitude and to realize that "criticism is part of the world of letters, and has its own mixed philosophical and literary, reflective and figural strength."[46] It is no wonder that Hartman should find in Wilde a forerunner in this respect. After quoting Wilde's contemptuous remark on the silly vanity of those writers and artists who would have the critic accept as primary function to chatter about their second-rate work, Hartman says: "The English tradition in criticism is sublimated chatter; but it is also animated by its fierce ability to draw reputation into question. Even Shakespeare had once to be made safe; and Milton is restored, after Leavis, to his bad eminence. This power to alter reputations is formidable, and it shows that criticism has an unacknowledged penchant for reversal in it, which is near-daemonic and which brings it close to the primacy of art."[47] In the critical evaluation, or rather, devaluation of works of art, Hartman sees the power of criticism that is capable not only of creation but of reversal, of destruction, and, quite appositely, of deconstruction.

In deconstructive criticism as reversal, however, the idea of creative criticism is perhaps pushed in a direction Wilde may not have expected and may not endorse. While the deconstructive critic takes great pains to pull the text apart by exposing its fissures or internal inconsistencies, Wilde's aesthetic critic is much more interested in the pleasure of the text, the enjoyment of the beautiful. As Wilde says in the preface to *Dorian Gray,* art is beautiful, and "those who find beautiful meanings in beautiful things are the cultivated. For these there is hope." One of the advantages the critic has over the artist, as Wilde specifies it, lies precisely in the catholicity of artistic tastes because, while the artist's taste is limited, "the aesthetic critic, and the aesthetic critic alone, can appreciate all forms and modes" (206). It is this catholicity of artistic temperament, the true spirit of cosmopolitanism, Wilde argues, that makes the aesthetic critic the superb preserver of culture.

In his emphasis on impression, subjectivity, artistic temperament, and personality, Wilde's critical theory is not characterized by well-balanced reasoning or scrupulous scholarship. But a cool and unspirited objectivity is neither his style nor his ideal. He regards preconceptions as the very condition of criticism: "One should, of course, have no prejudice; but, as a great Frenchman remarked a hundred years ago, it is one's business in such matters to have preferences, and when one has preferences one ceases to be fair. It is only an auctioneer who can equally and impartially admire all schools of Art" (189). Here Wilde is coming to an important truth, so often ignored outside of the humanities because it does not conform to the ideal of objectivity; namely, the truth that our understanding and appreciation are never impersonally objective, but always colored by tradition or our conscious rebellion against it, by social and historical conditions, personal taste, cultivation, and so on; that we never read a book with a blank mind, but always with a set of rules, principles, and conventions as *fore*-understanding. Hans-Georg Gadamer's philosophical reha-bilitation of *das Vorurteil* most powerfully demonstrates that "the prejudice against prejudice" is merely a prejudice in itself, a fundamental prejudice of the Enlightenment.[48]

However, without the support of profound philosophical reasoning, Wilde's argument seems more witty than substantial, bending, as it were, deliberately on a kind of shocking sensationalism. It did more to bewilder and amuse his contemporaries than to convince and enlighten them. "I throw probability out of the window for the sake of a phrase," Wilde confessed to Arthur Conan Doyle, "and the chance of an epigram makes me desert truth."[49] But that confession itself reads suspiciously like an epigram, and we feel we have to read all of Wilde with a conscious effort to see what is going on underneath, or within, his highly polished, sparkling language. To read Wilde is never to read literally but to be sensitive to the workings of language. "Beauty has as many meanings as man has moods," says Wilde; "Beauty reveals everything, because it expresses nothing" (144). His style of writing constantly invites doubt and rethinking and reveals the complexity and indeterminacy of literary language.

And yet, there is always something deeper than the mere play of language and the seemingly paradoxical in his paradox, something that comes from a deep seriousness. In his pursuit of paradoxes, maxims, and aphorisms, Wilde is, to quote what Ernest says of Gilbert, "quite incorrigible" (100). Therefore, it is quite easy to ignore his serious search for truth and his brilliant insight into the nature of art and criticism if we take them as a mere "patchwork affair or as a polished form of public entertainment."[50] We are liable to forget his emphasis on the self-culture of the critic, as "criticism demands infinitely more cultivation than creation does" (126), or his perfectly sane and solid enumeration of the essentials of Shakespearean criticism, which includes practically everything a Shakespearean scholar should know (154–55). We are liable to neglect his theory by seeing only his wit, and this, as Beerbohm indicates, is simply a fallacy. "In point of fact," says Beerbohm, "wit was the least important of his gifts. Primarily, he was a poet, with a life-long passion for beauty; and a philosopher, with a life-long passion for thought. His wit, and his humour (which was of an even finer quality than his wit), sprang from a very solid basis of seriousness, as all good wit or humour must."[51]

To see Wilde as both a poet and a philosopher is to appreciate the graceful style of his writing that gives him an indisputable advantage over some of our contemporary critics whose a-bit-too-French French discourse can hardly ever match the ease and brilliance of Wilde's not-too-French French gestures. His aestheticism needs to be understood in its historical context, as a revolt against the kind of moralistic criticism we find in Arnold and Ruskin, and his creative criticism needs to be taken as a defense of the artistic temperament. After all, most original and insightful criticism is creative in precisely the way Wilde has described it; that is, it "fills with wonder a form which the artist may have left void, or not understood, or understood incompletely" (144). Pater's Mona Lisa may reveal more of Pater than of da Vinci or his painting, but we can hardly avoid its influence on the way we see and think about that painting. Goethe's Hamlet as a sensitive artist, Coleridge's as a melancholy philosopher, and even Freud's as a neurotic patient are all valuable in one way or another, and a reading of the great Shakespearean play without awareness of all such interpretations would indeed miss a lot of the play itself. Creative criticism is thus a recognition of the richness and the excess of meaning in the great work of art. As Wilde puts it, "The aesthetic critic rejects those obvious modes of art that have but one message to deliver, and having delivered it become dumb and sterile, and seeks rather for such modes as suggest reverie and mood, and by their imaginative beauty make all interpretations true and no interpretation final" (148). Wilde's creative criticism, in other words, seeks to open the text of an artistic work and its inexhaustible meaning rather than close it once and for all with a seal of authority.

Yet Wilde's remarks will continue to irritate many people's sense of fairness, seriousness, or truthfulness. There are undoubtedly overstatements and exaggerations, bias, slant, and prejudice, but the essence of Wilde's critical thinking, the independence of Art and of Criticism as art, will endure as valuable insights which protect art against the encroachment too often perpetrated by moral, political, or religious interests. All the rest is not essential; all the seemingly absurd extravaganzas come from the desire to achieve a striking effect, the need to make a strong point and drive it home. But if criticism is an art as Wilde argues, he has then already given the most effective defense for himself: "Art itself is really a form of exaggeration; and selection, which is the very spirit of art [and so also of criticism], is nothing more than an intensified mode of overemphasis" (23).

Notes

1. Sir Max Beerbohm, "A Lord of Language," Appendix C, in H. Montgomery Hyde, *Oscar Wilde: The Aftermath* (New York: Farrar, Straus, 1963), 205.

2. Jerome Hamilton Buckley, *The Victorian Temper: A Study in Literary Culture* (Cambridge: Cambridge University Press, 1981), 219.

3. Richard Ellmann, *Oscar Wilde at Oxford* (Washington, D.C.: Library of Congress, 1984), 5.

4. René Wellek, *A History of Modern Criticism, 1750–1950*, vol. 4: *The Later Nineteenth Century* (New Haven: Yale University Press, 1965), 408.

5. Ibid., 409.

6. Ibid.

7. Oscar Wilde, "The Decay of Lying," "The Critic as Artist," in *Intentions* (New York: Brentano's, 1950), 5, 185. All further references to this edition will be included in the text.

8. Wellek, 413, 414.

9. René Wellek, "The Poet as Critic, the Critic as Poet, the Poet-Critic," in *Discriminations: Further Concepts of Criticism* (New Haven: Yale University Press, 1970), 256.

10. René Wellek, "Destroying Literary Studies," *New Criterion* 2.4 (1983): 1–8.

11. Roger Shattuck, "Viva Voce: Criticism and the Teaching of Literature," in *What Is Criticism?* ed. Paul Harnadi (Bloomington: Indiana University Press, 1981), 99.

12. Wellek, "Destroying Literary Studies," 8.

13. Murray Krieger, "Criticism as a Secondary Art," in *What Is Criticism?* 280.

14. Ibid., 282.

15. Karlfried Froehlich, trans. and ed., *Biblical Interpretation in the Early Church* (Philadelphia: Fortress Press, 1984), 1.

16. Wellek, *History of Modern Criticism*, 411.

17. Henri Peyre, *Writers and Their Critics: A Study of Misunderstanding* (Ithaca: Cornell University Press, 1944), 228.

18. Eugenio Donato, "Historical Imagination and the Idioms of Criticism," *Boundary 2* 8 (Fall 1979): 52, 50.

19. Giambattista Vico, *The New Science of Giambattista Vico*, sec. 363, trans. Thomas G. Bergin and Max H. Fisch (Ithaca: Cornell University Press, 1968), 110.

20. Sir Philip Sidney, *An Apology for Poetry,* ed. Forrest Robinson (Indianapolis: Bobbs-Merrill, 1970), 14.

21. Ibid., 57.

22. John Allen Quintus, "The Moral Implications of Oscar Wilde's Aestheticism," *Texas Studies in Literature and Language* 22 (Winter 1980): 567.

23. William K. Wimsatt and Cleanth Brooks, *Literary Criticism: A Short History* (New York: Knopf, 1957), 495, 496.

24. Northrop Frye, *The Secular Scripture* (Cambridge: Harvard University Press, 1976), 45, 46.

25. Northrop Frye, *Anatomy of Criticism: Four Essays* (Princeton: Princeton University Press, 1957), 5.

26. William K. Wimsatt and Monroe C. Beardsley, "The Intentional Fallacy," in *The Verbal Icon* (Lexington: University of Kentucky Press, 1954), 4.

27. Frye, *Anatomy of Criticism,* 4, 5.

28. Ibid., 6.

29. Wimsatt and Beardsley, "The Affective Fallacy," in *Verbal Icon,* 21.

30. Roland Barthes, "The Death of the Author," in *Image-Music-Text,* trans. Stephen Heath (New York: Hill & Wang, 1977), 146.

31. Northrop Frye, *Fables of Identity: Studies in Poetic Mythology* (New York: Harcourt, Brace & World, 1963), 1: Frye, *Anatomy of Criticism,* 99.

32. Frye, *Anatomy of Criticism,* 97.

33. Oscar Wilde, *The Artist as Critic: Critical Writings of Oscar Wilde,* ed. Richard Ellmann (Chicago: University of Chicago Press, 1968), introduction, x.

34. Edward W. Said, "Roads Taken and Not Taken in Contemporary Criticism," in *The World, the Text, and the Critic* (Cambridge: Harvard University Press, 1983), 154.

35. Ibid., 156, 157.

36. Ibid., 157.

37. Edward W. Said, *Beginnings: Intention and Method* (New York: Basic Books, 1975), 58.

38. Harold Bloom, *A Map of Misreading* (New York: Oxford University Press, 1975), 3.

39. Harold Bloom, *The Anxiety of Influence: A Theory of Poetry* (New York: Oxford University Press, 1973), 5.

40. Ibid., 5–6.

41. Ellmann, introduction, *Artist as Critic,* x.

42. Frank Lentricchia, *After the New Criticism* (Chicago: University of Chicago Press, 1980), 321.

43. Bloom, *Anxiety of Influence,* 13.

44. Geoffrey H. Hartman, *Criticism in the Wilderness: The Study of Literature Today* (New Haven: Yale University Press, 1980), 1.

45. Ibid., 9, 20.

46. Geoffrey H. Hartman, Preface, *Deconstruction and Criticism,* ed. Harold Bloom et al. (New York: Continuum, 1984), vii.

47. Hartman, *Criticism in the Wilderness,* 199.

48. See Hans-Georg Gadamer, *Truth and Method,* Eng. trans. ed. B. Garden and J. Cumming (New York: Crossroad, 1975), 235ff.

49. Wilde, Letter to Arthur Conan Doyle, in *The Letters of Oscar Wilde,* ed. Rupert Hart-Davis (New York: Harcourt, Brace & World, 1962), 291–92.

50. Epifanio San Juan, Jr., *The Art of Oscar Wilde* (Princeton: Princeton University Press, 1967), 74.

51. Beerbohm, "A Lord of Language," 205.

Semiotics and Oscar Wilde's
Accounts of Art

IAN SMALL

One of the most influential ways that recent literary criticism has attempted to re-describe writing at the end of the nineteenth and beginning of the twentieth centuries is in terms of an antithesis between the representational qualities of literature and its self-consciously fictional or artefactual elements. Generally, this argument runs, the more modernist a text, the more self-consciously artefactual it is. The corollary of this argument is the proposition that Victorian literary culture held to the naïve view that literary texts (and art works generally) could unproblematically represent the world and in so doing embody a form of knowledge about it. Most of the historians who hold this argument allow of significant exceptions but in general they maintain that such a taxonomy corresponds broadly speaking to literary "periods." But their case rests not on arguments about periodicity but on a simple distinction about the ontology of art works. Within this particular view of the relationship between the "Victorian" and the "modern," any art work which embodies within itself an ontological critique of itself as representation is defined as axiomatically modernist.[1] Aestheticism and the English decadence stand as key transitional moments, for it is maintained that then the nature of literature as representation first began to be seriously and systematically questioned. Typically it is Oscar Wilde who is credited with being the profoundest and most influential if not the most consistent critic of the assumptions about representation that underlie Victorian literary culture.[2] There are two kinds of argument about Wilde the proto-modernist. The first, weak form of the argument was the most usual until the 1970s.[3] It claims that Wilde is a simple formalist or a simple subjectivist (in his case a formalist and a subjectivist being one and the same thing). In this argument it is alleged that Wilde suggests that the spectator of a work of art responds to its compositional values, its patterns, its formal elements; or reads on to the art work whatever is in him or her. The strong version of the argument connects Wilde's remarks about form to his remarks about subjectivity in a causal way: the formal patterns of a work of art, it is claimed, are determinant of the spectator's subjective responses. Whatever specialized form the argument takes, it invariably sets up a simple antithesis between, in Wilde's terms, Art and Life, or Art and Nature, by isolating in Wilde's criticism the following line of logic. The formal, patterning effects of art embody the *cultural* in its most significant aspects (Wilde's term for what we would now call "culture" is "civilization"; to avoid confusion I will consistently employ the modern term). The effects of a culture at any one historical moment, according to this description of Wilde's case, organize the perception or conception of nature in a wholly derivative way. What determines the *cultural* determines in what kinds of way men will conceive of the *natural*. So, in Wilde's phrase, "Nature imitates Art" in the sense that man's conception of the natural is determined by art.

This particular view of Wilde as the midwife of modernism may be correct in the general emphasis it places upon Wilde's influence. But it is only partly true in the sense that it over-simplifies Wilde's arguments. His account of art is never simply dyadic, embodying an antithesis between art and nature. In fact, whenever Wilde talks of art—in *Dorian Gray,* in the critical dialogues, fleetingly in his plays—he specifically discusses or refers to art under three general headings. In the first place Wilde always broaches the relationship of art to its subject and to its author: the mimetic and expressive features of art are often glancingly and always paradoxically mentioned, but they always *are* mentioned. In the second place Wilde discusses particular art forms (usually pictorial art and literature) in terms of their compositional elements: he talks, that is, of what some modern theorists call the grammars of particular art forms. In the third place Wilde discusses at considerable length the variety of uses that art has in a culture at any moment—in the terminology of some crude Marxist accounts of art, that is, he talks of its social function, its consumption, its embodiment and replication of an ideology and so forth. (I shall use as a shorthand the term "cultural uses" to describe this particular interest of Wilde, although I am aware it is both clumsy and imprecise.) The shortcoming of what I called the dyadic account of Wilde's art criticism is that it collapses the third category into the first—the representational aspects of art, that is, become confused with its "cultural uses." Of course, few would deny that these two aspects of pictorial art and literature are indeed connected. All representation, it is often argued, works by conventions which are in themselves culturally given. But it does not follow from such an observation that the notion of representation is exactly commensurate with that of art's "cultural uses," far less that both sum up the concept of art which can, in its turn, be crudely opposed to the natural in the way that Wilde's critics have assumed. More importantly it is not a confusion of categories that Wilde anywhere makes. So, in order to uncover some of the complexities—and in passing some of the lost subtlety— of Wilde's thinking about art, I should like to apply to it some of the distinctions derived from two theories of semiotics: those developed by Charles

Morris and Umberto Eco, because they discriminate how and what pictorial art signifies in any particular cultural moment in a way that does more justice to Wilde than the naïve ontological distinctions made by his recent critics.

Charles Morris in *Foundations of the Theory of Signs* (1938) discusses the concept of the sign in semiotics under three specific headings: semantics, syntactics and pragmatics. Signs for Morris designate and they can also denote. The *designatum* of a sign is the kind or class of objects referred to, while the *denotatum* is the actually existent object of reference. For Morris a sign which is similar in some respects to what it denotes is iconic. Morris claims that iconicity is thus a feature of portraits, photographs, maps and models (although, as I shall show, this concept of iconicity has been profoundly questioned recently by Umberto Eco). The way a sign relates to one or more signs within a sign system or systems—its code, to use the accepted modern term—is called by Morris the syntactic dimension of semiosis. A sign implicates all the other signs to which it relates or can relate. The third feature of signs in Morris's account is pragmatics. Morris's "pragmatic dimension of semiosis" is the uses made of the sign by its interpreter or interpreters. Morris sums up his three-fold distinction thus: "[P]*ragmatics* is that portion of semiotic which deals with the origin, uses, and effects of signs within the behaviour in which they occur; *semantics* deals with the signification of signs in all modes of signifying; *syntactics* deals with combinations of signs without regard to their specific significations or their relation to the behaviour in which they occur."[4]

In particular Morris describes a painting as being itself a sign, but also composed of signs, and existing within a larger sign system. It is a description remarkably helpful in teasing out some of the complexity in Wilde's writings about art in the sense that it seems to answer fairly closely to the positions towards which Wilde, in his last years as a serious writer, was tentatively moving. In giving some examples, I shall, for the sake of clarity, reverse Morris's order of discussing the features of semiotics. The brief allusions that most semioticians make about a possible "grammar" for pictorial art[5] have their counterpart in Wilde's delphic utterances about composition. "Phrases and Philosophies for the Use of the Young" and the Society comedies abound in references to the primacy of style.[6] The idea is common, too, in the critical dialogues. Gilbert in "The Critic as Artist" pontificates in Wilde's voice: "The harmony that resides in the delicate proportions of lines and masses becomes mirrored in the mind. The repetitions of pattern give us rest. The marvels of design stir the imagination. In the mere loveliness of the materials employed there are latent elements of culture."[7] That art embodies, in addition to all of its other elements, certain principles of composition, is an idea that appears too in "The Decay of Lying." Wilde, this time through his mouthpiece Vivian, declares: "Art begins with abstract decoration, with purely imaginative and pleasurable work dealing with what is unreal and non-existent . . . Art itself is really a form of exaggeration; and selection, which is the very spirit of art, is nothing more than an intensified mode of over-emphasis."[8]

But Wilde was not the simple formalist he is often made out to be. The notions of representation and iconicity fascinated him. (*The Picture of Dorian Gray* is indeed a novel devoted to playing with the concept of iconicity.) As I shall show, the evidence of Wilde's revisions of "The Decay of Lying" suggests that his thoughts on the subject were not as straightforward or simple as most commentators have assumed.

Umberto Eco in *A Theory of Semiotics* (1977) presents a partial critique of Morris's definition of iconicity. He argues that in Morris's definition the only truly iconic sign would be the object itself, a proposition which, he notes, would dispose of semiotics entirely. Iconic signs, for Eco, are only a matter of convention and he cites the famous example of Constable's rendering of the effects of light given by Gombrich in *Art and Illusion* as an instance of the formative relationship between conventional representations and constructions of "reality." Eco concludes that we understand a "given technical solution as the representation of a natural experience because there has been formed in us a codified *system of expectations,* which allows us to enter into the semantic world of the artist. . . . At a certain point the iconic representation, however stylized it may be, appears to be more true than the real experience, and people begin to look at things through the glasses of iconic convention."[9]

However true this observation might be generally, it seems to me that Wilde in the years between 1889 and 1891, the years, that is, that saw the composition and publication of *Dorian Gray* and *Intentions,* was moving, hesitatingly perhaps, and certainly unsystematically, to a strikingly similar position. In any case, Eco's account of signs, by describing much less rigidly Morris's distinction between the syntactic and iconic aspects of semiosis, allows a modern reader to analyse Wilde's arguments in his critical dialogues in a way that avoids the risks inherent in the naïve accounts that I have described above. In semiotic theory it is possible to describe the manner in which the *cultural* predetermines our expectations or conceptions of the *natural* while still taking account of the other elements of art that relate to its cultural significance. In Eco's terms a culture possesses a codified system of graphic expectations through which and by means of which iconic convention and iconic representation portray our actual knowledge of the real world. This particular notion seems to me to be the burden of the most famous lines in "The Decay of Lying"—Wilde's account of how Impressionist painting of London fogs actually brought about their "recognition" by his contemporaries.

Where, if not from the Impressionists, do we get those wonderful brown fogs that come creeping down our streets, blurring the gas-lamps and changing the houses into monstrous shadows? To whom, if not to them and their master, do we owe the lovely silver mists that brood over our river, and turn to faint forms of fading grace curved bridge and swaying barge? The extraordinary change that has taken place in the climate of London during the last ten years is entirely due to a particular school of Art. You smile. Consider the matter from a scientific or a metaphysical point of view, and you will find that I am right. For what is Nature? Nature is no great mother who has borne us. She is our creation. It is in our brain that she quickens to life. Things are because we see them, and what we see, and how we see it, depends on the Arts that have influenced us. To look at a thing is very different from seeing a thing. One does not see anything until one sees its beauty. Then, and then only, does it come into existence. . . . There may have been fogs for centuries in London. I dare say there were. But no one saw them, and so we do not know anything about them. They did not exist until Art had invented them.[10]

Vivian's speech goes on for a further five hundred words. The history of that particular passage in Wilde's essay is interesting and in a sense demonstrates the appropriateness of his argument. The passage[11] did not appear in the essay's first publication in *The Nineteenth Century*. Wilde was a tireless reviser of his work and made numerous other stylistic revisions to "The Decay of Lying" between its periodical and book publication, although these were of a minor sort. But nowhere in Wilde's *oeuvre* is there an addition to his text of such proportions. It is a profound and provocative elaboration of the basic thesis of the essay.

But of course such an account of art as one of the central ways in which iconic conventions make knowledge about the world possible does not exhaust Wilde's thoughts about pictorial art. The pictorial artefact is also, to revert to Morris's terms, a sign within a larger cultural system of signs; and as such it occupies a place in a system of values that has little or nothing to do with its artistic or aesthetic values simply conceived *as* artistic or aesthetic values. Wilde more than any figure in the last decades of the nineteenth century knew of the way a man's possessions spoke for him. The Louis Seize cane or furniture, the gold-tipped cigarettes, the carefully selected button-hole were possessions that spoke for Wilde and for the central characters in his social dramas. But what best announces to the world the tastes and values of the clever man are the art objects he selects: they locate him in political and social spheres. In *The Picture of Dorian Gray* Dorian's and Lord Henry's connoisseurship defines how they are placed in the power structures of nineteenth-century society generally. In this respect Wilde's most interesting work is *An Ideal Husband*. In the first act Wilde introduces his characters by describing them, in the stage directions of the first printed edition of the play, in terms of their most appropriate portraitists. The artists mentioned are Boucher, Watteau, Lawrence and Van Dyck. Wilde is designating aspects of character by reference to the cultural significance that attaches to the work of specific painters and by extension locating those characters on a social and political (as well as a dramatic) spectrum of values. The pictures are not operating as graphic or iconic signs within an aesthetic code but within other social codes. The central contrast is a political one and is between Van Dyck, the putative portraitist of Sir Robert Chiltern, the play's main character, and Watteau, used to depict two minor female characters of great prettiness and "exquisite fragility." Some of the relevant passages from the stage-directions are these: *"Sir Robert Chiltern . . . A personality of mark. Not popular—few personalities are. But intensely admired by the few, and deeply respected by the many . . . It would be inaccurate to call him picturesque. Picturesqueness cannot survive the House of Commons. But Van Dyck would have loved to paint his head."* Earlier Mabel Chiltern's modernity is characterized by her being compared to a (recently discovered) Tanagra statuette and Mrs. Cheveley, clearly marked out as a "fast" and thus socially dangerous woman, is "a work of art, on the whole, but showing the influence of too many schools."[12] A nineteenth-century reading public would quite clearly grasp the distinction between the established portraitist, connoting order, tradition and authority, the gentle pastoralism of Watteau, suggestive, to the Decadent sensibility, of a delicate eroticism, the modernity of a Tanagra statuette and a style-less eclecticism. The art objects that Wilde selects, that is, themselves implicate the political values that are central to the play's development.

If such an account of Wilde has any merit it is to suggest that the taxonomy of modes of writing and pictorial representation that sets the "modernist" against the "Victorian" *solely* in terms of a critique of the concept of representation is misplaced. Such a view is true, but only partly so. Wilde's *oeuvre* suggests that early modernists well knew that pictorial or literary art could embody interpretative "openness" and thus invite questions about their functions as representation; but that they also knew that these features in themselves did not prevent art objects from being assigned specific social value or being used with a specific social function.

Notes

A version of this paper was given to a postgraduate seminar in the English Department of Reading University. I am grateful to the participants for the comments I received and especially for advice from Dr. Barrie Bullen.

1. This thesis has been presented in a variety of ways by a number of critics. See for example, Robert Alter, *Partial Magic* (London, 1975); David Lodge, *The Modes of Modern Writing* (London, 1977); and Colin McCabe, *James Joyce and the Revolution of the Word* (London, 1979). The idea, in a more general form, runs through works like Gabriel Josipovici's *The World and the Book* (London, 1971). Its most influential formulation, made in terms of a contrast between the "openness" of modernist texts and the "closure" of the classic realist text was made by Roland Barthes in *S/Z* (Paris, 1970).

2. The description of the '90s and the English decadence as "proto" or early modernist has also been made in a variety of ways by a variety of critics. See, for example Edward Said, "The Text, the World, the Critic," in J. V. Harari (ed), *Textual Strategies* (London, 1980), or the overall thesis contained in Malcolm Bradbury and Ian Fletcher (eds), *Decadence and the 1890s* (London, 1979) and G. Hough and E. Warner (eds), *Strangeness and Beauty* (Cambridge, 1983).

3. The first form of the argument I have in mind was made by Hilda Schiff, "Nature and Art in Oscar Wilde," *Essays and Studies by Members of the English Association* (London,

1965). For the second see Bruce Bashford, "Oscar Wilde, his Criticism and his Critics," *English Literature in Transition*, 20 (3, 1977) 181–7; and "Oscar Wilde and Subjectivist Criticism," *English Literature in Transition*, 21 (4, 1978) 218–34.

The line of argument is similar to one put forward by Richard Wollheim on Pater in *On Art and the Mind* (London, 1973). See also R. J. Green, "Oscar Wilde's *Intentions:* An Early Modernist Manifesto," *British Journal of Aesthetics*, 13 (Autumn, 1973), 397–404.

4. The quotation is from a later essay, *Signs, Language and Behaviour* (1946). See Charles Morris, *Writings on the General Theory of Signs* (The Hague, 1971), p. 302.

5. The term derives from a debate about the nature of narrative in France in the 1970s. Morris is frustratingly modest about what might be expected from such a "grammar" of pictorial art.

6. See, for example, Gwendolen's advice in *The Importance of Being Earnest:* "In matters of grave importance, style, not sincerity is the vital thing," *The Importance of Being Earnest*, ed., Russell Jackson (London, 1980), III, 28–9; or Lord Illingworth's belief that "The future belongs to the dandy. It is the exquisites who are going to rule." *A Woman of No Importance* in Oscar Wilde, *Two Society Comedies*, ed., Ian Small and Russell Jackson (London, 1983), III, 56–7.

7. Oscar Wilde, *Intentions* (1908), p. 206.

8. Ibid, pp. 22–4.

9. See Umberto Eco, *A Theory of Semiotics* (London, 1977), pp. 204–5.

10. *Intentions*, pp. 41–2.

11. The passage is too long to quote in full. It ends with the words "dissatisfaction, which is better," *Intentions*, p. 44. Wilde made numerous stylistic revisions to this particular essay and his plays have copious examples of his readiness to adapt material from his other work. But this revision is untypical. Moreover, to all intents and purposes London Galleries had ceased to exhibit Impressionist work by the late 1880s. There was, however, a lively debate about Impressionism, and Wilde's revision shows every indication of being influenced by that debate.

12. See *An Ideal Husband* in Oscar Wilde, *Two Society Comedies*, I, 84 and I, 50.

Framing Wilde

GERHARD JOSEPH

An off-hand list of the figures who obviously count these days in the undermining of a simple view of representation—say, Saussure, Heidegger, Derrida, Lacan, Foucault, Althusser—suggests the extent to which Anglo-American criticism has been swamped by a continental tradition, one in turn inspired by such nineteenth-century continental giants as Hegel, Marx, Nietzsche, and Freud. But if such be the mainstream of contemporary theory, this is not to deny the existence of a native English tributary that has had its influence. That nineteenth-century English line, to simplify, goes from Arnold to Pater to Wilde. "To see the object as in itself it really is," Arnold tells us is the Function of Criticism at mid-century, as if the Kantian "thing in itself," what Arnold's contemporary Henry James called the Real Thing were readily accessible to perception. But already in the Victorian heyday of a belief in "disinterestedness" or "objectivity," in the possibility of unmediated vision for either the empiricist or the idealist, Arnold's famous dictum deconstructs itself by a self-framing—by a redundancy ("in *itself*," "as it *really* is") that betrays cognitive uncertainty. It is thus but a short step to Pater's qualification in *The Renaissance* that the function of criticism is to know one's impression of the object as it really is (since the "thick wall of personality" will cut off an unobstructed view of the object)—and an even shorter distance to the full Wildean reversal in "The Critic as Artist" to the effect that "The highest Criticism . . . is more creative than creation, and the primary aim of the critic is to see the object as in itself it really is not" (*Artist as Critic* 369). Wilde's pivotal role in the critical tradition, his true importance for us today, resides in that single sentence—in his *English* assertion that criticism is neither subordinate to creation nor even mimetic of the aesthetic object that is its apparent occasion. "To the critic," continues Wilde's spokesman Gilbert in the same speech from which I have quoted, "the work of art is simply a suggestion for a new work of one's own, that need not necessarily bear any obvious resemblance to the thing it criticizes." As Pater had framed Arnold's key sentence, so Wilde had stepped back to frame the sentences of both his predecessors, but especially that of Arnold.

It is this act of critical framing, the engine of Wilde's aggressive wit, that I

Reprinted from *Victorian Newsletter* (Fall 1987): 61–63.

would like to examine, for it is that process which makes him our contemporary. As Mary Ann Caws has recently demonstrated in *Reading Frames in Modern Fiction,* her study of the novel from Jane Austen to Virginia Woolf, a concern for conceptual framing and meta-framing is a homology—may even be *the* most resonant homology—that cuts across literary theory, art history, psychology, sociology, the history of science, indeed, all of the human sciences these days. And the effect of such framing is to undercut in all of them a binary opposition of form and content, of surface and substance, of what Gombrich has usefully distinguished as "frame" and "fill." Differentiating "pre-modernist" from "modernist" texts, Caws suggests that in the former certain passages generally frame or stress an "inner" substance or field under investigation, while the principal texts of modernism (particularly the novels of James, Proust, and Woolf) emphasize the very act of framing as it calls attention above all to itself, scanning the surface frames rather than what they include "beneath" or "within" themselves. It is my contention that such a concentration upon the outer frame was forecast by Wilde's own attack upon depth analysis—or at any rate by his systematic transvaluation of various Victorian hierarchies—those of earnestness over acting, of the natural over the artificial, and, preeminently, of substance over surface. "I am on bad terms with Nature; I see in her neither intellect nor passion—the only two things that make surfaces possible" (letter to H. C. Pollitt [1898] in *Letters* 774), said Wilde, for whom the survey of life's surface was the essential aesthetic project. What existed below the surface sign was at best problematic and most likely impervious to representation. He did of course admit that the sign—the word, the image, the portrait—might stand for something else, that it might approach the condition of symbol. But the attempt to explicate that symbolic meaning he thought both an epistemological and moral mistake. "All art is at once surface and symbol," one of the opening epigrams of *The Picture of Dorian Gray* has it. But the two sentences that follow insist upon the priority of surface: "Those who go beneath the surface do so at their peril. Those who read the symbol do so at their peril" (viii).

Although Wilde's dramas, novels, and critical essays all demonstrate the importance of making do with surfaces, with the "Truth of Masks," "The Portrait of Mr. W. H." from the critical volume *Intentions* may do as well as any of them as a paradigm for Wilde's exploration of the "intentionality" of a text's surface. The narrative of this homosexual romance disguised as a tale of literary detection begins with a discussion of literary forgeries. The narrator, an unnamed young aesthete, tells his friend and interlocuter Erskine that such forgeries "are merely the result of an artistic desire for perfect representation." If we agree that we have no right to object to the conditions under which an artist chooses to present his work and regard art as "a mode of acting, an attempt to realize one's own personality on some imaginative plane out of the reach of the trammeling accidents and limitations of real life," then "to censure an artist for forgery was to confuse an ethical with an aesthetical problem" (152).

The impulse to forge in both the honorific and pejorative senses of that word arises out of a desire for origination, of a passion by the writer to render his subject first—to forge in the smithy of *his* soul rather than to frame the utterance of a predecessor (as I have thus framed Joyce's). The forger—again, in both senses—claims to be giving his audience a direct expression of personality, his "perfect representation" of the world's object as in itself it really is—or in the case of Mr. W. H.—was, an artifact bathed in what Walter Benjamin called its authenticating aura (217–51). In contrast, the framer not only admits the layered and derivative quality of his utterance but flaunts it in quotation or, as with Wilde, allusive transvaluation. Forgery and framing thus apparently stand in an inverse relationship to each other. The artist either frames or forges, and while the framer who more or less explicitly acknowledges his source seems honest (though, as we shall see by the end of my argument, "seems" is the operative word here), the forger, like his brother the plagiarist, seems to be involved in a morally reprehensible act. But "the fact of a man being [a forger or] a poisoner is nothing against his prose," Wilde had averred in "Pen Pencil and Poison" (339), an essay in *Intentions,* a defense of the writer Thomas Griffiths Wainwright, who had been both. At any rate, the opening generalization of "The Portrait of Mr. W. H." concerning the equivocal nature of forgery stands as an aesthetic principle which the story examines by way of recursive frames. For it's the work of art at a remove, the imagistic portrait framed by the story of a portrait (as the imagistic picture of Dorian Gray is framed by its textual frame) that exemplifies Wilde's paradoxical principles of representation.

The opening discussion of forgery in "The Portrait of Mr. W. H." leads Erskine to show the narrator a painting done of a young man in Elizabethan dress. That portrait, we learn, is the "proof" of a theory fashioned by a young friend of Erskine's, Cyril Graham, which identifies the inspiration of Shakespeare's sonnets as a boy actor named Willie Hughes. Cyril, whose beauty turns out to equal that of Willie in the portrait, has devised a story of Shakespeare's relations with the young actor, with the rival poet (identified as Marlowe), and with the Dark Lady, which constitutes the essential narrative within the outer narrative.

At the beginning of that outer framing tale, Cyril Graham is already dead, a modern Chatterton who had had the "Elizabethan" portrait forged in order to support his Willie Hughes theory and then in despair at his friend Erskine's skepticism had killed himself as a final attempt at persuasion. We learn that Cyril, like Willie Hughes, was "wonderfully handsome," and that he had been an actor in his Oxford days, taking young women's parts and having had his special triumph as Rosalind in *As You Like It.* The dead Cyril, that is, has become the double of the Willie Hughes he invented, and the outer framing plot is basically an account of the phases of Erskine and the narrator's belief and disbelief, a "dance of shifting credence,"[1] in Cyril's theory. For Erskine, on discovering that Cyril had had the portrait forged, loses *his* belief and falls away from him, but the narrator for whom the "wonderful portrait [has] already begun to have a strange fascination" is converted and devotes himself to a careful study of the sonnets. He then *re*converts Erskine to belief but in the course of doing so loses his own conviction. In the story's final act of meta-framing Erskine attempts to reconvert the now skeptical narrator by means of a letter, written from Cannes, in which he explains that he has decided to follow Cyril Graham in giving his life for the theory and to atone for the skepticism that had driven Cyril to his death. The narrator rushes to Cannes, finds that Erskine is indeed dead, but soon learns that he has died not by his own hand but of consumption. Erskine's attempt to forge (in both senses) his own suicide has failed, but he has won the narrator over, bequeathing to him the portrait of Willie Hughes in which the narrator, in the story's final turn of the screw, now "believes." "There really is a great deal to be said for the Willie Hughes theory of Shakespeare's Sonnets," the narrator affirms in the story's closing sentence (220) as he attempts to tease the reader into belief.

In thus retelling the plot, I have intentionally stressed an absurdist quality that is easy to miss because of a life-and-death seriousness of narrative tone, especially in the opening didactic generalizations about forgery and representation. For in this tale of a forgery that for Wilde expresses "the artistic desire for perfect representation," we can see his parodic examination of the death instinct behind such a desire. In that sense, I see this tale as a comic pendant to an earnest "Lady of Shalott," or at least my sense of that Tennyson poem. In two recent essays on that work as a paradigm of what is being done with representation theory these days in the criticism of Victorian poetry, I cited Geoffrey Hartman's Lacanian reading of the Lady's passion for direct, unmediated contact with the world's substance, her unwillingness to rest outside of the frame and within mere surface representation, as *the* single best poetic expression of "a Western desire for reality-mastery as aggressive and fatal as Freud's death instinct" (8). "I am half-sick of shadows," says the Lady and thus turns from her mirror of representation to the supposed reality of Lancelot, an attempt at advent which turns out to be suicidal. Wilde had given his own cautionary version of that desire in Sybil Vane, the music hall actress in *The Picture of Dorian Gray*. "My love, my love! Prince Charming, Prince of Life. I have grown sick of shadows. You are more to me than life can ever be," she says to Dorian, echoing Tennyson's Lady very directly, as she (Sybil Vane) prepares to descend from her theatrical heights of represented life into the Real Thing, a descent that precipitates *her* suicide. ("Those who go beneath the surface do so at their peril," as both the Lady of Shalott and Sybil Vane learn.)[2] In the forged suicides of "The Portrait of Mr. W. H.," we may have a further exemplification of the death instinct that Hartman has defined—but in a comic register. As Shakespeare's, Willie Hughes', and Cyril Graham's Rosalind might have said, "Men have died from time to time and worms have eaten them, but not for a literary theory." That is, Wilde undoubtedly feels that it is important to be earnest about first critical principles, and critics have taken quite seriously this tale of young aesthetes willing to put their lives on the line for a theory of homosexual love generated by an actor (Sybil Vane no longer disguised as a woman). But the story's domino effect of suicides reminds us (or at least me) of nothing so much as the mass suicides caused by the illusiveness of another theatrical performer, Zuleika Dobson.

In striving to reach the imaginative plane out of the reach of life's vagaries, the Wilde artist does erect a series of comic frames in *mis en abyme* fashion, and we are meant to admire the elaboration of textual forgery piled upon forgery by which this occurs. (One might at this point mention that the Mr. W. H. theory is itself a plagiarism by Wilde, having first been advanced in 1766 by the Shakespearean scholar Thomas Tyrwhitt and then incorporated into Malone's 1780 edition of the *Poems of Shakespeare*. Moreover, in the *Woman's World* of September 1888 Wilde had edited an article by Amy Strachey entitled "The Child Players of the Elizabethan Age," from which he had borrowed significantly [see Gagnier 41].) But the ultimate pathos of Wilde's life and work, two texts inseparable from one another, is the revenge of Nature upon the artist who would escape "the trammeling accidents and limitations of life" into the redoubt of art. "Nature has good intentions, of course, but . . . she cannot carry them out," says Wilde in "The Decay of Lying," (291) the first essay in *Intentions*—and if that volume has any single thesis, it is the subordination of Nature's "purposes" to those of the artist. If Nature's intentions seem relatively clear, the artist's are oblique and layered, entailing a frame-within-a-frame crystallization that evades a gross reality, a nuanced textualization of life that "The Portrait of Mr. W. H." demonstrates to perfection. At the most complex of meta-frames that the artist's imagination can achieve, he sits forging an artifice of freedom to the very edge of belief but never quite passing over as he asserts his control over his layered fiction. And to whatever depth he goes, he will always remain on the surface and on the frame.

But of course Nature will have its answer—and one which reminds the artist that his assertion of control over his texts is a delusion, since there will always be unanticipated meta-frames of more and less hostile readers proliferating beyond his intention's outer-most edge—hostile at the very least in the Derridean sense that all inscription and re-inscription is aggressive (see Derrida 101–40). At the outset of this [essay] I provisionally set up a "criminal" forgery and an "honest" framing in opposition, but I would now like to suggest that they move toward each other as problematic moral categories. For if forgery may be ethically defended (and "The Portrait of Mr. W. H." undertakes precisely such a defense) frames approach the condition of the criminal frame-up—and nowhere more so than in the practice of literary criticism. For the framer of the Wildean critic's frame, the "critic as artist's" critic, as it were, always has a greater cognitive leverage that comes from his vantage point of belatedness, a degree of control that he can—and frequently does—use for *his* skeptical purposes. Hoist by his own critical petard, the exhibitionist framer of the clever paradox becomes the victimized framee of other people's voyeuristic frames.

Let me by way of illustration close with a parable of such critical revenge that Wilde came to know through the circulation of a purloined letter (in Lacan's sense) that he had sent to Alfred Douglas. As he recalls that circulation for Douglas in *De Profundis,*

> You send me a nice poem, of the undergraduate school of verse, for my approval: I reply by a letter of fantastic literary conceits. . . . Look at the history of that letter! It passes from you into the hands of a loathsome companion: from him to a gang of blackmailers; copies of it are sent about London to my friends, and to the manager of the theatre where my work is being performed: every construction but the right one is put on it: Society is thrilled with the absurd rumours that I have had to pay a huge sum of money for having written an infamous letter to you: this forms the basis of your father's worst attack: I produce the original letter myself in Court to show *what it really is;* it is denounced by your father's counsel as a revolting and insidious attempt to corrupt Innocence: ultimately it forms part of a criminal charge: the Crown takes it up: the Judge sums up on it with little learning and much morality: I go to prison for it at last. That is the result of writing you a charming letter. (34–35, italics added)

In our post-Wildean theories, we may be asked to believe that the function of criticism is to see the object, the "original letter," as what in itself it really is not. But we instinctively rebel when *our* charming texts are so purloined and then misprisioned, when they elude our intentions. For Wilde at any rate the return of Nature against the Text has an appropriately ironic and *un*intended Arnoldian ring to it, as he produces the original letter in the Court of history in the naive attempt to show what it *"really* is." Arnold has the latest frame after all.

Notes

1.   The phrase is G. Robert Stange's from an unpublished manuscript on the prizing of the Artificial over the Natural in nineteenth-century aesthetics, to which my own formulations are indebted.

2.   For a fuller comparison of the Lady of Shalott and Sybil Vane, see Joseph, *Tennysonian Love: The Strange Diagonal* 49–50.

Works Cited

Benjamin, Walter. "The Work of Art in the Age of Mechanical Reproduction." *Illuminations.* Trans. Harry Zohn. New York: Schocken Books, 1969: 217–51.
Caws, Mary Ann. *Reading Frames in Modern Fiction.* Princeton: Princeton UP, 1985.

Derrida, Jacques. "The Violence of the Letter: From Lévi-Strauss to Rousseau." *Of Grammatology*. Baltimore: The Johns Hopkins UP, 1976: 101–140.

Gagnier, Regenia, *Idylls of the Marketplace: Oscar Wilde and the Victorian Public*. Stanford: Stanford UP, 1986.

Hartman, Geoffrey. "Psychoanalysis: The French Connection." *Psychoanalysis and the Question of Text*. Ed. Geoffrey Hartman. Baltimore: The Johns Hopkins UP, 1978. Rpt. *Saving the Text: Literature/Derrida/Philosophy*. Baltimore: The Johns Hopkins UP, 1981.

Joseph, Gerhard. "The Echo and the Mirror *en abyme* in Victorian Poetry." *Victorian Poetry* 23 (1985): 403–12.

———*Tennysonian Love: The Strange Diagonal*. Minneapolis: U of Minnesota P, 1969.

———"Victorian Weaving: The Alienation of Work into Text in 'The Lady of Shalott.' " *The Victorian Newsletter* No. 71 (Spring 1987): 7–10.

Wilde, Oscar. *The Artist as Critic: Critical Writings of Oscar Wilde*. Ed. Richard Ellmann. Chicago: U of Chicago P, 1969.

———*De Profundis*. New York: Vintage, 1964.

———*The Letters of Oscar Wilde*. Ed. Rupert Hart-Davis. New York: Harcourt, Brace, 1962.

———*The Picture of Dorian Gray*. New York: Random House, n.d.

Aesthetic Criticism, Useless Art:
Wilde, Zola, and
"The Portrait of Mr. W. H."

Patrice Hannon

[Ruskin's] prose also reminded all susceptible to its influence that "prose" might be rich in imagination, that words have colour as well as meaning, that they could suggest as well as speak, and need not be condemned to the hodman's work of conveying information.

—Osbert Burdett, *The Beardsley Period*

Don't degrade me into the position of giving you useful information.

—Gilbert, in "The Critic as Artist"

In 1874 Oscar Wilde was one of a group of Oxford students engaged in building a road under John Ruskin's direction. Wilde later bragged that during this time "he had enjoyed the distinction of being allowed to fill 'Mr. Ruskin's especial wheelbarrow.' "[1] The image of Wilde carrying Ruskin's wheelbarrow itself carries a suggestion—that the aesthete can do hodman's work (or close enough to it) for aesthetic ends when it suits him. Or, as Richard Ellmann puts it, "it was not much of a road, but for Wilde it was the road to Ruskin" (Ellmann, 50). For Wilde as for Ruskin, however, mere utility—the conveyance of "useful information"—was not the end of language in either art or criticism. In this essay I will show how Wilde's antiutilitarian aesthetics for literary criticism runs counter to what he saw as a realistic model based—in theory at least—on the observation of the object aimed at the discovery of deeper truths. The naturalist branch of realism in particular, as its precepts are outlined in Zola's "Experimental Novel," published in 1880, furnishes useful information by ascertaining and revealing the specific knowledge necessary for the control of human behavior. The artist-as-scientist is in the service of maintaining the health of the social body. While, as George Levine notes, "there was no precise analogue in England to Zola's epical 'scientific' enterprise," Levine also shows that the scientific model of detached observation was nonetheless the ideal for major Victorian realists.[2] Wilde's criticism offers

This essay is published here for the first time by permission of the author.

alternative models to the scientific one—less utilitarian and authoritarian—both for the artist and for the critic-as-artist. (Zola himself proposes the experimental method for criticism, drama, and even poetry, in addition to novels.) In Wilde's critical dialogues the value of criticism lies in the process and not the product, and the form of those dialogues runs counter to a critical method that seeks the status of a scientific inquiry.

Throughout "The Decay of Lying" Wilde aligns realism with "relevant" (i.e., useful) subject matter, carefully observed and analyzed as if under a microscope. The irony is that this kind of observation is concerned not with the visible surfaces, with the forms, but with seeing *through,* seeing *past* the surfaces. The meaning is always somewhere else, never on the surface, which means that the meaning is ultimately in the control of the observer.[3] This empowerment of the interpreter, as Susan Sontag has said, is above all what makes art usable (Sontag, 101). For the aesthete, however, "all art is quite useless" (preface to *Dorian Gray*).[4] For Wilde, the undesirable distribution of power just described is found most readily in realistic art, where it is manifestly a part of the structure, of the narrative technique. While other types of art, such as lyric poetry or symbolist drama, may appear to demand interpretation in a way realism does not, they fail to hold out the same promise for the power and social utility of that interpretation. Wilde's critical prose, by emphasizing surface and process, through its structure resists reducing the meaning of a work of art to useful interpreted "content."

In "The Decay of Lying," his most important critique of realism, Wilde, through the fictional critic Vivian, names Zola numerous times as an aesthetic opponent while being careful to dismiss the widespread moral outrage against him, with which he has "no sympathy at all."[5] A look at Zola's artistic project will, however, make clear the reasons for Wilde's antipathy to it.[6]

In "The Experimental Novel" Zola proposes an exact analogy between the scientist and the novelist. So completely identical are the two that Zola feels free to lift entire passages in which Claude Bernard, his scientific source, speaks of experimental science and to apply them to the experimental novel. In "The Decay of Lying" Vivian sketches this less favorable image of the realistic novelist as scientist:

> The modern novelist presents us with dull facts under the guise of fiction. The Blue-Book is rapidly becoming his ideal both for method and manner. He has his tedious "*document humain,*" his miserable little "*coin de la création,*" into which he peers with his microscope. He is to be found at the Librairie Nationale, or at the British Museum, shamelessly reading up on his subject. . . . [B]etween encyclopaedias and personal experience, he comes to the ground, having drawn his types from the family circle or from the weekly washerwoman, and having acquired an amount of useful information from which never, even in his most meditative moments, can he thoroughly free himself. (293–94)

For Vivian, scientific facts, as they appear in realistic art, are specifically connected to the artist's store of *useful* information. For Zola, too, facts are utilitarian, things in nature that can be observed by the artist-scientist, who stands distinct from them. The identity Zola posits between the scientist who observes the facts of nature and the novelist is one not only of means but of ends, and the end of both is control: "I shall also quote an image of Claude Bernard's which has greatly struck me: 'The experimenter is the examining magistrate of nature.' We novelists are the examining magistrates of men and their passions" (168).[7] This art does not even pretend to be disinterested observation. The purpose of Zola's project is to discover the laws of human behavior, which are as deterministic as the laws that govern the material world. Naturalistic novelists experiment "in order to analyze the facts and become master of them" (Zola, 169). But it is not only the facts that are to be mastered: again and again throughout "The Experimental Novel" we see an emphasis on social control through observation and interpretation.

In defending this method from charges of immorality leveled because, as Henry James put it, it "[represents] nature to us as a combination of the cesspool and the house of prostitution,"[8] Zola insists that naturalism is, on the contrary, a highly moral enterprise:

> This then is the goal, this the morality of physiology and of experimental medicine: to master life in order to direct it. . . . That is the role of intelligence: to penetrate the why of things in order to become superior to things and reduce them to the state of obedient mechanisms.
>
> Fine! This dream of the physiologist and the experimental doctor of medicine is also that of the novelist who applies the experimental method to the natural and social study of man. Our goal is theirs; we wish, we too, to be masters of the phenomena of intellectual and personal elements in order to direct them. We are, in short, experimental moralists showing by experiment in what fashion a passion behaves in a social milieu. The day when we have an understanding of the mechanism of this passion we will be able to treat it and reduce it or at least render it as inoffensive as possible. That is where the utility and the high morality of our naturalist works lie; they experiment on man, take apart and put together the human machine piece by piece in order to make it function under the influence of environment. When time shall have passed, when we shall have the laws, we shall have only to act on individuals and milieux if we wish to reach better social conditions. . . . To be master of good and evil, to regulate life, to regulate society, in the long run to resolve all the problems of socialism, above all to bring a solid foundation to justice by experimentally resolving questions of criminality, is that not to do the most useful and moral human work? (Zola, 176–77)

The determinism of social phenomena must be discovered by the novelists so that the legislators can control and direct them. Thus is the artist's vision degraded into the position of giving useful information: the objective scientific gaze can be used to hunt out the unhealthy in a society in the name of the "high morality" that demands the enforced cure—or the rendering inoffensive—of the corrupt members.[9]

It is easy to see why Wilde would object to the suggestion that art should reflect some external order of absolute truth determined through analysis so that—worst of all—the artist might perform "useful and moral" human work through a kind of social engineering. Wilde's objection to this scientific art is multifaceted. Throughout "The Decay of Lying" he satirizes and subverts conventional notions of health and sickness, the latter especially as it is perceived as a taste for the decadent and "unnatural" in art and life. In a further point of difference, Wilde rejects the split between spectator and object necessary for Zola's scientist-novelist's experimentations. Wilde had been too strongly influenced by those for whom vision could no longer be considered entirely and objectively trustworthy to maintain such a position.[10] Finally, whereas realism depends for its effectiveness on our willingness not to notice its artificiality, throughout Wilde's critical dialogues he emphasizes that our experience of art is (or should be) with the form, the surfaces. And so it is that music is the type—it has no "content," it is all form, it cannot be paraphrased or interpreted, except in the sense peculiar to music, and in that sense "interpretation" is more closely related to what Wilde's aesthetic critic does: Pater's extraordinary prose poem on the *Mona Lisa* and Ruskin's fervid and fiery-colored criticism of Turner are virtuoso interpretive performances *inspired* by the works of art. Rejecting the view that the art itself is a reflection of some preexistent, nonartistic reality that the critic must reconstruct, in a grandly anti-interpretive gesture Vivian says, "Art never expresses anything but itself" ("Decay," 313). Art does not—should not and cannot—express merely the artist's message or the age in which it was produced. That is, it cannot be reduced to these things through the critic's interpretation, in defiance of what it materially is. What's interesting about people, Vivian says in criticizing Bourget's literary "psychoanalysis," is the mask they wear, not what's underneath, and the same can be said for art (297). In literature, the linguistic surface is where the action is—the most important knowledge is invariably superficial.

Yet in his dialogues Wilde's position is not that critics are an undesirable breed (though they are ideally "useless"); rather, he redefines criticism, most elaborately in "The Critic as Artist," so that it is no more realistic—in the ways I have been describing that term—than the best art. Like that art, criticism rejects the dominating, controlling gaze that interprets in any utilitarian or reductive way. In "The Soul of Man under Socialism" Wilde denounces any such attempts at control by the press and the public, or the public through the press: "If a man approaches a work of art with any desire to exercise authority over it and the artist, he approaches it in such a spirit that he cannot receive any artistic impression from it at all. *The work of art is to dominate the spectator: the spectator is not to dominate the work of art*" (279; Wilde's emphasis).

In the critical dialogues Wilde's critic doesn't "desire to talk learnedly" and is determinedly antiutilitarian: "Don't let us discuss anything solemnly. I am but too conscious of the fact that we are born in an age when only the dull are treated seriously, and I live in terror of not being misunderstood. Don't degrade me into the position of giving you useful information," he says to his interlocutor. Immediately, as if to close off the source of useful information in an illustration of his own precepts, he moves into a "Symbolist" style (or a parody of one), into language that manifestly does not give information but, rather, generates its own "ineffable" meaning through its material surface: "Through the parted curtains of the window I see the moon like a clipped piece of silver. Like gilded bees the stars cluster round her. The sky is a hard hollow sapphire" ("Critic," 349–50).[11] When Ernest insists that they return to *discussing* the matter, the play between two forms of critical discourse is foregrounded. This emphasis on the linguistic surface draws our attention to the formal qualities of critical language instead of trying to make that language disappear, transparent in its "merely" useful role of information carrier.

Criticism, for Wilde, far from being useful, just another part of vulgar means-end living, as Zola's experimental novel is socially useful, is "its own reason for existing, and, as the Greeks would put it, in itself, and to itself, an end. Certainly, it is never trammelled by any shackles of verisimilitude. No ignoble considerations of probability, that cowardly concession to the tedious repetitions of domestic or public life, affect it ever" ("Critic," 365). Wilde wants criticism to work by precisely *not* discovering those laws, systems, and formulas that guarantee repetition as it is guaranteed in Spencer's nature. In fact, the "nature" found in art is a different creature from Spencer's altogether: "Nature has, in [art's] eyes, no laws, no uniformity" ("Decay," 306). The attempt to impart useful knowledge in the sphere of art always bears with it the danger that one will lapse into predictable and formulaic reiteration. Thus, the "man who has spent his life in trying to educate others" rather than himself has a mind that "wearies us, and must weary himself, with its endless repetitions and sickly reiteration" ("Critic," 387). His failure is that he has formed habits. Zola, we recall, proposes that the artist should penetrate the why of things and people in order to reduce them to the state of obedient mechanisms, but this is possible only if the latter are "human machines" to begin with, working by immutable laws that lie waiting to be discovered. Wilde's critical dialogues reflect the view that even if such laws exist—and at times he seems to fear they do, particularly in the realm of heredity—they are not the concern of art or criticism. In fact, art and criticism are what work against such codification; therein lies their value.[12]

When Wilde, unlike Zola, uses the organic metaphor for society it is to deny that what is conventionally taken to be the "health" of the status quo is a good thing: "The security of society lies in custom and unconscious instinct, and the basis of the stability of society, as a healthy organism, is the complete absence of any intelligence amongst its members" (388).[13] Custom and instinct, which consist of laws and foster repetition, are what a society's "health" consists of. But consistency, far from establishing one's identity, is what kills it: criticism is "simply a mood, and . . . we are never more true to ourselves than when we are inconsistent" ("Critic," 390). "Intelligence" rebels against custom. Art and criticism present us with an opportunity for this kind of inconsistency: in art thought is "fluid rather than fixed, and . . . cannot be narrowed into the rigidity of a scientific formula or a theological dogma" (392). Rather than establishing laws, "Criticism . . . [recognizes] no position as final" (405). To Ernest's suggestion that the critic will at least be sincere, Gilbert replies, "A little sincerity is a dangerous thing, and a great deal of it is absolutely fatal. The true critic . . . will never suffer himself to be limited to any settled custom of thought, or stereotyped mode of looking at things" (393). In fact, Gilbert says, "We are dominated by the fanatic, whose worst vice is his sincerity" (406).

Wilde wrote much sensible and sensitive criticism that might be classified as neither impressionistic self-indulgence nor "penetrative," dominating analysis. The critical-theoretical prose of *Intentions* and "The Portrait of Mr. W. H." is not of the same genre as Wilde's "real" criticism of contemporary literature and art. It should be emphasized that the former prose works are patent fictions. I am not suggesting that Wilde thought the two genres the same, or that we should. Neither, then, am I proposing that the "method" of "Mr. W. H." should serve as a prescriptive example for a critical method; for one thing, it does not appear to contain Wilde's reading of Shakespeare's Sonnets. Nevertheless, these pieces do present fictions that are concerned with those critical issues of authority, interpretation, and methodology which were important in the Victorian fin de siècle and remain so today.

The setting of "The Portrait of Mr. W. H." is characteristic of Wilde's dialogues, though this is not, strictly speaking, a dialogue, but a story told by a narrator who re-creates scenes of dialogue between typical Wildean aesthetes. At the narrator's urging, Erskine tells him the story of Cyril Graham, a friend whose theory about the "real meaning" of Shakespeare's Sonnets is based on the discovery of the true identity of Mr. W. H., to whom the poems were dedicated. Graham holds this to be one Willie Hughes, a young actor in Shakespeare's company. The major problem with this theory, however, is that there is no evidence that such a person ever existed. Finding this problem otherwise insurmountable, in a last-ditch effort to corroborate his theory Graham has a portrait of "Willie Hughes" painted, pretending to have found an Elizabethan original. Erskine is persuaded by the portrait, and so, he says, "for three months we did nothing but go over each poem line by line, till we had settled every difficulty of text or meaning" (164). The forgery is discovered, however, and in despair over the failure of his theory Graham commits suicide—"the youngest and the most splendid of all the martyrs of literature" (166).

Erskine was urged on in his telling of this story by the narrator's admission that he "[loves] theories about the Sonnets" (154). That he doesn't expect to be converted by any theory is irrelevant—he just wants the theory to be "delightful." The "Willie Hughes" theory is announced as false at the outset; moreover, it is an old theory Wilde himself is plagiarizing quite openly.[14] Thus the truth of the theory is shown to be a matter of indifference right from the start. What the narrator says in the very beginning about Chatterton's forgeries can be taken to apply to this theory too: "all Art being to a certain degree a mode of acting, an attempt to realise one's own personality on some imaginative plane out of reach of the trammelling accidents and limitations of real life, to censure an artist for a forgery was to confuse an ethical with an aesthetical problem" (152). Worrying about the historical truth of this theory is to make the same confusion.

Erskine relates Cyril's theory to the narrator and in the process converts him to it, despite the fact that in Erskine's words it is a "perfectly unsound theory from beginning to end" and the narrator has known as much from the start (166). The narrator, now thoroughly persuaded, thinks it is the "perfect key to Shakespeare's Sonnets, . . . complete in every detail" (166). When he announces his determination to spread Cyril's gospel, Erskine objects: "His faith . . . was fixed in a thing that was false, in a thing that was unsound, in a thing that no Shakespearian scholar would accept for a moment. The theory would be laughed at. Don't make a fool of yourself, and don't follow a trail that leads nowhere. You start by assuming the existence of the very person whose existence is the thing to be proved. Besides, everybody knows that the Sonnets were addressed to Lord Pembroke. The matter is settled once for all" (167). But the narrator disagrees: " 'The matter is not settled,' " I exclaimed. " 'I will take up the theory where Cyril Graham left it, and I will prove to the world that he was right' " (167).

The narrator holds not only to Cyril Graham's theory but to his method as well. That method, for the most part, is to analyze the sonnets as though they are a description of events and people in Shakespeare's "real world" and to find corroborating evidence to this effect. The language of the sonnets, that is, is read "realistically" rather than as "merely a dramatic utterance" ("Decay," 306). "Each poem," says the narrator, "seemed to me to corroborate Cyril Graham's theory" (168). The narrator, like Cyril, interprets the sonnets using sober scientific terms like *evidence, corroboration,* and *hypothesis.* The sonnets are chopped up into couplets, lines, phrases, and single words to make them fit the theory. The experience of reading the sonnets in this context shows how diminished they become as poetry. Where they succeed, however, is in adding to the pleasure of reading this parable of interpretation. The interpretation, while clearly inferior to the sonnets as art, ultimately has little to do with them. Thus the creation of the theory itself—and not the mastery of the real meaning of the sonnets—is what captures our interest.

The narrator hits on the "true interpretation" of the sonnets, making the "great discovery" that even Cyril Graham missed (171–72). He easily sums up the meaning of the sonnets, which according to him, "simply are" one thing: "The whole cycle of the early sonnets is simply Shakespeare's invitations to Willie Hughes to go upon the stage and become a player" (172). He quotes lines of poetry and begins paraphrasing their meaning. Then, the line between the two things, the sonnets and the theory, begins to blur as he intersperses single lines of his own with the text of the sonnets—as connectors, as paraphrase. The poetry is woven throughout so that at times we hear but one voice, as if lines of Shakespeare's poetry and lines of prose narrative—criticism —were parts of equivalent and interchangeable discourses, both "realistic." Yet neither is realistic, and we are equally aware—or should be equally aware—of that. The usefulness of "The Portrait of Mr. W. H." as criticism—insofar as utility is connected to realism—eludes us.

Throughout part 2 momentum builds and the theory seems to be evolving "inevitably." The meaning of the sonnets does indeed seem to be materializing as the sum total of these quoted bits and pieces, fragments that come together as a new whole: "I collected together all the passages that seemed to me to corroborate this view, and they produced a strong impression on me, and showed me how complete Cyril Graham's theory really was" (175). The word *corroboration* is used many times in this piece—so many times that its insistent presence cannot be ignored. In "The Decay of Lying" Wilde had proposed that the true liar—the true artist and, by extension, critic—would not be troubled by such matters as "cowardly corroboration." Corroboration belongs to realism, to the artist-as-scientist, earnestly engaged in research at the British Museum in order to do that which Wilde proposes cannot be done: re-create history from art, except insofar as we can re-create the history of art itself—conventions, schools, and so on. But for the narrator of "Mr. W. H.," the sonnets are not simply what they are, their world on an imaginative plane, but, rather, refer at each point to something else in the "real world." He assumes the authority to break up the text because he believes he knows the correspondences between the language and that something else: "it was quite easy to separate those lines in which Shakespeare speaks of the Sonnets themselves, from those in which he speaks of his great dramatic work" (175). Later he will rearrange the order of the poems so that they fit his theory: "My whole scheme of the Sonnets was now complete, and, by placing those that refer to the dark lady in their proper order and position, I saw the perfect unity and completeness of the whole" (205). "Perfect unity and completeness" are imposed on the sonnets and then "discovered" in them. The best-known sonnet of all gets absorbed in the critic's own sentence here:

> When he says to Willie Hughes:
>> But thy eternal summer shall not fade,
>> Nor lose possession of that fair thou owest;
>> Nor shall Death brag thou wander'st in his shade,
>> When in *eternal lines* to time thou growest:

> So long as men can breathe or eyes can see,
> So long lives this and this gives life to thee;—

the expression "eternal lines" clearly alludes to one of his plays that he was sending him at the time, just as the concluding couplet points to his confidence in the probability of his plays being always acted. (175–76; Wilde's emphasis)

The critic has no use for the sound and shape of the poet's language, and so he moves past the linguistic surface to assert—ever so briskly and economically—the meaning determined by his own scheme. Still, when the narrator says shortly after this, "Every day I seemed to be discovering something new" about the sonnets, we are signaled that at some later point he will see something illusory in his interpretation, and will not be so sure that he was discovering meanings "intended" by the sonnets at all (177).

True literary scholarship demands footnotes, and Wilde's interpreter is obliging:

Willie Hughes! How musically it sounded! Yes; who else but he could have been the master-mistress of Shakespeare's passion,[1] the lord of his love to whom he was bound in vassalage,[2] the delicate minion of pleasure,[3] the rose of the whole world,[4] the herald of the spring,[5] decked in the proud livery of youth,[6] the lovely boy whom it was sweet music to hear,[7] and whose beauty was the very raiment of Shakespeare's heart,[8] as it was the keystone of his dramatic power? . . .
[1] Sonnet XX. 2.
[2] Sonnet XXVI. 1.
[3] Sonnet CXXVI. 9.
[4] Sonnet CIX. 14.
[5] Sonnet I. 10.
[6] Sonnet II. 3.
[7] Sonnet VIII. 1.
[8] Sonnet XXII. 6. (177)

This is corroboration of the most absurd kind—the carefully documented matching up of a "real" person with the most extravagant romantic metaphors, each pulled out of its original context and each taken from a different poem. Wilde's playful documentation has the virtue—as does the whole piece—of constructing a thoroughly delightful critical fiction that criticizes its own form.

The narrator, putting the sonnets in a historical context, proposes that Shakespeare's love for Willie Hughes has to do with Renaissance Neoplatonism:

When he says to Willie Hughes [who is now a given],

> he that calls on thee, let him bring forth
> Eternal numbers to outlive long date,

he is thinking of Diotima's theory that Beauty is the goddess who presides over birth, and draws into the light of day the dim conceptions of the soul: when he tells us of the "marriage of true minds," and exhorts his friend to beget children that time cannot destroy, he is but repeating the words in which the prophetess tells us that "friends are married by a far nearer tie than those who beget mortal children, for fairer and more immortal are the children who are their common offspring." (184)

As charming as the narrator's interpretation is, we are aware that its appeal is not that of the sonnets, which are palpably diminished by being forced to "mean" only this. The continual cataloging, the listing, not only of "amatory phrases" but of Renaissance personae who reflect a similar preoccupation with Neoplatonism has the curious effect of impoverishing rather than enriching the culture under discussion—as well as the sonnets—by suggesting that all these various artists and works of art really mean the same thing. But this is only a problem if we read this criticism not as a brilliant fiction, as play between two literary texts, answering only to an internal truth and to the artist's last mood, but as a serious exposition of the real meaning of the sonnets. This is criticism that sees the object as in itself it really is not; it is a critical illusion.

The narrator will similarly list all the boy players and their histories as well as all the names, dates, places, quotations, critics, and theories having to do with the identity of the Dark Lady. In trying to determine her identity, he turns to "the Harleian MSS. at the British Museum" for corroboration of his version of her history: "Manningham's Table-book seemed to me to be an extremely strong link in the chain of evidence, and to place the new interpretation of the Sonnets on something like a secure historic basis" (203–4). Thus this critic is rather like those realistic artists who can be found at the British Museum, shamelessly reading up on their subjects. But the manipulation of "history" necessary to make the facts fit the theory is made amusingly obvious: when there is a discrepancy at one point, for example, we are assured that the apparent contradiction can be ignored because "tavern gossip . . . is proverbially inaccurate" (203). The theory's historical basis is made secure only at the cost of such equivocation.

By part 3 the narrator can document his discovery that Willie Hughes is an Elizabethan name, and he goes on to recite yet another catalog of Elizabethan names and dates. As close as he is to clinching the case, he can't quite do so: "But the proofs, the links—where were they? Alas! I could not find them. It seemed to me that I was always on the brink of absolute verification" (188–89). When he lists all the Elizabethan boy players, in one more logical slipup he asserts that "foremost, naturally, among them all had been [Willie Hughes]" (189). This, however, as we know, is what he's supposed to be proving. The names, dates—all "corroborating evidence"—are brought in after this fact. The theory is advanced first; then "historical proof" is found for it. He even claims that the romantic movement in English literature was indebted to W. H., "whose very name the dull writers of his age forgot to chronicle" (187). The absence of Willie Hughes's name in this instance is not seen as much of a problem. If the scientific artist is an "examining magistrate," as Zola suggests, then the judge this critic most resembles is the King of Hearts in *Alice in Wonderland*.[15] Here the King examines a set of verses presented as evidence of the Knave's having stolen some tarts:

> "Are they in the prisoner's handwriting?" asked another of the jurymen.
> "No, they're not," said the White Rabbit, "and that's the queerest thing about it." (The jury all looked puzzled.)
> "He must have imitated somebody else's hand," said the King. (The jury all brightened up again.)
> "Please, your majesty," said the Knave, "I didn't write it, and they can't prove that I did: there's no name signed at the end."
> "If you didn't sign it," said the King, "that only makes the matter worse. You *must* have meant some mischief, or else you'd have signed your name like an honest man."[16]

In this theory the absence of Willie Hughes's name similarly proves not only his existence but his role as begetter of the sonnets. (And that, we might say, is the queerest thing about it.) Erskine will continue pursuing this course of illogic: "It is quite true that his name does not occur in the list given in the first folio; but, as Cyril pointed out, that is rather a proof in favour of the existence of Willie Hughes than against it, if we remember his treacherous desertion of Shakespeare for a rival dramatist" (215). Moreover, since it is extremely likely that Willie Hughes acted under a stage name, it is only too obvious that his name would not appear on the rolls. In proposing a further embellishment of Willie Hughes's "history" the narrator will say that "there was certainly no evidence against it" (208), which hardly makes his claim secure. He notes several times in the same paragraph that the elements of this part of his theory are "fitting" (208). The theory, pretending to chart a correspondence between history and poetical text, is "fitting" rather than true—it is what *should* be true, which makes it art rather than science: "Words have their mystical power over the soul, and form can create the feeling from which it should have sprung. Sincerity itself, the ardent, momentary sincerity of the artist, is often the unconscious result of style" (199). What the narrator says of Shakespeare is of course equally true of himself: the sincerity found in his theory of the sonnets is momentary, the result of style. His belief in this theory did not precede the creation of the theory, since the theory itself—precisely as it is presented here—did not precede its creation in language. "Language," as we recall Wilde's Gilbert saying in "Critic," "is the parent, and not the child, of thought" (359). And the fanatic's worst vice is a sincerity that results not from style but from thought "narrowed into the rigidity of a scientific formula or a theological dogma" ("Critic," 392).

The narrator finally comes to the point where he can summarize "what happens" in the sonnets in one paragraph (205), but this synopsis has nothing to do with the art of the sonnets, with the experience of reading them. And the interpretation is so tidy that it looks like wishful thinking. It's too good—too fitting—to be true.

Having finished constructing his theory, the narrator writes a letter to Erskine to appeal to him "to give the world [Cyril Graham's] marvellous interpretation of the Sonnets—the only interpretation that thoroughly explained the problem. . . . I went over the whole ground, and covered sheets of paper with passionate reiteration of the arguments and proofs that my study had suggested to me. . . . I put into the letter all my enthusiasm. I put into the letter all my faith" (212). There is a sense in which this is literally true because no sooner does he do so than he reports, "It seemed to me that I had given away my capacity for belief in the Willie Hughes theory of the Sonnets, that something had gone out of me, as it were, and that I was perfectly indifferent to the whole subject. . . . Perhaps, by finding perfect expression for a passion, I had exhausted the passion itself" (212). The exercise of influence "produces a sense, and, it may be, a reality of loss. . . . [M]y enthusiasm having burnt out, my reason was left to its own unimpassioned judgment" (213). The theory is what has been "lost," spent in the telling, in its own creation. At the point at which the theory appears to afford total mastery of the text, the theory must be abandoned because it renders the text itself redundant, completely paraphrasable. It was only while he was on the *brink* of absolute verification that this marvelous interpretive theory had value for the theorist. Once the theory is complete, the meaning elucidated by the criticism, which "thoroughly [explains] the problem," cannot be a substitute for the meaning of the text, because such an equivalence puts the two into an economy from which Wilde would like to exclude both art and criticism.[17] All that corroborating historical "evidence," all those conventional methods of literary analysis, it turns out, were only momentarily "useful." The pleasure and the value of this criticism were in the creation of the theory, the weaving together of evidence, the process of mind interacting with world, and not in the end product, except as that might spark a similar process in the mind of the reader. This is useless theory because it cannot be used by anyone else—it's a one-shot deal, a kind of performance theory.[18]

The narrator, concerned about his sudden change of heart, wonders, "How was it that it had left me? Had I touched upon some secret that my soul desired to conceal? Or was there no permanence in my personality? Did things come and go through the brain, silently, swiftly, and without footprints, like shadows through a mirror?" (213). Was sincerity, then, only the momentary result of style? Wilde's critic is often marked by precisely this kind of impermanence. He evades the hardening into a fixed, rigid "personality" who amasses evidence in behalf of a formula or dogma—in behalf of what Erskine will call a hypothesis that "explains everything." Erskine had warned the narrator against embracing the theory in the first place, calling it (like sincerity in a critic) "fatal" (166). The narrator "saves himself" from the fatal theory by letting go of it in time. But not entirely, as we shall see.

In a last surprising twist, we find that Erskine now believes the argument, declaring that the narrator has shown him "that Cyril Graham's theory is perfectly sound" (214): "You have proved the thing to me. Do you think I cannot estimate the value of evidence?" The only "evidence," retorts the narrator, is the forged picture. "The one flaw in the theory," he now holds, "is that it presupposes the existence of the person whose existence is the subject of dispute" (215). But this circularity does not trouble Erskine: "Of course it is a hypothesis, but then it is a hypothesis that explains everything, and if you had been sent to Cambridge to study science, instead of to Oxford to dawdle over literature, you would know that a hypothesis that explains everything is a certainty" (216). ["The theory which carries the day," Zola says, "is the one which explains the most" (Zola, 189).] But this scientific approach to art is precisely the thing to which Wilde, who had been more than happy to dawdle over literature at Oxford, objects. The implication is that dawdling over literature, unlike studying science, is a thoroughly unproductive activity, and Wilde could not agree more.

The narrator now refuses the all-explaining hypothesis and gladly calls his a "moonbeam theory: where one thinks that one has got hold of it, it escapes one." We come to the end of analysis and have no product to take away and use again, no laws by which we can master art. Whereas for Zola's artist the "role of intelligence" is to "penetrate the why of things," for Wilde's artist there is evident satisfaction in the opposite result: "No. Shakespeare's heart is still to us 'a closet never pierc'd with crystal eyes,' as he calls it in one of the sonnets. We shall never know the true secret of the passion of his life" (216). While the self-serving nature of Wilde's conclusion may seem obvious in hindsight, coming as it does from someone whose own closet needed protection from piercing eyes, that does nothing to invalidate its broader application. Like their author, the sonnets are rescued from this theory, which, however fanciful it may be, threatens to obliterate them completely through interpretation. The meaning of the sonnets is in the sonnets, just as the meaning of "The Portrait of Mr. W. H." cannot be detached from the experience of reading it.

In this story the value of criticism does not lie in its utility, which would emphasize a product over a process, the reductive theory extrapolated from the sonnets over the rich experience of reading them. This position is underlined by the reversal that concludes "The Portrait of Mr. W. H." The narrator, gazing at the forged portrait, muses, "sometimes, when I look at it, I think there is really a great deal to be said for the Willie Hughes theory of Shakespeare's Sonnets" (220).[19] This criticism does not pretend to have pierced Shakespeare's heart (in the aggressive metaphor of the kind so often used in criticism), to have definitively explained the meaning of the sonnets with a formula. Yet the narrator reserves the right to entertain the theory now and again, leaving its validity in its indeterminacy, in the final suggestion that it continues to draw the narrator forth into the critical process, a process that here, at least, is in itself and to itself an end.

Notes

1. Richard Ellmann, *Oscar Wilde* (New York: Alfred A. Knopf, 1988), 49; hereafter cited in the text.

2. George Levine, *Darwin and the Novelists: Patterns of Science in Victorian Fiction* (Cambridge, Mass.: Harvard University Press, 1988), 12–13. As Levine writes, "The patient, ostensibly detached registration of human character and behavior is an aspect of the Darwinian ethos central to the experience of the Victorian novelist; it . . . tends to imply an ultimately material explanation for human behavior (14). The chapters of *Darwin* most significant for my argument are those on the role of observation in realistic art (56–83 and 210–37).

3. This aspect of interpretation has been discussed by several writers in recent years. As Susan Sontag argues, "The most celebrated and influential modern doctrines, those of Marx and Freud, actually amount to elaborate systems of hermeneutics, aggressive and impious theories of interpretation. All observable phenomena are bracketed, in Freud's phrase, as *manifest content.* This manifest content must be probed and pushed aside to find the true meaning—the latent content—beneath. . . . To understand *is* to interpret. And to interpret is to restate the phenomenon, in effect to find an equivalent for it" ("Against Interpretation," in *A Susan Sontag Reader,* ed. Elizabeth Hardwick [New York: Farrar, Straus and Giroux, 1982], 98; hereafter cited in the text). Realism and naturalism, because they are forms in which the artist and the audience take the role of analyst, are concerned, then, with this type of interpretation. The meaning of the work lies not in the experience of reading the words but in reading into them. One observes the object to know it in order to control it. Thus art is domesticated, controlled through analysis that is based on a subject-object split, whereby the interpreter acts on the work of art but is not acted on in return, remaining inviolable. James Guetti notes that a certain kind of Freudian reading of literature "implies that language and linguistic behavior can always be controlled by conversion" ("Freudian Slippage," *Raritan* 8, no. 1 [1988]: 57). Sontag similarly emphasizes that "by reducing the work of art to its content and then interpreting *that,* one tames the work of art. Interpretation makes art manageable, comfortable" (99).

4. Regenia Gagnier has pointed out to me that Wilde defended what he called the "propaganda" of *The Ballad of Reading Gaol.* But if the differences as I experience them between that poem and, say, "The Decay of Lying" or *The Importance of Being Earnest* are the result of Wilde's having changed his mind about the usefulness of art, I can only wish that he had not done so. Wilde's preprison writings, which reflect more closely his aesthetic as it is discussed in this essay, just seem more successful to me, though of course the criteria by which I make this judgment are not the only ones it is possible to apply.

5. Oscar Wilde, "The Decay of Lying," in *The Artist as Critic: Critical Writings of Oscar Wilde,* ed. Richard Ellmann (New York: Random House, 1968), 296; all quotations of Wilde's prose are from this edition.

Richard Ellmann tells us that when Wilde visited Zola in Paris in 1891, Wilde seemed to agree with Zola's insistence that one needed documents in order to write a good novel: said Wilde, "You cannot draw a novel from your brain as a spider draws its web out of its belly." The story, however, continues: "But with Max Beerbohm he was more candid: 'Do you know, whenever that man writes a book he always takes his subjects directly from life. If he is going to write about dreadful people in hovels he goes and lives in a hovel himself for months in case he shouldn't be accurate. It is strange. Take me for example. I have conceived the idea for the most exquisite tale that was ever written. The period is the eighteenth century. It would require a morning's reading at the British Museum. Therefore,' he sighed, 'it will never be written'" (Ellmann, *Oscar Wilde,* 323n).

6. Wilde, who deplored censorship of the arts, might well scorn the "moral indignation of [his] time against M. Zola" (296). In 1888 the National Vigilance Association, as part of its strenuous campaign against immoral literature in England, brought to trial Henry Vizetelly, the publisher of the English translation of Zola's work. Though he was released with a fine and a suspended sentence after agreeing to withdraw the works, he was retried and jailed later that year. For a transcript of the parliamentary debate and trial, along with contemporary newspaper accounts of the affair, see Becker, 350–82 (full citation in note 7).

7. Emile Zola, "The Experimental Novel," in *Documents of Modern Literary Realism,* ed. George Becker (Princeton, N.J.: Princeton University Press, 1963), 168; hereafter cited in the text.

8. Henry James, "Nana," in *Documents,* ed. Becker, 239.

9. It does not help for our purposes to speculate on how far Zola's own novels appear from the moralistic ideal he insists on here. In fact, Wilde might even have found the undoing of Zola's argument within itself, since at the end of the essay Zola appears to come down on the side of aestheticism rather than objective scientific truth. While on the one hand Zola complains that "an exaggerated emphasis is given to form" (192), he says in practically the same breath that "form is sufficient to immortalize a work; the spectacle of a powerful individuality interpreting nature in superb language will be interesting throughout the ages" (192). It makes no difference whether or not the scientist is "mistaken in his hypotheses" (192). Wilde advanced the same opinions regarding literary critics. In a further reversal, Zola ends up by "absolutely [repudiating]" (193) several of Claude Bernard's views on literature. And so, when Zola ends by saying, "If we except form and style, the experimental novelist is nothing but a special kind of scientist, who uses the tools of other scientists, observation and analysis" (193), he is excepting the very features that, according to him, confer immortality, and one is not inclined to except them at all.

10. As Pater wrote in one of those influential works, "It is only the roughness of the eye that makes any two persons, things, situations, seem alike" ("Conclusion to *The Renaissance,*" in *Selected Writings of Walter Pater,* ed. Harold Bloom [New York: New American Library, 1974], 60; all quotations from Pater are from this edition). And ironically, for Pater it is the "sciences of observation" with their emphasis on "delicate and fugitive detail" that will refine that roughness of the eye ("Coleridge," 144). But what kind of "science of observation" can be founded on a solipsistic base?

> If we continue to dwell in thought on this world, not of objects in the solidity with which language invests them, but of impressions unstable, flickering, inconsistent, which burn and are extinguished with our consciousness of them, it contracts still further; the whole scope of observation is dwarfed to the narrow chamber of the individual mind. Experience, already reduced to a swarm of impressions, is ringed round for each one of us by that thick wall of personality through which no real voice has ever pierced on its way to us, or from us to that which we can only conjecture to be without. (59–60)

Language, not vision, is what invests objects with solidity. In fact, what Pater says of Coleridge is the sort of thing Wilde might have said of Zola, if we substitute (à la Zola) the word *artistic* for *scientific:* "Scientific truth is a thing fugitive, relative, full of fine gradations: he tries to fix it in absolute formulas" ("Coleridge," 147). Fugitive rather than formulaic, truth in art, says Wilde's Gilbert, "is one's last mood" ("Critic," 391).

11. Regenia Gagnier sees the "jeweled" prose in the dialogues as a way of creating and addressing "a select audience of artful young men" (*Idylls of the Marketplace: Oscar Wilde and the Victorian Public,* [Stanford, Calif.: Stanford University Press, 1986], 19). "Undoubtedly," she

writes of "Critic," "the heightened purpleness of the prose throughout the lengthy dialogue is intended as a seduction" (46).

12. Here is Gilbert on heredity: "By revealing to us the absolute mechanism of all action, and so freeing us from the self-imposed and trammelling burden of moral responsibility, the scientific principle of Heredity has become, as it were, the warrant for the contemplative life" ("Critic," 382–83).

13. In "The Decay of Lying" Vivian connects this kind of "health" with realism, which the Greeks disliked "on purely social grounds. They felt that it inevitably makes people ugly, and they were perfectly right. We try to improve the conditions of the race by means of good air, free sunlight, wholesome water, and hideous bare buildings for the better housing of the lower orders. But these things merely produce health, they do not produce beauty" (308). In Wilde's view, a plan for social progress that does not include aesthetics is not worth even glancing at.

14. For the history of this plagiarized theory, see Gagnier, 41. She also tells us that Wilde stole material from an article he had edited entitled "The Child-Players of the Elizabethan Age."

15. James Guetti notes that Freud takes on the role of judge when he considers the motives of someone who has "committed" a parapraxis. It is as a judge, then, that he determines the real meaning of the slip, that he interprets it ("Freudian Slippage," 45).

16. Lewis Carroll, *Alice's Adventures in Wonderland*, in *The Annotated Alice*, ed. Martin Gardner (New York: Bramhall House, 1960), 157.

17. It is another of Wilde's contradictions that few artists were, in another sense, more commercial. See Regenia Gagnier for an analysis of these tensions in Wilde's work.

18. In using this term I am referring to the kind of performance described by Richard Poirier in *The Performing Self*. Linda Dowling has said that Wilde's belief in the superiority of spoken to written language led to a "performative ideal of language." For Dowling, this ideal "requires both enormous, self-depleting skill and an entire assent to the evanescence and final extinction of the spoken work of art" 187). Dowling correctly notes that "literature was for Wilde the greatest of the arts precisely because, as G. E. Lessing had said, it existed as a series of articulated tones in time, and thus could treat of time and change: . . . 'It is Literature that shows us the body in its swiftness and the soul in its unrest' " ("Critic," 187). But she goes on to argue that artistic authority "must be repeatedly enacted or enunciated through speech, for . . . it cannot according to Wilde be secured or made permanent through the petrifactions of written language. . . . Wilde's own trials and imprisonment were to suggest (with a certain melodramatic vividness) some of the constraints upon the performing self" (188). Dowling uses Poirier's phrase without seeming to want to enlist his views in behalf of her argument. I am interested in the ways Wilde manages repeatedly to enact and enunciate authority *despite* the petrifactions of written language. See Linda Dowling, *Language and Decadence* (Princeton, N.J.: Princeton University Press, 1986), and Richard Poirier, *The Performing Self: Compositions and Decompositions in the Languages of Contemporary Life* (New York: Oxford University Press, 1971).

19. Gagnier says of the theory that "the narrator's ambivalence at the end emphasizes its unfinalizability" (33).

Protoplasmic Hierarchy
and Philosophical Harmony:
Science and Hegelian Aesthetics
in Oscar Wilde's Notebooks

PHILIP E. SMITH II

My title suggests an association that critics might ordinarily dismiss: Oscar Wilde and *science?* Given the received view of Oscar Wilde as brilliant, self-promoting, homosexual *poseur,* the unlikely combination of scientific awareness with decadent celebrity seems more appropriate as material for an anecdote like the one in Charles Blinderman's recent article, "Huxley, Pater, and Protoplasm." Retelling the story of Oscar Wilde's visit to T. H. Huxley's home as an example of "the attitude that the Darwinists must have held towards the decadent personages," Blinderman notes that "there is no record of what the two gentlemen said to each other from the first limp handshake of corpulent Oscar to the final goodnight, but the meeting could well have been hilarious" (477). The hilarity would presumably arise from the incongruous confrontation of Wilde's superficial wittiness and Huxley's high seriousness. Blinderman reports only as much as his source tells us: after the meeting, Huxley remarked to his daughter Nettie, "That man never enters my house again" (477). Blinderman passes on to his real subject, Walter Pater's use of Huxley's ideas, remarking later in the article, "It would be stunning were anyone to demonstrate that Pater read Huxley's essay ["On the Physical Basis of Life"] and took from it the materials conducive to an exposition of aestheticism" (481). As Blinderman argues persuasively that Darwinism "was part of the network of ideas leading to the full expression of Decadence" (485), he notes that both the central image and the conclusion of Wilde's *The Picture of Dorian Gray* are "faithful" to Huxley's idea of protoplasm and Pater's appropriation of it (486). Because Blinderman does not explain how corpulent, limp-handed Oscar might have learned about protoplasm by any other route than its currency as a "household word" in late Victorian England (484), I

Reprinted from *Victorian Newsletter* (Fall 1988): 30–33. This essay reflects the results of collaborative research done with Michael S. Helfand of the University of Pittsburgh. See the edition and commentary, *Oscar Wilde's Oxford Notebooks: A Portrait of Mind in the Making* (New York: Oxford University Press, 1989).

take it that he, and most modern critics and historians of ideas, would agree with Peter Morton's remarks about Wilde in his 1984 study, *The Vital Science: Biology and the Literary Imagination 1860–1900.* Having quoted the passage on Heredity from "The Critic as Artist," Morton says: "Oscar Wilde . . . attempts to make the fearful facts of human heredity as the late nineteenth century revealed them a subject of aesthetic contemplation; to turn them into art. Despite his confident definitions we may well suppose that in reality he knew little and cared less for the specific difficulties which biology found itself in by the early 1890s; yet shorn of its flamboyances his strongly emotional attitude was shared by his more sober and better-informed peers" (149).

Wilde may not have been as sober as some of his peers, but, contrary to supposition, he was considerably better informed about science than most of them. My collaborative research with Michael Helfand for our annotated edition with commentary of Wilde's Oxford notebooks shows how much Wilde's knowledge of nineteenth-century science has been underestimated or misunderstood. In the commentary we argue that Wilde's aesthetic theory, as manifested in his critical essays and creative writing, was based upon a carefully developed synthesis of science, especially evolutionary theory, with Hegelian philosophy. In the notebooks, Wilde began to develop his syncretic view of science and philosophy in order to accommodate and consolidate modern scientists' latest theories and experimental findings. Our major arguments will appear more fully in the commentary; here, however, I want to suggest how they will apply to Wilde's knowledge of science, and I will add some significant details which will not appear in the book.

I hope it will be "stunning" to demonstrate about Wilde what Blinderman wished to find about Pater: that he read and made use of T. H. Huxley's "On the Physical Basis of Life." More importantly, Wilde's Commonplace Book and Notebook kept at Oxford in the late 1870's reveal extensive readings not only in Huxley, but also in John Tyndall, W. K. Clifford, Herbert Spencer, and others who explored the ability of modern science to explain the world.[1] Finally, I will propose that Wilde's aesthetic and critical theory envisioned the progressive and self-conscious development of human culture through evolutionary mechanisms recognized as valid by Victorian scientists. As Helfand and I argue in our commentary, an understanding of Wilde's synthesis not only should prove his knowledge and use of science in his aesthetic theory, but also should produce a comprehensive revaluation of his importance as a critical theorist, creative writer, and representative Victorian humanist.

Wilde's notebook entries on topics such as "the Unity of the Principle of Life," "The Protoplasmic Hierarchy," "Limits of the Investigation of Nature," and "The Realistic assumptions of modern science" demonstrate his interest in the details of contemporary scientific debates. For example, Wilde's early Commonplace Book entries on biology, especially those pertaining to

Bathybius haeckelii, show how a young and brilliant scholar of classics at Oxford in the 1870's read, recorded, and appropriated for his own critical purposes the latest findings of experimental science. The story of *Bathybius haeckelii,* especially as told by Loren Eiseley in *The Immense Journey,* sounds like a quaint eccentricity of Victorian science—he calls it "one of the most curious cases of self-delusion ever indulged in by scholars. It was the product of an overconfident materialism, a vainglorious assumption that the secrets of life were about to be revealed" (35). If it is a fossil of scientific thought, however, it has high value as an indicator of how interpretation functions to determine constitutive arguments and warrants for acceptance of evidence in scientific discourse (Rehbock 533).

T. H. Huxley's announcement in 1868 of the discovery of an organic compound at the bottom of the Atlantic seemed to many nineteenth-century scientists the proof of an advanced theory. At last, one could *see* under the microscope a bit of that *Urschleim,* "protoplasm," upon which Huxley founded his theory of "the physical basis of life." Like the hoped-for discovery of the "missing link" in primate evolution, biological proof of the existence of protoplasm would mean a solid warrant for a contested theory. *Bathybius haeckelii* (named by Huxley to recall its origin in the sea and to honor his German colleague and friend, Ernst Haeckel) was a verified part of scientific evidence for seven years, until 1875, when it was proven to be an inorganic compound, and Huxley retracted his acceptance of it as protoplasm. Despite Huxley's recantation, *Bathybius haeckelii* continued to be accepted by other scientists, including Haeckel himself, for years afterwards: it had been written into published scientific texts, and whole descriptions of the development of life assumed that this inorganic compound was a simple deep-sea organism, which validated the protoplasmic theory.

Wilde read such accounts and wrote notebook entries based on them that provide a fascinating case study of his interest in science. He accepted the organic interconnectedness of all life as a principle unifying the highest and lowest forms. In his Commonplace Book entry on "the Unity of the Principle of Life," he wrote: "As regards the hierarchy of protoplasmic phenomena we can ascend gradually by increased differentiation of function and division of labour from the structureless albumenoid matter (Bathybius Haeckelii) which the depths of the north Ocean hide, to the elaborate cerebral cells of the human brain which if they are not themselves consciousness are at least the organs by which consciousness manifests itself" (CB 19). Wilde also believed that this hierarchy represented the evolutionary development of human intelligence. In another entry he wrote: "Comparative anatomy shows us that, physically, man is but the last term of a long series which leads from the highest mammal to the almost formless speck of living protoplasm which lies on the shallow boundary between animal and vegetable life • so does comparative psychology or the anatomy of the mind" (CN 51).

In his appropriation of evolutionary theory in the notebooks, Wilde accepted and used a hypothesis discredited in the twentieth century, the inheritance of acquired characteristics. He credits Herbert Spencer for the idea of "the generalistic empiricism of hereditary transmission of concepts: Innate Ideas have thus returned to the mind . . . on Biological Grounds" (CB 61). He takes from W. K. Clifford the notion that "the experience of the race having been substituted for the experience of the individual, necessary truths are admitted to be a-priori to the individual, though a-posteriori to the race" (CB 137). He sums up the ideas in an entry titled *"Heredity"*: "Religion tells us that the father has eaten sour grapes and the children's teeth shall be set on edge—and the latest word of modern science is that the fact of our ancestors having held peculiar views on the three angles of any triangle is an inheritance from which we cannot escape" (CB 145).

Wilde's notebook references to evolutionary theory, protoplasm, *Bathybius haeckelii,* and heredity do not indicate his endorsement of the overconfident materialism Eiseley criticizes. He studied carefully the work of John Tyndall, for example, noting in an entry entitled *"Limits of the investigation of Nature"* (CB 93) exactly where the materialist scientist feared to tread. Wilde found nothing in Tyndall's atheism or Huxley's agnosticism to contradict his own belief that "spirit is that which thinks, so the spirit must be an indivisible entity" (CN 57). Even though Wilde believed in the existence of soul, he also could accept protoplasm as the physical basis of life without accepting materialism; his notebooks record several comments on the insufficiencies of materialist, positivist, and empiricist explanations of life, including Huxley's famous remark from "On the Physical Basis of Life," "Positivism may be described as catholicism without Christianity" (CB 214). Another entry suggests Wilde's view that the materialist camp lacked a metaphysical foundation: "Modern Positivists are as men who while they deny the existence of the sun yet worship the sunlight on the Earth, who acknowledge that the fruit is sweet to eat, and the flower goodly for sight yet insist that the root is rotten, and the soil barren" (CB 89).

The missing sun, roots, and soil may be found in Wilde's development of a philosophical and critical synthesis in the notebooks and in his later critical prose. This synthesis enabled him to appropriate and legitimate the facts and theories of "hard science" which most other Victorian humanists found puzzling or distasteful. As several notebook entries reveal, Wilde read the scientists and their results through the dialectical lens of Hegelian philosophy;[2] this way of reading enabled him to find in the scientists' discourse and experimental results some of the warrants for his own critical synthesis of evolutionary theory and Hegelian philosophy. Its metaphysical basis incorporated both empirical and rational truths, and in one of the few entries containing a personal reference, Wilde stresses the need for such a foundation: "Metaphysics seems to me the one science which has a future • for the acquiring of the new methods of science and reasoning to which we look forward must rest always on a metaphysical basis" (CB 151). Such a basis gave Wilde a powerful and inclusive synthetic philosophy; his reading in Hegel and the Oxford Hegelians (William Wallace and Benjamin Jowett) gave him access to a logic and dialectic which could resolve the major opposition in the history of western philosophy, the conflict between idealism and realism. In his entry on this subject, Wilde writes: "The opposition between Idealism and Realism is a shallow one belonging to the onesided method of the understanding: Every true philosophy must be both idealist and realist: for without realism a philosophy would be void of substance and matter • for with idealism it wd. be void of form and truth: Realism is the assertion of the claims of the . . . particular, the detail, the parts: Idealism is the grasp of the whole and the universal • In the rhythm of both the line of dialectic finds its true course of progress" (CB 101).

Wilde reasoned by analogy that the Hegelian dialectic explained the development not only of absolute idea, but also the progressive physical and mental evolution of man, and of human thought in any of what he called "spheres" of history, religion, philosophy, art, criticism, and aesthetics. Wilde wrote about the power of analogy in an entry titled "Physical Science": "The influence of physical science is rather the attracting influence of a new analo[g]y than a practical disproof of any particular belief . . . but the force of analogy[,] the desire to bring all one[']s thoughts into harmony, and mutual correspondance [sic], have led men to infer that the reign of Law which is the first message of physical science, is also to be extended to those phenomena which seem the most remote from Law" (CN 105). Those phenomena include human thought, and in a Commonplace Book entry, Wilde adopts an analogy from evolutionary theory to explain his preference for Hegelian dialectic. Marking three X's in the margin as a sign of importance, he writes: "Hegelian dialectic is the natural selection produced by a struggle for existence in the world of thought" (CB 204). Elsewhere in the notebooks, Wilde writes about the necessity of a critical method to make sense of facts, and remarks, "nothing is easier than to accumulate facts, nothing is so hard as to use them" (CN 28). A few pages later he adds, "Rem[ember] what every great man has prided himself on is, not the results he attains to, but the *method* he follows" (CN 39); twice in the notebooks he quotes aphoristically Leibniz's thought that "The attaching too high a value to mere facts is often a sign of a want of ideas" (CN 27 & 44).

Several entries also show that the ideas and method of his aesthetic theory owed much to Hegel's *Aesthetik,* which he may have read at first hand, and certainly knew through J. A. Symonds' and Walter Pater's works based on it. Our forthcoming commentary will more fully explain Wilde's use and occasional revisions of Hegel's aesthetic and historical theory of art. Here I want to stress the importance of a master idea, what Wilde called "one high law, the law of form or harmony" ("English Renaissance" 445). The imagination, understood as a faculty of mind, intuits the harmonies, sees the analogies, and constructs the correspondences. Wilde's synthesis itself is an example of the aesthetic urge toward order, harmony, and, as he phrased it in the entry on analogy, "mutual correspondance" of thought (CN 105). This law of harmony does not eliminate or foreclose artistic and critical disagreements, oppositions, and conflicts; instead, it assumes the dialectical necessity for them in a progressive, but not necessarily orderly, development. Just as Wilde accepted the analogy of mental development (the evolution of mind) with biological evolution, so also he believed that the artistic and critical spirits evolved dialectically and manifested themselves through racial inheritance in imaginative individuals.[3]

Wilde's several notebook entries on science and poetry understand imagination as the defining mental characteristic of both scientists and poets. For example, he writes of the need for a more imaginative scientific method, "Rem[ember] how the early Greeks had mystic anticipations of nearly all great modern scientific truths; the problem really is what place has imagination and the emotions in science: and primarily rem[ember] that man must use all his faculties in the search for truth: in this age we are so inductive that our facts are outstripping our knowledge—there is so much observation, experiment, analysis—so few wide conceptions: we want more ideas and less facts: the magnificent generalizations of Newton and Harvey cd. never have [been] completed in this mod. age where eyes are turned to earth and particulars" (CN 43). His remarks to an American reporter in 1882 echo this entry's insistence on the imaginative basis of science and poetry: "Poets, you know, are always ahead of science; all the great discoveries of science have been stated before in poetry. So far as science comes in contact with our [aesthetic] school, we love its practical side; but we think it absurd to seek to make the material include the spiritual, to make the body mean the soul, to say that one emotion is only a secretion of sugar, and another nothing but a contraction of the spine" (Mikhail 1:45).

Wilde's theory of science and aesthetics resists the production of such reductive, materialist conceptions and provides instead a site for the spirit, the soul, and the emotions to influence the imaginative, contemplative development of thought, and indeed, for the hereditary transmission of such developments. The early expressions of these ideas in the notebooks and lectures of the 1870s and 80s are coherent with their later formulation in Wilde's most famous dialogue, "The Critic as Artist." I will conclude by drawing attention to those remarks in which, Peter Morton supposes, Wilde "knew little and cared less" about the science he invoked. When Gilbert, Wilde's *raisonneur,* contends that "the scientific principle of Heredity has become, as it were, the warrant for the contemplative life" and that "the imagination is the result of heredity. It is simply concentrated race-experience" (1040–41), he speaks from Wilde's demonstrable familiarity with contemporary evolutionary hypotheses about heredity. This idea of imagination, as Gilbert suggests, gives tremendous scope and power to the creative artist and writer: "We have merely touched the surface of the soul, that is all. In one single ivory cell of the brain there are stored away things more marvelous and more terrible than even they have dreamed of, who, like the author of *Le Rouge et le Noir,* have sought to track the soul into its most secret places, and to make life confess its dearest sins" (1055).

Gilbert does not speak in hyperbole: Wilde's theory has the largest possible consequences for the development of life and culture; it does not reduce into a shallow aestheticism of art for art's sake, as critics have often contended. Gilbert claims that the nineteenth century is "a turning point in history . . . one of the most important eras in the progress of the world" (1058) because the work of Charles Darwin and Ernest Renan demonstrates the emergence of human thought into critical self-consciousness about its scientific and aesthetic basis. Self-consciousness has tremendous implications for the development of the race, such that it would enable humans to "reach the true culture that is our aim . . . the perfection of which the saints have dreamed." Gilbert explains Wilde's master revaluation, the claim that "AEsthetics are higher than ethics," with a crucial analogy based on evolutionary theory: "AEsthetics, in fact, are to Ethics in the sphere of conscious civilization, what, in the sphere of the external world, sexual is to natural selection. Ethics, like natural selection, make existence possible. Aesthetics, like sexual selection, make life lovely and wonderful, fill it with new forms, and give it progress, and variety and change" (1058).

This analogy of aesthetics to sexual selection is squarely based in Wilde's synthesis. Its assumptions about physical and mental evolution are drawn from Darwin's *Origin of Species* and *Descent of Man,* from Spencer's and Clifford's theories of the hereditary transmission of culture, and from the unity of the organic principle of life described by Huxley and Tyndall. Hegel's philosophy of dialectical spiritual progress drives its metaphysical assumptions: the realization of critical and imaginative self-consciousness in individuals gives humans the power to choose, to select on aesthetic and scientific principles, the course of their future development. As Gilbert concludes in his presentation of the theory, "The Critical Spirit and the World Spirit are one" (1058).

Notes

1. In page references the Commonplace Book will be referred to as CB and the Notebook kept at Oxford as CN.

2. As J. E. Chamberlin remarks, "Many Oxford students in the 1870s claimed that for a long period they never saw Darwin except through Hegelian bifocals" (58).

3. He conceded, however, that regression or stagnation might follow periods of historical progress: for example, he viewed Roman culture as such a period in the history of art and literature (CB 41).

Works Cited

Blinderman, Charles. "Huxley, Pater, and Protoplasm." *Journal of the History of Ideas,* 43:3 (1982): 477–486.

Chamberlin, J. E. *Ripe Was the Drowsy Hour: The Age of Oscar Wilde.* New York: Seabury, 1977.

Eiseley, Loren. *The Immense Journey.* New York: Vintage, 1959.

Mikhail, E. H., ed. *Oscar Wilde: Interviews and Recollections.* 2 vols. New York: Barnes & Noble, 1979.

Morton, Peter. *The Vital Science: Biology and the Literary Imagination, 1860–1900.* London: George Allen & Unwin, 1984.

Rehbock, Philip F. "Huxley, Haeckel, and the Oceanographers: The Case of *Bathybius haeckelii,*" *Isis* 66 (1975): 504–533.

Wilde, Oscar. "The Critic as Artist." *The Complete Works of Oscar Wilde.* New ed. London and Glasgow: Collins, 1966. 1009–1059.

———."The English Renaissance in Art." *The Essays of Oscar Wilde.* New York: H. S. Nichols, 1916.

PART 4
WILDE AND SUFFERING,
OR UNIVERSALITY

◆

The Ballads of Reading Gaol:
At the Limits of the Lyric

Leonard Nathan

When he decided to include *The Ballad of Reading Gaol* in his *Oxford Book of Modern Verse* (1937), Yeats took it on himself to edit its 109 stanzas down to 38. It is small wonder that he felt called on to defend so radical an excision:

> That young man [i.e., the young Yeats "struggling for expression"] . . . felt contempt for the poetry of Oscar Wilde, considering it an exaggeration of every Victorian fault, nor, except in the case of one poem not then written, has time corrected the verdict. . . . Now that I have plucked from the *Ballad of Reading Gaol* its foreign feathers it shows a stark realism akin to that of Thomas Hardy, the contrary to all its author deliberately sought. I plucked out even famous lines because, effective in themselves, put into the Ballad they become artificial, trivial, arbitrary; a work of art can have but one subject. . . . I have stood in judgment upon Wilde, bringing into the light a great, or almost great poem, as he himself had done had he lived; my work gave me that privilege.[1]

There is much in this majesterial pronouncement that a contemporary reader and Wilde himself might accept. Yeats's towering reputation may even seem to justify the cool arrogance of the final assertion. Surely Yeats's version of the poem is in many respects more comfortably readable than Wilde's. Richard Ellmann is probably not alone among critical readers in thinking that Yeats's drastic operation saved the poem from its worst self, delivered its Hardy-like strength from the burden of "foreign feathers": "The *Ballad* is strongest when it concentrates on the trooper and prison conditions, weakest when it deals with capitalized abstractions like Sin and Death, and imports imagery from *The Rime of the Ancient Mariner*."[2] It is precisely these "strongest" parts that Yeats preserves in his version.

Wilde's likely agreement with Yeats's judgment is to be inferred from remarks he made about the poem during and after its composition. To Robert Ross he writes that the "poem suffers under the difficulty of a divided aim in style. Some is realistic, some is romantic: some poetry, some propaganda."[3] And again to Ross: "I think I shall call the whole thing *Póesie et Propagande* or *Dichtung und Wahrheit*" (*Letters*, 661). Though it is not wholly clear to what

This essay was written specifically for this volume and is published here for the first time by permission of the author.

parts of the poem Wilde would apply these terms, there is no doubt he regretted what he saw as an unbridgeable stylistic rift in the *Ballad,* the very one that invited Yeats's recension.

But the implicit agreement of Wilde with his (posthumous) editor is based on a deeper agreement than that of style. This agreement—or perhaps *settlement* is the word—concerns the nature of poetry and is grounded on a romantic aesthetic that perceived lyric—above all, personal lyric—as the most authentically poetic of poetry. John Stuart Mill offers one (Victorian) version of this view, defining the true poem as "feeling confessing itself, in moments of solitude, and embodying itself forth in symbols which are the nearest possible representations of the feeling in the exact shape in which it exists in the poet's mind," and so it follows that "all poetry is of the nature of soliloquy."[4] Which is to say that true poetry is the expression of personal pathos isolated from active intercourse with others. This is the aesthetic of the cry of the heart, passive victim of circumstance.

Though Mill is asserting theory, the theory does describe many poems we think of as most typically romantic, poems that begin in all-but-helpless pathos, like "Dejection: An Ode" and "Resolution and Independence." The hope in such poems is that the poet can break through passive suffering into active joy. Such breakthroughs seemed less available to the authors of "Dover Beach" and "Tears, Idle Tears."

Though Yeats, twentieth-century Yeats, found ways to escape passivity in his poetry, he nevertheless held to the view that what was essentially poetic was also essentially lyric, for Yeats a passionate personal utterance of an active self. In the same introduction in which he justifies his editing of Wilde, he gives as his reason for excluding war poets that "passive suffering is not a theme for poetry" (Yeats, xxxiv). Part of his task of saving the *Ballad* was to trim away its passive suffering. This meant sacrificing some of its lyric intensity for the sake of the narrative and sharp detail. Yeats's revision brings the poem closer to preromantic ballad tradition, in which the emphasis is less on direct expression of pathos than on vivid action, the pathos mostly implied.

Wilde too put lyric at the center of his poetics, and it is for this reason that the *Ballad* seemed so contrary a project. To his publisher, Leonard Smithers, he complains that "I should not like to die without seeing my poem as good as I can make a poem, whose subject is all wrong, and whose treatment too personal" (*Letters,* 675). Most any one of Wilde's preprison poems reveals why the subject of the *Ballad* is wrong, the style too personal. In almost all his earlier poems he worked in the conventions of the English pastoral in its romantic and Victorian phases. The typical result was Alexandrian: classical myth serving erotic themes, spangled with ornament, and loaded with cultivated pathos. Even his religious poems partake of these conventions.

It is with classical myth that Wilde explains one aspect of his intention in the *Ballad.* The myth is that of the music contest between Marsyas and Apollo, in which Marsyas, as punishment for his presumption, is flayed alive. Wilde brings this myth into play as far back as 1888 in a review of W. H. Henley's poems, finding in them more Marsyas than Apollo, that is, more the voice of pain than of beauty (*Letters*, 232–233; 233n). In his *De Profundis* letter to Alfred Douglas the myth provides Wilde with a way of describing much of modern art, its pervasive tone of trouble, doubt, and suffering in the work of poets like Baudelaire, Lamartine, Verlaine, and Arnold (*Letters*, 490). Finally, the myth becomes an explanatory metaphor for his intentions in the *Ballad* and why its subject is wrong for him, why its treatment is foreign to his practice. He writes Frank Harris that "I, of course, feel that the poem is too autobiographical and that *real* experiences are alien things that should never influence one, but it was wrung out of me, a cry of pain, the cry of Marsyas, not the song of Apollo" (*Letters*, 708). Wilde, for all his career the Apollonian poet of the art lyric, now finds that he must submit to the imperative of the suffering heart, crying out not for art's sake but because it cannot help itself, because it has no leisure for beauty in the cruel world of Olympian gods or human authority.

This is the great "aesthetic" lesson of prison, which Wilde sums up in remarks to Chris Healy: "It is the cry of Marsyas and not the song of Apollo. I have probed the depths of most of the experiences in life, and I have come to the conclusion that we are meant to suffer . . . and it was only when I was in the depths of suffering that I wrote [i.e., "conceived of"] my poem."[5] It is unsurprising that a poet for whom poetry was removed from daily life, let alone prison experience, would feel dread not just at a new style but at a subject that destroyed all possibility of an ideal distance from intractable reality, a subject that also demanded it be treated not as some new literary choice but as moral and psychological necessity.

But the harsh Marsyan cry was not the only novelty that beset Wilde. Besides some purplish Apollonian passages (which came under Yeats's knife), there was the propaganda. What precisely that term signified is not, as noted, self-evident; however, Wilde offers a clue, one isolating one aspect of the poem as pure polemic. In a letter to Ross already quoted from, Wilde concedes his friend's criticism that the poem has gone on too long *as a poem* but gives a reason why it must: "the poem should end at 'outcasts always mourn [stanza 89],' but the propaganda, which I desire to make, begins there" (*Letters*, 661).[6]

What "begins there" are two more cantos, themselves divided into sets. Canto 5 addresses the law and its effects on its victims. The following is a fair specimen from the first set:

> But this I know, that every Law
>   That men have made for Man,
> Since first Man took his brother's life
>   And the sad world began,
> But straws the wheat and saves the chaff
>   With a most evil fan.

> (*Works*, 279)

After four stanzas in this manner, a more grainy, less sententious set follows; these concern the consequences of the law, the brutal degradation of prison life. But the physical horror and humiliation described here are not the worst of it. The next set takes up the spiritual effects of inhuman punishment:

> But though lean Hunger and Green Thirst
> Like asp with adder fight,
> We have little care of prison fare,
> For what chills and kills outright
> Is that every stone one lifts by day
> Becomes one's heart by night.
>
> (*Works,* 281)

But there is a sudden shift of emphasis in this set from the evil consequences of the law to one good one—heartbreak, true surrender to God, which brings "peace of pardon." Yet if harshness of punishment is the occasion, if not the cause, of this conversion, Wilde's line of argument veers perilously near a justification of the inhuman cruelty the poem has been written to protest. This seeming contradiction—and it is not the only one—is never resolved.[7] Perhaps Wilde understood that it was merely another version of the ancient effort to explain the mysterious necessity of evil to the Providential plan. He might have justified it less as theology than as an effort to redeem some hope out of what otherwise—so long as the law was "a most evil fan"—was irretrievably hopeless.

The concluding set of this canto narrows attention to the condemned man, reduced now to a corpse, to the epithet "he of the swollen throat," victim of an institution that permitted him three weeks to "heal/His soul" and prepare for Christ. As so often in the more sententious parts of the *Ballad,* Wilde becomes heavily schematic: here, red for the judge's gown and guilty blood set against white for purity, "Christ's . . . seal." It is very likely Wilde believed that, in using such bold metonymies, he was getting close to the ballad convention of presenting pathos indirectly through strong detail (say, the "golde kems" and "cork-heild schoone" of "Sir Patric Spens"). The difference, of course, is that Wilde's details have become abstractions that his usage, in this case, fails to redeem.

The final canto consists of three stanzas that attempt to bring into some relationship the main subjects or concerns of the poem. First are the shameful debasement and judicial murder of the guardsman, who is the moral stand-in for all the other prisoners and all other victims of man's inhumanity to man. Next is the appropriate response to inhumanity, which is the unstinting pity that Wilde, with heavy irony, recommends be withheld from the hanged man:

And there, till Christ call forth the dead,
  In silence let him lie:
No need to waste a foolish tear,
  Or heave the windy sigh:
The man had killed the thing he loved,
  And so he had to die.

                (*Works*, 285)

The third concern of the poem, universal guilt, is here embodied in the sardonic variation on the refrainlike motto "each man kills the thing he loves," the universal explanation for all "capital" crimes (except those committed by institutions), crimes that, literally or figuratively, destroy life.

Yeats may have omitted all allusions to this motto for reasons other than he gave in his introduction.[8] Like many of Wilde's paradoxes, this one comes off badly if read straight, with full seriousness, as it seems to demand. To insist that all men kill what they love (and does that "men" include "women"?) suggests helplessness of all the parties to the crime, a notion that could seem to trivialize murder, shifting it from the category of sin to that of folly. If killing is in many instances figurative, then the exaggeration can weaken the literal horror of actual murder. The claim itself is so sweeping it could fatally reverse the effect Wilde surely intended. Nothing could be so subverting to his intention as the raised eyebrow and the sighing comment, "Old Oscar is at it again."

More, many more, objections to this and other parts of the poem can be, and have been, raised, but perhaps the most serious of them—the damning implications of Yeats's editing—deny the *Ballad* its ambition, its heroic straining after a style beyond the aesthetic limits of the time and of the poet's profoundest poetic instincts, compelling him to work with alien matters and in uncongenial ways. Against the thrust of his whole career, Wilde aspired now to create a social poetry that could enter the public domain with every hope of having consequences in the real world. It is as though Walter Pater had undertaken a new "Areopagitica" or as though the author of "The Lake Isle of Innisfree" had composed "Easter 1916."

But however noble, Wilde's ambition was doomed before it began, and doomed by, among other things, his own poetic prejudices, those which prompted him to damn as propaganda the concluding stanzas of the *Ballad*. In calling them propaganda Wilde was consigning them to a lower order of discourse, at best what Mill might have termed "eloquence," at worst, vulgar journalism, not the sort of expression the Apollonian poet would be proud to own.[9] Wilde's view here reflects a more general one of serious poets at the end of the century: that no acceptable public language seemed available (or for the austere poets of the Rhymers' Club, to which both Wilde and Yeats belonged, even desirable) to poetry. The closest thing to such a language was found in a sort of loose classification of "realistic" verse dealing with "low" subjects in a "plain" style, what Wilde, as we have seen, termed Marsyan. In this grouping—not a genre so much as a decorum rooted in older conventions developed in certain poems of Wordsworth and Crabbe—would be found work by Hood, Davidson, Henley, Kipling, and Hardy.[10] But during the 1890s such work did not constitute a serious counterbalance to the Apollonian in its various manifestations. And the realist poem was still largely confined to the first-person lyric voice, whose public character was found in its directness, in the need to attend to things as they are (the lesson Wilde had to learn in prison). Beyond tough-minded facing of the harshness of life among the poor and afflicted, they had no aspiration, no program for change or reform of things as they are.

The personal voice was the only legitimate one for poets composing within the limits of romantic aesthetics. One of these limits was a debilitating contradiction (or paradox). Romantic aesthetics was committed to a war of the deep, spontaneous self against convention, committed thus to an adversarial stance. But the deep, spontaneous self may not avail itself of the strongest weapon of its adversary—deliberative eloquence, the power of direct argument. Poets found themselves in what amounted to an (undeclared) public debate without a public rhetoric of their own. Deprived of this instrument, they resorted to the weapons at hand, intense pathos or allegory, "The Idiot Boy" or "The French Revolution." Neither of these modes comfortably enters public debate, and if either works change, it does so indirectly, slowly, by altering the "feel" of experience. But pathos also can satisfy its aims in pity, and allegory can exhaust its effect in the search for concealed meaning long before any political action is called for. In its Victorian and Edwardian version, the romantic aesthetic seemed even more insulated from action. Art-for-art's-sake, whatever else it signified, was the harsh dismissal of even the modest "realist" strain that valued a poetry, in Wordsworth's phrase, "belonging rather to nature than to manners."

But whether Apollonian or Marsyan, the lyric was the mode Wilde inherited, along with the aesthetic contradiction of an adversarial end without adversarial means.[11] The strain shows up in the *Ballad,* which adopts lyric pathos as its main line of argument. Though Wilde concentrates his attention on another, a stranger, and achieves personal pathos indirectly, by identifying with the stranger, the emotion is not an adequate base for discursive argument. Ross (and Yeats) correctly saw that the last sections of the poem add very little to its force. The concluding two cantos circle and repeat, as though in search of a commanding, all-unifying summary and conclusion. But nothing new is discovered: hope for broken hearts, denunciation of the system, the shaky assertion of universal guilt, but in terms no more effective than those in Shelley's "The Mask of Anarchy," whose personifications, like Wilde's in the *Ballad,* lack the mythic power of those in the *Rime.*

The cry of Marsyas, no more than the song of Apollo, can take Wilde where he wants to go, and that is why he has such mixed feelings about the last cantos of the *Ballad:* that on the one hand they are in a style unworthy of the name poetry; that on the other, they are absolutely necessary, made so by a decorum more urgent and overriding (perhaps even more profound) than that permitted by romantic aesthetics. That Wilde overrode every objection to the last sections, even his own, suggests not a faulty ear but an imperative that it would be folly to ignore. His determination makes it very unlikely that, as Yeats so confidently assumes, had he lived on, he would have edited the *Ballad* down to its true poetic size, sparing others the task.

For all Wilde's grumbling about the poem, about the endless trouble it gave him, and despite his scornful labeling of parts of it as mere propaganda, he cared for this work with passion and truly believed he had hold of something large, larger than any Apollonian lyric. He is more matter-of-fact than boastful (or ironic) when he writes to Reginald Turner, "I have finished the great poem" (*Letters,* 656), and he is plainly proud when he writes to W. R. Paton, "It is a new style for me, full of actuality and life and in the directness of message and meaning" (*Letters,* 630). Actuality and life are expressions of the Marsyan cry, message and meaning, the propaganda. But for all its divided intention, Wilde regards the work as a whole and is willing to stand by it without shame or apology, even though it may not measure up to Apollonian (or Yeatsian) standards. And for all we know, despite its many failings, among them its effect as a call to action, it may have had a considerable share, belated and indirect, on penal reforms in England.

Yeats's version is, in any case, not the last word on the *Ballad;* it is only one of many possible versions, one of which might well be composed of what he left out of his. But the version that must never be slighted in favor of some "real" or "better" one, or one that Wilde, had he had the chance, would eventually have done, is the one Wilde left us. This is the "almost great poem," propaganda and all, that the author meant to be authoritatively first in any consideration, critical or otherwise, and, I think, not just first but also last.

If any conclusion is to be drawn from Wilde's failure to make an effective public poetry, it should be balanced against Yeats's success in the same enterprise, for success here required more than Marsyas's cry of pain. Yeats's assertion that "passive suffering is not a theme for poetry," while it excludes a whole range of authentic poets, does suggest what is required to achieve an active, a public, poetry: a fundamental change in poetic ethos, an abandonment of the conventions of the Millite lyric in its various modes, including the Marsyan, whose voice could carry only so far into the world of action—not very far in Henley and Davidson, quite far in Hardy and Kipling, but not far enough for Yeats, far enough, that is, to make a poetry that could be factored into public debate, could move people to action, or could stamp some social group with a unifying identity.

The poet who—with a century of aesthetic attitude behind him— pronounced that the aim of rhetoricians is to deceive their neighbors could also insist, "In my present mood I am all for the man who, with an average audience before him, uses all means of persuasion."[12] The poet, that is, will take as a model the orator and exploit a range of means unavailable to the pure poet, this to persuade some audience, some vital presence (real or imagined). The poet-orator, not confined to soliloquy, will pitch into the arena of public debate, accepting the impurities of the world of action, using them as instruments to make points.

Why Wilde could not and Yeats could abandon the passive lyric ethos is not at issue here (though Yeats's willingness to do so had much to do with his longtime practical involvement in a living theater and with his growing conviction that identity was an artifice, something made and therefore something that could be remade). That it *could* be done—that someone could see that ethos was in fact a collection of conventions and that conventions might be modified or even abandoned—is the moral I wish to draw in this essay. The dogma of romantic aesthetics, the aesthetics of sincerity, proclaimed that true poetic ethos is natural and, as such, not subject to change. Yeats taught that there was a good deal more freedom in being who we are than we had thought, more freedom in the kind of poet we might be than had been imagined.

But having said this, I must add that Yeats's lesson has been largely ignored in our century, in Anglo-American poetry, except in a few cases—W. H. Auden, Marianne Moore, Richard Wilbur, and Howard Nemerov come readily to mind. Modernist, and now postmodernist, poets seem to have preferred to stay with various modes of Marsyan lyric, occasionally trying to build on it something like epic superstructures—*The Cantos,* for example, or *Paterson,* even *The Waste Land.*[13]

There are current calls for a more accessible poetry, a poetry willing to go beyond image, beyond objective correlative, beyond the no-ideas-but-in-things doctrine, beyond showing to telling.[14] These I take to be signs of dissatisfaction with the limits of passive lyric. Though this kind of lyric is not bound to the purity of Mill's ideal—since Marsyas is perforce a realist—it is constricted to a narrow if intense range of feeling. The poetry of James Wright is perhaps the most brilliant testimony of what such a poetry can and cannot do. What it cannot do is comfortably turn outward to the public realm, as so many modern poetry anthologies dedicated to some great political or social occasion have shown.

But for those who would see poetry become, among other things, public again, there is another hope, one coming from literary criticism and philosophy: the theory of self as a social construct, the integration of conventions that we recognize as personal identity. To see that selves are less born than made, and that making implies unmaking or remaking, is to lift an enchantment that has enthralled poets and critics for more than a century. And if it is argued that before poetry can become public, there has to be a public, a forum, a community for it to address, this might serve as a reply: that the poet, by imagining these social necessities, can perhaps help create them. If that seems a hopeless task in light of the poet's many successful competitors in "the media," nevertheless it must be undertaken, unless we want our poetry to sit in the same old yew shade weeping the same old tears, overheard by the same old happy few and taken for preservation (or deconstruction) into the same old seminar.

Notes

1. W. B. Yeats (ed.), *The Oxford Book of Modern Verse* (New York: Oxford University Press, 1937), vi–viii; hereafter cited in text.

2. Richard Ellmann, *Oscar Wilde* (New York: Alfred A. Knopf, 1988), 533.

3. Oscar Wilde, in *The Letters,* ed. Rupert Hart-Davis (New York: Harcourt, Brace and World, 1962), 654; hereafter cited in text as *Letters.*

4. J. S. Mill, "What Is Poetry?" in *Mill's Essays on Literature and Society,* ed. J. B. Schneewind (New York: Collier Books, 1965), 109. The power and persistence of this position are demonstrated by their echoes in modernist theory. T. S. Eliot, self-proclaimed classicist, put it thus: "If the author never spoke to himself, the result would not be poetry, though it might be magnificent rhetoric" [T. S. Eliot, "The Three Voices of Poetry" (New York: American Book–Stratford Press, 1954), 33]. The other voices of poetry—the dramatic and the rhetorical—are compromised by the poet's consciousness of audience expectation. Only "the poet speaking to himself—or nobody" creates the authentic stuff of poems (Eliot, 6).

5. Quoted by Ellmann in *Oscar Wilde,* 532–33, from "Oscar Wilde and Zola," *To-Day,* 26 November 1902. For another statement of the myth, see *Letters,* 714.

6. The full stanza is as follows:

> Yet all is well; he has but passed
> To Life's appointed bourne:
> And alien tears will fill for him
> Pity's long-broken urn,
> For his mourners will be outcast men,
> And outcasts always mourn.

(Oscar Wilde, *The Works,* Sunflower edition [New York: Lamb Publishing, 1909], 1:278; hereafter cited in text as *Works.*)

Yeats's version cuts off nine stanzas earlier:

> They think a murderer's heart would taint
> Each simple seed they sow.
> It is not true! God's kindly earth
> Is kindlier than men know,
> And the red rose would but blow more red,
> The white rose whiter blow.
>   (Yeats, 45)

7. For example, if institutional oppression is the cause of evil, of capital crime, how is the guardsman's murder of his wife to be explained, a crime that neither society nor its cruelest instrument, the law, compelled? Wilde's silence on this matter might be justified by the *Ballad's* traditional reticence about the causes of human acts, but silence in this instance makes for ambiguity rather than psychological authenticity.

8. It is quite likely that Yeats is referring to the motto when he speaks of "famous

lines . . . effective in themselves, put into the Ballad" becoming "artificial, trivial, arbitrary" (Yeats, vii).

9. What propaganda (or "eloquence" or "rhetoric") meant to Wilde and his contemporaries was no doubt a complex of qualities associated with public discourse, the most obvious being overt assertion of position, the strong sententia, what we have come to call "telling" as opposed to "showing." See Regenia Gagnier, *Idylls of the Marketplace* (Stanford, Calif.: 1986), for discussion of propaganda understood as "the effort to enforce an either/or dichotomy" (135).

10. As Regenia Gagnier notes (230), reviewers were quick to light on the *Ballad*'s derivativeness, a quality notorious in Wilde's Apollonian poems. Kipling's "Danny Deever," Hood's "The Dream of Eugene Aram," Henley's "In Hospital," and Housman's *A Shropshire Lad,* along with *The Rime of the Ancient Mariner,* were all perceived as grist for Wilde's mill.

11. Even Yeats's severe pruning does not obscure the lyric cast of the poem, many of whose stanzas give narrative or descriptive detail through the medium of personal wonder, as in "I never saw a man" or "And strange it was to see him pass." But the power that lyric exercised over Yeats never diminished through all his career, even when he was working in another genre. In a letter to his father written in 1909, Yeats says, "Wilde wrote in his last book 'I have made my drama as personal as a lyric,' and I think, whether he has done so or not, that is the only possible task now" (W. B. Yeats, in *The Letters,* ed. Allan Wade [London: Rupert Hart-Davis, 1954], 524).

12. W. B. Yeats, "The Musicians and the Orator," *Essays and Introductions* (New York: Macmillan, 1961), 268.

13. See Jeffrey Walker, *Bardic Ethos and the American Epic Poem* (Baton Rouge: Louisiana State University Press, 1989).

14. See, for example, *Expansive Poetry: Essays on the New Narrative and the New Formalism,* ed. Frederick Feirstein (Santa Cruz, Calif.: Story Line Press, 1989).

Wilde and Huysmans: Autonomy, Reference, and the Myth of Expiation

JAMES WINCHELL

L'art n'a rien à faire . . . avec la pudeur ou l'impudeur. Un roman qui est ordurier est un roman mal fait, et voilà tout.
—Joris-Karl Huysmans, "Emile Zola et *l'Assommoir*," 1876

There is no such thing as a moral or an immoral book. Books are well written, or badly written. That is all.
—Oscar Wilde, preface to *The Picture of Dorian Gray*, 1891

In this essay I will attempt to develop two central ideas: first, that the "contagious" intertextual relations between these authors and their fictional characters derive precisely from the anxiety and mimetic rivalry provoked by claims of autonomy and self-referential "plenitude of being" made by aestheticism itself,[1] and second, that the recourse of both writers to sacrificial logic (or the "romance of Christ") marks a culminating crisis central to modernism as both an aesthetic and a sociopolitical moment.[2]

The careers of Oscar Wilde and Joris-Karl Huysmans present uncannily parallel destinies. As men of letters (in the public sphere) and as private individuals, their fates might be drawn at the intersection of two affinities: aestheticism and a mystique of transgression. Neither preoccupation stood as a fixed creed, however, and both preoccupations should therefore be approached critically as dynamic, interpenetrating fields bound by a shared problem: the social life of signs and the paradoxes of mediated autonomy.[3]

Indeed, any clear distinction between public and private is effaced in the lives and arts of both writers: textually, their real-life public personas (culminating most poignantly in Wilde's trials, imprisonment, and exile) are largely indistinguishable from the personages who haunt their works. Similarly, the autobiographical alter egos of Huysmans's early writing coalesce in one authorial persona, the novelist-initiate Durtal, who will appear repeatedly in novels written after 1891. Moreover, Wilde's oft-quoted witticisms on the

This essay was written specifically for this volume and is published here for the first time by permission of the author.

breakdown in the art-life split are well known: "I have put only my talent into my works," he often stated; "I have put all my genius into my life."[4] Or this: "To become a work of art is the object of living."[5]

Aestheticism and the apotheosis of paradox characterize Oscar Wilde's oeuvre, as has often been noted in the critical tradition. But these rarefied practices belied self-reference, revealing in their deep structure a profound preoccupation with "the other." From his "exhibitions," writes Regenia Gagnier in her ground-breaking study on his relation to his audience, "Wilde wants public recognition as a Professor of Aesthetics who is able to lead the public toward art, and he wants a private life in which young men may realize their personalities . . . 'on some imaginative plane out of reach of the trammeling accidents and limitations of real life.' "[6]

Likewise, the mystique of transgression and the "intensification of personality" enacted by criminality provide the individual with an arena in which this "imaginative plane" might productively collide with the limitations of real life, providing a riposte to "earnestness" and positivist historiography: "There is no essential incongruity between crime and culture," Wilde states. "We cannot re-write the whole of history for the purpose of gratifying our moral sense of what should be."[7]

In both these fields, a critical preoccupation with the claims of autonomy for symbols (in the tradition of *l'art pour l'art*) and the nagging persistence of heteronomy (in contingent social determinations) marks the central tension in the production and reception of "aestheticism" throughout the period, in France as well as in England. Indeed, their resistance to each other veritably dictates intertextuality, resulting in the quintessentially modern crisis of mimesis and reference. "In a very ugly and sensible age," Wilde states, "the arts borrow, not from life, but from each other."[8]

For Wilde-the-professor-of-aesthetics as for Baudelaire, Huysmans, and the generations of their successors, the primary status of knowledge and judgment derives from an Apollonian faith in the "eternal of the transitory," the ineffably declining possibility of modern tragedy, and a classicist's trust in language as the self-governing stuff of symbols.[9] Claims of absolute liberty for representation, freed from real-world referentiality and especially from moralizing censure, would surpass Victorian (or, in France, naturalist) representations based on earnestness, psychologizing "depth," and a politics of edification or disillusionment. This aestheticism would be postulated in terms of a faith in sheer visibility (surface, artifice, and appearance itself) and, at the same time, in a transcendental cult of amoral beauty. For Wilde, these ideas find programmatic statement in such essays as "The Decay of Lying: An Observation," "The Truth of Masks: A Note on Illusion," and "The Critic as Artist."

Wilde's antinomies, however, like those of Huysmans, find their highest complexity in fiction. Unlike the essays and dialogues, these parables of alterity and transgression are often characterized by Dionysiac pleasures and sufferings motivated not only by the ambiguities of symbols and self-reference but also by the insoluble tension between self and other. It is not so much the body that becomes the locus of this struggle, however; this conflict is enacted, rather, on the ideological site of the traditional body-spirit split: a somatic-symbolic amalgam of desire and responsibility, haunted by mediation, criminality, memories of innocence, and the romance of sacrificial expiation. When asked in 1894 about spiritual life, Wilde reportedly said, "There is no hell but this—a body without a soul, or a soul without a body."[10]

The paradox of reflexive specularity—the intersubjective play of mirrors—is pronounced by Lord Henry Wotton, the dandy/spectator in *The Picture of Dorian Gray* (1890), for he is the eponymous character's model, his "professor of aesthetics": "It is only shallow people who do not judge by appearances. The true mystery of the world is the visible, not the invisible."[11]

Despite this claim, invisibility triumphant (as the heuristic secret of surface beauty) emerges allegorically at the conclusion of both *Dorian Gray* and Huysmans's *A Rebours*. Here the aesthete Des Esseintes, also obsessed with objects and surfaces, finds himself overwhelmed by the tides of history and "human mediocrity . . . rising to the heavens," the floodgates of which he has opened himself, against his own will. Likewise, Lord Henry Wotton's specular, "contagious" doctrine of surface aestheticism works fantastically to suspend the visible results of crime and suffering on the body of his disciple Dorian, only to find them revealed in the play of images on the profoundly superficial surface of an unviewable painting.

Throughout his works and life, culminating in the epistolary prison autobiography *De Profundis,* Oscar Wilde grapples with the invisible, in private images of self-sufficiency surrounded by the public mediations of Victorian moral codes. His aestheticism and the "mystique of transgression" in which it finds parabolic expression both attest to the possibility that, contrary to what modern theorists claim for self-referentiality in literature as a "self-engulfing artifact," literature manifesting such highly conscious self-reference actually "refers twice: first, to itself; and second, to . . . self-reference itself, understood here as a property of the world and in particular of human desire."[12]

This, then, constitutes the real-world paradox of aestheticism's parables, as Kafka demonstrates in "On Parables":

Concerning this a man once said: Why such reluctance? If you only followed the parables you yourselves would become parables and with that rid of all your daily cares.

Another said: I bet that is also a parable.

The first said: You have won.

The second said: But unfortunately only in parable.

The first said: No, in reality: in parable you have lost.[13]

This double mediation of conscious self-reference—of itself and of the problem of *self-reference in the world*—"goes critical" when its "contagion" spreads from one ontological level to another, from characters in novels to their authors and readers. Wilde's biographical transformation replicates just such a promotion: because of the necessarily public role played by aesthetic autonomy, he is (self-)advertised, commodified, therefore implicated, prosecuted, and ultimately incarcerated not only in symbols but also in the flesh. By publishing *The Ballad of Reading Gaol* in *Reynolds's,* as Wilde writes after his release from prison in a letter to editor Leonard Smithers, he would be read "widely among the criminal classes—to which I now belong—so I shall be read by my peers—a new experience for me."[14]

The endemic hypocrisy of this "vulgar" heteronomy in modernity is total and totalizing, yet fin de siècle aestheticism posits a transgressive, "supernatural negativity" as a would-be antithesis to socially overdetermined reality.[15] Borrowing one of Wilde's favorite tropes, Theodor Adorno writes: "Against the background of an illusory, social totality, art's illusory being-in-itself is like a mask of truth."[16] In the parallel fates of Wilde and Huysmans, this mask of self-reference is eventually lifted to reveal a truth about desire in history and the world.

For the decadence, the mask and the mirror emerged as the reflexive metaphors of self and other, each faithful to the most hermetic standards of aestheticism: symbolic self-sufficiency and the utter uselessness of the lie that tells the truth.[17] By their interactions and metamorphoses, they embody the crisis of indifferentiation shared by reflection and illusion; by their forms as *"identity surfaces,"* they embody both aspects of the paradox of reference in autonomy, as noted earlier: their self-reference refers first to themselves (mask and mirror) and at the same time to self-reference itself, as a problematic property of human desire.

As Jean-Pierre Dupuy has shown, the fact that self-reference now enjoys a special status in scientific disciplines demonstrates that this claim need not be rejected out of hand: "At least this fact indicates that the very literature wishing to segregate itself within itself has, through the cunning of reason in the humanities, joined a general problematic exterior to itself."[18]

In this light it is easy to grasp the seemingly contradictory fact that the series of prefatory aphorisms composed in 1891, in which Wilde asserts the absolute moral autonomy of literature, was composed as a *response* to the public outcry against *The Picture of Dorian Gray.* Moreover, they reveal in some instances the same terms and phrase rhythms used by Huysmans in his 1876 essay on Zola: "There is no such thing as a moral or an immoral book. Books are well written, or badly written. That is all." Within the novel these aphorisms preface, however, Dorian Gray is corrupted, at the profoundest level of his being, by a book.[19]

This "poisonous" novel, in the context of its role in Dorian's development, therefore comprises a third term for the misleading art/reality dichotomy: not only does Dorian learn from the epigrammatic verbal brilliance of his

"Professor of Aesthetics," but he also makes contact, by reading the contagious book, with the *external* source of his mediator's mediations.[20] Hypnotized as if in a dream of truth, Dorian Gray discovers the realm of the third term, of the triangular mediations that simultaneously adore and immolate the idols of self-sufficiency: "It was a novel without a plot, and with only one character, being, indeed, simply a psychological study of a certain young Parisian, who spent his life trying to realize in the nineteenth century all the passions and modes of thought that belonged to every century except his own, and to sum up, as it were, in himself the various moods through which the world-spirit had ever passed."[21]

For the nineteenth century, this "world-spirit" exemplifies the external mediator par excellence. It is never content to float in its own autonomy, however; it seems to require formal access to subjective cognition, and like the *pharmakon* associated with writing since Plato,[22] the French text left for Dorian Gray by his dandy-mediator works simultaneously through the channels marked "remedy" and "poison," conflating all physical and spiritual dichotomies in a novelistic allegory of criminal sensuality and ascetic renunciation: "The life of the senses was described in the terms of mystical philosophy. One hardly knew at times whether one was reading the spiritual ecstasies of some medieval saint or the morbid confessions of a modern sinner. It was a poisonous book."[23]

The continual recourse to metaphors of contagion and poison points up the power of these ideas seemingly to intervene panhistorically and against nature, in the form of nerve storms or epidemic agents of mediated and mimetic desire. As a reader, Dorian Gray is caught in the double bind of the master's mediation: "Imitate me, but do not obey me, for I am inimitable." As if under a magic spell, he cannot *not* take the advice he is advised to eschew: fascinated, he therefore approaches the unapproachable plenitude of aesthetic being incarnated by the "young Parisian" in the "poisonous book."

The ontological difference between author and character, or the subject-object difference between Pygmalion character and Galatea character, collapses here in a rarefied atmosphere of indifferentiation and decadent self-reference. The mechanism by which Dorian Gray inculcates this whirlwind of alterity and identity is explicitly spelled out:

> Yet one had ancestors in literature, as well as in one's own race, nearer perhaps in type and temperament, many of them, and certainly with an influence of which one was more absolutely conscious. There were times when it appeared to Dorian Gray that the whole of history was merely the record of his own life, not as he had lived it in act and circumstance, but as his imagination had created it for him. . . . He felt that he had known them all, those strange terrible figures that had passed across the stage of the world and made sin so marvellous, and evil so full of subtlety. It seemed to him that in some mysterious way their lives had been his own.[24]

Further demonstrations of this procedure, which might be called decadent *Bovarysme* (for Flaubert's heroine's propensity to model her life after images encountered in romantic novels), are found in Dorian's historical ruminations on, in turn, the historical ruminations of the character in the novel. "The hero of the wonderful novel that had so influenced his life had himself known this curious fancy," the narrator tells us, leading into a lengthy description of the scenes and meditations of the contagious novel's "seventh chapter."[25]

Although Oscar Wilde would identify this "yellow-backed French novel" as Huysmans's *A Rebours* under cross-examination by Edward Carson in 1895 at the Queensberry trial,[26] in the original typescript of *Dorian Gray* sent to Lippincott's he identified this book as the nonexistent *"Le Secret de Raoul* par Catulle Sarrazin."[27] Leaving this book's title unnamed in the novel makes good sense, but there is no doubt regarding Wilde's admiration for Huysmans's novel and for its hero, the Duc Jean Floressas des Esseintes. Ironically enough, the book appeared a mere two weeks before and marked its literary explosion during Wilde's problematic honeymoon.[28] As he told the *Morning News* at the time, "This last book of Huysmans is one of the best I have seen."[29] Because one of des Esseintes's sexual memories revolves around a homosexual experience, Richard Ellmann claims that the novel "summoned him [Wilde] towards an underground life totally at variance with his aboveboard role as Constance's husband."[30]

By its focus on issues of judgment and transgression, and by its tortured ruminations on the transhistorical status of the decadent Subject, the contagious book would also pose for Wilde not only the dilemma of his marriage but also the aporia of the aesthetic parable he would write in *The Picture of Dorian Gray:* the criminality, violence, and death inherent in the double-bind relationship between the aesthetic master and his disciple.

Turning from Wilde to Huysmans, the reader sees that the aforementioned chapter 7 of *A Rebours* begins precisely after the account of the crucial episode involving Auguste Langlois. Indeed, it begins with this resonant, single-sentence paragraph: "Beginning on the night when, for no apparent reason, he had conjured up the melancholy memory of Auguste Langlois, Des Esseintes lived his whole life over again."[31]

It is significant—and this is my central thesis—that the ensemble of this "fantastic chapter, and the two chapters immediately following,"[32] as cited by Dorian Gray, begins in *A rebours* with this conjunction of the name Auguste Langlois and the tormented act of recalling "his whole life over again" by des Esseintes. The critical tradition has focused on the aesthete's musings over bibelots and books without decoding this crucial episode. The very name, which might be translated as "Venerable Englishman" and thus interpreted as an epithet for the first dandy to import his "germ" into France, Beau Brummell, is now *itself* a germ that contagiously spreads back out of France into yet another "Venerable Englishman," this time Dorian Gray in all his fictional selfhood.

There is an important difference between the two cases, as noted earlier: des Esseintes undertakes the formation of his young charge without the aid of "a contagious book," and fails miserably. Harry Wotton mediates Dorian Gray's nascent criminal personality both by means of his own model mentorship (as an internal mediator) and with the help of the contagious text: for this reason, his mediation is all the more heteronomous, violent, and fatal.

Unlike his French counterpart, Lord Henry Wotton takes " 'Human life' [as] the one thing worth study; and so, like the 'true critic,' but with none of the purity of motive . . . lives vicariously on the emotions and experiences of other people."[33] Based on his aestheticism and the Auguste Langlois episode, des Esseintes becomes Lord Henry's external mediator in transgressive Pygmalionism. This "young Parisian" maintains the greater "purity of motive" by focusing primarily on art objects rather than people, however, thereby guaranteeing a greater degree of a decadent form of Kantian disinterestedness. Yet des Esseintes's lone project violating this distinction, and the one that would become central for the allegory of Dorian Gray, is his plan for the criminalization of "the other," Auguste Langlois, by "forming" his very sense of desire.

This episode marks, curiously enough, the world-weary des Esseintes's lone sociopolitically explicit project: the creation of an avenging, class-warfare criminal. Auguste Langlois is treated by des Esseintes to carte blanche at a brothel, which privilege he then instructs the madam to withdraw, thereby forcing the young man into a life of crime in order to support his "habits of desire" in the fashion to which he has artificially grown accustomed: "And to get the money to pay for his visits here, he'll turn burglar, he'll do anything if it helps him on to one of your divans in one of your gaslit rooms. . . . Looking on the bright side of things, I hope that, one fine day, he'll kill the gentleman who turns up unexpectedly just as he's breaking open his desk. On that day my object will be achieved: I shall have contributed, to the extent of my financial resources, to the making of a scoundrel, one enemy the more for the hideous society which is bleeding us white."[34]

This "anarchic" gesture is qualified authorially by the irony of des Esseintes's reservations about the extent of his *"engagement"* ("to the extent of my financial resources") and by the comic reaction of the prostitutes gathered around the outspoken criminal mediator: "The women gazed at him with open-eyed amazement."[35] Such authorial irony is largely lacking in Wilde's novel, however; in fact, the narrator's voice itself often resembles Harry Wotton's, and vice versa.

The embarrassed future criminal Langlois, now conditioned in the hothouse of the dandy's favorite bordello, emerges from his erotic exercise; back on the street, des Esseintes addresses this stupefying speech to his criminal creation: "We shan't see each other again. Hurry off home . . . and remember this almost evangelic dictum: Do unto others as you would not have them do unto you; with this maxim you'll go far."[36]

Just how far des Esseintes intends for his prototype to go is limited only by the infinite possibilities of crime, a realm of activity bearing the same open-endedness and imaginative liberty as delectation, connoisseurship, and art itself. "Whatever you do, show a little gratitude for what I've done for you," des Esseintes tells Auguste Langlois on parting, "and let me know as soon as you can how you're getting on—preferably through the columns of the *Police Gazette*." The boy disappoints his creator, however: "The little Judas! To think that I've never once seen his name in the papers!"[37]

By his failure to commit a crime sufficiently infamous to merit the attention of popular journalists, Auguste Langlois has betrayed his sermonizer-on-the-*mons-veneris* ("Do unto others as you would not have them do unto you"); thus des Esseintes is betrayed by his criminal subject because the latter does not sufficiently trespass to meet even the low standards of the sensational journalism of fin de siècle crime.

Retrospectively meditating on this failed political project, the aesthete reveals its key, an organizing idea simultaneously oriented toward societal trends and artistic ends, revealing a profound preoccupation with history and the shifting ground of intersubjectivity for the autonomous dandy: "All I was doing was parabolizing secular instruction, allegorizing universal education, which is well on the way to turning everybody into a Langlois: instead of permanently and mercifully putting out the eyes of the poor, it does its best to force them wide open, so that they may see all around them lives of less merit and greater comfort, pleasures that are keener and more voluptuous, and therefore sweeter and more desirable."[38]

Thus Auguste Langlois viewed in retrospect comes to incarnate the infernally democratic idea of universal education, which Des Esseintes bitterly views as an all-too-concrete manifestation of popular resentment, misguided republicanism, and desires "inappropriate" to the lower classes.

Des Esseintes's reasoning assumes a dialectical cast as he further meditates on this anarchic allegory-in-flesh. Where he had initially intended the "refinement" of the boy as a revolutionary act against a corrupt society, he now realizes that the criminality of his "naturalism" (wherein the bordello serves as the corrupting *moment* and *milieu*) is in fact perfectly consonant with the values of that very society, and that therefore the Auguste Langlois project, if criminally successful, would be a triumph of conformity rather than anarchy: "The fact is that, pain being one of the consequences of education, in that it grows greater and sharper with the growth of ideas, it follows that the more we try to polish the minds and refine the nervous systems of the underprivileged, the more we shall be developing in their hearts the atrociously active germs of hatred and moral suffering."[39]

This particular failure and Huysmans's authorial irony about its futility as an "aesthetic," mark the ground for his break with his naturalist master, Emile Zola, itself occasioned by the publication of *A rebours* in 1884. The whorehouse project is like a parody-in-miniature of Zola's *roman expérimental;* Auguste

Langlois becomes a willful caricature of the members of the Rougon-Macquart, Zola's mythic familial figures of degeneration and preordained transgressions. He simply refuses, however, to degenerate.[40]

As the novel progresses, des Esseintes is less and less convinced of his own autonomy. By his public-anarchic Auguste Langlois project, he would like to "universalize" and "industrialize," in René Girard's terms, desire for the sake of desire. Although des Esseintes's aristocratic origins are posited as the source of his mental and physical decline and his attitudes clearly derive from an aristocratic mystique of superiority, Girard might well be describing him and his plan for Auguste Langlois when he states: "There is nothing less aristocratic than this undertaking; it reveals the bourgeois soul of the dandy. This high-mannered Mephistopheles [the inverted Christ of the sermon on the mound of Venus] would like to be the capitalist of desire."[41]

The aesthetic criminal mastermind therefore becomes like Lord Henry Wotton and Dorian Gray, a figuration of the dandy in a state of crisis. As Walter Benjamin puts it, the Baudelairean dandy finds no consolation in having been dropped from the calendar: his vaunted isolation from contemporaneity ultimately leaves him desolated and redundant on an island of ahistory.[42] Des Esseintes, watching his criminal prototype vanish into law-abiding oblivion, witnesses yet another hothouse idea wither and fail under his touch. This "naturalist" experiment in personality formation fails as surely as his experiments in tortoise husbandry fail. The dandy-in-crisis attempts a project in the public sphere and finds that the allegory of universal education, which he thought to control in the figure and criminal future of Auguste, is in fact already "well on its way to turning everybody into a Langlois."[43] Not only has des Esseintes been dropped from the calendar, but he has even been dropped from the *Police Gazette:* the vast, democratized, secularly instructed public has already surpassed in criminal reality his supposed breakthrough in transgressive aesthetics.

In her study of the cultural and material bases for Wilde's aestheticism Regenia Gagnier distinguishes between Wilde and Huysmans in the following terms: "Wilde as a dandy is often erroneously compared to Huysmans's hero in *A Rebours,* yet the comparison is negatively instructive. If Des Esseintes is solitary, neurotic, reactive against the bourgeoisie he despises, formally monologic, and concerned with perversion, Wilde is public, erotic, active, formally dialogic, and concerned with the inversion of middle-class language and life. (The French decadents may also be more engaged than critics have made them out to be, but Wilde should not be treated as French.)"[44]

Clearly the critic is correct here: the significant parallel is not between the author Wilde and the fictional des Esseintes but, rather, between the latter and Harry Wotton, both "Professors of Aesthetics" for their respective disciples. Just as Balzac's archcriminal Vautrin creates the beautiful criminal Lucien de Rubempré by mimetically informing his desires, thereby endowing him with social and sexual ambiguity, so does Des Esseintes attempt (and fail) to create

Auguste Langlois as he would an art object, and so, finally—and with fatal success—does Harry Wotton create Dorian Gray. Ultimately, these mediated desires come full circle. Fictional characters create authors: "One of the greatest tragedies of my life is the death of Lucien de Rubempré," Wilde writes in an oft-quoted passage. "It is a grief from which I have never been able to completely rid myself."[45]

Des Esseintes's relationship with his prototype is relatively anodyne in terms of the virulence of the germ of mediated desire; indeed, its failure contributes to his desperation, and his desperate prayer, in the last lines of the novel. But the stakes are much higher for the characters in Wilde's novel, in the form of violence and fatality, murder and suicide, of the monstrous doubles caught in Lord Henry's aesthetic machine. Where Auguste Langlois has but one internal mediator, his English counterpart has two: while the painter Basil Hallward's medium is art, Lord Henry's medium is life itself.[46] As Rodney Shewan writes, "He plays on Dorian as on 'an exquisite violin' . . . and his 'poisonous theories,' which Dorian unwisely and uncritically puts into practice, make 'the lad . . . largely his own creation.' "[47] The fantastic and avenging portrait is ostensibly the creation of Basil, but the picture, the artist, and the subject himself are all inevitably the victims of Lord Henry's mediations.

The relation between self-reference as a *procedure* (in aesthetic autonomy) and self-reference as a *problem* was adumbrated by Huysmans, fleshed out by Wilde, and lived out by both of them. Startlingly, both would reinscribe the issue during the last years of their lives in personal refigurations of traditional myths of sacrifice, mystical substitution, and expiation. Instead of merely reiterating aestheticism, however, these shared mythologies signal efforts to bootstrap the Subject out of the grinding machine of history, out of declining societies, and into a realm of not autonomy but referential totality. As I shall demonstrate, this shift—from Subject-as-spectator to Subject-as-object—is no less problematic and is far more "contagious" than the paradoxes of Harry Wotton or the sociology of Des Esseintes, for the impossibility of unmediated experience endemic to modernity creates an objectification of the individual in all realms of existence, often englobing and surpassing even the literary.

The parallels between the literary fates of Joris-Karl Huysmans and Oscar Wilde might most economically be illustrated by an allegorical work by Félicien Rops, *La Tentation de Saint Antoine* (1878).[48] This *dessin en couleurs* presents a parable of ascesis, or renunciation of desire in the name of metaphysical desire, and is mentioned by Freud as an illustration of the mechanism by which repressed material returns to the life of the subject in complex yet direct ways. In the case of Rops's *Saint Antoine,* as in the cases of Huysmans and Wilde, the dreamlike, haunting yet triumphant return of

Félicien Rops, *La Tentation De Saint Antoine* (1878). Copyright Bibliothèque royale Albert 1er, Bruxelles (Cabinet des Estampes). Reprinted by permission.

banished material occurs at the very site where it was originally repressed: "Other painters of less psychological insight have, in such representations of temptation, depicted sin as bold and triumphant and relegated it to some place near the Savior on the cross. Rops alone has allowed it to take the place of the Savior on the cross; he seems to have known that the thing repressed proceeds, at its recurrence, from the agency of repression itself."[49]

Huysmans would assume the role of the penitent yet tormented ascetic during the last years of the century, while Oscar Wilde would promote himself into the very center of the circle of social and judiciary violence, assuming the position of surrogate redeemer/excruciating Eros on the allegorical cross as depicted by Rops. After the publication of *Là-Bas* in 1891—corresponding precisely to Wilde's annus mirabilis[50]—Huysmans would begin a process of religious conversion that he would chronicle in a series of autobiographical novels.[51] He would also publish one of the most astonishing documents of the period, a hagiography titled *Sainte Lydwine de Schiedam,* in 1901, the year after Wilde's death.

This account of a fifteenth-century saint's life is an attempt to rival in prose the pictorial effects Huysmans so admired in the Primitive painters of the late Middle Ages, especially Mathaeus Grünewald. Huysmans's luminous meditation on the latter's scene of the crucifixion, as described in the opening pages of *Là-Bas,* marks the birth of the writing technique he would call *"supra-naturaliste"*: "Grünewald was the wildest of all idealists. Never had a painter so magnificently exalted the heights and so resolutely leapt from the summit of the soul into the distressed sphere of heaven. He had passed through both extremes and from triumphant wastes had extracted the finest mints of affection, the sharpest steel essences of tears. In this painting the masterpiece of a desperate art is revealed, summoned to render the invisible and the tangible, to give form to the disconsolate filth of the body, to sublimate the distress of the soul."[52]

The delectation and high connoisseurship in this description are self-evident, but the aesthetic of reference has shifted from the self to the overdetermined corpse of the sacrificial victim. This emergence of a new *écriture* of suffering is further developed in the 1901 hagiography: Sainte Lydwine comes to enact, in her suffering and her martyrdom, the heterodox doctrine of mystical substitution and reparation of sins.

By means of an aesthetic procedure designed to partake of naturalism's descriptive powers yet transcend it in supernaturalist metaphysics, Huysmans would represent her life as a fifteenth-century variation on demonic possession and expiatory victimization particularly significant for the history of the "world spirit" and the modern world. "Rather than insisting as some have that Modernism constitutes the uniquely ascetical art," writes Geoffrey Harpham, "we should say that asceticism constitutes the perennial modernism of art."[53] Only in the realm of a supermodern ascetic renunciation, Huysmans believed, would the totalizing desacralization of modern life be understood and its horror expiated.

The hagiography begins with a somber and gruesome account of the violent turmoil and political upheaval in Europe in the fifteenth century; from several sources, including a letter dated 6 December 1897, we know that Huysmans considered the nineteenth century a time of universal criminality and degradation comparable in many ways to the late Middle Ages but even worse under the curse of the rampant bourgeoisie: "There is a rage to 'enjoy,' to 'live high' from the top to the bottom of the social scale; then throw in the lack of religious ideas, the only control possible, all things considered. Here we are having prepared for us generations raised without God, and the results are already visible in the increase of alcoholism and convictions for theft. In a few years, the people will be but a holding tank for bandits. It is true, of course, that they will never exceed in vileness the *bourgeois* who govern us."[54]

How is it that Huysmans would project himself, by the same sort of mystical substitution, into the position of the aesthetic saint? His conversion trilogy (*En Route,* 1895; *La Cathédrale,* 1898; *L'Oblat,* 1902) marks his progress through the Trappist monastery at Ligugé and the transformative power of the symbology of the liturgy, architecture, music, and practice of monastic devotion. Moreover, during his final illness he made several statements elucidating his yearning for martyrdom and expiatory suffering. Ravaged by excruciating cancers, he refused morphine injections from his doctors, stating, "Ah! You want to prevent me from suffering! You want me to exchange the sufferings of God for the evil pleasures of the earth! I forbid you!"[55] Most tellingly, he then remarked to a friend, in obvious remembrance of Léon Bloy's criticism of the last, desperate prayer of Des Esseintes ("Who would have guessed that all that talk was just another literary trick?"),[56] "I hope that this time they won't say that this is only " 'literature.' "[57] Like Wilde's, Huysmans's life was ultimately haunted by aesthetic and literary criteria: "to become a work of art" was the object not only of living but also of dying.

Wilde would undergo a series of disasters in his personal life in the years after 1895, as is well known. It is also a commonplace in the critical literature to concede the ascetic gesture of mystical substitution he hoped (consciously or not) to effect because of his martyrdom at the hands of an unworthy lover (the "Judas" Lord Alfred Douglas of *De Profundis*) and Douglas's unworthy, irate father intent on persecuting him.[58]

"Think of what we owe to the imitation of Christ," Wilde had written in "The Decay of Lying." But his mimetic Christ is problematically " 'Hellenic,' derived from Renan, noble, an exponent of Love over Law," writes Stoddard Martin. "Because of his very goodness, Wilde's Christ is doomed."[59] The manifestations of the "romance of Christ" occur in numerous works, including "The Soul of Man under Socialism" (in which Christ stands for both the ideal of suffering and "the rejection of private property"), the prose poems, the stories, and *Salome*.[60] This female figure of transgression, however, like Huysmans's Sainte Lydwine, joins Wilde's redeemer figure in an androgynous, non–gender-specific composite version of the central figure in his personal mythology.

The hermeneutic fluidity represented by the figures in Rops's illustration —their interchangeability and the dynamism by which they attract and replace one another—recounts the decadent crisis of indifferentiation, or desacralization, in a particularly compact way. It also succeeds at bringing to consciousness the nascent psychoanalytic critique of repression and asceticism later remarked by Freud. The image of mystical substitution emerges, both in Huysmans's "supra-naturalist" hagiography and in Wilde's elaborate erotic-expiatory "romances" of *The Ballad of Reading Gaol* and *De Profundis*, as the most potent allegory-making substance in the artist's arsenal. Both writers, in works that make up the respective culminations of their creative lives, seek the allegorical relations between the enactment of reparation for the crimes and sins of entire social groups, corporeal anguish, and the apocalyptic spectacle of the turning century. "As the mediator approaches," writes Girard, "the phenomena connected with metaphysical desire tend to be of a collective nature."[61] And "the truth of metaphysical desire," Girard concludes, "is death."[62]

Wilde's downfall need hardly be rehearsed here. *De Profundis* remains, however, an astonishing account of a consciousness informed by suffering and nearly broken by punishment, yet strangely puzzled by the continuing riddle at its center. Like Huysmans's hagiography, *De Profundis* crosses the boundaries of genres: it stands as an auto-hagiography, a reiteration of the struggle and agony of a narcissistic Christ, recounted in the rhetoric of prison autobiographies conditioned by incarceration and hard labor.[63]

Addressed to his "Judas," Lord Alfred Douglas, this epistolary Christology recounts the past, the present, and the futureless future in tones alternately moving and stoic. The vertiginous narcissism in the relationship, viewed retrospectively by the author, is revealed in such sentences as these: "In the morning you were quite yourself. I waited naturally to hear what excuses you had to make, and in what way you were going to ask me for the forgiveness that you knew in your heart was invariably waiting for you, no matter what you did; your absolute trust that I would always forgive you being the thing in you that I always really liked best, perhaps the best thing in you to like."[64]

Here the author states the astonishing sentiment that the loved one's trust that he would always forgive him was the one quality he (the author) always loved best, "perhaps the best thing in you to like." (Merely writing this sentence is difficult because of the complexity involved in this autotelic trust.)[65] The author's ability to trigger this favorite quality in the loved one's behavior, then, depended on his own willingness to forgive the transgressor whose absolute faith in exacting the author's eventual forgiveness, as it were, charmed the subject in advance and thereby was fulfilled in advance by itself.[66] So who is imitating whom? After Dorian Gray complains about Sybil Vane's fall from a "great artist" to a mediocrity as an actress (a change brought on by her love for Dorian), Basil Hallward tells him not to talk in such a way about a loved one, saying, "Love is a more wonderful thing than Art." To which Lord Henry characteristically replies, "They are both simply forms of imitation."[67] This situation has changed in *De Profundis,* however: "And as the gods are strange, and punish us for what is good and humane in us as much as for what is evil and perverse," Wilde writes, "I must accept the fact that one is punished for the good as well as for the evil that one does."[68]

The curse and the blessing for Wilde's strangely autonomous Christ take the form of this endemic punishment. Just as the coquette Salome is "attracted to Iokaanan less for his spiritual purity than for his imperviousness to the fascination she is able to exercise over other men,"[69] the character type in Wilde's works "who cannot be controlled by Beauty—Iokaanan, Basil Hallward, Christ, Wilde himself—becomes the martyr-masochist."[70]

This public figure in turn embodies a final metamorphosis, even an apotheosis, of the transgressor; as stated in *De Profundis,* "For I have come, not from obscurity into the momentary notoriety of crime, but from a sort of eternity of fame to a sort of eternity of infamy."[71] The martyr-masochist in the "romance of Christ" requires not a following of the faithful but, rather, a following of the faithless like Alfred Douglas, or Dorian, or Auguste Langlois, or the end of the nineteenth century itself, all those whose temples are structurally indistinguishable from a bare prison: "When I think about religion at all, I feel as if I would like to found an order for those who cannot believe: the Confraternity of the Faithless one might call it, where on an altar, on which no taper burned, a priest, in whose heart peace had no dwelling, might celebrate with unblessed bread and a chalice empty of wine."[72]

This inversion or emptying out of redemptive ritual, here accomplished in punishment, marks Wilde's relation to the displaced Christ held in place by the hybrid figure of Madness and Satan in Rops's allegory; the synthesis, for Wilde, will be accomplished by his own substitution for his imprisoned equivalent of excruciated yet autonomous Eros, highly visible, pleasurably crucified, and eternally impervious.

To the end of *De Profundis,* however, Wilde seems confused about the cause-and-effect relation between these roles. Wilde states that he "awoke the imagination of my century so that it created myth and legend around me," and concludes by stating, "But I let myself be lured into long spells of senseless and sensual ease. I amused myself with being a *flâneur,* a dandy, a man of fashion."[73] Clearly, these two "opposites" do not oppose each other: the expiatory legend—as scapegoat and redeemer—precisely elaborates the problem of the public life of the self-referential dandy.

As the avatar of modernity, the decadent dandy is also the victim of the "literary schizophrenia" of modernity itself: erotic love of desire and ascetic hatred of desire.[74] Roland Barthes has argued that modernity begins with the search for an impossible literature.[75] The "modernism" of aestheticism lies precisely in its capacity for testing the impossible bounds of reference and the equally impossible claims of autonomy. The aesthetic transgressor, like the dandy, pronounces himself autonomous in a renunciation of desire, then slips inexorably toward his own objectification as the ascetic redeemer, culminating in the return of the repressed, heteronomous material.

As Félicien Rops demonstrates, however, this last phase bifurcates in the decadent, triangulated version of *imitatio Christi*. Tormented monk or excruciated Eros, both Huysmans and Wilde seek surcease from their roles as aesthetic spectators and become instead incarcerated martyrs through whose ever-more-objectlike bodies pass the impossible expiations for an impossible community.

Notes

1. René Girard, *Deceit, Desire and the Novel: Self and Other in Literary Structure*, trans. Yvonne Freccero (Baltimore: Johns Hopkins University Press, 1965).

2. Cf. Regenia Gagnier, *Idylls of the Marketplace: Oscar Wilde and the Victorian Public* (Stanford, Calif.: Stanford University Press, 1986), especially chapter 5, "*De Profundis*: An Audience of Peers."

3. Richard Ellmann, *Oscar Wilde* (New York: Alfred A. Knopf, 1988), 310; on the "mystique of transgression," cf. René Girard, *Des Choses cachées depuis la fondation du monde* (Paris: Grasset, 1978), published in English as *Things Hidden since the Beginning of the World* (Stanford, Calif.: Stanford University Press, 1987).

4. Cited in Ellmann 1988, 341.

5. Cited in Ellmann 1988, 310, note 12; cf. also page 191.

6. Gagnier, 21.

7. Oscar Wilde, "Pen Pencil and Poison," in *The Artist as Critic: Critical Writings of Oscar Wilde*, ed. Richard Ellmann (Chicago: University of Chicago Press, 1969), 339.

8. Wilde, 330.

9. Cf. especially Charles Baudelaire, "Le Peintre de la vie moderne," in *Oeuvres complètes* (Paris: Gallimard Pléiade, 1975).

10. Ellmann 1986, 583.

11. Oscar Wilde, *The Picture of Dorian Gray* (Harmondsworth, England: Penguin, 1949), 29.

12. Jean-Pierre Dupuy, "Self-Reference in Literature," *Poetics* 18 (1989): 491–515.

13. Franz Kafka, *Parables and Paradoxes* [trans. unnamed] (New York: Schocken, 1961), 11.

14. Cited in Gagnier, 195; for the effect of prison on Wilde's writing, see her chapter 5.

15. Cf. Jean-Paul Sartre, *Saint Genet, Comédien et martyr* (Paris: Gallimard, 1952), published in English as *Saint Genet, Actor and Martyr* (New York: Braziller, 1963): "Even if, in his dying moment, the criminal should go so far as to repudiate his crime, he remains, in his ignorance and fear, haunted by a supernatural negativity."

16. Theodor W. Adorno, *Aesthetic Theory*, trans. C. Lenhardt, ed. Gretel Adorno and Rolf Tiedemann (London: Routledge and Kegan Paul, 1984), 323; cf. also page 402.

17. Cf. the composite autograph composed for Wilde by Loüys and Gide, in Ellmann 1986, 353: "Il ne faut regarder que dans les miroirs. Car les miroirs ne nous montrent que les masques." (We must look only at mirrors. For mirrors show us nothing but masks.) Cf. also James Winchell, "Murdered Sleep: Crime and Aesthetics in France and England, 1850–1910," diss., University of Washington, 1988, chapter 3, *passim*.

18. Dupuy, 493.

19. Ellmann 1986, 322. Translation of epigraph my own, from Huysmans, *Oeuvres complètes*, (Paris: Crès, 1928), 1:165.

20. Girard 1965, 9. Lord Henry Wotton is Dorian's "internal mediator" because he, unlike the young Parisian, shares the same physical *and* spiritual proximity. Des Esseintes, or his fictionalized shadow, would be Dorian's "external mediator."

21. Wilde, *Picture*, 140.

22. Jacques Derrida, *Dissemination*, trans. Barbara Johnson (Chicago: University of Chicago Press, 1981), 101: "The noxiousness of the *pharmakon* is indicted at the precise moment the entire context seems to authorize its translation by 'remedy' rather than poison."

23. Wilde, *Picture*, 140.

24. Wilde, *Picture*, 161.

25. Wilde, *Picture*, 161.

26. *The Three Trials of Oscar Wilde*, ed. H. Montgomery Hyde (New York: University Books, 1956), 130.

27. Gagnier, 65 and note 35; 219.

28. Cf. Ellmann 1986, 252: "he intends to set an example of the pervading influence of art on matrimony."

29. Ellmann 1986, 252.

30. Ellmann 1986, 253. This claim, relatively unsophisticated in its account of the formation of Wilde's sexuality, nonetheless pertinently stresses the importance of the French text in Wilde's personal life.

31. Joris-Karl Huysmans, *Against Nature*, trans. Robert Baldick (Harmondsworth, England: Penguin, 1959), 81.

32. Wilde, *Picture*, 161.

33. Rodney Shewan, *Oscar Wilde: Art and Egotism* (London: Macmillan, 1977), 115.

34. Huysmans, 82 (translation corrected).

35. Huysmans, 82. Richard Shryock has demonstrated the extent, perhaps surprising, of Huysmans's involvement in contemporary anarchism in "Joris-Karl Huysmans and the Politics of *A rebours*" (unpublished).

36. Huysmans, 82 (translation corrected).

37. Huysmans, 82.

38. Huysmans, 83.

39. Huysmans, 83. Shryock reminds me that "conformity" and "anarchy" may not form the cleanly oppositional pair they seem to form in Des Esseintes's reflection; this ambiguity, too, contributes to Huysmans's authorial irony regarding his character.

40. Wilde, too, criticized Zola's brand of realism, notably in "The Decay of Lying." Cf. Ellmann 1986, 302.

41. Girard 1965, 162.

42. Walter Benjamin, *Charles Baudelaire: A Lyric Poet in the Era of High Capitalism*, trans. Harry Zohn (London: New Left Books, 1973), passim.

43. Huysmans, 83.

44. Gagnier, 5.

45. Wilde, *Artist*, 299.

46. Shewan, 115.

47. Shewan, 115.

48. Félicien Rops, *La Tentation de Saint Antoine*, in *Aquarelles, Dessins, Gravures* (Bruxelles: Centre Culturel de la Communauté Française de Belgique, 1980), 53. For the artist's own account of the allegorical "machine" of this work, cf. Thierry Zeno, *Les Muses sataniques: Félicien Rops, Oeuvre graphique et lettres choisies* (Bruxelles: Jacques Antoine, 1985), 76–81: "Le sujet est facile à comprendre; le bon St-Antoine, poursuivi par des visions libidineuses, se précipite vers son prie-Dieu, mais pendant ce temps-là, Satan—un drôle de moine rouge—lui a

fait une farce: il lui a ôté son Christ de la croix et l'a remplacé par une belle fille, comme les Diables qui se respectent en ont toujours sous la main." (The subject is easy to understand: good Saint Anthony, pursued by libidinous visions, hurls himself at his lectern. At that very moment Satan, a funny kind of red monk, plays a trick on him: having taken the Saint's Christ from the cross, he has replaced Him with a beautiful woman, as all self-respecting devils have on hand at all times.)

49. Sigmund Freud, *Delusion and Dream and Other Essays,* ed. Philip Rieff (Boston: Beacon Press, 1956), 56.

50. Stoddard Martin, *Art, Messianism, and Crime: A Study of Antinomianism in Modern Literature and Lives* (London: Macmillan, 1986), 37.

51. Cf. the convenient annotated bibliography in Philippe Audoin, *J.-K. Huysmans* (Paris: Henri Veyrier, 1985), 163–171.

52. Joris-Karl Huysmans, *Là-Bas* (Paris: Garnier-Flammarion, 1978), 40; translation my own. On the relation between Huysmans and Grünewald, cf. Geoffrey Galt Harpham, *The Ascetic Imperative in Culture and Criticism* (Chicago: University of Chicago Press, 1987), 137–73.

53. Harpham, 141.

54. Joris-Karl Huysmans, *Lettres à Arij Prins* (Geneva: Droz, 1977), 310; translation mine.

55. Robert Baldick, *The Life of J.-K. Huysmans* (Oxford: Clarendon Press, 1955), 347.

56. Léon Bloy, "Sur la tombe de Huysmans," in *Le Salut par les Juifs* (Paris: Union Générale d'Editions, 1986), 264; translation my own.

57. Baldick, 347.

58. Ellmann 1986, 437.

59. Martin, 36.

60. Roger B. Henkle, *Comedy and Culture: England 1820–1900* (Princeton, N.J.: Princeton University Press, 1980), 300.

61. Girard, 280.

62. Girard, 282.

63. Gagnier, chapter 5, passim.

64. Oscar Wilde, *De Profundis* (New York: Philosophical Library, 1960), 34–35.

65. Gagnier, 187: "In the first half of the letter, Wilde forces the presence of Douglas in the prose in order to make the pre-prison Wilde a reality. Sometimes he becomes hopelessly confused, as in the crazy syntactical subordination of subject and object, e.g., 'But most of all I blame myself for the entire ethical degradation I allowed you to bring on me.'"

66. Girard, 105.

67. Wilde, *Picture,* 96–97.

68. Wilde, *De Profundis,* 83.

69. Martin, 37.

70. Martin, 37.

71. Wilde, *De Profundis,* 84.

72. Wilde, *De Profundis,* 81.

73. Wilde, *De Profundis,* 77.

74. This formula has been slightly changed from an idea by A. E. Carter, *The Idea of Decadence in French Literature, 1830–1900* (Toronto: University of Toronto Press, 1958), 90.

75. Dupuy, 492; cf. also page 503: "Reflexive literature, in wishing to be seen as a total discourse, self-sufficient, *per causa sui,* is a disguised theology."

The Christ of Oscar Wilde

JOHN ALBERT, O.C.S.O.

The following essay attempts to explore the meaning of Christ for Oscar Wilde, in his art and in his life. It is my intention also to provide the reader with ample texts from Oscar Wilde, which will allow the richness of his thought and style to emerge. Secondly, it is hoped that this essay will provide material for the monastic exercise of *lectio* that leads to meditation, prayer and contemplation. . . .

CHRIST IN THE ART OF OSCAR WILDE

Oscar Wilde used his art to reveal himself in a way impossible in real life (until he was found out), and, at first glance, Wilde appears to be a pagan author. But a careful reading of the canon of his works with the intention of taking him seriously demonstrates to us an Oscar Wilde of intense religious feeling. Wilde's art was his interpretation of ultimate reality and his writings, replete as they are with biblical concepts, themes and even elements of style, express his genuine religious sentiments and his own authentic religious experience. In the art of Oscar Wilde we find a fully developed doctrine of Christ.

The 1895 tragedy of Wilde's trials and imprisonment can serve us as a line of demarcation in our investigation of his writings. First, we can refer to the writings before 1895 as the "early writings," thus looking for the place of Christ in Wilde's poems, fairy tales and essays. Secondly, we can designate Wilde's later work as the "prison writings," and look to *De Profundis* and "The Ballad of Reading Gaol" as the fullest sources of Wilde's doctrine of Christ.

THE EARLY POEMS OF OSCAR WILDE   As a young Oxonian visiting Greece and Italy, Wilde wrote the following poems descriptive of a suffering Christ, an outcast Christ; and he conveys his identification with this Christ because of his own recognized sinfulness.

In *"E Tenebris"* Wilde pleads:

Reprinted in part from *American Benedictine Review* 39, no. 4 (December 1988): 372–403.

> Come down, O Christ, and help me! reach thy hand
>> For I am drowning in a stormier sea
>> Than Simon on the lake of Galilee:
>> The wine of life is spilt upon the sand,
>> My heart is as some famine-murdered land
>>> When all good things have perished utterly,
>>> And well I know my soul in Hell must lie
>> If I this night before God's throne should stand.
>> Nay, peace, I shall behold, before the night,
>>> The feet of brass, the robe more white than flame,
>> The wounded hands, the weary human face. (*CW*, p. 619)

The forgotten, tortured Christ is brought again to mind in "Sonnet—Written in Holy Week in Genoa":

> Ah, God! Ah, God! those dear Hellenic hours
>> Had drowned all memory of Thy bitter pain,
>> The Cross, the Crown, the Soldiers and the Spear. (*CW*, p. 616)

In *"Ave Maria Gratia Plena,"* Wilde contrasts the imagined splendors and triumph of the coming Messiah with "this supreme mystery of Love":

> Some kneeling girl with passionless face,
>> An angel with a lily in his hand,
>> And over both the white wings of a Dove. (*CW*, p. 615)

And "Easter Day" contrasts the pageantry of the Roman Pontifical Mass with:

> . . . one who wandered by a lonely sea,
> And sought in vain for any place to rest:
> "Foxes have holes, and every bird its nest.
> I, only I, must wander wearily,
> And bruise my feet, and drink wine salt with tears." (*CW*, p. 619)

In "Sonnet—On Hearing the *Dies Irae* Sung in the Sistine Chapel," Wilde foreshadowed that spiritual ambivalence that would cause his ruin:

> Nay, Lord, not thus! white lilies in the spring,
>> Sad olive-groves, or silver-breasted dove,
>> Teach me more clearly of Thy life and love
> Than terrors of red flame and thundering.
> The hillside vines dear memories of Thee bring:

A bird at evening flying to its nest
Tells me of One who had no place of rest:
I think it is of Thee the sparrows sing.

Come rather on some autumn afternoon,
    When red and brown are burnished on the leaves,
And the fields echo to the gleaner's song.
Come when the splendid fulness of the moon
    Looks down upon the rows of golden sheaves,
And reap Thy harvest: we have waited long. (*CW*, pp. 618–19)[1]

In *"Humanitad,"* perhaps his most lyrically beautiful writing on this theme, the young Oscar Wilde composed these lines descriptive of the unity of Christ and all humankind in suffering:

To make the Body and the Spirit one
    With all right things, till no thing live in vain
From morn to noon, but in sweet unison
    With every pulse of flesh and throb of brain
The Soul of flawless essence high enthroned,
Against all outer vain attack invincibly bastioned,
Mark with serene impartiality
    The Strife of things, and yet be comforted,
Knowing that by the chain causality
    All separate existences are wed
Into one supreme whole, whole utterance
Is joy, or holier praise!

But we have left those gentle haunts to pass
    With weary feet to the new Calvary,
Where we behold, as one who in a glass
    Sees his own face, self-slain Humanity,
And in the dumb reproach of that sad gaze
Learn what an awful phantom the red hand of man can raise.

O smitten mouth! O forehead crowned with thorn!
    O chalice of all common miseries!
Thou for our sakes that loved thee not hast borne
    An agony of endless centuries,
And we were vain and ignorant nor knew
That when we stabbed thy Heart it was our own real hearts we slew.

Being ourselves the sowers and the seeds,
    The night that covers and the lights that fade,
The spear that pierces and the side that bleeds,
    The lips betraying and the life betrayed;
The deep hath calm: the moon hath rest: but we
Lords of the natural world are yet our own dread enemy.

Nay, nay, we are but crucified, and though
    The bloody sweat falls from our brows like rain,

Loosen the nails—we shall come down I know,
  Staunch the red wounds—we shall be whole again,
No need have we of hyssop-laden rod,
That which is purely human, that is Godlike, that is god.
                               (*CW*, pp. 685, 686)

FROM VERSE TO PROSE   The Poem *"Les Jardin Des Tuileries"* and the fairy tale entitled *The Selfish Giant* reflect Wilde's maturing thought and his transposition of a particular Christian theme from poetry to the story form. In *"Les Jardin Des Tuileries"* Wilde is speaking of the children playing in the garden, and here implicitly the author is the Christ figure:

And now in mimic flight they flee,
  And now they rush, a boisterous band—
  And, tiny hand on tiny hand,
Climb up the black and leafless tree.
Ah! cruel tree! if I were you,
  And children climbed me, for their sake
  Though it be winter I would break
Into the spring blossoms white and blue! (*CW*, pp. 695–96)

How important this theme of the flowering tree and Christ was to Wilde is demonstrated again in his alternate version in *The Selfish Giant*. Michael Neugebauer, in his Picture Book Studio edition of *The Selfish Giant*, called it unique among the prose tales: ". . . for the skillful manner in which elements of traditional fairy tales and Christian symbolism are combined in such a way that they perfectly complement each other, and achieve a depth of meaning that neither story type would possess alone."[2] Here the Child Jesus, the Crucified Jesus and the Resurrected Christ all appear with the Cross-Tree of Death and Life in the giant's garden. Once again, Wilde's sensitivity and self-identification is apparent. *The Selfish Giant*—as all of Wilde's stories—needs to be read in its entirety.

THE FAIRY TALES   Oscar Wilde's play *Salome* (banned because biblical subjects could not be dramatized on the English stage);[3] the poems in prose ("The Doer of Good," "The Disciple," "The Master," and so on); and the play fragment about the monk of the Thebaid and the prostitute, entitled *La Sainte Courtisane;* all evidence that *bizarrerie* of decadence that gave Wilde the reputation of perversity as a writer.[4]

But if we look to Wilde's fairy tales (ostensibly written for children and read to his small sons as entertainment), we discover works filled with Christ figures and Christian moral values. Read Oscar Wilde's fairy tales as Christian allegories; consider the metonymy of *heart* for "sacred heart" or "wounded heart" of Christ and "broken heart" of Wilde himself, and we find poignant portraits of their author's spiritual sensibilities.

In *The Nightingale and the Rose*, the nightingale is the Christ-figure:

And the Tree cried to the Nightingale to press closer against the thorn. "Press closer, little Nightingale," cried the Tree, "or the Day will come before the rose is finished." So the Nightingale pressed closer against the thorn, and the thorn touched her heart, and a fierce pang of pain shot through her. Bitter, bitter was the pain, and wilder and wilder grew her song, for she sang of the Love that is perfected by Death, of the Lord that dies not in the tomb. . . . "Look, look!" cried the Tree, "the rose is finished now"; but the Nightingale made no answer, for she was lying dead in the long grass, with the thorn in her heart. (*CW*, pp. 568–69)

In *The Happy Prince*, it is the statue which is the representation of Christ. Rather than allow them to suffer want and need, the statue has completely sacrificed itself for others:

Early the next morning the Mayor was walking in the square below in company with the Town Councillors. As they passed the column he looked up at the statue: "Dear me! how shabby the Happy Prince looks!" he said. "How shabby indeed!" cried the Town Councillors, who always agreed with the Mayor, and they went up to look at it. "The ruby has fallen out of his sword, his eyes are gone, and he is golden no longer," said the Mayor; "in fact, he is little better than a beggar!" "Little better than a beggar," said the Town Councillors. "And here is actually a dead bird at his feet!" continued the Mayor. "We must really issue a proclamation that birds are not to be allowed to die here." And the Town Clerk made a note of the suggestion.

So they pulled down the statue of the Happy Prince. "As he is no longer beautiful he is no longer useful," said the Art Professor at the University. Then they melted the statue in a furnace, and the Mayor held a meeting of the Corporation to decide what was to be done with the metal. . . .

"What a strange thing," said the overseer of the workmen at the foundry. "This broken lead heart will not melt in the furnace. We must throw it away." So they threw it on a dust heap where the dead Swallow was also lying. (*CW*, p. 565)

Being more than a fable treating events in the lives of animals and inanimate objects, *The Birthday of the Infanta* is the saddest of the stories: it is based on human experience—with coloring and detail from the art of Velasquez—and it foretells Wilde's doom. In this tale a dwarf discovers his ugliness and the reason for the laughter of the Royal Court; all along he had thought they laughed in delight at his playing for them. Here we find an expression of the great sadness at the heart of Oscar Wilde, and perhaps some indication of a fundamental inferiority complex that was at the root of his homosexual self-identity:

When the truth dawned upon him he gave a wild cry of despair, and fell sobbing to the ground. So it was he who was misshappen and hunchbacked, foul to look at and grotesque. He himself was the monster, and it was at him that all the children had been laughing, and the little Princess who he thought loved him—she too, had been merely mocking at his ugliness, and making merry over his twisted limbs. . . . He crawled, like some wounded thing, into the shadow, and lay there moaning.

And at that moment the Infanta herself came in with her companions. . . . "His dancing was funny," said the Infanta; "but his acting is funnier still. Indeed he is almost as good as the puppets, only, of course, not quite so natural."

. . . "But why will he not dance again?" asked the Infanta, laughing. "Because his heart is broken," answered the Chamberlain. And the Infanta frowned, and her dainty rose-leaf lips curled in pretty disdain. "For the future let those who come to play with me have no hearts," she cried, and she ran into the garden. (*CW*, pp. 526–27)

AN ESSAY ON CHRIST AND SOCIETY   Religion and morality were themes treated by Oscar Wilde throughout his critical essays, but it is in his *The Soul of Man Under Socialism* that we find Wilde's fullest pre-prison reflection on Christ. It has been said that Wilde wrote this essay after attending a lecture on Marx and communism given by George Bernard Shaw.[5] *The Soul of Man Under Socialism* showed his readers Wilde's increasing identification with those sectors of English society at once scorned by the aristocracy and ministered to by those in the Social Gospel Movement. The wealthy who condescended to assist the poor, and those practical Christians who sought to impose their morality on the downtrodden and lower elements (foreign missionaries included) were satirized by Wilde. When published in *The Fortnightly Review* in February of 1891, this essay "aroused the secret enmity of the rich and powerful class at whose house parties Wilde was an invaluable entertainer."[6]

Here Wilde wrote that the personality of man in its full development will be wonderful, as wonderful as the personality of the child. "In its development," says Wilde, "it will be assisted by Christianity, if men desire that; but if men do not desire that, it will develop nonetheless surely. For," writes Oscar, "it will not worry itself about the past, nor care whether things happened or did not happen. Nor will it admit any laws but its own laws; nor any authority but its own authority. Yet it will love those who sought to intensify it, and speak often of them." Wilde includes Christ as one of these and continues: " 'Know thyself!' was written over the portal of the antique world. Over the portal of the new world 'Be thyself!' shall be written. And the message of Christ to man was simply 'By thyself.' That is the secret of Christ" (*CW*, p. 920).

Wilde then goes on:

When Jesus talks about the poor he simply means personalities, just as when he talks about the rich he simply means people who have not developed their personalities. Jesus moved in a community that allowed the accumulation of private property just as ours does, and the gospel that he preached was not that in such a community it is an advantage for a man to live on scanty, unwholesome food, to wear ragged, unwholesome clothes, to sleep in horrid, unwholesome dwellings, and a disadvantage for a man to live under healthy, pleasant, and decent conditions. Such a view would have been wrong there and then, and would, of course, be still more the wrong now and in England; for as a man moves northward the material necessities of life become of more vital importance, and our society is infinitely more complex, and displays far greater extremes of luxury and pauperism than any society of the antique world. What Jesus meant was this. He said to man, "You have a wonderful personality. Develop it. Be yourself. Don't imagine that your perfection lies in accumulating or possessing external things. Your perfection is inside of you. If only you could realize that, you would not want to be rich." (*CW*, p. 920)

Continuing to speak in the words of Christ, Wilde says: "Ordinary riches can be stolen from a man. Real riches cannot. In the treasury-home of your soul, there are infinitely precious things, that may not be taken from you. And so, try to so shape your life that external things will not harm you. And try also to get rid of personal property. It involves sordid preoccupation, endless industry, continual worry. Personal property hinders Individualism at every step" (*CW*, p. 920).

Thus Wilde in this essay articulated his own Christian anthropology: "Man is complete in himself . . . And so he who would lead a Christlike life is he who is perfectly and absolutely himself" (*CW*, p. 921).

THE CHRIST OF *DE PROFUNDIS*   Oscar Wilde was released from prison on May 19, 1897. In the months that preceded his departure from Reading Gaol, Wilde wrote *De Profundis* as his own *apologia pro vita sua*, with Alfred Douglas as the intended recipient. The textual history of this long letter is as troubled as the life of its author; and its full reading is extremely important for our understanding of Oscar Wilde's religious nature.

De Profundis is an immense work, and the Christ section of itself is a self-contained textual unit.[7] Wilde's presentation of Christ and Christ's teachings must be read as a composite of unified paragraphs within the context of Wilde's self-explanation to Lord Douglas (and a projected larger audience to come).

Following six years after *The Soul of Man Under Socialism*, *De Profundis* shows us the development of Wilde's thought. In this later work, Wilde expands ideas previously expressed. Here, for Wilde, Christ's place is with the poets: "His whole conception of humanity sprang right out of the imagination and can only be realized by it. What God was to the pantheist, man was to him. He was the first to conceive the divided races as a unity" (*Lts*, p. 477). According to Wilde, Christ more than anyone else in history wakes in us that temper of wonder to which romance always appeals. In Wilde's Christ, sorrow and beauty are made one in their meaning and manifestation. He is the leader of all lovers: "He saw that love was the first secret of the world for which the wise men had been looking, and that it was only through love that one could approach either the heart of the leper or the feet of God" (*Lts*, p. 479).

And for Wilde, Christ is above all the "most supreme of individualists." Humility, says Wilde—like the artistic acceptance of all experiences—is merely a mode of manifestation: "It is man's soul that Christ is always looking for. He calls it 'God's Kingdom,' and finds it in every one. He compares it to little things, to a tiny seed, to a handful of leaven, to a pearl. That is because one realizes one's soul only by getting rid of all alien passions, all acquired culture, and all external possessions, be they good or evil. . . . When one comes in contact with the soul it makes one simple as a child, as Christ said one should be" (*CW*, p. 479).

In *De Profundis*, Wilde portrays Christ as going beyond the artist's mode of expression by which he conceives life. As we now know, in prison Wilde continued to read John Henry Newman's writings. The influence of Newman —whom Wilde revered from the beginning of his Oxford years—is evident in *De Profundis*. Far more than just the *genre* of the confessional mode,[8] Oscar Wilde also found in Newman a mode of thinking that becomes a doctrine of Christ's nature for Wilde: universal sympathy.

In his *Idea of a University*, Newman had argued that all branches of knowledge are connected together, because the subject matter of knowledge is intimately united in itself, as being the acts and the work of the Creator. Newman wrote: "Hence it is that the Sciences, into which our knowledge may be said to be cast, have multiple bearings one on another, and an internal sympathy, and admit, or rather demand, comparison and adjustment. They complete, correct and balance each other."[9] In *De Profundis*, Wilde describes Christ with these words:

> With a width and wonder of imagination that fills one almost with awe, he took the entire world of the inarticulate, the voiceless world of pain, as his kingdom, and made of himself its external mouthpiece. Those of whom I have spoken, who are dumb under oppression and "whose silence is heard only of God," he chose as his brothers. He sought to become eyes to the blind, ears to the deaf, and a cry in the lips of those whose tongues had been tied. His desire was to be to the myriads who had found no utterance a very trumpet through which they might call to heaven. And feeling, with the artistic nature of one to whom suffering and sorrow were modes through which he could realize his conception of the beautiful, that an idea is of no value till it becomes incarnate and is made an image, he made of himself the image of the Man of Sorrows, and as such has fascinated and dominated art as no Greek god ever succeeded in doing. (*Lts*, p. 481)

Then Wilde develops this theme through a further interpretation of Christ and love:

Christ, like all fascinating personalities, had the power of not merely saying beautiful things himself, but of making other people say beautiful things to him. . . . Most people live for love and admiration. But it is by love and admiration we should live. If any love is shown us we should recognize that we are quite unworthy of it. Nobody is worthy to be loved. The fact that God loves man shows us that in the divine order of ideal things it is written that eternal love is to be given to what is eternally unworthy. Or if that phrase seems to be a bitter one to bear, let us say that every one is worthy of love, except him who thinks that he is. Love is a sacrament that should be taken kneeling, and *Domine, non sum dignus* should be on the lips and in the hearts of those who receive it. (*Lts*, p. 484)

All the morality of Christ, according to *De Profundis,* is all sympathy. "Christ," continues Wilde, "had no patience with the dull lifeless mechanical systems that treat people as if they were things, and so treat everybody alike; for him there were no laws: there were exceptions merely, as if anybody, or anything, for that matter, was like aught else in the world!" (*Lts*, pp. 476, 485)

Wilde speaks of Christ's love of the ignorant (for them there is hope of a great idea) and scorn of philistines, who, having the key of knowledge to open the gates of God's Kingdom, do not use it themselves, and allow no others to use it. And those he saved from their sins, "are saved simply for beautiful moments in their lives": e.g., Mary Magdalen's anointing of the feet of Christ. Wilde develops this:

All that Christ says to us by the way of a little warning is that every moment should be beautiful, that the soul should always be ready for the coming of the bridegroom, always waiting for the voice of the lover. . . . But it is when he deals with a sinner that Christ is most romantic, in the sense of the most real. The world has always loved the saint as being the nearest possible approach to the perfection of God. Christ, through some divine instinct in him, seems to have always loved the sinner as being the nearest possible approach to the perfection of man. His primary desire was not to reform people, any more than his primary desire was to relieve suffering. To turn an interesting thief into a tedious honest man was not his aim. . . . Indeed, that is the charm about Christ, when all is said: he is just like a work of art. He does not really teach one anything, but by being brought into his presence one becomes something. And everybody is predestined to his presence. Once at least in his life each man walks with Christ to Emmaus. (*Lts*, pp. 486, 487)

"THE BALLAD OF READING GAOL"   During one of the many humiliating experiences of his prison years, Oscar Wilde turned to his warders and said: "If this is how the Queen treats her convicts, she doesn't deserve to have any!" Wilde, as we know, was devoted to Victoria his entire life and celebrated her diamond jubilee from exile in 1897. The saying above and many of Wilde's post-prison letters show Wilde's characteristic attempt to see above any human tragedy (particularly his own), and to assure friends of his newly-found happiness; but Stanley Weintraub is correct in calling these letters "his final works of fiction."[10]

Oscar Wilde's suffering and real compassion for others is reflected in the letters he wrote for publication concerning the cruelties of prison life, especially with regard to young children (those who endured the greatest hardships of all). Eventually, these letters would have an effect in the revision of the English penal code, as did Wilde's own inhumane treatment eventually cause a rethinking of the specific punishments involved in his case.

But it is "The Ballad of Reading Gaol"—the last published work of his lifetime—that stands as Oscar Wilde's final testimony to the love of Christ the Outcast. No professional publishing house in England would have considered bringing it out, of course, and Wilde resorted to the services of Leonard Smithers, a pornographer. The poem was released in a limited edition, with the author anonymously given as "C.3.3."—Wilde's cell-block number at Reading Gaol.

"The Ballad of Reading Gaol" is a nineteenth-century document of protest against capital punishment. In it Wilde is describing the hanging and burial of a young trooper of the Royal Horse Guards, sentenced to death for murdering the woman he loved (she had been unfaithful to him). In this poem Wilde says:

> They hanged him as a beast is hanged:
>   They did not even toll
> A requiem that might have brought
>   Rest to his startled soul,
> But hurriedly they took him out,
>   And hid him in a hole.
> The warders stripped him of his clothes,
>   And gave him to the flies:
> They mocked the swollen purple throat,
>   And the stark and staring eyes:
> And with laughter loud they heaped the shroud
>   In which the convict lies.

These implicit allusions to Christ's passion and death then give way to an explicit identification of the hanged victim with the crucified Christ, the Christ who remains on the outside of Victorian Christianity:

> The Chaplain would not kneel to pray
>   By his dishonoured grave:
> Nor mark it with that blessed Cross
>   That Christ for sinners gave,
> Because the man was one of those
>   Whom Christ came down to save.

Many times, in many ways and situations, Oscar Wilde described the unchristian behavior of a purportedly "Christian" society. Nowhere has Wilde done this more forcefully than in "The Ballad of Reading Gaol." Here he says:

> This too I know—and wise it were
> If each could know the same—
> That every prison that men build
> Is built with bricks of shame,
> And bound with bars lest Christ should see
> How men their brothers maim.
>
> With bars they blur the gracious moon,
> And blind the goodly sun:
> And they do well to hide their Hell,
> For in it things are done
> That Son of God nor Son of Man
> Ever should look upon![11]

CHRIST IN THE LIFE OF OSCAR WILDE

How Oscar Wilde's portrayal of Christ might be understood in its Victorian context—that is, in relation to the German *Das Leben Jesu* (3rd ed. 1838) of David Friedrich Strauss; the French *Vie de Jésus* (1863) of Ernest Renan; the British *Life and Times of Jesus the Messiah* (1883) of Alfred Edersheim; in relation to the portraits of Christ by such poets as Robert Browning, Francis Thompson, John Ruskin—is the concern of critical Christology and the sociology of religion: the matter for fuller treatment in another essay.

At this juncture in our present study, having examined problems and perspectives in an interpretation of Oscar Wilde and the Christ presented by him in his art, we are able to move directly to Wilde himself and ask what place Christ might have had in his life. Two points of fact concerning Oscar Wilde and Christ must be acknowledged from the start. One, in the time of his tragedy Oscar identified himself with the Outcast Christ portrayed in his art. Secondly, and most important for our understanding of his relationship with Christ, Wilde was received into the Roman Catholic Church on his deathbed.

WILDE AND CHRIST IN PRISON AND IN EXILE   In his second to last month in Reading Gaol, in a letter to his friend Robert Ross (dated April 1, 1897), Oscar Wilde wrote of life in prison with these words: "In point of fact, Robbie, prison-life makes one see people and things as they really are. That is why it turns one to stone. It is the people outside who are deceived by the illusion of a life in constant motion. They revolve with life and contribute to its unreality. We who are immobile both see and know" (*Lts*, p. 514).

In a passage in *De Profundis* (written at approximately the same period of time as the above letter), Wilde repeated these emotions and implicitly identified with Christ. Here, Wilde is describing what happened one day when, as a prisoner, he was transported to and from bankruptcy court. In this section Wilde recalls the hardship endured by all prisoners and his own personal experience:

> Everything about my tragedy has been hideous, mean, repellent, lacking in style; our very dress makes us grotesque. We are zanies of sorrow. We are clowns whose hearts are broken. We are especially designed to appeal to the sense of humour. On 13th November 1895, I was brought down here from London. From two o'clock till half-past two on that day I had to stand on the centre platform of Clapham Junction in convict dress, and handcuffed, for the world to look at. I had been taken out of the hospital ward without a moment's notice being given to me. Of all possible objects I was the most grotesque. When people saw me they laughed. Each train as it came up swelled the audience. Nothing could exceed their amusement. That was, of course, before they knew who I was. As soon as they had been informed they laughed still more. For half an hour I stood there in the grey November rain surrounded by a jeering mob.
>
> For a year after that was done to me I wept every day at the same hour for the same space of time. That is not such a tragic thing as possibly it sounds to you. To those who are in prison tears are part of every day's experience. A day in prison on which one does not weep is a day on which one's heart is hard, not a day on which one's heart is happy.[12]

On his first day of freedom after two years of imprisonment, Oscar Wilde appealed to a Jesuit retreat house on Farm Street in London, seeking refuge there. He received a reply saying he could not be accepted on the impulse of the moment and the matter must be considered for at least a year.[13] We can speculate how different history might be had Wilde been received with compassion.

On that same day, before his final departure from England, Wilde told friends that he looked on all the different religions as "colleges in a great university" and that he regarded Roman Catholicism as "the greatest and most romantic of them."[14] Traveling to Rome once again in what proved to be the final year of his life, Oscar wrote to his friend More Adey on April 24, 1900: "My position is curious: I am not a Catholic: I am simply a violent Papist. No one could be more 'Black' than I am. I have given up bowing to the King. I need say no more."[15]

WITH CHRIST IN DEATH   A detailed account of Oscar Wilde's final days and deathbed conversion to Roman Catholicism was drawn up by Robert Ross in the form of a letter to More Adey, dated December 14, 1900.

This text and information gathered from other sources over the years since Wilde's death tell us the following. On the night of November 29, 1900, Oscar Wilde was visited in his room at the *Hotel d'Alsace* by Father Cuthbert Dunne, a priest of the Congregation of the Passion from Dublin attached at this time to Saint Joseph's Church, in the Avenue Hoche, Paris. He had been brought there at the urgent appeal of Robert Ross, himself having just returned in haste to Paris to assist his friend. That night, Wilde, lying *in extremis,* was conditionally baptized. On November 30, the day of his death, he received at the hands of Father Dunne the Sacrament of Extreme Unction.[16] Through the kind ministrations of this priest, Oscar Wilde fulfilled his lifelong desire to enter the Roman Catholic Church, delayed for whatever reasons. These reasons, and the reactions to Wilde's conversion on the part of others, need fuller examination elsewhere.

Though he lacked the moral courage of Elizabeth Seton or John Henry Newman, Oscar Wilde surely experienced his entire life the Baptism of "Desire," and in his final years the Baptism of "Blood." Of his real Baptism of "Water and the Spirit" Father Cuthbert Dunne himself has left us this testimony:

As the man was in a semi-comatose condition, I did not venture to administer the Holy Viaticum; still I must add that he could be roused and was roused from this state in my presence. When roused, he gave signs of being inwardly conscious. He made brave efforts to speak, and would even continue for a time trying to talk, though he could not utter articulate words. Indeed I was fully satisfied that he understood me when told that I was about to receive him into the Catholic Church and give him the Last Sacraments. From the signs he gave as well as from his attempted words, I was satisfied as to his full consent. And when I repeated close to his ear the Holy Names, the Acts of Contrition, Faith, Hope and Charity, with acts of humble resignation to the Will of God, he tried all through to say the words after me.

At a later visit, I was if anything more convinced as to his inward consciousness when, in my presence, one of the attendants offered him a cigarette which he took into his fingers and raised to his face, although, in the attempt to put it between his lips, he failed. On his head above the forehead, there was a leech on either side, put there to relieve the pressure of blood upon the brain. At these subsequent visits, he repeated the prayers with me again and each time received Absolution.[17]

I carry in my mind an image of a room in the *Hotel d'Alsace.* In it a man is dying. With him are two distraught friends. Into this room comes a priest with the Sacraments of the Church. But into this room also comes the Gentle Christ. He and the dying man converse. What they share is unknown. When the conversation is complete, Christ takes this man, as he did the Good Thief, into his arms and carries him Home.

Oscar Wilde suffered the disgrace of his public trials and the horror of his imprisonment during the days of Lent and Paschaltide in 1895. He died at the time when the liturgical year turns from Ordinary Time into Advent, the time of new hope. Few in history have participated in the life and death of Christ as he did. And a passage from the *Letter to the Hebrews* (12:5–6) seems most fitting in his regard: "My son, despise not thou the chastening of the Lord, nor faint when thou are rebuked of him; for whom the Lord loveth he chasteneth, and scourgeth every son whom he receiveth."

Notes

1. It was Mozart's composition Wilde heard in the Sistine Chapel. Contrast the pastoral mood of this Christic poem with that of "Wasted Days" wherein a youth is warned against the quick coming of age and death, symbolized by sunset and night (*CW*, p. 692).

2. Illustrated by Lisbeth Zwerger (Natick, MA: Picture Book Studio USA 1984) dust jacket, inside flap of back cover. The pure wisdom of the child and the Christ-figure of the fool find their resonance in this poem. Oscar Wilde himself embodied both. In the Tarot, the hood of *Le Fou* satirizes the cowl of the monk: the fool, like the monk, is neither relevant nor non-relevant. For a fuller interpretation, see *Meditations on the Tarot: A Journey into Christian Hermeticism* (Amity, NY: Amity House 1985) pp. 589–621; Sallie Nicols, *Jung and the Tarot: An Archetypal Journey*, with an introduction by Laurens van der Post (York Beach, ME: Samuel Weiser, Inc. 1980) pp. 23–43. I have treated this theme with regard to Saint Bernard of Clairvaux in "Saint Bernard as Self-Fashioned Fool: A Look at Letter Eighty-Seven," *Monastic Exchange* 7:3 (Fall 1975) 24–31. See also John Saward, *Perfect Fools* (New York: Oxford University Press 1980).

3. See *Salome (A Tragedy in One Act)*, translated from the French of Oscar Wilde by Lord Alfred Douglas, pictured by Aubrey Beardsley, facsimile edition of the 1894 publication by Elkin Mathews and John Lane, with additions by the publisher and "A Note on 'Salome'" by Robert Ross (New York: Dove Publications 1967). On Wilde's interpretation of the biblical narratives and *Salome* as opera, see Rudolf Hartman, *Richard Strauss: The Staging of His Operas and Ballets* (New York: Oxford University Press 1981). Strauss' opera was originally published in Berlin in 1905 by Adolf Furstner. It is now available in the following edition: *Salome in Full Score* (New York: Dove Publications 1981). For a study of Beardsley's illustrations, see: *The Collected Drawings of Aubrey Beardsley*, with an appreciation by Arthur Symons, edited by Bruce S. Harris (New York: Bounty Books 1967).

4. See John Guest's introduction in *Oscar Wilde: Stories* (London: Heron Books n.d.) pp. 9–10. Guest comments: "As the pursuit of experience for its own sake, irrespective of the quality of the experience, it [decadence] leads, in literature at any rate, to a process of refinement which develops until finally it topples into the absurd, the distasteful or the futile. Before doing so it may produce works of rare beauty, but the artist who attempts to intensify his work further along the same lines, does so at his peril. Refinement can lead in the end only to rarer moods, and stranger sensations, and in that way madness lies." Oscar Wilde's novel is of course his most famous decadent work. See *The Picture of Dorian Gray*, edited with an introduction by Isobel Murray (New York: Oxford University Press, The World's Classics Series, 1982). Another example of Wilde's treatment of evil is his short story "Lord Arthur Savile's Crime." Beside the text available in *The Complete Shorter Fiction of Oscar Wilde*, there is an easily accessible reprint in *Lord Arthur Savile's Crime and Other Stories* (New York: Penguin Modern Classics 1984). In "The Canterville Ghost" (found in both editions just cited), Oscar demonstrated his wonderful wit and sense of irony in the inversion of fear and fascination, life and death.

5. On the Wilde-Shaw relationship, see *Bernard Shaw and Alfred Douglas: A Correspondence*, ed. Mary Hyde (New York: Ticknor & Fields, 1982); Hesketh Pearson, *George Bernard Shaw: His Life and Personality* (New York: Atheneum 1963) pp. 446–47; H. Montgomery Hyde, *Oscar Wilde, A Biography* (New York: Farrar, Straus & Giroux, n.d.; Da Capo reprint, 1975) pp. 307–08.

6. Pearson, *Oscar Wilde: His Life and Wit* (New York: Grosset & Dunlap, 1946) pp. 136–37. Pearson writes that during the period when he was the darling of the aristocracy, it was customary for formal invitations to be printed with the inscription: "To Meet Mr. Oscar Wilde."

7. This document fills pages 423–511 of *The Letters of Oscar Wilde* ed. Rupert Hart-Davis (New York: Harcourt, Brace & World, 1962). *De Profundis* (the title later given by Robert Ross) was written January–March 1897 at Reading Gaol as Wilde prepared himself for the next phase of his life. See letter to More Adey (February 18) on its progress, and letter to Robert Ross (April 1) on its completion. The petition of April 2 to the Prison Commission that Wilde be allowed to post the letter from prison was denied on April 6. Governor Nelson of Reading Gaol (who had stretched prison rules to allow its composition in the first place) kept the letter to Douglas, handing it to Wilde upon his release from that prison on May 18 (Wilde was transferred to Pentonville Gaol to avoid public notice) and Wilde handed it to Robert Ross when they met at Dieppe, France, early on the morning of May 20, 1897. In his April 1 letter to Ross, Wilde gave marvelous detailed instructions on how the Douglas letter was to be transcribed: ". . . the lady type-writer might be fed through a lattice in the door like the Cardinals when they elect a Pope, till she comes out on the balcony and can say to the world '*Habet Mundus Epistolam.*'" Ross had two typed copies made (typed original and carbon). Going against Wilde's instructions, Ross sent not the autograph document but the first typed copy to Lord Alfred Douglas. Douglas destroyed it thinking it was the only extant copy. Ross kept the autograph and carbon manuscripts and these formed the texts for the published editions. In 1905 Ross published the letter as *De Profundis* (Douglas later published a refutation of Wilde called *In Excelsis*), the contents being about one half the original length. In 1908, a slightly expanded version was published in the revised edition of the *Collected Works*. Neither of these editions contained any reference to Douglas, the suppressed material being considered too libellous. Subsequently—to guarantee its safety—Ross as Wilde's literary executor had the autograph letter sealed up and presented to the British Museum where it was to be kept hidden for sixty years. During litigation involving Douglas and Wilde biographer Arthur Ransome, it was unsealed and used in court; though libellous, the evidence against Douglas was true and Ransome won the case. The carbon copy was eventually given to Wilde's son Vyvyan Holland and this supplied the text for the 1949 "first complete and accurate version." A comparative study of this text with the original autographic text made by Rupert Hart-Davis revealed several hundred errors of misreading, misprinting, editing (deletions, etc.) and arranging (paragraph displacement, etc.). In 1962 Hart-Davis published the definitive critical full text based on Wilde's original letter (though even here courtesy to still-living family members required the brief deletion of offensive material). See *Letters*, pp. 419, 423–24, n. 2; 512, n. 1; 513. For a survey of the literary and legal history of Wilde's manuscript, see *Bernard Shaw and Alfred Douglas: A Correspondence*, Appendix II: "The publication of *De Profundis*," pp. 211–13. For Vyvyan Holland's introduction to his father's most famous letter, see *De Profundis and Other Writings of Oscar Wilde* (New York: Penguin, 1983) pp. 91–95. In this edition, Wilde's meditation on Christ occupies fifteen pages of tiny print. Roy Gasson has used the Christ section as one of the chapters, "On Christ from *De Profundis*," in his *The Illustrated Oscar Wilde* (Dorset, England: Jupiter Books: New Orchard Editions, Ltd. 1977) pp. 9–21.

8. See Jan B. Gordon, "Wilde and Newman: The Confessional Mode," *Renascence* 22 (Summer 1970) 183–91.

9. Newman: *Prose and Poetry*, edited by George N. Shuster (Boston: Allyn and Bacon 1925) p. 36. Newman died on August 11, 1890. On August 29, Wilde wrote to Wilfrid Meynell: "In what a fine 'temper' Newman always wrote! the temper of the scholar. But how subtle was his simple mind!" (*Letters*, p. 274). At that same period, Wilde wrote about Newman in *The Critic as Artist*: "Forms are the food of faith, cried Newman in one of those great moments of sincerity that made us admire and know the man. He was right, though he may not have known how terribly right he was. The Creeds are believed, not because they are rational, but because they are repeated. Yes, form is everything. It is the secret of life" (*CW*, p. 893).

Rupert Hart-Davis reported that among the books Wilde read in prison were *Newman's Grammar of Assent, Apologia Pro Vita Sua, Two Essays on Miracles, The Idea of a University,* and *Critical and Historical Essays* (*Letters*, p. 399, n. 4; p. 405, n. 1). For comments from Wilde about Newman in Oscar's Oxford years, see: *Letters*, pp. 17, 19, 20, 31, 33; also p. 41, n.1.

10. *The Portable Oscar Wilde,* revised edition, edited by Richard Aldington and Stanley Weintraub (New York: Viking Penguin, Inc. 1981) p. 1. The first edition edited by Richard Aldington was published in 1946; the revised edition contains the full text of *De Profundis* and substitutes other material. My essay emphasizes the more serious side of Wilde, and the tragic aspects of his later life. In happier times, Wilde was delighted to be satirized, and his status as celebrity was assured by the spoofing of others. He was the true-life personality behind Gilbert and Sullivan's "Reginald Bunthorne (A Fleshly Poet)" in *Patience.* See William Gilbert and A. S. Sullivan, *The Complete Plays of Gilbert and Sullivan,* illustrated by W. S. Gilbert (New York: W. W. Norton 1976) pp. 155–97. In his *roman à clef* novel, *The Green Carnation,* Robert Hichens spoofed Wilde in the character of Esmé Amarinth. The portrayal was so accurate some felt Wilde had written the book. Hichens had the sensitivity to remove his novel from circulation during Wilde's period of sorrow. See *The Green Carnation,* edited with an introduction by Stanley Weintraub (Lincoln, NE: University of Nebraska Press 1970). This novel was first published in 1894. Ada Leverson secured a deep and lasting friendship with Oscar when she parodied his poem "The Sphinx" with her own "The Minx" (published in *Punch,* July, 1894). Again, it was thought that Wilde was the anonymous author. These two authors had first met in 1892, and later Wilde said he had been "caught in the net of her jade eyes." Ada became affectionately called "The Sphinx" by Wilde, and she and her husband were a great source of comfort and assistance to Oscar during the public scandal. My source, along with the Wilde biographies and his letters, is Ada Leverson's *The Little Ottleys,* with an introduction by Sally Beauman (The Dial Press/A Virago Modern Classic 1982). For an entertaining presentation of Wilde's brilliant epigrams, see *The Wit and Humor of Oscar Wilde,* edited by Alvin Redman, with an introduction by Vyvyan Holland (New York: Dover Publications, Inc. 1959).

11. For an edition of stark beauty and haunting power, see *The Ballad of Reading Gaol by C.3.3. (Oscar Wilde),* with woodcuts by Frans Masereel (London & West Nyack: The Journeyman Press 1978). I am quoting from the text in *De Profundis and Other Writings,* pp. 247–48, 249, which contains variant readings and a different typography.

12. *Letters,* pp. 490–91; see also pp. 529, 531. Wilde was accused by some of dramatizing his sufferings, but those who actually visited him in prison reported differently. Constance Wilde met with Oscar for the last time on February 19, 1896, having the empathy to travel from Genoa to tell Wilde personally of the death of his mother on February 3. Constance wrote of his meeting: "They say he is quite well, but he is an absolute wreck compared with what he was" (*Letters*, p. 399, n. 2). Wilde's trustee Arthur Clifton saw him on Oct. 8, 1896, and later described the prisoner's condition: "I was very much shocked at Oscar's appearance, though scarcely surprised. Fortunately he had his ordinary clothes on: his hair was rather long and he looked dreadfully thin. You can imagine how painful it was to meet him; and he was very much upset and cried a good deal; he seemed quite broken-hearted and kept on describing his punishment as savage. . . . He was terribly despondent and said several times that he did not think he would be able to last the punishment out" (*Letters*, p. 409, n. 2). For a detailed account of Wilde's circumstances in prison, see Pearson's *The Life of Oscar Wilde,* pp. 315–35. For Wilde's letters describing the conditions of British prisons and their need of reform, see "The Case of Warden Martin, Some Cruelties of Prison Life," *Daily Chronicle,* May 28, 1897, and "Don't Read This If You Want To Be Happy Today," *Daily Chronicle,* March 24, 1898, in *Letters,* pp. 568–74; pp. 722–26.

13. *Letters,* pp. 563–64. Hart-Davis is quoting from *Letters to the Sphinx from Oscar Wilde, with Reminiscences of the Author* (1930) by Ada Leverson, who with her husband were among the first friends to see Oscar upon his release. She said Wilde in fact was refused, "Then he broke down and sobbed bitterly." Up to that moment he had triumphed in all his efforts to

put his friends at ease. In a letter of May 6, 1897, discussing what to do immediately upon his departure from prison, Wilde teased his friend More Adey: "I still suspect you of wishing to incarcerate me in a Trappist monastery . . ." (*Letters*, p. 536).

14. Hyde, *Oscar Wilde*, p. 324.

15. *Letters*, p. 825. See also *Oscar Wilde and the Black Douglas*, p. 119.

16. *Letters*, pp. 847–49; continued pp. 853–56.

17. For Father Dunne's narrative and entry number 547 in the Register of St. Joseph's Church (Dated "1900: No. 29," with *addendum* on Wilde's death the following day), see *Letters*, p. 857. Wilde died at 10 minutes to 2, Friday afternoon, November 30. Concerning Wilde's death, Rupert Hart-Davis wrote in 1962: "The latest medical opinion is that [Wilde] died of an intercranial complication of suppurative *otitis media,* or middle-ear disease, of which his illness in prison . . . was an earlier symptom." He cited as his source: Terrence Cawthorne, F.R.C.S., "The Last Illness of Oscar Wilde," *Proceedings of the Royal Society of Medicine* (February, 1959) (*Letters*, p. 854; also p. 404). Doctors attending Wilde also diagnosed cerebral meningitis. Robert Ross contended that Wilde also suffered the meningitis as "the legacy of tertiary syphilis." H. Montgomery Hyde however wrote: "But it is practically certain that neurosyphilis was in no way responsible for his terminal illness" (*Oscar Wilde*, p. 374).

After his body was washed and dressed, Wilde was vested in a blessed rosary and a Franciscan medal, given by the Franciscan sisters who guarded the corpse before Oscar's burial. The funeral Mass took place at the Church of St. Germain des Prés at 9:00 a.m. Monday, December 3. The Office of Burial was assisted at by Father Dunne at a temporary grave in Bagneux cemetery. In 1909, after sufficient funds had been raised and the literary reputation of Oscar Wilde restored through the publication of his collected works, his body was moved to a permanent grave in the cemetery of Père Lachaise in Paris.

Robert Ross, who before Wilde had converted to Roman Catholicism, died in 1918. In 1911, having married, Lord Alfred Douglas joined the Roman Church along with his mother, his sister and his nine-year-old son Raymond. Neither Douglas' marriage nor his new religion brought him happiness in this life. He spent six months in prison after losing a lawsuit for libel against Winston Churchill. Douglas died at Old Monk's Farm, Lancing, on the morning of Wednesday, March 20, 1945, at the age of seventy-four. His funeral Mass took place at the Franciscan Friary at Crawley, where he is buried alongside his mother. Raymond died in St. Andrew's Mental Hospital, Northampton, in 1964. Constance (Wilde) Loyd died April 7, 1898, in Genoa and was buried in the Protestant cemetery. Oscar visited her grave in February, 1899. First son Cyril died as a British soldier in combat in World War One. Vyvyan in his youth became Roman Catholic, fulfilling his great desire for the Eucharist. Since Vyvyan's recent death, Oscar Wilde is survived by grandson Merlin and great-grandson Lucian Holland.

Selected Bibliography

◆

Beckson, Karl, ed. *Oscar Wilde: The Critical Heritage*. London: Routledge & K. Paul, 1970.

Bird, Alan. *The Plays of Oscar Wilde*. London: Vision Press, 1977.

Bloom, Harold, ed. *Oscar Wilde: Modern Critical Views*. New York: Chelsea House, 1985.

——. *Oscar Wilde's "The Importance of Being Earnest": Modern Critical Interpretations*. New York: Chelsea House, 1988.

Chamberlin, J. E. *Ripe Was the Drowsy Hour: The Age of Oscar Wilde*. New York: Seabury Press, 1977.

Cohen, Ed. *Talk on the Wilde Side: Toward a Genealogy of the Discourse on Male Sexuality*. New York: Routledge, 1991.

Cohen, Philip. *The Moral Vision of Oscar Wilde*. London: Fairleigh Dickinson University Press, 1978.

Croft-Cooke, Rupert. *The Unrecorded Life of Oscar Wilde*. New York: D. McKay, 1972.

Dowling, Linda. *Language and Decadence in the Victorian Fin de Siècle*. Princeton, N.J.: Princeton University Press, 1986.

Ellmann, Richard. *Oscar Wilde*. London: Hamilton, 1987.

——, ed. *Oscar Wilde: A Collection of Critical Essays*. Englewood Cliffs, N.J.: Prentice-Hall, 1969.

Gagnier, Regenia. *Idylls of the Marketplace: Oscar Wilde and the Victorian Public*. Stanford, Calif.: Stanford University Press, 1986.

Hyde, H. Montgomery, ed. *The Annotated Oscar Wilde*. New York: C. N. Potter, 1982.

——. *Oscar Wilde: A Biography*. London: Methuen, 1976.

Jackson, Holbrook. *The Eighteen-Nineties*. N.p., 1913.

Jackson, Russell, ed. *The Importance of Being Earnest*. New York: Norton, 1980.

Lawler, Donald. *An Inquiry into Oscar Wilde's Revisions of The Picture of Dorian Gray*. New York: Garland Pub., 1988.

Mason, Stuart [Christopher Sclater Millard]. *Oscar Wilde: Art and Morality: A Record of the Discussion Which Followed the Publication of "Dorian Gray."* London: F. Palmer, 1912.

Mikhail, E. H. *Oscar Wilde: An Annotated Bibliography of Criticism*. London: Macmillan, 1978.

Nassaar, Christopher. *Into the Demon Universe: A Literary Exploration of Oscar Wilde*. New Haven, Conn.: Yale University Press, 1974.

Pearson, Hesketh. *Oscar Wilde: His Life and Wit*. New York: Harper and Brothers, 1946.

Powell, Kerry. *Oscar Wilde and the Theatre of the 1890s*. Cambridge: Cambridge University Press, 1990.

Raby, Peter. *Oscar Wilde*. Cambridge: Cambridge University Press, 1988.

Roditi, Edouard. *Oscar Wilde*. Norfolk: New Directions Books, 1947.

San Juan, Epifanio, Jr. *The Art of Oscar Wilde*. Princeton, N.J.: Princeton University Press, 1967.

Schroeder, Horst. *Annotations to Oscar Wilde, "The Portrait of Mr. W. H."* Braunschweig, 1986.

———. *Oscar Wilde, "The Portrait of Mr. W. H."—Its Composition, Publication and Reception*. Braunschweiger Anglistische Arbeiten, 1984.

Sedgwick, Eve Kosofsky. *Between Men: English Literature and Male Homosocial Desire*. New York: Columbia University Press, 1985.

Shewan, Rodney. *Oscar Wilde: Art and Egotism*. London: Macmillan, 1977.

Showalter, Elaine. *Sexual Anarchy: Gender and Culture at the Fin de Siècle*. New York: Penguin, 1990.

Small, Ian, ed. *Lady Windermere's Fan*. London: E. Benn, 1980.

Small, Ian, and Russell Jackson, eds. *Two Society Comedies*. New York: Norton, 1983.

Smith, Philip E., II and Michael Helfand, eds. *The Oxford Notebooks of Oscar Wilde: A Portrait of Mind in the Making*. Oxford: Oxford University Press, 1989.

Stokes, John. *In the Nineties*. Chicago: University of Chicago Press, 1989.

———. *Oscar Wilde*. Essex: Longman for the British Council, 1978.

Von Eckardt, Wolf, Sander L. Gilman, and J. Edward Chamberlin. *Oscar Wilde's London*. New York: Doubleday, 1987.

Index

261